Irmi Maral-Hanak

Language, discourse and participation:
Studies in donor-driven development
in Tanzania

Irmi Maral-Hanak

Language, discourse and participation: Studies in donor-driven development in Tanzania

LIT

Umschlagbild: Bild und Grafik: Birgit Englert

Gedruckt mit Unterstützung des Bundesministeriums
für Wissenschaft und Forschung in Wien

Bibliographic information published by the Deutsche Nationalbibliothek
The Deutsche Nationalbibliothek lists this publication in the Deutsche
Nationalbibliografie; detailed bibliographic data are available in the Internet at
http://dnb.d-nb.de.

ISBN 978-3-643-50014-4

A catalogue record for this book is available from the British Library

©LIT VERLAG GmbH & Co. KG Wien 2009
Krotenthallergasse 10/8
A-1080 Wien
Tel. +43 (0) 1-409 56 61
Fax +43 (0) 1-409 56 97
e-Mail: wien@lit-verlag.at
http://www.lit-verlag.at

LIT VERLAG Dr. W. Hopf
Berlin 2009
Fresnostr. 2
D-48159 Münster
Tel. +49 (0) 2 51-620 32 22
Fax +49 (0) 2 51-922 60 99
e-Mail: lit@lit-verlag.de
http://www.lit-verlag.de

Distribution:

In Germany: LIT Verlag Fresnostr. 2, D-48159 Münster
Tel. +49 (0) 2 51-620 32 22, Fax +49 (0) 2 51-922 60 99, e-Mail: vertrieb@lit-verlag.de

In Austria: Medienlogistik Pichler-ÖBZ GmbH & Co KG
IZ-NÖ, Süd, Straße 1, Objekt 34, A-2355 Wiener Neudorf
Tel. +43 (0) 22 36-63 53 52 90, Fax +43 (0) 22 36-63 53 52 43, e-Mail: mlo@medien-logistik.at

In Switzerland: B + M Buch- und Medienvertriebs AG
Hochstr. 357, CH-8200 Schaffhausen
Tel. +41 (0) 52-643 54 85, Fax +41 (0) 52-643 54 35, e-Mail: order@buch-medien.ch

Distributed in the UK by: Global Book Marketing, 99B Wallis Rd, London, E9 5LN
Phone: +44 (0) 20 8533 5800 – Fax: +44 (0) 1600 775 663
http://www.centralbooks.co.uk/html

Distributed in North America by:

Transaction Publishers
New Brunswick (U.S.A.) and London (U.K.)

Transaction Publishers
Rutgers University
35 Berrue Circle
Piscataway, NJ 08854

Phone: +1 (732) 445 - 2280
Fax: + 1 (732) 445 - 3138
for orders (U. S. only):
toll free (888) 999 - 6778
e-mail: orders@transactionpub.com

Contents

Acknowledgements	11
1. Introduction	13
1.1. Introduction: Language, discourse and participation	13
1.2. Research process, data collection and text corpora	16
1.3. On actors, targets and interventions – the terminology of development co-operation	16
1.4. Contents	18
2. Participatory rural development in Tanzania	21
2.1. Participatory rural development in Tanzania: Introduction	21
2.1.1. Historic background: Rural development, customary law and the gendered division of labour in agriculture	22
2.2. The postcolonial state: Participation 'from above'	27
2.2.1. From Independence to the Arusha declaration	27
2.2.2. Arusha Declaration and Villagization	31
2.2.3. Aid and dependency	33
2.2.4. Economic crisis and structural adjustment	34
2.2.5. The crisis in agriculture and the peasant agrarian transition	36
2.2.6. Peasant economy in Zanzibar: Dependence on imported staple foods	39
2.2.7. Summary: The state as initiator of participatory development in Tanzania	40
2.3. NGOs, development and the state in Tanzania: Changing relationships	41
2.3.1. The influence of mother cultures: Organizations affiliated to religious institutions	46
2.3.2. The options of local subsidiaries of international organizations	47
2.3.3. The changing background of community development activities	50
2.3.4. The emergence of Tanzanian-based advocacy organizations	52
2.3.5. The new role of NGOs in national policy dialogue	56
2.3.6. Summary: The contribution of NGOs to participatory development in Tanzania	59
2.4. Conclusion	61
3. Donors' agendas and transformatory concepts in development discourse	63
3.1. Participatory rural development: an alternative to top-down technology transfer	65

3.1.1. Robert Chambers' concept of Participatory Rural Appraisal (PRA) 66
3.1.2. Experience from development practice:
setbacks despite 'best intentions' 69
3.1.3. Success as a challenge: institutionalisation and mainstreaming 71
3.2. Are 'mainstream' planning tools compatible with
participatory approaches? 76
3.2.1. Project Cycle Management (PCM) 76
3.2.2. The Logical Framework Approach (LFA) 78
3.2.3. LFA components: Stakeholder and SWOT Analysis as examples 83
3.2.3.1. Stakeholder Analysis 83
3.2.3.2. SWOT Analysis (Strength-Weakness and
Opportunities-Threats Analysis) 85
3.2.4. Planning concepts and the 'reality of aid' 86
3.3. Theoretical concerns: conceptual backgrounds and critical comments 87
3.3.1. Human relations and organizational development 88
3.3.2. Freire's 'Conscientization' and adult education 89
3.3.3. Critical development studies: beyond good intentions 90
3.3.3.1. Power 90
3.3.3.2. Myths of local community and local knowledge 91
3.3.3.3. Expert dominance and the construction of 'knowledge' 92
3.3.4. Postcolonial perspectives 93
3.3.5. Post-developmentalism 95
3.3.6. Donors and participation 96
3.4. Gender Planning: feminist concerns in development co-operation 97
3.4.1. Gender discrimination, colonialism, and notions of development 98
3.4.2. 'Women in Development' and the role of the United Nations 99
3.4.3. Donors and the implementation of the 'Women in Development'
(WID) approach 100
3.4.4. 'Gender Planning' as a tool in development co-operation 102
3.4.5. Donor practice and the DAC (OECD) policy markers 104
3.5. Feminist theory: intersectional analysis 106
3.5.1. The emergence of gender studies 106
3.5.2. Postcolonial feminism: deconstructing WID and nationalism 107
3.5.3. Transnational feminisms:
working towards autonomous feminist practices 109
3.5.4. Donors and Gender Planning 111

3.6. Conclusion: Transforming relationships?	112
4. Sociolinguistic background: Participation and language use	115
4.1. Multilingualism, colonialism, racism	115
4.2. Sociolinguistic approaches and postcolonial challenges	119
4.3. Tanzania: a critical perspective on linguistic choice	127
4.4. Language use and inequality in two agricultural development programmes	136
4.4.1. The Sustainable Rural Agriculture Programme (SRAP)	137
4.4.2. Linguistic preferences of individual actors (SRAP)	139
4.4.3. The Rice Cultivation Mechanization Programme (RCMP)	147
4.4.4. Linguistic preferences of individual actors in the RCMP	152
4.4.5. Conclusion: Language competence and training in the working environment	153
5. Swahili-English codeswitching in development communication in Tanzania – an obstacle for participatory development?	157

5.1. Introduction 157

5.2. Theorising codeswitching in the East African context: the work of Carol Myers-Scotton	159
5.3. Lexical borrowing and terminology development	163
5.4. Bilingualism and codeswitching in formal meetings: attitudes and language use	166
5.4.1. Rural development communication as a Swahili domain	167
5.4.2. Negotiating language use and activities for the week	169
5.4.3. Personal style, technical terms and development jargon	171
5.4.4. Rendering technical information	173
5.4.5. Rural contexts - mitigating codeswitches by translation	175
5.4.6. Lost for words - the dominance of English in teaching and learning contexts	177
5.4.7. Searching for words – preparing Swahili terminology for rural outreach	181
5.4.8. Discussion of results	182
5.5. Conclusion	184
6. Discourses on participation: negotiating programme implementation	189
6.1. Donor dominance in development discourse	189
6.1.1. Critical Discourse Analysis – an influential 'school' in critical linguistics	190

6.1.2. Theoretical and methodological diversity in CDA 192
6.1.3. CDA and poststructural critics 196
6.1.4. Research issues and approaches to analysis 197
6.2. Participation as dialogic exchange 199
6.2.1. The importance accorded to meetings in development work 200
6.2.2. Access and organization: Who participates where, when and how? 205
6.2.3. Egalitarian communication and democratic decision-making 211
6.3. Participation as an obligation to contribute: Time, labour
and user fees 213
6.3.1. Communicating obligations: The framework set by
organizational policy 214
6.3.2. The need to plan 217
6.3.3. Beneficiaries' contributions as an indicator of programme success 219
6.4. Participation as entitlement to material benefits 222
6.4.1. Individual expectations and the wider policy context 222
6.4.2. Requests in circumstances of need 227
6.4.3. Inner-organizational processes 232
6.5. Discussion and results 235
6.5.1. Participation as dialogic communication 235
6.5.2. Participation as obligation 236
6.5.3. Participation as entitlement to material benefits 237
6.5.4. Conclusion 237
7. Participation, language and discourse: ways forward 239
7.1. The examples of the SRAP and the RCMP:
How do participatory processes interact with social inequality? 239
7.1.1. Peasant farmers encountering development intervention:
exclusion of the needy 240
7.1.2. Gendered power differences: superficial progress,
underlying gaps 242
7.1.3. Development workers: creating subaltern voices? 242
7.1.4. The changing role of the state as an actor in participatory
development 243
7.1.5. Asymmetries in global aid relations and tangible local
repercussions 245
7.2. Language use in development organizations:
Can recommendations be made for practice? 245
7.2.1. Organizations and language use 245

7.2.2. Mainstream discourse and the power to define	246
8. Bibliography	249
Notes on Transliteration	277
List of Abbreviations	279

Acknowledgements

The research and analysis presented here would have been impossible without the support of many people and institutions in Tanzania and Austria. I am deeply grateful to all the 'actors in development' in Mara Region, Zanzibar and Vienna who provided information and allowed their voices to be recorded. Several Tanzanian institutions have facilitated this research. I would like to thank the Tanzania Commission for Science and Technology, the Zanzibar Research Committee and the Kiswahili Department of the University of Dar-es-Salaam for their invaluable co-operation.

The research was funded by the Austrian Science Fund (FWF) at several stages: The FWF sponsored the research projects Communication and Development (10/1993-9/1995) and Communication and Consulting (11/1996-10/1999), during which part of the data for this research was collected. From 10/2004 to 3/2006, the FWF granted me a 'Charlotte-Bühler-Habilitationsstipendium' that enabled me to complete the data collection and to undertake a renewed analysis of the extensive data corpus.

At the African Studies Department of the University of Vienna, I want to thank Walter Schicho for his tireless efforts to place contemporary social challenges at the centre of academic engagement. His unorthodox approach to research and teaching, especially in co-ordinating the study programme 'Internationale Entwicklung' (International Development), greatly enriched the intellectual space in which the study of language, communication and development could be pursued. I am very grateful for his readiness to discuss all aspects of this research, and for the many helpful comments and suggestions he made for the manuscript.

Inge Grau and Karsten Legere encouraged me at every stage of the research, read through several drafts of the text and gave valuable advice. Florian Menz and Norbert Cyffer made helpful comments. Among the many other colleagues and friends who supported me I want to mention Birgit Englert, Bea Gomes, Betty Kwagala, Kathrin Bromber, Daniela Waldburger, Birgit Peter, Astrid Nolte, Kaseza Lukumbuzya, Claudia Kragulj, Berta Macha, Ina Ivanceanu, Ulrike Auer, Marcelina Chijoriga, Peter Indalo, Edith Soura and Barbara Nöst. Furthermore, I am also indebted to the students of the 2007 and 2008 seminars on 'Discourse on Participation' for many stimulating challenges and contributions. Needless to say, any shortcomings or errors are my responsibility alone.

As I was writing up the research, my daughters Selvi and Idil engaged into first experiments with language, and developed their own theories on why I spent all that time on the computer. I am grateful to them and Ertürk for patience and curiosity. Last but not least I want to thank the many people who took care of our children as I worked on the text. I remain greatly impressed with the pioneering approach of the Kinderbüro at the University of Vienna. Of the many supportive people of our family in Turkey and Austria, I am particularly grateful to Demet Holly-Kavut, Eylül Sarioğuz and to my parents.

1. Introduction

1.1. Introduction: Language, discourse and participation

The most used aid form is still the project: an externally formulated intervention in local development processes (Degnbol-Martinussen and Engberg-Pedersen 2003:188).

Research for this study was undertaken in the mid-1990s, at a time when the 'participatory turn' began to have an impact on development co-operation (Hickey and Bracking 2005:852; Hickey and Mohan 2005:238). In order to document the role of language in the implementation of participatory approaches in social development, data was collected in two development programmes: the Sustainable Rural Agriculture Program1 (SRAP) in Western Tanzania and the Rice Cultivation Mechanization Programme (RCMP) in Zanzibar. As elsewhere, participatory 'tools' such as the 'Participatory Rural Appraisal' (PRA) had become popular in both programmes. Drawing on theoretical and methodological approaches from critical linguistics (Pennycook 2001) and critical discourse analysis (Chilton and Wodak 2007, Fairclough 2006; 1995; Wodak and Weiss 2003), my analysis aims to gain a better understanding of the way participatory approaches interact with power relations manifest in language and discourse.

While some NGOs promoted participatory approaches from the 1970s and 1980s onwards, it was not until the 1990s that principles and practices like the 'Participatory Rural Appraisal' (PRA) became the expected standard in aid delivery. The PRA's major concern was a reversal of top-down hierarchies in project co-operation through an appeal for a more egalitarian attitude and corresponding behaviour among development workers (Chambers 1997b). While the emerging academic debate approved of an approach that promised to "put the last first" (Chambers 1983), it soon also became critical of the way participatory approaches effectively interacted with power relations, especially at the community level (Nelson and Wright 1995). By the end of the 1990s, the challenge of extending participatory practices to organizations and institutions in development co-operation became evident (Blackburn and Holland eds. 1998). In subsequent years, fundamental doubts about the concept began to be voiced. Arguing that participatory approaches in some cases superseded existing legitimate decision-making processes, and that group dynamics in participatory processes can often work more in the interest of the powerful, poststructural critics have since denounced participation approaches as 'tyranny' (Cooke and Kothari 2001:7-8). In particular, doubt has been cast on across-the-board claims for the capacity of participatory approaches to fundamentally transform asymmetric social relations. Hickey and Mohan

---

1 The names of persons, organizations and programs involved in the research have been changed in order to ensure anonymity of those interviewed.

(2004c:168), who have committed themselves to critical modernism, maintain that, while participatory approaches have the potential to effectively challenge unjust power relation, in their view this potential is limited to highly specific contexts, such as Freirean literacy programmes, participatory governance, social movements and NGO advocacy. In any case, the critical debate has contributed to keeping participation on the agenda, even if as a highly contested topic, with most authors still confident of its ability to contribute to positive change (Parfitt 2004). In the realm of development practice, participatory approaches have grown to encompass aid frameworks that allow for a stronger role of the recipient states and their institutions. "Advocates of participatory alternatives are no longer confined to the grass roots, but promote participation at the macro level" (Lewis and Mosse 2006:4). For example, the implementation of PRSP programmes has been widely accompanied by a debate on the merits of NGO participation in the process.

At the same time, as participatory concepts have proliferated and adapted to newly emerging domains of development co-operation, they have also consolidated their position as an important part of mainstream development. Donors and implementing organizations have adopted participatory approaches as a principle in implementation (cf OEZA 2006b:9) and, as Degnbol-Martinussen and Engberg-Pedersen remind us, the 'project' is still the primary format in which aid is delivered. In their view, "the project co-operation form has been able to survive", as the "institutional framework for the 'programme aid' is also the project" (2003:188). Participatory concepts used in aid implementation have changed little over the last decades (Chambers 2007). They continue to feature as both technical instruments (such as PRA) and general policy principles, the implementation of which is difficult to appraise. It is from this perspective that the challenge of understanding how participatory approaches are implemented at the project or programme level is of continued relevance.

In recent years the interdependency of language, communication and participatory development has been addressed from various linguistic perspectives. In his reflections on problems experienced by mother tongue programmes for minority languages, Christopher Stroud (2001) advocates participatory planning for language support programmes in order to achieve greater acceptance and effectiveness. Stroud develops a concept of 'linguistic citizenship' that envisages an active role for speakers of minority languages in corpus and status planning for their language. Discussing recent developments in language planning in South Africa, Kathleen Heugh (2003) points to the continuing exclusion of the majority of the population who are unable to access public services in a language they understand (2003:139). "Linguistic citizenship seeks to overcome narrow monolithic ethnic identity markers and to uncover the ownership of multiple languages and discourses typical of ordinary people in Africa" (2003:142). Commenting on the effect of using English as a medium of instruction for secondary education in Tanzania, Martha Qorro concludes that "In Tanzania ... worth-while development discourse and formal education have been packaged in the medium of English, a language that is foreign to the majority of students and the majority of people in the wider society" (2003:192). She argues that, in order to enable peasant farmers to participate in a discourse on innovation and development, the language of science and education needs to change to Swahili. In her study on language use in a participatory project in Namibia, Rose-Marie Beck has pointed to the dominant role of English in the construction of development expertise. Farmers who actively participated in the discussion as long as it was conducted in their language, Otjiherero, became passive when they were required to write their thoughts on cards in English. "While English has a high esteem and the preferential uses of it are well understood by those who do not speak or write it, those same actors also resent its use, because it excludes them from participating fully in development processes at any level, from the local to the international" (2006:322).

The study presented here takes a broad methodological approach: it combines sociolinguistic perspectives, including an analysis of codeswitching phenomena, with discourse analysis of interviews and planning meetings. For the purpose of analysis, the following 'working definitions' of participation was adopted: Participation is understood as an equitable sharing of knowledge, decision-making as well as the fruits of development, for the benefit of all. As such, participation implies a deep-rooted appeal to justice and humanity, as well as a clear commitment towards more egalitarian human relations. Underlying this definition is an awareness that, as Cooke and Kothari argue, participatory processes described in terms of sharing knowledge and negotiating power relations may "conceal and reinforce oppressions and injustices" (Cooke and Kothari 2001:13). And, as Cooke and Kothari add, this constitutes a systemic rather than a technical problem.

The challenge for this research on two programmes is multilayered: What do outcomes in regard to particular cases tell us? How do participatory processes interact with social inequality in the examples of SRAP and RCMP? What generalisations can be made from the two examples? What are the insights made about methodology and theory in the course of the research process? How can participatory processes be accounted for in their complexity? Finally, there is also the question whether any recommendations can be made for practice.

1.2. Research process, data collection and text corpora

The data for the empirical analysis of this study was collected by Irmi Maral-Hanak and Barbara Nöst during two research periods in Western Tanzania (Mara Region) and Zanzibar in February, March July, August and September of 1994. Throughout the research, which focussed on organizational and communicative patterns in the Sustainable Rural Agriculture Programme (SRAP) in Western Tanzania and in the Rice Cultivation Mechanization Programme (RCMP) in Zanzibar, more than 90 people were interviewed and over 30 meetings were attended and recorded. From this transliterated data corpus, 33 interviews and 9 meetings in the SRAP programme and 11 interviews and 6 meetings pertaining to the RCMP programme were used for linguistic analysis. The selected data provided a comprehensive source covering the various communicative events in the two programmes.[2] (Hanak/Nöst/Schicho 1995, Hanak 1997 and 1998).

Information on the two development networks was updated during two stays in Tanzania in August 2000 and June 2001. These shorter visits were also used to supplement the compiled text corpora with literature research at the University of Dar es Salaam. The main literature search, text analysis and writing was carried out in Vienna between 2005 and 2007.

1.3. On actors, targets and interventions – the terminology of development co-operation

Development co-operation is characterized by discrepancies between targeted objective and actual performance, as well as wide-spread use of idealizing language. A few remarks must therefore be made on the terminology used in this book. On the one hand, development co-operation is primarily negotiated in terms of a material transaction, measurable in monetary terms from donors to recipients. On the other hand, mutual obligations and gratifications often play an important role, both on the level of openly acknowledged values such as intercultural learning and on the level of covertly pursued economic, strategic or political agendas. This leads to complex, multilayered forms of interaction that do not necessarily facilitate mutual understanding. The problem may be exacerbated in the context of participatory approaches. Claims to make relations balanced, transparent and democratic, stated in a language full of optimism and progressive attitude, often stand in stark contrast to top-down practices widespread throughout the aid industry.

Much of the current terminology in the practice of social development continues to reflect the technical, economic or military contexts from which some of the

---

2   The research referred to here was part of the research project 'Communication and Development' which was directed by Prof. Walter Schicho and sponsored by the Austrian Science Foundation. The author of the study was involved throughout the collection of the set of data selected for linguistic analysis here.

most relevant ideas and concepts have originated. The realization of technical 'projects' such as bridges or hospitals has dominated ideas of development from the 1950s onwards. At present, 'intervention' is a word commonly used to refer broadly to any type of project or programme activity, as development continues to be seen as a process primarily conceptualized and managed from the outside. When people became an important focus of efforts in social development from the late 1980s and 1990s onwards, they were initially identified as 'beneficiaries' or 'target groups', the underlying assumption being that they were the passive recipients of development programmes designed and implemented by others. When so-called 'participatory' approaches gained ground, the appellations became more diverse, including terms like 'people', 'actors', 'women', 'marginalized groups' and 'stakeholders'. The concept of 'actors' is often restricted to donors, experts and development workers. In this study, the term 'actors' will be used as a collective term for all human beings who are involved in the two types of programmes discussed. This use of the term recognizes that the agency of all people involved is important, and should be the subject of critical analysis. At the same time, the term 'beneficiary', is also retained to refer specifically to the peasant farmers who took part in the SRAP and RCMP programmes. Alternatively, terms specific to each of the programmes are also employed, such as 'peasant farmers' (wakulima) or 'rice farmers' (wakulima wa mpunga) in RCMP. In SRAP the phrase 'peasant farmers' (wakulima) was used, as well as specifications such as 'group members' (wanakikundi), 'follow-up group', 'youth' (vijana) or 'women' (wanawake). The origins and backgrounds of such denominations are often enmeshed in the project's history, such as the fact that the senior 'follow-up group' consisted mostly of men, while women only formed a group years later.

Moving on to the people who work in the aid industry, a similar diversity in terminology can be observed. The Zimbabwean aid programme co-ordinator and feminist activist Everjoice Win has aptly caricatured the imbalances in the careers of national and expatriate development professionals. In her "Open letter to my donor friend" (2004:123), she describes how a US-American graduate can rise to become a 'South-Africa expert' in a development organization by virtue of a few months' stay in the region. In colloquial Tanzanian English, the terms 'expat'(riate) and 'expert' are at times ironically collapsed into one, reflecting the observation that qualified foreign development workers enjoy comparative advantages over their often equally or better qualified Tanzanian counterparts. In the present study, 'development worker' is preferred as a broad term to encompass everyone from junior volunteers to senior specialists, irrespective of their nationality and the terms of their contracts, which may be 'local' or 'international', or the significant differences in their respective salaries. Differences in working conditions, such as different income levels or organizational links with donor organizations are pointed out wherever necessary. When the term 'expert' is used in this study it refers to senior aid workers who enjoy privileged status within the aid network. Finally, specific terms used within the organizations are also

employed. In the context of the SRAP development workers referred to themselves as counsellors (washauri), while in RCMP the terms 'specialist' (mtalaamu) and 'extension agent' (bwanashamba) were used.
Finally, it is worth noting here that both the SRAP and the RCMP included the term 'program' in their official designation. At the same time, both the beneficiaries and the development workers used the term 'project' interchangeably with 'program'. The preference of the term 'program' over 'project' in both cases reflected claims about the scope of activities, as well as an awareness of wider policy changes in favour of 'program' approaches. In this study, the term 'network' is also sometimes used, referring to the organizational set-ups related to the implementation of programmes (Schicho and Nöst 2006:53).

1.4. Contents

Chapter One provides an introduction to the highly asymmetric multilingual environment in which development co-operation takes place. Contemporary development discourse tends to emphasize participation and gloss over inequalities. In planning, aid organizations generally focus on technical and economic aspects and do not address language issues. The purpose of this book is to explore practices of language use in the everyday implementation of aid programmes. This study further offers a critical linguistic perspective on language choice and discourses of participation. In its analysis, it draws on the postcolonial critique of development as well as the recent debate on the 'tyranny of participation'.

Chapter Two offers an overview of participatory approaches throughout Tanzania's postcolonial history. For the Tanzanian government, participatory development constituted an important policy goal. Tanzania committed itself to the policy of Ujamaa, accorded priority to rural development, and gave substantial support to Swahili, the national language spoken by the majority of the population. A number of achievements were made in the era of 'Tanzanian Socialism' before this state-centred approach was eventually discarded in favour of economic and later political liberalisation. In the 1980s and 1990s, development actors in the emerging 'civil society' could build on a public consciousness in which the ideas of equal access, participation, empowerment and women's rights had acquired legitimacy. Some NGOs took over tasks in social service provision, others focussed on advocacy. Retaining an independent position towards the government or foreign donors, for example, in the process of negotiating Poverty Reduction Strategy Papers (PRSPs), remains a challenge for development NGOs in Tanzania.

Chapter Three analyzes donors' commitment to participatory development, which has emerged on a larger scale from the 1990s onwards and entails multiple expectations. The purpose of the beneficiaries' enhanced participation was to render programmes more effective, to add legitimacy to neo-liberal cost-sharing measures and to make recipient governments more accountable. Planning techniques such as the 'Participatory Rural Appraisal' promised swift implementation and tangible results. Multilateral agencies including the World Bank and the OECD's Development Assistance Committee (DAC) assumed a leading role in rendering 'participation' part of the mainstream development approach – without effectively questioning asymmetries in aid relations. A similar process occurred with regard to 'Gender Planning'. Complex feminist demands were reduced to a planning tool that promised manageable change and measurable progress. However, improvements were superficial and came at the cost of ambivalent overall impacts on gender relations.

Chapter Four turns to the communicative dimensions of participatory development, as well as the linguistic challenges involved. In Sub-Saharan Africa, the legacy of colonial language policies continues to shape stereotypes about the potential of African and European languages. Critical linguistic analysis needs to go beyond conventional socio-linguistics, as concepts of attitude, appropriateness or prestige potentially raise more questions than they answer. An integrated social, political and linguistic perspective is in a better position to explain the linguistic predicament of Tanzania, where Swahili has become a popular resource of inclusive development communication while English has in many respects retained a dominant position. From the analysis of interviews with aid workers and beneficiaries in two agricultural programmes, distinct patterns of language use and preference emerge. Although Swahili is the working language of development organizations, the use of English persists when technical matters are discussed. At the same time, Tanzanians readily accommodate the communicative needs of English-speaking foreign aid workers or visiting co-operation partners.

Chapter Five analyzes the linguistic strategies of aid workers, in particular practices of codeswitching. Speakers are proficient in at least 2-3 languages and adapt to a variety of communicative situations. Analysis of language use in meetings illustrates that, for aid workers, switching between languages is part of a shared code. Communicating largely in Swahili, while resorting to English for technical terms, is a wide-spread practice of Tanzanian professionals. The study documents that this phenomenon was also common among development workers in SRAP and RCMP programmes. It is a pragmatic choice, as Swahili is the language of wider communication in Tanzania, while secondary and higher education continue to operate in English. However, in the practice of participatory development, development workers' failure to diligently work on their technical vocabulary in Swahili has its pitfalls. When communicating technical information to beneficiaries, the option of switching to English can not work. On the contrary, failure to express relevant concepts in Swahili excludes the majority, who do not understand English, from innovative discourse. This is particularly regrettable, as much of the required terminology development for Swahili has been accomplished and only needs to be put into practical use.

Chapter Six deals with the meanings given to 'participation' in discourses on programme implementation. In meetings that bring together development workers and peasant farmers, a diversity of interpretations regarding participation in development emerges. Discourse analysis of these meetings as well as related interviews allows for the identification of three main dimensions in the way participation is perceived: First, participation is understood as dialogic exchange, a sharing of ideas and opinions. A participatory communicative culture is considered an essential prerequisite for a holding a stake in planning and decision-making. However, the peasant farmers' influence in planning processes was largely confined to technical details, that is, they were consulted rather than involved in decision-making. A second interpretation of participation concerned the commitment in time, labour or financial means expected of peasant farmers. Development workers were found to link notions of working morale and industriousness to their perception of the farmers' engagement. The third dimension of participation involved the material benefits that peasant farmers expected from taking part in the programmes. The inclusion of beneficiaries in participatory planning processes clearly raised expectations, however, in many cases the farmers' priorities differed significantly from the program's objectives.

Chapter Seven sums up the results and provides recommendations. From a theoretical perspective, the study found that the linguistic dichotomy of English and indigenous languages which is typical of postcolonial states in Sub-Saharan Africa is a hindrance to true participation in development endeavours. It also found that addressing the inequality of actors in terms of their power to define key concepts of co-operation yields important insights into the interrelationship of power and participation. Furthermore, in the process of planning a program's activities, outlining the terms of implementation and negotiating work processes the actors redefine their relationships. A reflexive approach towards language use is therefore recommended.

With respect to the practice of development co-operation, the study concludes that development programmes should not only react and accommodate linguistic environments, but also consider measures of active support for the corpus development of languages that facilitate participatory development. Aid workers often have a clear understanding of the problem. Their specific experience of language constraints should be considered and systematic institutional support and motivation offered.

2. Participatory rural development in Tanzania

2.1. Participatory rural development in Tanzania: Introduction

During the 1990s, participation, empowerment and gender were cutting-edge concepts of international development co-operation in Tanzania. In rural development, they largely replaced modernist approaches to agriculture that had dominated much of the 1960s and 1970s. However, a closer look reveals that programmes emphasising community development and participation for rural development have a long history and continuity in what constitutes today's Tanzania. The objective of the following chapter is to show that, from the perspective of Tanzanian peasant farmers, participatory approaches of the 1990s often did not have much new to offer. Despite the change in actors and discourses, propositions made and contributions required by development agencies were familiar from earlier 'development encounters' with the state. This historic contextualisation is important in understanding the principal dilemmas and challenges of participatory rural development in present-day aid networks: is it possible to empower people by outside intervention? Moreover, how can adverse macro-economic and political conditions be dealt with?

Both development programmes analyzed in this study are set in rural Tanzania of the mid-1990s and both aim at improving peasant farmers' income and productivity, albeit with different approaches. Both programmes primarily support peasant agriculture, concentrating on staple food production, an aim the SRAP (Sustainable Rural Agriculture Program) in Musoma pursues through organic farming, while the RCMP (Rice Cultivation Mechanization Program) in Zanzibar provides means for conventional agricultural mechanisation. In order to adequately appreciate the socio-economic context of the respective programmes, the historic background of participatory approaches to rural development in Tanzania is outlined in this chapter. As agriculture has always been vital for the country's fortunes as a whole, the issues raised are complex and often go beyond the scope of this work. The socio-historic overview offered here is necessarily limited to the more relevant aspects.

In the last 30 years, the general picture of African agriculture is one of stagnation and decline. Between 1971 and 2004, Sub-Saharan Africa has generally experienced a 15% fall in per capita production (Wiggins 2005:17). Nevertheless, during two extended periods in the 20th century, from the start of the century until 1929, and from the late 1940s until the early 1970s, African agriculture experienced sustained growth driven by strong demand for exports. However, in recent decades, success stories are few and far between, and most of them do not last beyond 5-10 years.

This chapter is essentially divided in two parts. After a short review of the colonial history, the first part looks at the postcolonial state's performance in participatory rural development. It focuses on political events, their influence on development policy as well as the particular characteristics of the Tanzanian rural economy, the interaction of the Tanzanian state with foreign donors, socio-economic change and the peasant agrarian transition, gender relations in the rural economy as well as on the specific situation in Zanzibar. The second part of the chapter turns to NGOs' achievements in participatory development from the mid-1980s onwards. It discusses the emergent state-NGO relationship, the peculiarities of organizations originating in influential mother cultures such as religious institutions, the dependency of local subsidiaries of international NGOs, the changing background of community development activities, the emergence of Tanzanian-based advocacy organizations, as well as the new role of NGOs in policy dialogue. The role of donors, the third major group of actors in Tanzania's history of participatory development, is followed up in both parts of the chapter.

Despite recent encouraging economic growth rates, Tanzania remains among the poorest countries in the world, its agriculture caught up in structural problems of intransparent marketing authorities and an unfavourable world market. The situation in Tanzania and many other parts of Sub-Saharan Africa poses challenges that require far-ranging social and political solutions. Genuine participatory development means that governments in the South and the North will have to address people's priorities through adequate policy frameworks, otherwise intervention at programme or project level will continue to have a very limited impact.

2.1.1. Historic background: Rural development, customary law and the gendered division of labour in agriculture

The present-day rural economy of Tanzania originated in the 19th century when agricultural systems combining food and cash crops emerged and a number of new crops and farm implements were introduced. By the late 19th century, the German colonial state increasingly tried to introduce export crops, partly by setting up plantations, but more effectively by forcing small-scale farmers to pay taxes, and to raise money through the cultivation of cash crops such as coffee.

The establishment of colonial rule from the end of the 19th century onwards was characterized by dominance and coercion. "Development" initiatives in colonial contexts, especially infrastructural projects such as the building of roads or bridges, often relied on forced labour. Taxation combined with regional bans on cash-crop production were used to create labour reserves providing migrant labour according to the need of the plantation economy (Havnevik 1993:31). In other areas such as Kilimanjaro, peasants were urged to cultivate cash crops for export. In both cases, discriminatory legislation that enforced distinct social hierarchies was instrumental in safeguarding the colonial government's economic interests.

An important part of this oppressive regime was customary law as implemented by the colonial authorities. Customary law consisted of social norms that originated in oral traditions and were codified during the colonial period. In the process of codification, some norms were reinterpreted and instrumentalized so as to suit the requirements of the colonial economy. The social model of the extended patrilineal family meant that it was largely male elders who took decisions on the allocation of resources and labour force for a larger family unit. While ensuring the economic viability of peasant family production (cf. Bryceson 1999), this model reinforced gendered and age-based hierarchies. Women largely remained dependent on men for access to land. They worked primarily in subsistence and retained only limited control over what they produced. Customary law also meant that the older generation to a certain extent had means to control younger family members. When migration began to offer young men alternative sources of status and income, customary law was instrumentalized to "keep the younger generation in its place". The ideology underpinning these policies made ample use of constructs such as "tribe" in the sense of a rigid social entity of rural Africa that in the view of colonial anthropology existed unperturbed by historical processes. Urban migration, it was feared, posed a challenge to this supposedly static social order. While codified customary law does reflect some of the social norms of African societies in the 19th (a period in which the area that constitutes today's Tanzania was fraught with war, slavery, famine and disease and rather authoritarian social and political structures emerged) and the 20th century (in which the colonial influence dominated), it had developed specific characteristics which served the interests of the colonial government and were often of particular disadvantage to women and youths (Grau 2006:84).

Customary law had a structural influence on agricultural production that extended far beyond the colonial era. For a large part of the 20th century, combined peasant food and cash crop production meant that subsistence and food crops were women's domains, while the more prestigious cash crops were men's prerogative. Land ownership in most areas was controlled through the patrilineage and women had little access to cash income from the sale of export crops. Under these circumstances, women were often hesitant to contribute work to men's cash crop fields (Kabeer and Whitehead 2001:4), a factor that some authors assume to have hampered economic growth. In some cases, women preferred to work as waged labourers instead of being helpers on 'family' farms where cash income was controlled by men. While there is obviously a bias against women's participation in agricultural production, the situation was and is by no means uniform throughout Tanzania. Relationships between women and men in households have been found to include co-operative along with competitive aspects, comprising "complex and shifting arenas of separation and interdependence" (Kabeer and Whitehead 2001:10). Moreover, geographical conditions, population density, availability of land, cultural factors such as patrilineal or matrilineal family and inheritance patterns as well as individual preferences are factors that shape varying local conditions.

Nevertheless, in most areas, a more or less strict gendered division of labour prevailed, with women primarily responsible for subsistence, whereas men either migrated or tended to cash crops. In order to illustrate an example of this division of labour, some aspects of Kate Crehan's study of a settlement scheme in Chizela in rural Zambia in the late 1980s will be summed up here. Crehan's account gives a detailed insight into the complex interdependence of gendered peasant agriculture. In the village she studied, women cultivated sorghum, the primary subsistence crop in the region, and it was also their responsibility to store and distribute food to household members. They performed numerous household tasks such as fetching water and fuelwood, pounding grain, cooking as well as looking after the children. Men also worked in subsistence agriculture and housework, but rather with occasional tasks such as clearing fields and building houses. Otherwise, they engaged in commercial farming, especially of maize which was sold rather than consumed locally. Women were not principally barred from engaging in cash-crop production. However, because of their considerable workload in subsistence production, household chores and childcare, women had little time to do so (Crehan 1997:148). Another factor barring women from cash crop production was the bureaucratic language surrounding commercial farming. Extension services, marketing facilities as well as participation in a development project providing support to commercial farming was "policed by endless forms - usually in English - that operated according to rules and conventions that local women, most of whom were illiterate even in Kaonde, let alone English, found alien and intimidating" (Crehan 1997:167). Crehan comes to the conclusion that women were systematically disadvantaged when it came to commercial agricultural production.

Naturally, ethnographic descriptions such as Crehan's work depict temporary conditions. They reflect the interaction of a community's norms with outside influences and circumstances and individual everyday practice by its members. Neither the community's norms nor everyday reality can be generalized for the region at large. Relationships are multidimensional and continuously subject to change; what may have been an adequate description of gender relations at a certain point of time, often turns out to be irrelevant at a later stage. Additionally, the study quoted here concerns a community organized along matrilineal kinship ties, a social pattern that constitutes an exception in Eastern Africa where in most areas patrilineal family patterns predominate. While the study's findings are therefore not to be generalized, Crehan's account allows a helpful insight into how competition and co-operation in complex household and family relations take concrete shape.

A differentiated approach is all the more important as African agriculture, including its gendered division of labour, has been subject to numerous stereotypes and inappropriate generalizations. Ann Whitehead (2000:41), for example, reveals how Eurocentric stereotypes about 'lazy' African farmers have often been veiled in a language of feigned commitment to women's emancipation. Comparing development approaches of British Colonial Governments in Eastern and Southern Africa in the 1920s and 1950s, as well as World Bank documents of the 1990s, she demonstrates how rural African men have repeatedly been stereotyped as 'idle' or 'lazy', particularly when they refused to work for agricultural export production under unfavourable conditions. Whitehead points to the continuity in the argument throughout the 20th century. In the 1920s, British colonial economists eager to boost cash crop production labelled African peasants as inert and idle, implying that measures to force them to work were required. In the 1950s, Nobel-Prize winner Arthur Lewis (1954), an influential economist with the Colonial Office in London, identified the "unlimited supply of labour" as a key feature of developing economies, working with the presumption that rural men are largely 'underemployed'. In 1998, the authors of a World Bank report on the Special Programme of Assistance for Africa hold that if control of agricultural means of production was passed from men to women, growth could be boosted to up to 15% (Blackden and Bhanu 1999:3;20; quoted from Whitehead 2000). Again, the underlying argument is that men fail to respond to opportunities in cash crop production because they are unwilling to work adequately. At the same time, by unfairly forcing a larger share of the daily workload on women, men prevent women from utilising their potential in the cash crop domain. Single case studies, for example, one focusing on a particular community in Zambia where men are found to engage in no more than two hours of productive work per day, were quoted in support of the argument which is then generalized for the whole continent (Blackden and Bhanu 1999:72; quoted from Whitehead 2000). While the preoccupation with gender issues may be a minority position within the International Financial Institutions, an inappropriate instrumentalization of feminist arguments in this case works to divert attention from other reasons for the poor performance of cash crop agriculture. Among these, problematic agricultural policies imposed by the IMF and World Bank as part of Structural Adjustment Programs would feature significantly. However, instead of questioning deterrent costs for inputs, unfavourable world market prices or disadvantageous marketing conditions, it may be more convenient to blame African men's 'idleness' and their 'unfair' behaviour towards women for the crisis in cash crop production. Whitehead criticizes this approach as implicitly racist. She points out that as long as household work and childcare are taken into account - as is done in East African data referred to above – statistics on the gendered divisions of labour in Sub-Saharan Africa and Europe are similarly skewed. In both cases, men enjoy significantly more leisure and relaxation time than women. Yet, economic and social policy discourse rarely portrays European men as underemployed or lazy, particularly when they work in the formal sector. While neo-liberal argumentation in the report has replaced the 'male breadwinner vs. female housewife' cliché with models of co-operative and competitive intra-household relations, some of the arguments presented are reminiscent of ideology justifying colonial labour policy.

Tanganyika was subject to British rule after Germany lost WWI in 1918. Agricultural policy had initially been driven by Germany's, and after 1918 by Britain's need for export crops such as coffee, tea, sisal and cotton. Some areas were turned into labour reserves, and in others cash crop production by African farmers was encouraged. Agricultural policy focussed on extension and support for 'model farmers' who would supposedly become examples for the large numbers of other farmers. The cultivation of "cash crops" became attractive in an increasingly monetized economy, with the necessity to pay taxes constituting a major motivating factor. In regions such as Kilimanjaro, Bukoba and Sukumaland, the production of maize, coffee and cotton increased dramatically between 1924 and 1934 (Hyden 1980:48ff.). With the introduction of new crops, agricultural extension officers became relevant as advisors for peasant farmers. However, peasants were in some cases reluctant to plant new crops, especially as changes in agricultural practices often led to soil erosion and pest infestation. People became even more cautious when the British administration coerced peasants into communal labour for respective soil conservation measures or activities to prevent the spread of the tsetse fly.

Nevertheless, cash-crop production by small-scale farmers took root in many regions, and from the mid-1950s, rising demand for agricultural products on the world market was met by an adequate response: "For African peasants, the postwar period was dominated by the cash-crop boom" (Illiffe 1979: 453).

The British administration supported this development with extension based on agricultural research. It also began to engage in community development projects in the 1940s and 1950s. Widespread discontent with social and political conditions gave rise to a growing anti-colonial movement. Community development was an attempt to improve living conditions and create popular compliance. Programmes required some measure of popular participation, even if in the colonial context the primary aim was to prevent possible forms of resistance. In particular, community development was intended to counteract any tendencies towards urbanisation, which was regarded as an undesirable development: it was feared that this could lead to political engagement of Africans in nationalist movements. However, in the long run the strategy failed: "The colonial regime in Tanganyika failed to achieve the aim of simultaneously ensuring compliance and popular support, and peasant resistance succeeded in forcing the state to abandon its rural development strategy in 1956/7" (Jenning 2003:185). Peasants' resistance was in part expressed in a refusal to comply with conservation measures, such as maintaining terraces, dipping and destocking their cattle (Coulson 1979:17). Thus, while some development activities in colonial contexts anticipated the importance of the involvement of communities, of gaining their commitment and approval, this idea of popular participation was clearly limited to a context that would facilitate the dissemination of top-down knowledge and introduce the idea of cost-sharing, both entrenched within a hierarchically structured system of foreign dominance.

In contrast, opportunities to participate in the anti-colonial movement met with broader popular enthusiasm. This included both membership in and commitment to TANU (Tanganyika African National Union), as well as the labour and co-operative movements (Havnevik 1993:32). From the 1950s onwards, TANU also initiated self-help schemes, in particular to meet social needs such as schools in areas neglected by the colonial government (Jennings 2003:166).

2.2. The postcolonial state: Participation 'from above'

2.2.1. From Independence to the Arusha declaration

After Independence in 1961, the Tanganyika government under the leadership of Julius K. Nyerere attempted to reach out to the large majority of smallholder peasant farmers. However, the early years after Independence were characterized by conventional economic policy that did not fundamentally differ from the preceding approach of the British administration. Just prior to Independence, the British had invited a World Bank mission to assess Tanzania's economic potential. The resulting report and its recommendations became the basis for the independent government's first three-year plan (1962-65) and the subsequent five-year plan (1965-1970) (Rugumamu 1997:112). Despite his conventional economic policy, as early as 1962, Nyerere also began to popularise some of his ideas on African Socialism (Nyerere 1962, quoted from Havnevik 1993:196). By propagating the Ujamaa concept, he evoked the notion of mutual support within the traditional African extended family. Ujamaa placed an emphasis on rural development, aiming to achieve progress by addressing the concerns of peasant farmers who constituted the large majority of the Tanzanian people. Communal efforts and settlement schemes were seen as the most promising steps towards self-reliant development. In his inaugural address as President in the same year, Nyerere also introduced the idea of villagization, arguing that the provision of schools, hospitals and wells, as well as the widespread use of modern farm implements such as ploughs and tractors, would not be feasible as long as people continued to live in isolated homesteads. Instead, people should move to villages which would then be provided with the necessary infrastructure (Nyerere 1966:183-184, quoted from Havnevik 1993:196).

Irrespective of this early commitment towards what were to become core elements of "Tanzanian Socialism", in the first years after Independence, Nyerere's government essentially implemented the two strategies for rural development that the World Bank had recommended, the "improvement approach" and the "transformation approach". Both conformed to the modernization theory of the 1960s, including the expectation that the example of a few progressive farmers and as well as mechanisation on large scale farms and settlement schemes would eventually lead to widespread technological innovation and growing agricultural output. The 'transformation approach' related to the setting up of commercial agriculture in government-controlled settlement schemes. Farmers retained individual land titles and were expected to engage in modern commercial farming under the guidance of agricultural extension officers. The 'improvement approach' provided better inputs for commercial agriculture to a few farmers whose example was supposed to be a model for others; their example was then expected to persuade the large majority of rural peasants into modernization. Additionally, it invited popular participation in self-help schemes where the government gave support to communal efforts of building schools, dispensaries, water schemes and other rural infrastructural programmes (Jennings 2003:165). The communal settlement schemes established under the transformation approach proved a failure and were abandoned by 1966 (Lyimo 1999:162). The major problem had been that technology introduced in these settlement schemes was used uneconomically, making production far too expensive.

The improvement approach, especially the expected model effect, was extremely slow to produce results. While moderate growth in agriculture continued, the share of subsistence agriculture increased, a sign of decommercialisation caused by falling prices on the world market and inefficient management through governmental marketing structures.

Nevertheless, even in the early years after Independence, some developments already set a trend towards more sustainable approaches, while in some ways anticipating possible contradictions between the objective of broad democratic participation and the realization of equal social standards for all. One illustrative example in this regard relates to the participatory self-help initiatives that were encouraged as part of the improvement approach. The principal idea was that communities should organize themselves into building schools, dispensaries or other projects. The government would then support the effort by providing running costs such as salaries for teachers and nurses. "In theory, it was a policy of development from below, a consensus-driven model in which projects would both be initiated and implemented by the communities themselves" (Jennings 2003:166). The promise of government support led to an intensive response by rural communities. People constructed roads, bridges, schools, clinics, dispensaries, community centres and markets, achievements that were at least partly documented in annual reports from the districts and regions (Jennings 2003:168). In some areas, activities reached an intensity that began to worry governmental development planners coordinating programmes on a regional or national level. Communities began to compete against each other for financial resources, for instance, by hurrying to build a primary school or water scheme before the neighbouring community managed to do so and ensuring that "development" resources went there instead. This resulted in duplication (such as water schemes or schools being constructed unnecessarily close to each other) and uneven distribution of essential services. As comparatively affluent regions were more successful in mobilising self-help initiatives, disproportional amounts of government funding were channelled there rather than into poorer areas. At times, projects were initiated without being registered with local or regional planning authorities, with the hope of gaining acceptance and support later as buildings approached completion. Government bureaucrats were irritated by the local and at times chaotic nature of the process, aspiring to more centralized forms of planning instead. By the end of the 1960s, the self-help schemes began to lose their voluntary character as some overzealous bureaucrats implemented coercive measures to compel villagers to work in community projects. The government intensified its control of development planning, strengthening bureaucrats' and politicians' means to direct development processes from above. As Jennings observes, unlike in many other cases of participatory processes initiated by governmental institutions, it was not lack of interest by the peasants, but rather the very success of achieving broad popular commitment that finally led to the relinquishing of this approach (Jennings 2003:185).

Another notable development concerned the settlement schemes that were promoted as part of the transformation approach. Most of these settlements were state run and, as mentioned above, not very successful in their objective of rationalizing agricultural production. Some, however, had a more autonomous character, the most remarkable being the villages that formed the Ruvuma Development Association (RDA). Founded in 1961, the RDA was a co-operative body that had been established by committed TANU youth leaders and peasant settlers. Educating critical, independent minds and cultivating democratic decision-making were core principles of the RDA villages. The constitution of the RDA specified that the peasant farmers fully controlled and owned the co-operative and its assets. This meant for example that in contrast to other settlement schemes, technical innovations in agricultural production were implemented unhurriedly and at the deliberation of the villagers themselves. The RDA was relatively independent from the local party bureaucracy, but received support from foreign donors, in particular from Oxfam. Many of the RDA villages, in particular Litowa, achieved substantial results in communal agricultural production. Nyerere was said to refer to Litowa as an exemplary village that embodied the essential principles of Ujamaa in practice (Hyden 1980:75; 100). The success of the RDA villages was certainly due to a number of factors, among them progressive leadership, but most importantly the fact that villagers did in fact manage and determine their own affairs democratically.

However, it was precisely this autonomy and success that had raised ill feelings on the part of party bureaucrats over the years (Havnevik 1993:198-200, Hyden 1980:106). Villagers in Litowa were self-confident, informed and outspoken, and more than once argued publicly against party directives. For instance, they opposed the compulsory growing of tobacco as they had found the crop to be labour-intensive while offering little reward. "The RDA was an autonomous organization, receiving funds and personnel from abroad, and promoting a form of socialism that did not depend on a strong central party" is Coulson's plain assessment of a situation that gravely annoyed party officials and eventually led to the dismantling of the RDA by TANU's central committee in 1969 (1985:271). Although by the end of the 1970s the Arusha Declaration's principles had only begun to be implemented in a few regions in Tanzania, TANU party bureaucracy had already grown unable to tolerate self-determined communities that had made tremendous advances in rural development, communal efforts and self-reliance. The party obviously felt threatened by what could be termed a successful 'empowerment' process, namely one in which peasant farmers had begun to hold real power and control over their lives. TANU subsequently decided to place all Ujamaa villages under its direct control, de facto annihilating the achievements of the model communities that had been essential in inspiring Nyerere's philosophy of Ujamaa and self-reliance.

While some of the villages of the RDA had started to implement principles of communal work soon after Independence, in most other areas Ujamaa was first heard of after the Arusha Declaration of 1967 when the establishment of Ujamaa villages in which people were encouraged to engage in communal activities for the benefit of all had become an official policy. Nyerere had outlined the features of Ujamaa in rather utopian terms, stressing the importance of education and personal autonomy for achieving true development. The absence of exploitation and the fulfilment of basic needs such as access to food, housing, education, health and other social services were held as major development objectives. Communal effort and self-reliance in agricultural production were the starting points to achieve progress. Ujamaa appealed to the African culture of mutual assistance within the extended family, while not necessarily idealising traditions.

For example, Nyerere frequently pointed to the subdued position of rural women who, on average, worked far more than men, an exploitative relationship that was to be overcome in the newly established Ujamaa villages (Nyerere 1968). To a certain extent, this argument once again took up colonial stereotypes of the "lazy African man" and "problematic city women", giving political leaders the opportunity to criticize male peasant farmers while drawing attention away from their own privileged position. However, emancipatory arguments were not limited to mere rhetoric. Women benefited considerably from welfare programmes in health, education and infrastructure. From the seventies onwards, legal reforms gradually alleviated women's discrimination in family, inheritance and labour laws as well as in the domain of political participation. Progress was slow enough, and probably largely irrelevant for the majority of rural women. Nevertheless, in the domain of legal reform Tanzania advanced considerably faster than other countries in the region.

This example shows that Nyerere's political rhetoric was at the same time promisingly progressive yet evasive, with few concrete notions of implementation. This flaw may be one of the root causes of the often considerable difference between ideological promise and everyday reality, as it was often left to civil servants' discretion of what to make of policy guidelines.

It should also be noted here that Paulo Freire, a pioneer of radically participatory approaches to literacy and education was invited to Tanzania in 1971 to present his method of literacy teaching at the Institute of Adult Education at the University of Dar es Salaam (Hall 1997:3). The idea of liberation through education had been essential to President Nyereres ideas on Ujamaa and Self-Reliance, and

Freire was enthusiastic about participating in an adult education programme implemented by a postcolonial socialist state. He positively appraised the role of charismatic political leadership for the development of popular conscientization and political culture. In his presentation at the Institute of Adult Education in Dar es Salaam, he emphasized that in his view, "adult education in Tanzania should have as one of its main tasks to invite people to believe in themselves" (Freire 1971:1-5, quoted from Hall 1997:2) to overcome the devastating effects of colonization. As Budd Hall observes, Freire at this occasion even pointed out that methodological issues were secondary to ideological foundation. Freire was not only drawn to the ideas of Julius Nyerere, but also towards the thoughts of Amilcar Cabral during his later, better-known work in Guinea-Bissau, Sao Tomé and Cabo Verde (Torres 1993:132). While Freire was clearly more critical of state authority in other contexts, he was obviously unaware or unwilling to be concerned about the emerging conflict between the Tanzanian government bureaucracy and peasant farmers.

2.2.2. Arusha Declaration and Villagization

The Arusha Declaration in 1967 marked a fundamental re-orientation towards socialist policies. More than before, the government's development policy focussed on peasant households, which held 97.4 percent of all cultivated land in Tanzania in 1971 (Lyimo 1999:182). A core element of the Ujamaa policy was the introduction of communal farming in rural areas. Co-operatives and later parastatal organizations were put in control of agricultural marketing. From 1967 to 1973, the government aimed to resettle the scattered rural population in villages where they could benefit from improved services in terms of health, education and infrastructure. Great efforts were made to expand medical service delivery, promotion of literacy and primary school enrolment.

As pointed out above, Nyerere's speeches and texts on the idealised Ujamaa model were not very concrete in terms of how the large-scale changes in peasant mode of production were to be brought about. Education, persuasion and material support were to be the major instruments which party representatives would use to encourage peasant participation; Nyerere was always very clear about the right to self-determination and democratic decision making by the members of the new Ujamaa villages. However, in the first years after the Arusha declaration, the pace of change in the rural areas was discouragingly slow. The rural peasantry refused to be "captured" by a project of modernization with an uncertain future (Hyden 1980), instead preferring established patterns of cash-crop and subsistence production. Government policy soon began to put party officials under considerable pressure. They had to ensure the initiation of Ujamaa villages and present productive outputs of the communal efforts. This resulted in a major contradiction, whereby a bureaucracy used to giving top-down directives and exercising central control was assigned the role of implementing a socio-political project that was essentially about bottom-up participation and democratic decision-making (Boesen 1979:128). In everyday practice, officials were often disinterested in the quality of the co-operative efforts taking place and were happy to simply present success in terms of mere numbers of newly established villages and members registered there. Officially, coercive measures were not condoned, and after incidents in 1968 Nyerere publicly affirmed Ujamaa villagers' right to determine their own affairs. However, contradictions began to emerge. Large-scale resettlement 'operations' in Rufiji District (1969), Dodoma Region (1970) and Kigoma Region (1972) marked the beginning of a pragmatic approach that relied on mass coercion rather than voluntary commitment.

In 1973-74, Nyerere officially shifted policy priority from collective economic efforts to resettlement in villages. In 1973, TANU decided that by 1976 all Tanzanians must live in villages or towns (Boesen 1979:128). With the official policy insisting on rigorous implementation of 'villagization', the government resorted to force and coercion to move peasants to communal settlements, clearly abandoning the idea of voluntary commitment based on individual conviction. Villagization meant different things to different areas in Tanzania, depending on regional differences in implementation, an area's population density, its social stratification and climatic conditions. In densely populated areas there was little need and space to resettle, while people in sparsely populated areas faced pressure to move together. In some areas, poorer peasants became the target of resettlement campaigns, while better-off farmers could use their influence to remain undisturbed. People were moved to places that were often inadequately prepared and planned. Villagization enjoyed little popular support and peasant farmers faced difficult conditions in settling in their new villages. Often, they had long distances to cover between their new homes and farms. It took time before houses were built or perennial crops could be harvested. Service provision, one of the main arguments used to justify villagization, could not keep up with soaring demand. An expanding, at times complacent, at times overzealous bureaucracy implemented the government's measures in a hierarchic top-down manner.

In 1976, the government took a further step to bring agricultural production under control. Farmers' co-operatives were abolished and replaced with parastatals. The government successively disbanded or co-opted all existing popular mass organizations. Co-operatives, trade unions, women's and youth associations were either banned or transformed into centrally administered party organizations. Increasingly, the state assumed a virtual monopoly in all socio-political spheres, thereby undermining individual initiative as well as voluntaristic association.

From 1970 onwards, agricultural productivity declined. Disruption caused by the villagization policy was only one of the underlying causes. External factors such as falling world market prices for export products, repeated droughts, as well as soaring oil prices led to an overall crisis in economic development. A period of self-imposed austerity measures from 1979-1982 meant that imported goods, including agricultural inputs, were scarce, with detrimental effects on agricultural production; the ensuing economic crisis was particularly felt in the rural areas.

2.2.3. Aid and dependency

During the early 1970s, Tanzania became a major recipient of aid, entering into co-operation with about 40 different bilateral donors. Support was particularly forthcoming from the Nordic countries, West Germany and Canada who were willing to encourage Tanzania's exemplary strategy of development, in particular the efforts towards promoting popular participation as well as social justice. Throughout the seventies, Tanzania engaged in comprehensive welfare undertakings, aspiring towards Universal Primary Education, providing free education from primary to university, free health care, medical services and free clean water for all its citizens. To some representatives of Western European leftist governments, Nyerere seemed a like-minded social democrat. Among the many corrupt leaders and predatory regimes in Sub-Saharan Africa, Nyerere's personal integrity was a welcome contrast. Ujamaa attracted enthusiasm of Northern NGOs and voluntary organizations. For many development practitioners, the Ujamaa model embodied the realization of their development ideals, to an extent that for many years organizations such as Oxfam failed to fully acknowledge problematic developments such as the villagization campaigns (Jennings 2001:110). "The Tanzanian government gained recognition because it emphasized social welfare, especially regarding health and education, and aspired towards an egalitarian society in which enrichment of the political elite was restricted" (Kiondo 1995:110). Among the donors from communist countries, China assumed considerable importance through facilitating the building of the TAZARA (Tanzania-Zambia Railway). TAZARA was a project of considerable political and economic relevance as it opened access to the port of Dar-es-Salaam for land-locked frontline states and emphasized the strategic importance Tanzania had for the region.

The total development assistance channelled to Tanzania after the Arusha Declaration was of an impressive scale. According to estimates, the country obtained more than $16 billion in external aid between 1967 and 1992, amounting to about 80% of net official flows of external capital (Rugumamu 1997:155). Irrespective of the Arusha Declaration's commitment to self-reliance, foreign aid was allowed to become the dominating factor of the Tanzanian economy. Much of the aid was donated under rather favourable conditions, with the proportion of grants as part of total aid averaging about 80% (Rugumamu 1997:156). Nevertheless, commitment to growing numbers of aid projects and programmes led to donor dependency in all socio-economic domains and to soaring foreign debts. Accepting aid projects usually obliged Tanzania as a recipient country to incur substantial expenses in contributing a national share of the total project costs. In many cases, projects supported by donors did not match Tanzania's priorities, were totally unnecessary or unreasonably costly. Routinely, large parts of the funds were spent on financing the donor countries' aid administration or foreign experts. Instead of insisting on Tanzanian national interests in aid negotiations, inexperienced civil servants often agreed to detrimental conditions, especially as long as funds was generously forthcoming. As a consequence, ministries and planning commissions shifted from policy-making to administration, authorising the transfer of aid resources, mediating between competing national actors, compiling reports as requested by donors as well as monitoring and evaluating aid activities.

In the 1970s, the dominant modernist paradigm held that development was to be co-ordinated by a "strong state" which initiated, implemented and supervised respective activities. In Tanzania this was true to some part, as a proliferating bureaucracy enforced an ever-growing tangle of rules and regulations. At the same time, Tanzania, as was the case with most other recipient governments, lacked the real authority to develop and enforce a genuine national policy to which foreign donors would have to conform. Rather, national actors competed to obtain aid funds, with the government merely supervising negotiations, devoid of real influence on relevant decision-making. In this context, it is somewhat ironic that by the beginning of the 1980s, when the IFIs began to dominate development policy with a neo-liberal agenda, donors identified the dominant role of the state as the primary reason for economic failure. However, with an emerging process of donor co-ordination under the guidance of the IMF and World Bank, other donors also complied with the demands for economic reforms, and Tanzania gradually lost its sources of financial support.

2.2.4. Economic crisis and structural adjustment

Domestically, the government faced a deepening economic crisis by the second half of the 1970s. Economic decline was due to a combination of internal and external factors. The economic downturn began with the first oil shock in 1973-74, followed by years of drought (1974-76). This exacerbated the disruptive effects of the villagization programme which the government had embarked on. Meanwhile, the State Trading Corporation proved inefficient and the reorganization of the marketing system showed poor results. Low producer prices meant that peasant farmers were demotivated. Agricultural production declined, social service provision deteriorated and foreign debt rose. From 1974 onwards, the government had embarked on an import-substituting industrialisation strategy. However, foreign exchange for spare parts and raw materials soon became scarce and factories operated at low capacity. The coffee boom from 1976-77 was insufficient to bring about significant economic recovery. Towards the end of the 1970s, some external developments further aggravated the situation. The break-up of the East African community in 1977 resulted in the need for increased infrastructure-related imports. The second oil shock in 1979-80 and the war with Uganda resulted in a growing budget deficit, while agricultural production continued to decline or stagnate (Gibbon 1995:11, Bigsten and Danielson 2001:16). A further factor was the fall in world market prices for export commodities while prices for imports rose (1979-1982).

With rising inflation, peasant farmers turned away from unprofitable cash crop production, while urban workers and employees experienced a drastic loss of purchasing power. At the same time, many basic consumer goods such as sugar, edible oils and soap were rationed or became unavailable and the provision of social services collapsed. In this climate of economic hardship, the public service became increasingly corrupt and unreliable.

Already by the second half of the 1970s, the IMF and the World Bank had become sceptical about Tanzania's economic policies. Nyerere, however, was determined to resist neoliberal reforms which were in stark contrast to his socialist convictions. He hoped to rely on his good relations with other donors who were willing to continue their support for his political principles. When by 1978, he eventually approached the IMF for a stand-by credit, co-operation failed soon after agreement was reached because the government did not comply with the stipulated conditionalities, among others the devaluation of its currency. A long-lasting conflict between the government and the IMF and World Bank ensued and was only settled in 1986, a year after Nyerere had resigned as president. In the meantime, the government had developed its own rather ambitious austerity programme, the "National Economic Survival Programme" (NESP 1981-82), an appeal to sympathetic donors proving the government's readiness to execute reforms. Its implementation, however, largely failed, and by 1983 most of the donors had withdrawn their support from Tanzania. Around 1980, donor countries that were members to the Development Assistance Committee of the OECD increasingly committed themselves to a co-ordinated policy under the guidance of the IMF and World Bank. Tanzania may have been one of the first countries that experienced rigorous consequences of the concerted action on the part of DAC members (Havnevik 1993:287). In 1984/85 Tanzania once again attempted to introduce major reforms: expenditure for agriculture was significantly raised, producer prices were boosted, the national currency was devalued and subsidies for staple foods abolished. Yet even the Nordic countries, long-term supporters of Tanzania's independent development orientation, refused to grant aid without a prior IMF agreement.

In 1985, Nyerere resigned as president, and in the following year his successor Ali Hassan Mwinyi reached an agreement with the IMF, resulting in a Structural Adjustment Program. Measures included the devaluation of the national currency and import liberalisation (Economic Recovery Programme ERP1 1986-89), followed by ERP2 (1989-1992). Government expenditure rose, and as the adjustment process was mainly financed through foreign aid, the country's dependence on outside support soared. Under pressure from various donors, the government in 1986 changed its policy from a socialist to a liberalised economy, including the restructuring of agricultural marketing. While in the first half of the 1980s, agricultural productivity had declined, the agricultural sector began to recover in the mid-1980s. The increased use of farm inputs, expansion of areas cultivated and a favourable climate were among the factors that contributed to this positive trend (Lyimo 1999:164). However, in 1990, subsidies to agricultural inputs were abolished, resulting in a decline in agricultural productivity. Agricultural growth remained under the target of 5% per annum and generally disappointing in the 1990s. At the same time, health care services, and school enrolment rates, for which Tanzania had gained wide recognition in the 1970s, were negatively affected by the generally poor economic performance.

A major restructuring of agricultural producers' infrastructure involved the reintroduction of farmers' marketing co-operatives. Co-operatives had been replaced by parastatals in 1976 and were only allowed to operate again from 1982 onwards. However, it required a longer reform process before they evolved into functional and attractive membership organizations. In 1985, co-operatives were further enhanced as multipurpose institutions with the aim of integrating agricultural production and marketing. But it was not until 1991 that a legal amendment to the co-operative act of 1982 enabled farmers to initiate co-operatives on their own, finally facilitating broad and popular participation on a voluntary and democratic basis (Lyimo 1999:163).

In 1992, structural adjustment was continued with the "Economic and Social Action Program" (ESAP). Performance in agriculture remained poor, while social services, especially in health and education, continued to be drained of resources. Nevertheless, the IMF agreement and the ensuing political and economic reforms had the effect of restoring donor support to the country. In the early nineties, Tanzania saw the peak of a second aid boom (Bigsten and Danielson 2001:20). However, this was again followed by a renewed crisis with donors, as the implementation of reforms was slow and levels of corruption remained high. In 1995, the first multiparty elections were held after the decision to allow the establishment of political parties since 1992. The newly elected government of President Mkapa was striving to improve its relationship with donors and pushing reforms was high on the agenda. International development discourse emphasized partnership and ownership, with the objective that Tanzania and not donors should be in charge of identifying development goals and formulating strategy (IMG 2005:8). Towards the end of the 1990s, the amount of aid received rose dramatically for a third time, doubling its volume between 1993 and 2003 (Lawson et al. 2005:3).

2.2.5. The crisis in agriculture and the peasant agrarian transition

During the 1990s, agriculture continued to play a central role for the large majority of Tanzanians who depended on it for subsistence and income. More than three-quarters of the population still lived in villages and relied on agricultural activities for survival, most of them as peasants engaging in small-holding agriculture. Declining economic development of the last decades had meant that they worked for stagnating incomes and were mostly poor. Cultivating small-scale plots, they relied largely on their own labour, unable to afford costly mechanised farming methods. The economic record in agriculture remained disappointing.

Among the factors contributing to this poor performance were low world market prices for export crops, lack of major technological improvements and inefficient marketing systems (Netherlands Ministry of Foreign Affairs 2004:32). Producer prices fluctuated and input prices rose to prohibitive levels. Private-sector traders did not develop the same outreach potential as parastatals, ignoring producers in locations off the main roads. As a result, farmers in some areas resorted to crops that needed few inputs, to fast crops that yielded crops all year around as well as to traditional food crops. The younger generation in particular lost interest in commercial farming (Bryceson 2002b:726). Research carried out in several regions in Tanzania indicated that structural adjustment in Tanzania did not have the intended effect of inducing agricultural growth, but rather motivated peasants to opt out of commercial agriculture. Increasingly, the younger generation of rural dwellers was instead seeking its income with non-agrarian activities such as petty trade (Bryceson 2002b:725). As the country's socialist policy had previously inhibited most forms of private trading, the changes brought about by economic liberalisation did actually offer a promising opportunity. Peasants disillusioned with commercial farming began to experiment with opportunities arising in trade and other non-agricultural activities (Bryceson 2002a:7). The trend towards de-agrarisation and economic activity diversification in several areas within Tanzania as well as other parts of Sub-Saharan Africa (Bryceson 1999) is evident and forms part of a far-reaching social and economic transformation process. Adapting a model from Shanin (1976), Deborah Bryceson (1999:4,5) sums up the following points that characterize peasants as a distinct group of agricultural producers:

> "farm - the pursuit of an agricultural livelihood combining subsistence and commodity production
> family - internal social organization based on the family as the primary unit of production, consumption, reproduction, socialisation and risk spreading;
> class - external subordination to state authorities and regional or international markets which involve surplus extraction and class differentiation; and
> community - village settlement and traditional conformist attitudinal outlook"
> (Bryceson 1999:4,5)

The process of de-agarisation and de-peasantisation involves the loss of one or more of these general characteristics. According to findings of the DARE (De-agrarisation and Rural Employment) research network based in Leiden, de-peasantisation has been accelerated by structural adjustment policies in the 1980s and 1990s in several Sub-Saharan African countries. DARE research referring to the late 1990s found that most rural households had one or more non-agricultural income sources, with 60-80% of their income originating from these activities (Bryceson 2004:619). Financial viability of these endeavours has of course varied, with most activities being little more than survival strategies yielding little profit. Yet peasants' readiness to experiment with new forms of income-generating activities, in particular to engage in various non-agricultural occupations, has been testimony to their willingness to adapt to changing social and economic conditions. However, while non-farm activities have multiplied, the economic situation of the majority has not improved. The diversification into non-farm activities has not proved a profitable option for most of those engaging in it. Corresponding economic activities are usually initiated to compensate for low productivity in agriculture (Kabeer and Whitehead 2001:11). Usually, options requiring little cash input, such as petty trading or beer brewing, tend to yield little profit. Households that successfully adopt diversification strategies both engage in more profitable as well as multiple activities. "The challenge is to source sufficient starting capital and avoid the ever-present danger of running down one's working capital by using it for necessary consumption rather than business operations" (Bryceson 2002a:11).

Kabeer and Whitehead (2001:12) come to the conclusion that non-farming activities are usually successful if undertaken in areas of prosperous farming activities. In localities of low-productive agriculture, non-farm activities are often not rewarding. This is again linked to the fact that profitable activities usually require some minimum initial capital that may be lacking in poorer areas.

Studies from various geographical areas in Tanzania also point to the problem that diversification of economic activities aggravates social division within rural communities. Profitable trading is an option that is only available to the more well-off part of the population. In research in the Uluguru mountains, carried out at the beginning of the 1990s, it was found that those who engaged in non-agricultural activities could increase their earnings, while those who remained solely in agriculture became even poorer. The opportunities offered by economic liberalisation were restricted to the better-off segment of the population (van Donge 2002:308). Only a few studies are optimistic about broader sections of the population being able to improve their living conditions by taking advantage of the opportunities offered by economic liberalisation (Ponte 2002:318, Booth et al 1993, Booth 2004:45).

The issue of women's prospects in the transition process is similarly complex and controversial. Division of labour in agriculture is usually distinctively gendered, with younger women often having few opportunities to exercise control over land ownership and income from production. The current transition has brought both hardship and opportunities for rural women and men. Kabeer and Whitehead (2001:16), summing up various studies on rural income diversification in Sub-Saharan Africa, come to the conclusion that women face a "gender disadvantage in relation to the non-farm sector". Relying on evidence from Tanzania, Deborah Bryceson shows how more and more young men migrate to urban areas to engage in petty trading, leading to an increase in poor and vulnerable female-headed households left behind in rural areas. However, she also points to the greater autonomy women develop and documents how they experience changing conditions in contradictory ways: "Many women bemoan the decline in their households economic welfare, but at the same time relish having more autonomy to earn money and spend as they see fit" (Bryceson 2002a:26). Detailed studies document individuals' and communities' ability to respond dynamically to changing conditions; however, the overall picture suggests that class, gender and regional differences have been aggravated in the current de-agrarisation process. This raises particular concern as "African rural-dwellers' recent market experimentation offers a meagre and uncertain existence for most of its practitioners" (Bryceson 2002a:26).

2.2.6. Peasant economy in Zanzibar: Dependence on imported staple foods

The history of agriculture in Zanzibar, which became a constituent part of the United Republic of Tanzania in 1964, differs significantly from the mainland. In the early 19th century, Sayyid Said, the Omani Sultan of Zanzibar, gave export commodity production, especially cloves, a boost to make up for the collapsing slave trade. Cloves had been introduced to the island from 1770 onwards and became the domain of Arab planters who relied on slave labour for production (Sheriff 1987:49). Both in Zanzibar and Pemba, land was appropriated from indigenous owners for the establishment of clove plantations (Sheriff 1987:55). The indigenous peasant economy was marginalized and the production of rice and other indigenous staple foods was undermined. In Pemba, an island that had acted as a regional 'granary' supplying staple food to Mombasa, clove plantations had become widespread by the end of the 19th century. While both islands had previously exported food crops to as far as the Arabian peninsula, Zanzibar had become a net importer of rice by 1860 (Sheriff 1987:54).

The abolition of slavery did not fundamentally change the economic system. German and British colonizers left the Omani Sultanate in power and supported plantation agriculture, its economic power base. The former slaves became landless squatters and labourers on the plantations. Colonial agricultural policy continued to neglect indigenous peasant farmers' production, resulting, for instance, in "many rice fields degenerating into swamps" (Cameron 2004:109).

In 1963, the Sultanate gained its Independence from the British colonial power. A few weeks later, the deep social divisions between the island's inhabitants erupted in popular upheavals. The Sultan was deposed and many inhabitants of Arab or Indian origin expelled or persecuted. A revolutionary government took power and later merged with the mainland to become the United Republic of Tanzania. The agrarian question was one of the main concerns of the new regime. Plantations were nationalised and a land reform programme granted small individual plots that could be held for the productive life of the cultivator (Cameron 2004:110). This enabled some of the former plantation workers to become peasant producers. It was the declared aim of the government to reduce the dependence on clove and coconut export production. In practice, however, little was done to enhance staple food production. The new government pressured peasants into cultivating and selling cloves for unfavourable prices and used profit margins for its own ends. Instead of investing in the diversification of agriculture, urban prestige projects were financed. In the following years, production and income from cloves steadily declined, both as a result of a lack of workers during the labour-intensive three-months period of clove-picking, unfavourable national pricing policies as well as falling world market prices. To date, clove marketing has not been liberalised.

Attempts at diversifying agricultural production through state farms had little success because of poor management. As Maghimbi (1999:100) points out, Zanzibar has a larger proportion of urban population than mainland Tanzania, with the result that the corresponding demand for staple food creates a unique opportunity for agricultural producers. However, due to poor planning and marketing by the government, the demand for staple foods is not met by local producers. Instead, imports, especially of rice and wheat, supply most of the required food (Maghimbi 1999:100).

As a result of unfavourable conditions for peasant producers in Zanzibar, processes of de-agrarisation are also common in Zanzibar. Young people leave agriculture and seek their fortune in trade and other non-agrarian occupations. The failure to address the problem of outdated modes of agricultural production perpetuates the deep social divisions in Zanzibar society (Cameron 2004:111).

2.2.7. Summary: The state as initiator of participatory development in Tanzania

The British colonial government tried to instrumentalize popular participation in community development as a means to ensure compliance and subdue resistance. People's attitudes, however, were cautious and dismissive. The anti-colonial movement, for its part, was more successful in mobilising enthusiasm and support for social improvement and self-governance.

The independent government initially largely followed donor-inspired development plans. Especially in agriculture, the programmes were not appropriate to Tanzanian circumstances and largely failed. Only a few of these first initiatives focusing on participatory development took root, among them the formation of the Ruvuma Development Association and its self-governed villages, as well as numerous infra-structural self-help initiatives established by the rural population.

With the Arusha declaration, programmes for self-reliance and autonomous development became official policy and were to be replicated countrywide - with the substantial support of foreign donors. However, implementation was authoritarian, working against the core objectives of Ujamaa and self-reliance. Coercion during villagization and economic mismanagement quashed popular enthusiasm. With external factors contributing to the economic downturn, social services declined. Donors demanded reform and adjustment, blaming the crisis on the failure of the government as an agent of development.

In Zanzibar, the bias towards the cash-crop economy at the cost of subsistence agriculture is more pronounced. Social classes are more divided, politics more confrontational and attitudes towards governmental development initiatives ambivalent.

The agrarian transition, that is the diversification of economic activities of peasant farmers into non-agricultural domains, has been accelerated by Structural Adjustment Programmes. Women and men have responded differently to changing conditions, but, on the whole, emerging opportunities have been less accessible to the poor and to women.

2.3. NGOs, development and the state in Tanzania: Changing relationships

> *How is it possible for external interventions to install internal capacities for autonomous action?" (Kelsall and Mercer 2003:294)*

With the collapse of many state-provided social services, NGOs increasingly strove to fill the gap throughout the 1980s. Religious-based institutions had always continued to work in the relevant fields and were well established. Other organizations that began to become active in social service provision were the local branches of international development organizations as well as Community Based Organizations. Institutions and actors supporting associational growth were multifaceted and at times even contradictory in their ideological orientation. For the World Bank and the IMF, a growing role for the NGOs was attractive as NGOs engaging in social services would facilitate a "roll-back" of the state from this domain and relieve public budgets from the costly realm of social service provision. According to neo-liberal ideology, the state was both incapable of managing business ventures and coping with welfare tasks. NGOs, on the other hand, were expected to deliver better services to the poorest, while remaining cost-effective and efficient (Mercer 1999:247). Because of this, the IMF's conditionalities routinely included demands for liberalisation of the economy as well as legal reforms to ensure associational and political freedoms. While the previous support of the Financial Institutions for the strong developmental state had included the acceptance of one-party states as an adequate political model for Sub-Saharan Africa, pressure for multiparty democracy rose during the 1990s.[3] A thriving "civil society" made up of associations and NGOs became a yardstick for the progress of states in transition. With the newly donor-induced focus on good governance and democratization, many Southern governments strove to establish a democratic image in order to make a new start as partners of Northern bilateral donors. It was thus increasingly in the interest of the government to foster NGO activity, or in terms of the newly established discourse, the government was to create an enabling environment that would allow voluntary organizations

---

3 In particular where one-party-states were of socialist persuasion as was the case in Tanzania - in Uganda, the one party system (euphemistically disguised as "movement" or "no-party system") encountered more tolerance from the Financial Institutions as well as the donor community.

to emerge and prosper. NGOs were in turn expected to exercise some control over the state. Undemocratic or authoritarian tendencies were to be curbed by strong autonomous organizations.

In Tanzania, many NGOs and social movements did not share the preoccupation of the International Financial Institutions (IFIs) with the free market economy. On the contrary, many of them voiced concern about diminished public spending on the social sector and protested strongly about the government's compliance with the IMF's austerity programmes and conditionalities. The 1980s were a time when NGOs and social movements began to emerge and grow on a global scale. Among others, feminist, environmentalist, human rights, socially disadvantaged and minority people's concerns came to the fore in many countries of the world. Many of them were inspired by radical emancipatory projects and catalysed by international networks and UN conferences. In Tanzania, numerous NGOs mostly concentrating on the social services sector began to emerge from the mid-1980s onwards. As in other Third World nations, development concerns were central to the political agenda and organizations with strong international support and substantial means to dispose of became politically influential. These larger organizations became a major factor in reshaping relations and operational modes in the development sector, including orientation along internationally prevailing discourses on participation, gender and empowerment. By and large, this had little effect on top-down structures in the aid sector, but was mostly limited to additional requirements and conditionalities imposed on target groups. Other, often smaller Tanzanian-based NGOs followed a more radical agenda of grass-root participation and empowerment, some of them engaging in advocacy work that was often critical of the government and its policies. While these organizations were seriously committed to engaging in empowering processes, results and success were mixed. Another large group of locally based organizations concentrated on providing material benefits for their members or target groups. While likewise paying lip service to the dominant discourse of popular participation, they were often not very concerned with grass-root democracy and social change, their organizational structure as well as their relationships to local or foreign donors being part of authoritarian patron-client networks. Therefore, while multilateral donors and the various groups of NGOs had very different interests and priorities, both worked for more space for third sector organizations in development. Similarly, both sides contributed to transforming participation, empowerment and community development into routine qualitative programme or project objectives, to an extent that these approaches are "perceived as the new orthodoxy [...] from NGOs to the World Bank" (Green 2000:67). However, as in other parts of the world, it was of course impossible for NGOs to live up "simultaneously to the neo-liberal and radical expectations" (Mercer 1999:248). While there is little substantial information available on the NGO sector in Tanzania, existing field research (for example, Green 2000; Kelsall 2001, Kelsall and Mercer 2003; Kiondo 1995; 2000; Mercer 1999; 2002b; Hanak 1998; 2000) provides evidence of many contradictions that have also been described for participatory approaches in other parts of the world (Mosse 2005, Cooke and Kothari 2001:3). Particularly challenging aspects include the fact that the poorest, towards whom the whole effort is geared, often remain excluded, that any consideration of the larger political context is suppressed and that decision-making processes in organizations are rarely inclusive, democratic or egalitarian. While the IFIs favoured a discourse where private voluntary organizations gradually replacing the state in service provision came to be valued as a positive trend as such, many Tanzanian NGOs are rather down-to-earth when appraising the situation. In the long run, the latest cutting-edge development discourse can hardly gloss over the fact that services provided in what is after all one of the world's poorest countries are in many cases either completely lacking or of appallingly low quality.

As living conditions worsened and Tanzanians realized the willingness of donors to give support to CBOs and NGOs, the number of organizations increased steadily (Mercer 1999:249). In 1993, there were 224 registered NGOs in Tanzania (Lange, Wallevik and Kiondo 2000.6). A 1997 estimate quoted in a parliamentary debate suggested that there may be up to 8000 NGOs in Tanzania - a figure probably including District Development Trust Funds and Community Based Organizations that are not registered (Kelsall 2001:135). In 2000, Tripp reports the number of registered NGOs as 8499 (Tripp 2000:200). Other authors indicate lower figures. While exact numbers are difficult to obtain, it is clear that the NGO sector is continuously growing in influence. Faced with an internationally changing political climate, demands from the donors and an emerging NGO community, in the mid-1980s, the government enacted legal reforms that enabled NGOs to organize and operate. Reforms of the public sector, including the civil service, parastatals, co-operatives and local government as well as the change to a multiparty system were other elements of the fundamental political reorientation of the government. However, for the NGOs the legal situation remained complex as they could be registered under five different legal provisions and legislation has never clearly defined what an NGO was (Mogella 2000:15). The fact that a number of NGOs were founded by people working in the public sector has in some cases secured amicable ties of mutual trust and co-operation. However, both the government and the NGO sector consist of heterogeneous interest groups and individuals and the occurrence of disagreements is not necessarily surprising.

In particular, whenever the government or the ruling party saw its interest threatened, it left no doubt about its determination to stay in control. Analysing documents and statements made by officials in the NGO unit situated in the vice-president's office, Mercer concludes that the government welcomed the economic benefit of having NGOs working in the service sector, but was more suspicious about the few existing attempts to represent the political interests of the poor (Mercer 1999:250). The de-registration of BAWATA (Baraza la Wanawake Tanzania), a high-profile women's NGO with the potential to appeal to women from all backgrounds of Tanzanian society, was a case in point. Prior to the 1995 elections, BAWATA had provided voters with detailed information on women's policies of contesting parties, urging women to use their vote accordingly. The government accused BAWATA of partiality in favour of the opposition and withdrew the NGO's registration. Ensuing appeals and protests were of no avail. Other organizations also faced de-registration because there were accused of being 'political', while others were told that there was no need for their NGO because a corresponding party affiliate already existed. Some organizations were denied permission to hold meetings or rallies. These examples illustrate that while there is some co-operation with the expanding NGO community, the government is keen to retain strong control over the emerging organizations (Tripp 2000:206).

It was therefore encouraging that in 1996 attempts to reform the legal framework for NGOs began with good will and commitment from both sides. A consultative process was initiated by the government. The policy dialogue took a bottom-up approach and was jointly facilitated by the government and international donors. It provided national and international NGO and government representatives with an opportunity to work out several versions of 'NGO policy drafts'. However, the government delayed the implementation for years, and finally in 2002, it passed an NGO bill that largely ignored the draft's progressive input. Tanzanian NGOs remained with little to do but register their protest about a bill that "threatened their existence" (Shivji 2004:4). The problematic aspects of the 2002 NGO bill include the following aspects: registration is compulsory and the prescribed procedure is rather cumbersome, requiring, for example, periodical re-registration. The government on its part has failed to offer any reciprocal benefits to NGOs (such as tax exemption) and it has not made transparent any reason for registration other than central control. Registered NGOs are compelled to become members of the NGO Council, a requirement that will possibly interfere with the functions of existing voluntary umbrella organizations. Finally, the law lacks an explicit reference to provisions for appeal in case registration is refused (Irish and Simon 2003:73-74). As of 2005, the agenda of the NGO umbrella organization TANGO prominently featured the "ongoing campaign for an enabling NGO law that caters for the interests of indigenous NGOs and not that of the government and international or foreign agencies" (http://www.tango.or.tz/dir.htm). The authoritarian manner in which the year-long consultative process pertaining to the NGO bill has been ignored and nullified shows how, despite growing co-operation with NGOs, the government has been deeply ambivalent about its policy.

So how can NGOs in Tanzania be characterized? While there is only patchy information available, a few trends can be summed up from existing research. It is important to realize, however, that researchers differ in their concept of what constitutes an NGO. Many studies focus on a particular type of NGO which is assumed to be of relevance to the Tanzanian setting. Often, results of specific studies are then generalized for NGOs at large, at times at times leading to unfounded conclusions. Before engaging in a closer analysis on Tanzanian NGOs' potential for facilitating participatory and empowering development, some consideration of terminology and context is indispensable.

For the purposes of this study, the rather broad definition of the term development NGO as a generic term for "all organizations within the aid channel that are institutionally separated from the state apparatus and non-profit distributing" (Tvedt 1998:16) will be adopted. Numerous other definitions exist, based on variations in the criteria adopted. The relevant considerations concern legal aspects (e.g. public registration), economic/financial (e.g. some definitions exclude organizations financed largely through state funds), functional (e.g. some approaches differentiate between NGOs who work 'for the people' and 'people's organizations' through which members represent themselves; others emphasize voluntarism as an essential characteristic of both organizational types and place all of them in the NGO category) and finally structural-operational factors (e.g. formalism, autonomy in decision-making, separateness from the state even if state funds are received, voluntarism and non-profit orientation) (cf. Salamon and Anheier 1992:135, quoted from Tvedt 1998:15).

Categorisations based on the above-mentioned criteria need not be universally valid; in fact, many of the prevalent terms for NGOs and their popular acronyms (such as Quango, Gongo, Bingo)[4] are diffuse and intersecting. However, they need to be appropriate and useful for the relevant context. Given the rather heterogeneous Tanzanian NGO community, the following aspects and details deserve close attention: organizational structure (for instance, membership organization/ professional charity/community-based organization), source of funds (various types of foreign or local donors/self help), geographical focus and interconnectedness (local/national/international), activity type (lobbying/service provision/ self-improvement) and influential mother cultures (religious communities/government/interest groups). For the purpose of this study, these criteria will not be used to develop a model for classification. As organizations are not static, they often do not neatly fit ready-made categories.

Rather, only a selected number of NGO characteristics discussed in research will be presented here. The objective is to provide a qualitative insight into the developments of recent decades. It is, however, important to bear in mind that most characteristics are not mutually exclusive and some organizations might fit several or none of the characteristics presented. Moreover, development networks involved in the implementation of particular programmes often link several NGO types with very distinct characteristics. The aim here is therefore to facilitate an understanding of the historic processes which favoured the development of certain characteristics over others. Aspects discussed will include the following: the influence of mother cultures, especially those originating in religious institutions, the options of local subsidiaries of international organizations, the changing back-

---

4 Short for: Quasi NGO, Governmental NGO, Big NGO

ground of community development activities, the emergence of Tanzanian-based advocacy NGOs and finally the new role of NGOs in national policy dialogue.

2.3.1. The influence of mother cultures: Organizations affiliated to religious institutions

The history of religious organizations in the area which today constitutes Tanzania reaches back centuries. Religious communities, whether based on indigenous, Muslim or Christian faith, often constituted eminent social and political forces. Islam probably reached East Africa around the 8th century. Religiously motivated welfare activities are reported from the 19th and 20th century. Christianity was first brought to East Africa by the Portuguese in the 15th century but did not really take root until the advent of the 19th and 20th century missionaries who were part of the German and British colonial conquest. It was Christian missions who engaged most systematically into what resembles today's social service provision, for example, by establishing schools and hospitals. Welfare activities by Muslim communities were less substantial and additionally constrained by colonial authorities (Bromber 2003). Christian missions had a fundamental role in the formation of the educational elite who took over power in independent Tanzania. Ethnic and religious restrictions on admission were abolished by the postcolonial government and some institutions were nationalised. Nevertheless, many schools and hospitals continued to be run by religious bodies such as churches or the Aga Khan Foundation. Religious communities faced some constraints, but by and large continued to control their often considerable organizational infrastructure and were able to maintain their international support networks. After 1985, a considerable rise in religious-based self-help groups and NGOs occurred as part of the general NGO boom. Before, administrative units within the church had often acted as implementing organizations of projects and programmes. Increasingly, some of these development units seized the opportunity to form independent organizations, a move facilitated by the legal reforms. Organizational independence gave them the opportunity to develop a more pronounced professional identity and the chance to improve their profile towards donors. At the same time, the formation of new development-oriented organizations within religious communities was encouraged, especially in terms of self-help groups at grass-root levels. Elements from the religious mother culture in many cases continued to dominate organizational practices, such as the maintenance of top-down hierarchical decision-making structures and in the adherence to traditional gender roles. In many settings, religious organizations also continued to exert direct influence on NGOs in their entourage. Studying women's groups initiated by the Lutheran Church in Kilimanjaro Region, Claire Mercer found that contrary to popular development discourses on women's groups, participation and empowerment, the poorest women were largely excluded from membership. Most of the groups focussed on income generation, and although they usually lacked substantial donors, modest material gains were an important motivation for individual participation. Group membership, however, was largely limited to better-off women in the community, described as those who dress well, have good homes, some education, husbands with regular income; mostly, members were older, married women. Young and poor women, in short those who could gain most from participatory development approaches, were de facto excluded from taking part. Poverty, illness, disability, poor education or unco-operative husbands were major impediments, with many women unable to raise the means required for group contributions or feeling that more well-off group members were discouraging them. Membership of women's groups is thus largely confined to those of average household wealth, while those identified as poor remain marginalized. Project activities thus tended to exacerbate rather than reduce existing social inequalities (2002a:118; 124). Mercer also found that groups strongly upheld cultural ideals on gender roles. Both women (group members) and men (church employees, husbands) expressed the opinion that activities assisted women in being "good housewives, mothers and community members". Some men even viewed women's groups as a "vehicle for 'correcting' the behaviour of women who exhibit 'undesirable' social traits". Mercer comes to the conclusion that over time, both church and state have, by encouraging the foundation of women's groups and shaping their agenda, established a link between "women, collective organization and community development" in Kilimanjaro (1999:254; 2002a: 113-116).

Various authors (Mercer 2002a, Kiondo 1995) also report that development activities initiated by Muslim communities are on the rise, both inland and on the coast. However, hardly any details are available on concrete trends.

2.3.2. The options of local subsidiaries of international organizations

Local subsidiaries of international NGOs experience more than the influence of a dominant mother culture or the interference of a strong founding institution. They are usually part of an international organization and as such subject to decision-making and organizational policy which is mostly worked out in Northern countries. In developing countries, international organizations are usually the most visible group among development NGOs. Most of them are well endowed with offices, cars and other resources bearing representative logos. Infrastructural provisions, especially in remote areas and in the context of emergency aid, may exceed or in extreme cases even substitute those of the state (Tvedt 1998:189). Able to rely on steady funding and professional staff, their interventions have the potential of a sustainable long-term impact. Many of them are popular as employers among national academics and have access to up-to-date expertise and technology. However, this material advantage is often compromised by structures that allow little consideration for local particularities, with the organizations agenda being by and large determined by supra-national head offices (a prominent example being micro-credit programmes, where "scaling-up" and "replication" have led to the implementation of very similar programmes targeting thousands of 'clients' in developing countries all over the world). Even where national organizations enjoy some formal organizational autonomy, they are often subject to directives from higher-ranking structures. These structural imbalances implicate international NGOs in the malaise of "developmentalism", that is foreign agendas shaping interventions that may in many ways disregard national or community interests. Based on foreign, usually 'Northern' initiatives, they have been a core part of what Kelsall has criticized as the establishment of an "ersatz, air-conditioned civil society" created by "the proliferation of governmental and non-governmental benefactors looking for NGOs to fund" (2002:598). International NGOs are usually well integrated into cutting-edge development discourse including that on participation, gender and empowerment. Yet practical implementation is often poor. This is not only due to the resilience of established hierarchical organizations towards innovative, egalitarian approaches, as Chambers (1997a) has argued. Equally important is the fact that often very reduced, naive or even contradictory concepts of participation, gender and empowerment are propagated within organizations. Consequently, contradictions between externally imposed agendas and the quest for local agency, as implemented by development workers, are rarely brought to the fore. Contrary to the rhetoric, members of target groups are usually not significantly involved in project planning or decision making; "participation" usually offers no more than an opportunity to become a beneficiary in projects or programmes implemented through external actors. The conviction that it is possible to "empower" beneficiaries through dissemination of knowledge is still widespread in most development agencies. The necessary intellectual input, it is assumed, will facilitate a change in conscience and eventually enable people to take part in processes of social transformation. At the same time, it is implied that poor people are not capable of initiating such developments on their own. Similarly, constraints caused by broader social and economic conditions are largely ignored - participatory approaches are depoliticised and reduced to tools in local implementation. As a result, people targeted by rural programmes hardly gain positive experience with community participation and often develop considerable reservations. Maia Green (2000:84) documents such processes for Ulanga District in South-Western Tanzania, where a large foreign donor-sponsored poverty reduction programme in 1996 failed to engage people in participatory community activities. While people valued material assistance through project interventions, their previous experience with development interventions made them wary about sacrificing time and energy for the common good. Green concludes that programmes advocating 'empowerment' and 'participation' are bound to fail as long as people have no chance to participate in decision-making structures in a wider political context. As long as development practice ignores the macro-economic environment and the politics which creates it, participatory approaches in development work will remain superficial and ineffective (2000:85).

Kelsall and Mercer (2003) carried out research on World Vision Tanzania's work in Arumeru district (Kilimanjaro Region) and Hai district (Arusha Region) in

1996/97. Similar to Green, they found that the contradictions of implementing empowerment through external intervention were not addressed in everyday project work (2003:294). Instead, development workers were found to have a very narrow interpretation of empowerment and participation. This was visible from everyday practice, as villagers had no say in the planning of development activities. It was also visible in their everyday language use. For example, development workers used the terms "kuhamasisha" (to mobilise, induce) and "kushiriki" (to co-operate, participate) as synonyms. When one of the aid workers was asked to explain the difference between the two expressions, she answered that they were both the same (Kelsall and Mercer 2003:298).

In order to ensure local institution building, Area and Village Development Programme Committees had been established to coordinate development planning. Membership of these committees was voluntary, and it was planned that these committees should eventually register as independent NGOs who would then become the local counterparts of World Vision Tanzania. Most informants agreed that the committees were more efficient in delivering development goods than government bodies. However, membership of the committees was de facto limited to members of the local elite. Ordinary village people had little knowledge of internal organizational structures or decision-making processes. Allocation of resources often did not relate to beneficiaries' level of need, but rather to being connected to people who were locally influential. Participation at grass-root level mostly related to the labour contributions beneficiaries were expected to provide, while villagers were not involved in initiatives and plans for projects. Rather, these usually originated from higher level committees and villagers were merely informed about them.

In conclusion, Kelsall and Mercer established that World Vision Tanzania was relatively successful in service provision. However, its methods of mobilising the community to contribute labour had parallels with colonial development schemes as well as postcolonialist efforts to recruit villagers into working for 'self-reliance'. Implementation of the programme relied mostly on local elites and little effort was made to break with local practices of patron-client relations (2003:301).

Kelsall and Mercer found that people targeted by social development projects in rural Tanzania do not necessarily think that participatory processes are conducive to whatever form of "development" they personally aspire to. Decades of experience with malpractice and fraud in self-help initiatives established first by the government and then by NGOs have left many rather disillusioned with any form of communal activity. Many peasants tend to regard development in terms of personal advancement as well as improving the standard of living of one's own family. Given the poor performance of implementing organizations in terms of participatory programmes, such attitudes are not surprising. As Green (2000:84) has pointed out, the consideration of the wider political context is indispensable.

Limiting concepts of participation and empowerment to a community perspective inhibits effective implementation.

In conclusion it is appropriate to bear in mind that subsidiaries of international NGOs engaged in service delivery often have a rather powerful position vis-à-vis government institutions. Their close connection to foreign donors and the volume of financial resources they command make them important players in national welfare. In recent years, the tendency towards budget support, government ownership, strengthening of local government as well as the preference given to programmes over projects has meant that the at times close links between international NGOs and donors have lost some of their importance, being replaced by the growing co-operation between donors and (local) governments. In the process, NGOs had to adjust to the more competitive environment, for example, by applying for tenders put out by local governments. Not all organizations managed to adapt to the changing conditions, but again, the better endowed and connected international NGOs generally did better than the Tanzanian-based organizations, with the result that very few of these Tanzanian-based organizations (excluding community-based self-help initiatives, who would often also call themselves NGOs) work in social welfare (Michael 2004:72).

2.3.3. The changing background of community development activities

In the early 1990s, Andrew Kiondo (1995) carried out research on the changing nature of development activities, such as the establishment of schools, dispensaries and other community services, in nine rural and urban districts that reflected Tanzania's economic and geographical diversity. He found that as local government and its affiliated organizations pulled out, alternative non-governmental organizations were increasingly present in social development activities. With multiparty politics, the compulsory entanglement of the single party, government and community based development activities was dismantled. Formerly party-controlled co-operatives and self-help groups withdrew from state control and re-organized independently, while other associations, for example, those aligned to religious institutions, were on the rise. The organizational background of actors in rural development changed, with control over funds, political influence and development planning in general shifting from party and government functionaries to private individuals. "Local elites that were previously linked to the central state through salaried employment or party position are now engaged in local struggles for influence over non-state institutions, the co-operative, the church, NGOs - which in places control relative large resources" (Kelsall 2001:141). While those individuals often retained some official functions which secured, after all, part of their power base, they no longer carried out development activities in their role as state representatives, but rather as chairpersons of newly founded development NGOs. Similarly, many groups could still trace their origins to the initiative of governmental bodies - such as the co-operatives served by the agricultural extension service - but they were no longer subject to government structures. Kiondo interprets the organizational shift primarily as 'privatisation of development', as some of the organizations, for example, District Development Trust Funds, assumed powers such as taxation that were previously the prerogative of local government (1995:169). However, in their operations these Funds were accountable neither to super-ordinate state structures nor to the people they collected the 'taxes' from. In operational respects, Kiondo's findings leave few illusions about the alleged abilities of NGOs as actors in social development, especially if tested against criteria such as responsiveness to the needs of the poorest, correction of regional imbalances, or participatory and transparent decision-making. First, poor and marginalized peasants continued to be excluded from development activities. Membership of groups demands input of time and fees, which the poorest often did not possess. Second, with regard to regional distribution, he found that organizations and social development programmes were unevenly spread – with affluent locations being privileged by intense activities of both foreign and local organizations. The geographical imbalance stems from the fact that funds for development activities often depend on patronage networks around affluent or successful individuals from the region who either act as sponsors themselves or facilitate contacts to donors. Third, the operational approach of NGOs did not significantly differ from earlier state-dominated patterns. While NGOs had raised high expectations about working in a participatory manner, for example, in close co-operation with the 'grass-root' population they served, records of decision-making and accountability left a lot to be desired. Kiondo comes to the conclusion that organizational practice had deteriorated when compared with earlier governmental approaches in the field. This conclusion refers specifically to his analysis of District Development Trust Funds. Based on private local initiative, these organizations engaged in various development activities, for instance in the sponsorship of secondary school students. They were run by members of the local elite who showed little inclination of accounting for the way they managed these funds. For the rural poor, this meant that they were compelled to contribute financially, while they usually did not have any influence on its decision-making processes and their own children were unlikely to benefit. District Development Trust Funds "seem almost deliberately designed to exclude popular participation" (Kiondo 1995.172). Kiondo thus comes to the conclusion that contrary to widespread expectation, the manner in which these services are provided has not been particularly inclusive towards rural dwellers. "If anybody is empowered in the process, it is the NGOs themselves" (1995:172). Of course, he contends that any social service such as education, health or clean water can always be said to have an empowering impact on beneficiaries as their capabilities and potentials are enhanced. However, while NGOs may differ considerably among themselves in the way they are organized and work, in service delivery none of them operated in a more participatory, democratic or transparent fashion than the state. In fact, the contrary was the case (1995:173). Patron-client relations were the core organizational pattern of most organizations.

2.3.4. The emergence of Tanzanian-based advocacy organizations

A number of Tanzanian-based advocacy NGOs have been founded from the 1980s and 1990s onwards. These organizations mostly originate from initiatives by urban professionals. Especially in their founding years, NGOs often command very limited financial resources. In many ways, they rely on their members' dedication, such as willingness to commit time, or infrastructural facilities, such as computers, telephones from private sources or other workplaces. With time, some advocacy NGOs have managed to attract substantial donor support. Throughout the 1990s, some observers criticized Tanzanian NGOs as elitist, urban and largely unable to respond to the needs of the rural majority (Mercer 1999:249) and as being engaged in "workshopocracy", removed from popular interests, and middle-class based (Kelsall 2001:140). On one hand, they obviously did not match the ideal expectations of NGOs as rural grass-root self-help initiatives. On the other hand, many of the organizations failed to make any real impact beyond district or regional level, most of them being confined to Dar es Salaam or urban areas in the more affluent regions such as Kilimanjaro or Arusha. Issa Shivji, a prominent law professor at the University of Dar es Salaam and founding member of the NGO "HakiArdhi" (Land Rights Research and Resources), goes even further in his (self)-criticism towards NGOs in Tanzania: "most of our NGOs are top-down organizations led by the elite [...] they are urban based [...] they did not start as a felt need of the large majority of the working people. [...] The relationship between us [the NGOs] and the masses therefore remains, at best, that of benefactors and beneficiaries [...] we (the NGOs) end up being more accountable to our donors, rather than to our own members, much less our people [...] In many direct and subtle ways, those who fund us determine our agendas" (Shivji 2004:1). While Tanzanian advocacy NGOs have definitely not managed to become broad-based grass-root organizations, a number of them have achieved a remarkable record in successfully conducting information, lobbying and networking campaigns. For example, the Tanzania Media Women's Association (TAMWA), a membership organization founded by journalists, has over a period of years coordinated a campaign against gender-based violence, the objective being popular awareness-creation and legal reform. In 1998, the government enacted the Sexual Offence Special Provisions Act, which contained numerous long overdue reforms, among them a timely redefinition of sexual violence as well as a ban on female genital mutilation (Kelsall 2002:604). After the government had passed the law, TAMWA stated that most of the relevant issues had been addressed (Kiondo 2000:15). While there is no doubt that the issue of gender-based violence cannot be solved by legislation alone, especially as long as implementation remains poor, the reform was an important first step. Throughout the campaign, TAMWA had networked and successfully brought together a number of NGOs concerned with gender-based violence. This approach reflected an emerging pattern in which coalitions are formed to work on particular issues, each of them co-ordinated by an NGO with specific skills, capacity and experience in the field. Other examples of issues around which NGOs organized included land rights (HAKIARDHI - Land Rights Research and Resources), the gender budget initiative (Tanzania Gender Networking Programme - TGNP), and debt relief (Tanzania Coalition on Debt and Development - TCDD). Records of the relationship between the government and the various NGOs are mixed - for example, in the process of drawing up a new land law, HAKIARDHI eventually backed out of the process as it could not agree with the government on policy and operational issues. Feminist NGOs, however, conclude that due to their demands at least essential provisions enabling women to inherit land were included. The above-mentioned case of BAWATA shows that the government, if it deems appropriate, also displays a more authoritarian stance. In another example, activists from the Lawyers' Environmental Action Team (LEAT) demanded an investigation into the forced eviction of artisanal miners from gold mines at Bulyanhulu in 1996, during which up to 65 miners were alleged to have been buried alive. As a result, in 2002, two environmental lawyers, Rugemeleza Nshala and Tundu Lissu, together with opposition politician Augustine Mrema, were charged with sedition (Kelsall 2002:604). The gold mining industry has in recent years become Tanzania's major factor of economic growth (Cooksey 2004:1). By revealing the questionable practices of foreign mining companies, of the World Bank and of the Tanzanian government's compliance with regard to the setting up of Tanzania's largest underground gold mining plant, the LEAT team had obviously touched a highly sensitive spot.

Tanzania's involvement in the World Bank's HIPC initiative and the ensuing PRSP process provided government and NGOs with another opportunity for critical interaction. From the perspective of the NGOs, the government's approach left a lot to be desired and offered the organizations little opportunity to state their concerns in the resulting policy papers. The PRSP process added a new dimension to the discourse on participation. It turned away from grass-root perspectives and instead focussed on established, highly articulate NGOs who became stakeholders 'participating' in the shaping of development-related policy. This 'discursive shift' around participation and empowerment will be discussed in further detail below. What matters here is that while NGOs might have had only limited influence on policy formulation, they were able to make their voice heard in the debate at a national level. Many seized the opportunity to criticize both the International Financial Institutions as well as the government's compliance with their conditionality.

A regional study comparing NGO activities in various African countries (Michael 2004:71), relying on an interview-based survey carried out in the year 2000, identified a number of specific characteristics of Tanzanian NGOs. In her study, the author did not subsume Community Based Organizations (CBOs) such as

District Development Trust Funds under the broader term NGO, rather, in her work the two categories are treated as mutually exclusive.[5] Michael's description of what she terms as 'indigenous NGO' in many ways matches the characteristics of Tanzanian advocacy NGOs. In her research, she found that most NGOs were highly specialised and concentrated in the domains of gender and environmental concerns, with each organization working in a specific field and little duplication occurring. She found only a few local NGOs working in "traditional welfare" fields (with international NGOs and CBOs being more prominent in this domain). Moreover, most of the Tanzanian-based NGOs were found to have a limited geographical target zone as they usually lack the means to work on a national base, let alone in remote areas - an area for which International NGOs are logistically better equipped. In comparison to NGO structures in other African countries, the study also showed that Tanzanian NGOs had few full-time professionally staffed organizations. Instead, organizations relied on part-time voluntary input of members as well as the use of office resources from members' other places of work. The lack of proper resources clearly affected NGO efficiency. Yet, considering the lack of wherewithal, many organizations achieved remarkable results, while others were briefcase NGOs that existed on paper only. Of the more active NGOs, many had particularly strong ties to academic institutions and media. They were well connected internationally, particularly to regional NGO networks and to Northern donor organizations.

Gender was found to be the thematic focus on which most Tanzanian-based NGOs concentrated (Michael 2004:71). In this field, networking as well as cooperation with the government were the most developed aspects. The focus on gender issues also marks some continuity with the post-independence period as the Tanzanian government had put gender equality concerns on its agenda earlier than other countries in the region. For example, the 'Law of Marriage Act 1971' constituted an important step in reforming discriminatory family law, presenting a viable alternative to the colonial legacy of discriminatory customary law. Girls' education was supported through affirmative action, an important attempt to balance women's poor representation in higher education. The all-pervasive public sector offered women and men at least nominally equal conditions of employment as well as social benefits such as maternity leave. From 1985 onwards, 'special seats' ensured women's representation in parliament (other interest groups represented through such quotas were young people, the army and workers) (Meena 2003:2). However, as in many other post-independence African countries, the women's movement was co-opted by the ruling single party, making sure that feminist concerns remained under control and subordinate to party policies (Tripp

---

5   Michael also notes that "the majority of local groups which call themselves NGOs are involved in caring for the sick, disabled and elderly, with varying degrees of professionalism and success. However, these social welfare organizations lack any engagement with the wider issues of underdevelopment, are tied to international movements or have no official organizational standing, and as such, were not considered local NGOs for the purposes of this study (2000:72).

2001:40). In Tanzania, even before Independence the largest women's mass organization had been the women's section of TANU. After Independence, it was renamed 'Umoja wa wanawake" (UWT) and formally affiliated to TANU in 1962 (Tripp 2001:40). Unlike in other countries in the region, UWT members were not confined to singing and cooking at official state functions, but could shape some political space of their own. They were comparatively well represented in the political and administrative elite and the idea of gender equality enjoyed some legitimacy in official political discourse. From the 1980s onwards, independent women's organizations came into being, an example of the first and smaller initiatives being the "Women's Research and Documentation Center" at the University Dar-es-Salaam. The 3rd United Nations Women's Conference in Nairobi 1985 represented an important regional impetus. However, it was in the 1990s when an interplay of emerging national NGOs and international activities generated more concerted networking activities. The 4th United Nations Women's Conference in Beijing was preceded by preparatory meetings in Kampala in 1993, bringing together 120 leaders of women's organizations from Kenya, Tanzania and Uganda. NGOs also prepared national plans for the preparatory All-Africa UN-Conference in Dakar in 1994. In Tanzania, the Tanzania Gender Networking Programme, established in 1992, played a major role in promoting national cooperation and dialogue ahead of the Beijing conference (Tripp 2005:6). Over the years, TGNP has been able to further expand this role of facilitating communication and exchange among NGOs, for example, by organizing biannual meetings (so-called 'Gender Festivals') which provide an opportunity to debate evolving challenges and to build objective-oriented coalitions. Being strongly linked to academic networks, TGNP and other Tanzanian-based NGOs have been able to offer highly skilled country-relevant gender expertise, in many ways outperforming foreign development experts' dominance in the field. At present, women's NGOs are numerous and because of the above-mentioned historical legacy, the government has largely been supportive of their agenda. Apart from gender issues being prominently placed on NGO agendas, women in general are well represented in the NGO sector; Michael found that "nearly half of the local NGOs are run by female directors" (2004:72).

Other well represented sectors among Tanzanian NGOs include human rights, natural resources and the environment. As in the gender domain, NGOs have been able to build their own infrastructure, conduct information campaigns and to lobby for political and legal change, but they have not engaged in building broad grass-root based social movements. Issa Shivji critically remarks that the present day development discourse conflates NGO presence with civil society activism, a practice that has undermined other civil society organizations, especially broad-based people's organizations such trade unions or peasant associations. Shivji further argues that this trend is all the more questionable as, under the name of good governance, NGOs "are cast in the role of partners" of the state and the donor community and involvement of NGOs has come to substitute popular participation. Shivji asserts that elitist NGOs have come to replace democratically-legitimised mass organizations and that unfortunately many NGOs tend to accept these new roles and powers without sufficiently questioning them (2004:2). At the same time, not being legitimised by a broad grass-root base may also have contributed to the limited political significance of NGOs. As Kelsall argued, NGOs have largely failed to meet expectations raised by proponents of the dominant development discourse such as the World Bank. The prospect that NGOs as an eminent part of civil society could develop the ability to control and hold the state accountable is clearly beyond the powers of existing Tanzanian organizations (2001:148). Advocacy NGOs have had some success in influencing government policy. Yet their activities may still have very little impact on the life of the rural majority facing the pressing challenges of day-to-day survival. Many NGOs simply lack the resources to engage in programmes on a national scale. However, even if legal reforms and information campaigns may be slow to take noticeable effect, NGOs have managed to involve themselves in issues of high relevance and political sensitivity. In some cases, they have succeeded in enforcing essential corrections. It may be true that "it is easier for the elite-based organizations to work for the grassroots than with them" (Lange, Wallevik and Kiondo 2000:28). Yet discourses emanating from some of the Tanzanian-based advocacy NGOs, elitist as they may be, must be credited as addressing Tanzania's most pressing social and political issues. They have raised highly relevant issues, encouraged productive debates and proposed viable solutions.

2.3.5. The new role of NGOs in national policy dialogue

In recent years, Tanzania has received ever-increasing volumes of development aid, presently amounting to more than twice the real value of the level of the early 1990s (Lawson et al. 2005:2). During this period, the trend in international aid relations has been favourable towards expanding general budget support. This has meant a stronger role for recipient governments as it supports 'country-led poverty reduction efforts'. General budget support has been associated with an increase in government spending in health and education. In 2005, it accounted for 36% of the Tanzanian aid volume (Lawson et al. 2005:2).
Since 1999, the compilation of Poverty Reduction Strategy Papers (PRSPs) has been mandatory for countries receiving funds under the HIPC (Heavily Indebted Poor Countries) initiative, the World Banks PRGF (Poverty Reduction and Growth Facility), and all other forms of concessional (IDA) finance (Brown 2004:237). For the World Bank, PRSPs constitute a major instrument in implementing the Comprehensive Development Framework (CDF) and working towards the achievement of the Millennium Development Goals (MDG). All these policy instruments emphasize the principle of "country ownership", namely the ability of recipient countries to realize autonomous, self-determined development planning. In addition, PRSPs emphasize the importance of broad participation. In the World Bank's PRSP Sourcebook (2000), a whole chapter is dedicated to par-

ticipation. Broad inclusion is mapped out in terms of "stakeholder participation", and it is especially recommended that marginalized groups ought to be actively involved. However, there is no precise clue as to who should be represented and by what criteria stakeholders are to be selected. While the International Financial Institutions expect "good governance" in developing countries to include democratic and representative processes, such standards are not necessarily part of the notion of participation in PRSPs. Rather, each country is to decide on its own the nature of the participatory process (Brown 2004:240). It is stated that civic engagement is to be enhanced by (personally) inviting individuals who need to be only broadly representative of the community. While consultations between civil society representatives and their constituencies are portrayed as desirable and the expectation is raised that they would make the PRSPs "truly participatory", it is at the same time stated that such negotiations need not necessarily be part of the process. As David Brown observes, "there is an interesting use of language here. If 'non-binding' consultations are said to be 'truly participatory', then the concept appears not to be seen by the bank as anything very substantial" (2004:241). Contrary to 'claimed' policy space, 'invited' spaces such as NGO participation in PRSP processes offer little real opportunity for influence since the agenda and terms of debate are defined by the powerful financial institutions rather than civil society organizations themselves (Miller, VeneKlasen and Clark 2005a:32).

Tanzania was one of the first countries that profited from the HIPC (Highly indebted poor countries) initiative, which offered preferential forms of debt relief. As elsewhere, PRSP has brought in a new dimension to local discourses on participation, with the World Bank and the IMF claiming significant progress, for example, in terms of the inclusion of women and marginalized groups in planning processes. In a comparative study by the World Bank analysing the incorporation of gender concerns in PRSP processes in various countries, Tanzania is commended for its reported model performance (cf. Bell 2003:10).

However, Tanzanian NGO representatives disagree with the World Bank's positive assessment of the consultation process. Mbilinyi remarks that while the interim PRSP paper expressed some concern about women's access to social services, it was at the same time characterized by a refusal to take on board any of the more constitutive feminist concerns, which would envision a transformatory process of development (Mbilinyi 2000:3).

NGOs involved in the process were highly critical of what they had been able to achieve in "consultations" that provided hardly any opportunity to voice their substantial concerns (Evans and Ngalwea 2003:277). First, the whole process of preparing the PRSP was firmly in the hands of the government machinery. Government officials were reluctant to share the preparatory documents with NGO representatives in time, regarding the process as donor-driven while downplaying the importance of the consultation process. The government did not allow some of the more vocal advocacy NGOs such as the "Tanzania Coalition for Debt and Development – TCDD" to have a share in the organization of the zonal workshops, dismissing them as "briefcase NGOs" without a popular base (Mbilinyi 2000:3). Put under pressure by the World Bank and the IMF by a tight time frame and demands for accountability, ministerial departments were not prepared to facilitate a participatory process that went beyond invitations to workshop attendance. The International Financial Institutions had from the beginning made it clear that participation was to be limited to technical issues, such as the identification of poverty indicators, while the more principal issues of the macro-economic reform process were never submitted to discussion.

TCDD still agreed to take part in the process of preparing the PRSP, well aware that the International Financial Institutions instrumentalized NGO involvement to legitimise their own agenda. As one TCDD members put it, the International Financial Institutions were arrogating the authority to reject or endorse the PRSP, which represented "a borrower's entire national plan ", while emphasising civil society participation and country ownership (Muna 2001:6). Mbilinyi remarks that the linkage between HIPC and PRGF meant that "in return for little, if any, additional debt relief, countries are going to be locked into 20 more years of structural adjustment and economic reform. A major change is that civil society organizations will be willing participants in the process" (Mbilinyi 2000:1).

Issa Shivji argues that in recent years donors have been increasingly assuming government functions, that is taking over the role of those who make policy in the name of the people, while the role of the government has become secondary. At the same time, the involvement of NGOs has had to replace popular participation. "I am urging that we need to re-examine our conceptualization and practices of these new and fancy roles that we are being given, that is, that of partners and stakeholders" (Shivji 2004:3).

The proliferation of NGOs in Tanzania has coincided with a growing assertion of political freedom and growing opportunities to voice criticism publicly without fear of repression. This development has been first of all due to the space opened by the government. While some NGOs used the climate of increasing political freedom to work for people's empowerment, others reinforced existing patterns of paternalism and inequality. However, both NGOs and government ultimately have little influence on cutting-edge development discourse dominated by the larger donors. The prevailing discourse of "empowering recipient governments" (Lawson et al. 2005:3), having "NGOs participate" in aid negotiations (Evans and Ngalwea 2003:277) and "mainstreaming gender" in institutions (Mbilinyi 2000:4) shows how far alternative development concepts have been alienated from their original objective of transforming power relations in favour of the poor and powerless. Leslie Groves points to the problems arbitrary policy change creates in concrete implementation. She documents how successful projects in Tanzania were stalled because donors refused to support projects that were not part of the national PRSP (Poverty Reduction Strategy Paper). Within a very short time span, some donors withdrew from commitments to ongoing projects, moving instead to support PRS (Poverty Reduction Strategies) that had become the preferred option of the day. In a child labour reduction project that had been diligently prepared for two years, recipient communities had a disappointing experience. "Community members involved in the project design and capacity-building workshops felt that they had completed their end of the bargain – they had attended workshops, hosted donors and donated land, time and resources to the project. Despite this, the result was that they were left with nothing but shattered expectations. In another case, a participatory water project was abandoned despite a successful mid-term evaluation" (Groves 2004:79). These examples show that while donors remained true to their participatory agendas, they arbitrarily breached long-term understandings. Complex issues of power and dependency are raised by these examples and they illustrate that stable continuity in egalitarian approaches is very far from realization.

2.3.6. Summary: The contribution of NGOs to participatory development in Tanzania

In the above focus on NGOs, some major organizational trends of the aid sector and their implication for development co-operation were discussed. Research data on aid practice in rural areas is available from various studies carried out in the last decade. In social development participation, empowerment and community commitment towards development have routinely become part of the qualitative programme and project objectives, with the respective approaches being "perceived as the new orthodoxy [...] from NGOs to the World Bank" (Green 2000:67). In implementation, hopes are particularly pinned on NGOs and their presumed abilities in delivering aid participatorily and effectively. However, evidence from Tanzania suggests that such expectations are largely unfounded.

Religious communities are, together with governmental institutions, among the most effective initiators of development-oriented groups and organizations. The 'mother culture' of the religious institution has been found to exert considerable influence on the organizational practices of organizations. This results, for example, in pervading gender and age-based hierarchies which hamper or inhibit bottom-up participatory work and empowerment.

Subsidiaries of Northern NGOs are important players in development and formally closely abide by cutting-edge development agendas, including gender, empowerment and participation. Yet implementation is usually biased by the priorities of the Northern centres, the agendas of which shape asymmetric aid relationships with all levels of Tanzanian development networks, from government to local groups. As concrete social and political constraints are usually excluded from everyday practice (e.g. unfair pricing of agricultural produce, undemocratic decision-making in committees, discriminatory legal conditions, etc), participation and empowerment often remain devoid of meaning. Studies have found that many rural dwellers have reverted to activities granting individual material advancement rather trusting in community efforts driven by irrelevant outside concepts. In recent years, NGOs in service provision have had to adapt to new conditions. While many previously worked through direct links with donors, they have had to compete for tenders due to the growing role of local governments. In practice, this often resulted in a comparative advantage for larger and better connected organizations international NGOs, with smaller Northern NGOs losing out.

In the 1990s, the organizational base of community development activities changed fundamentally. Whereas development activities previously took place under the control of party and government, groups and initiatives could now act independently. However, in everyday practice little changed since patron-client relationships remained the structuring element of the activities taking place. As a result, the emerging NGO usually do not include the poor and fail to balance regional disparities. In their everyday organizational practice, they are neither transparent nor democratic. As Kiondo (1995) sums up, it may be organizations and their proponents who are empowered in the process, but not the beneficiaries they are supposedly working for.

Some of the most dynamic developments have taken place among the emerging Tanzanian advocacy NGOs. Having strong links to professionals, especially in academia, their work often has a high relevance to national development policy. Successful interventions involved, for example, legal reform relating to gender-based violence. Other campaigns aiming at social justice and reallocation of national resources, e.g. land reform or protests about inhuman practices in the mining sector, proved more difficult as they led to confrontation with the government. Advocacy NGOs usually do not represent broad social movements and few of them can afford outreach on a national basis because of financial constraints. Yet some of their initiatives are of high relevance for the well-being of the large majority and the above-mentioned conflicts with government and IFIs are evidence that social inequalities and injustices are indeed being effectively addressed.

In recent years, the trend has been away from projects towards programmes and budget support as part of a restructuring of aid relationships. For instance, the HIPC initiative marks a new development in which the government plays an increasingly important role in development planning. Larger urban-based NGOs have also become involved in policy dialogue and high-level policy negotiations, such as in the context of the PRSP process. Being regarded as representatives of civil society, their inclusion has supposedly made the process more democratic and participatory; however, the organizations involved have pointed to the dangers of this development, warning that NGO participation has provided legitimacy for rather doubtful policy imposition by the International Financial Institutions.

NGOs are groups with heterogeneous backgrounds so it is therefore not conducive to generalize in relation to their performance. Yet the above synopsis has shown that in recent decades, NGOs have raised many expectations in social development which they have been largely unable to fulfil. In the postcolonial period, the state had little success in delivering on the hopes it had nourished in community development. After 1990, NGOs were extolled as the new main players in participatory development but largely failed to do any better. When it came to state-NGO relations, the Tanzanian government's primary interest was in co-opting the NGO sector into service provision as well as neutralising its progressive potential and political aspirations (Mercer 1999:251).

NGOs' role has subsequently been described in terms of "filling the gap the withdrawing state has left" in social development. Again, it is important to put the achievements into perspective. Although NGOs may have been vital in absorbing the worst repercussions of the crisis in social service provision, they have at no point been able to replace the state in the enormous task of providing basic needs in education, health or other social sectors.

In education, non-state run schools had been allowed to operate from the mid-1980s onwards. Nevertheless, this did little to stop the decline in educational quality.

> "Schools lacked sufficient classrooms, furniture and textbooks. Less than half of the teachers met the Ministry's minimum qualification requirements. Classrooms were overcrowded, teaching methodology was authoritarian and harassment of pupils, including sexual harassment, was common. The level of absenteeism among teachers was high. ... Many children dropped out of primary school or were never enrolled. Of those that lasted the seven years, around 80% failed the final examination" (Wedgwood 2005:4).

Significant improvement was not realized before the government, supported by the World Bank, abolished fees for primary schools in 2000, launching the Primary Education Development Plan. Meanwhile, primary school enrolment and performance has improved, with a huge challenge remaining in secondary education. In health, the user charges introduced in the mid-1990s have not been abandoned, although cost-sharing in healthcare constitutes a problem for over half of the population (Cooksey 2004:16).

2.4. Conclusion

This chapter has discussed various issues around the history of 'participation' as a key concept in Tanzanian development discourse. Even in the days of the colonial government, there was a reliance on participatory approaches when implementing community development projects. The independent government's Ujamaa policies were a major effort to develop rural areas with people-centred priorities. However, success was limited and social services could only be maintained at the cost of increasing dependency on foreign aid. With the donor fatigue of the 1980s, major political restructuring became inevitable. In the 1990s, NGOs became the main actors in social development, linking themselves to a dominant discourse on participation, gender and empowerment. More than a decade later, the NGOs' record on participation remains questionable. The peasant agrarian transition has meant that rural societies are increasingly turning away from agricultural production, with many of them unable to secure alternative livelihoods. Social service provision remains poor, while material inequality persists. Recently, the relationships between NGOs, the state and donors have been reshaped by changes in aid policy to increase budget support. Participation, empowerment and gender approaches, while remaining important potential challenges to existing inequalities and injustices, have made little impact on development practice. The problem remains twofold. Even at a conceptual level, participatory concepts are perverted by donor's priorities and requirements, while existing inequalities prevent transformations in practical implementation.

3. Donors' agendas and transformatory concepts in development discourse

Long before they meet the livelihood needs of rural people, aid projects satisfy the political needs of Western development agencies (Mosse 2005:22).

Having looked at the historical background of participatory development in Tanzania in the previous chapter, this section focuses on donors' approaches to transformatory concepts in development. The last chapter began with reflections on Tanzanians' first encounter with 'popular participation' in the context of colonial development policy. The British administration, rather unsuccessfully, had tried to impose participation as an obligation from above. During the anti-colonial movements, in contrast, people began to demand participation as their right. Broadening the perspective beyond Tanzania, one finds that participation played a role in development approaches throughout the 20th century, from the 'community development' approaches adopted by the British Colonial Office in the 1940s to present-day debates on participation, rights, and citizenship (for a detailed overview see Hickey and Mohan 2004a:7). Cooke (2003:47) traces continuities between the colonial policy of "Indirect Rule" and present-day participatory development management. Yet it was not before the 1990s that donors adopted participative planning tools as well as 'Gender Planning' approaches as an integral part of mainstream development policy. By the early 1980s, multilateral agencies such as the World Bank and IMF turned from the modernization approach to neoliberal policy. The state as a major actor of national development was put into question; at the same time, NGOs gained credibility as more relevant and efficient actors in aid delivery. For the most part, it was NGOs which took up demands from social and political movements and pioneered the use of participatory planning tools as well as Gender Planning. Northern development agencies, who by the 1990s were following the trend, proved very selective in what they adopted from concepts that originally aimed at radical social transformation. Essentially, they initiated a mainstreaming process that turned political demands into technical tools, obliterating their history of social contestation. Powerful donors and international financial institutions such as the World Bank have meanwhile created mechanisms to consult with them on selected issues. However, in important policy matters, including the setting of macro-economic frameworks, they still follow predetermined directions (Miller, Veneklasen and Clark 2005b:56). In preparation for the main empirical part of this study, which looks at the implementation of participatory tools and 'Gender Planning' concepts in everyday project work, the objective of this chapter is to gain an understanding of how the powerful actors in development could incorporate and mitigate radical concepts to suit their own interests and objectives.

The roots of participatory concepts in development co-operation can be traced to practitioners and scholars, who, from the 1970s onwards, were committed to a more people-centred form of rural development. Early concepts of participation included a greater respect for farmers' knowledge, more democratic and egalitarian communication between communities and development experts, a focus on local concerns and solutions instead of universal technical blueprints as well as a preference for environmentally-friendly 'appropriate' technology. Equally important, participation meant an empowering process for beneficiaries and a fundamental change in social relations, including the dismantling of hierarchies in development networks. Practitioners and communities developed a variety of approaches with different priorities. Over the years, Participatory Rural Appraisal (PRA), a planning tool developed by Robert Chambers (for example 1983, 1994a, 1994b, 1994c, 1997a, 1997b, 2004), has come to dominate practical implementation and theoretical debate (cf. Hickey and Mohan 2004a:11).

A similar process can be observed in regard to the objective of gender equity: feminist social scientists originally developed 'gender' as a broad analytical concept to question and dismantle patriarchal power relations (Oakley 1972:16). In development discourse, however, a single simplified planning tool, Caroline Moser's (1989; 1993) 'Gender Planning', has come to widely influence and shape practice and theory. Both in the case of PRA and Gender Planning, narrow and reduced tools are propagated under the name and image of originally more complex demands, ideas and theories. In the process, the transformatory potential of the concepts was lost to a large extent. The analysis of the broader social and political context shaping people's living conditions was abandoned, including the inequalities of the aid relationship that were excluded from consideration. While both Chambers and Moser provided a complex analysis of the status quo, they also recognized the need for simplified and effective tools in development co-operation. Northern donor agencies have been good at adopting these simple 'tools', while at the same time ignoring the elaborated social analysis from which they were developed. Numerous other participatory and gender-emancipatory tools were developed from the late 1980s onwards. Development organizations added to the variety as they combined and adapted different models. Yet one can say that Chamber's PRA and Moser's Gender Planning influenced mainstream development practice more than any other approach: First, they were adopted by powerful multilateral aid agencies that in turn influenced the practice of national donors and aid organizations; second, many of the other planning tools in the realm of gender and participation took over major tenets from PRA and Gender Planning.

Empowerment, a term closely related to participation, has similarly been subject to a variety of interpretations and uses (Schicho/Nöst 2006:45). The original understanding of empowerment promises profound social transformation and is based on a differentiated concept of the power relations involved. In aid practice, a variety of programmes, from those providing fishing nets to mobile phones, have been targeted to communities and individuals, especially women. Despite the inflationary use of the term, empowerment as a concept has in some way remained elusive, as unlike 'Gender Planning' or 'Participation' it has not come to be represented by a single methodological tool. As such, in the eyes of some practitioners it still holds the quality of not yet being ultimately defined, and possibly being less susceptible to manipulation by dominant actors (Kabeer 1999:436). The following reflections focus on donor's understanding of PRA and Gender Planning.

3.1. Participatory rural development: an alternative to top-down technology transfer

A key aspect in defining participation is popular agency. Participatory approaches put people, their aspirations and actions at the centre of interest. In mainstream development approaches, programme objectives are often at odds with the interests of the intended beneficiaries. Abstract overall objectives such as economic growth, industrialisation, mechanisation, higher productivity or economic sustainability have often taken priority over the actual aspirations of the people involved.

Rural and agricultural development was one of the domains where participatory approaches were put into practice early onwards. The main concern was to change the research and extension practices that were characterized by highly unequal relationships between agricultural scientists, extensionists and poor farmers. The bureaucratic and rigid operational structures in agricultural research, extension and teaching institutions were challenged. In particular, the idea of top-down technology transfer from scientists to farmers by extension agents was put into question (Scoones and Thompson 1994b:18; Nandi and Schaap 2005:643). Conventional agricultural research and extension was criticized as it tended to classify peasant farmers either as 'progressive' - as long as they were willing to adopt the new 'scientific' farming methods - or - if they preferred to stick to their own practices - as ignorant and 'conservative'. In the 1970s, researchers from various disciplines (anthropology, agriculture etc) proved that many 'local' farming practices were based on fairly accurate knowledge about the properties of seed, soil, climate and farming methods. Moreover, prevailing patterns of farming were found to take into account a complex variety of social and material conditions. Many development practitioners became enthusiastic about what they termed 'indigenous technical knowledge'. They demanded that it should be taken more seriously by formal knowledge systems and incorporated into agricultural research practice. Extension agents were to take on the task of 'extracting' respective knowledge from farmers, report it to research institutions and make it accessible beyond the 'local' context. The problem about this approach was that peasant farmers were still largely excluded from processes of knowledge appraisal and analysis (Pottier 1997:206). As "fundamental issues of power and knowledge" were not addressed, "critics charge that *Farmer First* initiatives often encounter many of the same problems as conventional transfer-of-technology strategies" (Scoones and Thompson 1994a:2).

By the 1980s and early 1990s, this early experience was critically reviewed. Many practitioners and scholars published their insights and recommendations in manuals and firsthand reports on participatory methods in rural development (e.g. Burbridge 1988, Bergdall 1993, Burkey 1993, Okali, Sumberg and Farrington 1993). Based on practical experience, these publications combined critique of existing aid relations with suggestions for 'alternative' practice. An important forum was the journal that started in 1988 as "RRA Notes", changed its name to "PLA Notes" in 1995 and again to "Participatory Learning and Action" in 2004; it was published by the International Institute of Environmental Development (IIED). Co-operation between practitioners and academics within the emerging field of development studies, for example, at the Institute of Development Studies in Sussex, was becoming instrumental to the development of participatory approaches that were based on dialogic and more egalitarian models of knowledge generation. Instead of imposing foreign blueprint models that ignored conditions relevant to peasants, foreign experts would first of all have to become more modest in their attitude. Sharing and exchanging knowledge, and, most importantly, joint sessions of knowledge appraisal and analysis should make sure that all participants had equal control over the knowledge produced. Participatory Rural Appraisal, an approach developed by Robert Chambers (1994a, 1994b, 1994c), offered a model for more equitable encounters between peasant farmers and outside experts. Chambers regarded the rural poor as marginalized and disempowered, and defined the reversal of hierarchies as one of his main objectives.

3.1.1. Robert Chambers' concept of Participatory Rural Appraisal (PRA)

In an article titled "The origins and practice of participatory rural appraisal" Chambers (1994a) traced five sources from which PRA developed. PRA is essentially a method of obtaining and analysing data. The origins specified by Chambers consist of various approaches to research and data collection. These include first of all activist participatory research (including Freire's 'Pedagogy of the Oppressed'), which contributed the idea that poor and marginalized people can do their own analysis, and do not have to rely on outside experts. Secondly, agro-eco-system analysis brought in various alternative methods of measurement and assessment: "transects (systematic walks and observations), informal mapping (sketch maps drawn on site), diagramming (seasonal calendar, flow and causal diagrams, bar charts, Venn or chapati diagrams), innovation assessment (scoring and ranking different actions)" (Chambers 1994b:954). Third, applied anthropology opened up perspectives on the validity and richness of rural people's knowledge, and on methods of flexible field research and learning, unhurried participant observation, extensive conversations, as well as the importance of attitudes and behaviour of outside researchers. Experience of these practices was important, even if PRA usually operated with a rather narrow time frame. Fourthly, field research on farming systems, carried out within various academic disciplines, has revealed the complexity, diversity but also the risk-prone nature of many cultivation schemes. Finally, Rapid Rural Appraisal (RRA), an approach that emerged from the late 1970s onwards, anticipated some of the methodical innovations. RRA originated mainly in the search for alternatives to research methods based on long-winded questionnaires and standard statistical norms. Additionally, many development practitioners were dissatisfied with the superficial nature of conventional visits of outsiders to rural projects and their biased nature that often neglected peripheral, poor and difficult contexts. The IDS in Sussex was vital in advancing RRA into a method that proved not only more cost-effective and time-saving, but also more relevant and valid in data collection. RRA constitutes, more than PRA, an extractive approach, as its "normal mode entails outsiders collecting data which is then taken away to be analyzed elsewhere" (Chambers 1994b:957). In contrast, PRA advocated an active role for rural project beneficiaries both during the collection *and* the analysis of data.

Many practitioners mention the change in attitude as the most important aspect of PRA in development work. As one aid worker from Kenya pointed out: "The most important thing about PRA was going in and listening [...] Just getting staff members to go to peoples houses and listening to them was the revolution" (Cornwall, Musyoki and Pratt 2001:14). A central element of PRA processes consisted in the organization of meetings in which communal decision-making processes would take place in a transparent, informed and democratic way. In order to elicit and visualise relevant information, the above-mentioned techniques such as mapping and diagramming were used and graphically illustrated with locally available material. Separate meetings with different sections of the community could be organized to obtain different perspectives and opinions, (taking into account different interests arising from differences in social class, gender, age, occupation or ethnic background, comprising for instance community leaders, youth, the poor, women, etc). Various intentions lay behind the use of PRA methodology. On the one hand, participatory approaches were expected to empower individuals and communities to become more self-reliant. On the other hand, the method also promised more efficient project implementation. The elaboration of specific tools to assist aid workers in implementation was important to facilitate widespread application in practice. Simple and easy-to-use 'methods' eventually found their way into the practice of development organizations, while complex social theory was regarded as having little relevance to everyday practice. Aspirations for transformation were channelled into moderate tracks and did not challenge broader political or social frameworks.

Chambers' writings are highly critical of prevailing practices in development co-operation, which he describes as biased, hierarchical and inefficient. He is particularly concerned about the role of foreign development professionals, reviewing in detail the approaches of information exchange various disciplines in development work have used (1983:28ff). His proposal for a more egalitarian practice centres on the demand for a fundamental change in attitude. Analysis of the status quo is repeatedly expressed in dichotomous oppositions. The following list of professional values and preferences is illustrative. It distinguishes conventional and participatory approaches and includes the following aspects: "urban – rural, industrial – agricultural, high-cost – low-cost, capital-using – labour using, mechanical – animal/human etc ..." (1983:173). Chambers links clear-cut value judgements to these opposing points. Yet beneath his urgent appeal for a change in attitude, many assumptions underlying conventional aid co-operation remain unquestioned. For example, prevalent practices of experts visiting villages are condemned as 'development tourism'. Yet the idea that 'outsiders' have to visit villages and gather information in order to adequately plan, monitor or evaluate development projects is not put into question. Chambers merely argues that a change in outsiders' attitudes and behaviour can make an essential difference. He is not concerned about the fact that the respective change is often minimal and that power differences still remain intact (1994b). Instead, he argues that in rural development "the beliefs, behaviour and attitudes of outsiders" explain failures in rural development rather than a lack of adequate methods (1995:1). In his view, the fact that outsider behaviour routinely denied the ability of 'local people' to carry out their own analysis is particularly detrimental. It is only when a change in behaviour is realized that development can take place. This includes the ability of the outsider of "sitting down, listening and learning, relaxing and not rushing, 'handing over the stick' (or pen, or chalk); 'embracing error' and 'failing forward', being transparently clear about who they are, their purpose and what can and what cannot be expected, and 'being nice to people'" (1995:2). The issue of outsiders' behaviour and abilities remains at the centre of considerations even in later publications, although the scope of responsibilities expands. In 2004, they include the following points: First, learning about and understanding rural living conditions; second, the adoption of innovative language use to facilitate attitudinal change; third, the reorganization of aid practice; and fourth, the facilitation of organizational change (Chambers and Pettit 2004:140). Throughout Chamber's writings, the 'primacy of the personal', that is the importance of personal qualities and commitment of aid workers and villagers, remains a constant concern, placing an urgent appeal for personal commitment and responsibility prominently on the agenda. While Chambers' demands often seem radical, the practical measures he suggests are those of moderate reform.

Many of the practical problems of PRA practice are anticipated in Chambers' writings. One of them concerns the assumption of homogeneous communities and the failure to accommodate antagonistic interests within groups. Another relates to the tendency to (mis)use participatory rhetoric in conventional top-down aid practice, especially as the concept gained prominence and acceptance throughout the 1990s. "The sudden popularity of PRA has generated huge problems and widespread bad practice. Quality assurance has become a massive concern" (Chambers 1997a:115). Critics have pointed out that these are not problems of practical implementation, but rather rooted in theoretical flaws of the concept. As PRA largely relies on dichotomous social categories (outsiders - local people, uppers - lowers, etc), it often fails to account for complex social relations. Equally, it assumes the need for outside intervention as a necessary impetus for initiating change. Concentration on local relevance has meant that the approach has largely been irrelevant to the broader political framework (Mohan and Stokke 2000:274). Finally, PRA evokes ambitious objectives that the applied method or tool often does not live up to.

3.1.2. Experience from development practice: setbacks despite 'best intentions'

There is widespread consensus that people-centred approaches demanded changes in development practice that were desirable and long overdue. How to achieve these changes, however, remains a contested issue. PRA are and related approaches continue to be popular, and many practice-oriented authors credit it with bringing positive change in aid co-operation (Cornwall, Musyoki and Pratt 2001:4). However, others report ambivalent experiences with the implementation of participatory programmes. Mosse's (2005) comprehensive study of the Indo-British Rainfed Farming Project, a participatory agricultural programme implemented between 1992 and 1999 in Western India, discusses a range of problematic issues that are not unique to the particular case.

In this rural programme, farmers soon became familiar with the rhetoric of participation, yet in everyday language use, the term came to signify a contribution of money or labour they were expected to make (Mosse 2005:114). Rather than having their own rationality and priorities acknowledged, villagers were more or less successfully adapting to a particular planning mode introduced from outside. Mosse found that it was not uncommon in participatory projects that staff selected people who already possessed the characteristics the project was supposed to create; the educated, the organized, the innovators, in short, independent, solvent, modernizing peasants who would guarantee a measure of success (2005:211). Initially, men rather than women participated in the programme. As implementation continued, the disadvantaged situation of women was to be addressed by targeting specific activities at them. Interestingly enough, this improved the relationships between aid workers and male farmers. As women were identified as those in most need of development intervention, men had an opportunity to negotiate their own status as needy beneficiaries. The more important women became within the intervention, "the more women became the signifiers of underdevelopment" (2005:171).

Field staff, despite better intentions, found themselves in the role of local patrons and benefactors rather than facilitators. The main reason for this was that it was them who decided about the distribution of subsidies such as improved seed or other technology on credit (2005:113). Staff who spent much of their time meeting expectations pertaining to participatory processes, such as investigating women's needs or insisting on slow build-up of skills, were seen as inefficient by the community and their superiors. Throughout the duration of the project, the contradictions between high-profile publicised participation processes on the one hand and vertical management control on the other developed into a major challenge. "In the wider market for development success [...] both participatory goals and their denial in practice are necessary to manage reputations" (2005:161). In everyday implementation, the 'profound but inevitable' internal contradiction between participation and patronage posed a considerable communicative task, especially in outward project representation. One of the many occasions where diverging messages had to be negotiated were visits by outside experts or donors to village communities. The rather rigid formality that often accompanied such visits is interpreted by Mosse as an attempt to come to terms with the insecurity of control senior outsiders had over everyday project life (2005:166). In everyday communication around the project, such as reports and meetings, the vagueness and lack of conceptual precision of many buzzwords of development policy discourse (including participation, partnership, empowerment) primarily had the function of concealing ideological difference and allowing compromise (2005:230).

A similarly challenging experience is reported by Pottier (1997) from PRA exercises carried out in Magindu, Tanzania. He gives an account of how participatory processes in practical implementation reproduced typical 'top-down' patterns of communication. During "the so-called participatory search for solutions" it turned out that "local participants suggested only those solutions the PRA team wanted to hear" (Pottier 1997:217). In the event, a common 'voice of the community' was being constructed, a process during which disparate opinions were largely excluded. Instead of facilitating the exchange of heterogeneous views and opinions, facilitators had silenced any opinion that did not comply with the dominant discourse they had established. Their assessments included the view that villagers were themselves responsible for their difficult situation (planting the wrong crops, getting pregnant frequently, not building toilets, etc). During the so-called participatory consultations, villagers saw no alternative to accepting this version of reality. Instead of presenting their own view of the situation, they engaged in extensive self-accusation and self-blame.

In a participatory water programme in Tanzania undertaken by the NGO HESA-WA (Health through Sanitation and Water), fieldworkers did not implement wealth ranking exercises when implementing PRA processes, anticipating that pointing out social difference could lead to conflict and endanger project results (Cleaver 2001:45). Reflecting on experience from various projects, Kothari remarks that "the use of PRA techniques often requires the taking out of anything complicated, making peoples lives and their social interactions linear and sterile as they fit into charts, diagrams and tables and conform to the boundaries and limitations of the methodological tools. There is also a process of controlling to produce the norm, the usual and the expected" (2001:147). This reflects the common experience that PRA, just like other tools and standard models in development co-operation, has the tendency to isolate projects from their wider socio-economic frameworks or historic contexts (Mosse 2005:97).

While the most common obstacle for popular participation is certainly the persistence of hierarchies, it should be considered that a radical reversal of power relations is also not without risks for those involved. As Mwajuma Masaiganah (2000:40) reports from an integrated rural programme in coastal fishing communities in Mtwara and Lindi in Tanzania in 1996, questioning the interests of well-connected dynamite fishers whom the communities had identified as a major obstacle to their welfare proved an impossible task. Processes of conscientization and organization of village communities left facilitators and participants enthusiastic, resulting for example in an encounter of an outspoken village committee with the then Tanzanian Prime Minister Frederick Sumaye. However, at a certain point, threats and acts of violence against aid workers and community members led to an abandonment of the programme. While local community members are most vulnerable to such acts of repression, this example shows that outside facilitators, if identified as 'ring leaders', may similarly face intimidation or violence. Foreigners are often less in danger (and usually the first to be offered a safe way out if developments get out of hand).

Finally, critical reflection of PRA practice raises the question of who benefits from the process. 'Handing over the stick', or putting in charge those who are affected by the intervention, may turn out to be a temporary affair after all. Community members will spend time and creativity on the process, but at the end of the day, it often turns out that results are by far more useful to aid workers and their agencies than to themselves.

3.1.3. Success as a challenge: institutionalisation and mainstreaming

In the course of the 1990s, the challenge of 'institutionalising' participation became a major concern (Blackburn and Holland eds. 1998). "Participation, if it is to be more than a palliative, involves shifts in power. These occur within communities, between 'people' and policy-making and resource-holding institution, and within the structure of these organizations" (Nelson and Wright 1995:1). The underlying rationale was that aid workers who were subject to rigid organizational hierarchies were unlikely to practise egalitarian or empowering behaviour in their interaction with community members. Institutionalising was part of an attempt to 'scale-up', extending PRA's quest for change beyond the limits of rural communities. In implementation, however, many existing organizational bureaucracies were only superficially reformed. The efforts at 'scaling-up' largely failed to address global asymmetric relations.

The spread of participatory approaches to mainstream aid organizations was accompanied by the tendency to implement the concepts of alternative development through technical blueprints rather than political transformation. Participatory processes became taken-for-granted components of the Project Cycle (Cornwall, Musyoki and Pratt 2001:5). Participation remained preoccupied with local project and programme realities, while the larger socio-political framework causing underdevelopment received hardly any attention. The asymmetries in international relations within development co-operation continued to be ignored. Instead, the preference for technical fixes and planning solutions meant that the transformatory potential of participatory approaches was undermined. As Hickey and Mohan remark, the recent trend to mainstream participation has further enhanced "the tendency [...] to treat participation as a technical method of project work rather than as a political methodology of empowerment" (2005:242).

Multilateral organizations played a major role in mainstreaming processes. For example, the Development Assistance Committee (DAC) of the OECD was founded as a member organization by bilateral donors in 1961. As mentioned in the second chapter, from the beginning onwards, its major function was the establishment of common standards and reciprocal mechanisms of control in order to ensure quality and co-ordination in development co-operation. For member countries, DAC standards provided a legitimising instance; conforming to the commonly set standards exonerated individual actors from debating or justifying critical aspects of their donor policy and practice (Gomes 2006:15). In the 1990s, the DAC added participation to its list of qualitative development objectives that Northern donors should consider in their development policy and report on regularly. In the "Guidelines on Participatory Development and Good Governance" (OECD-DAC 1995), participation is subsumed together with other objectives such as democratization, good governance and human rights into a common category of "Participatory Development and Good Governance". Any project or programme that has one of these four aspects as its principal objective (that is, the project or programme would not have been undertaken without this explicit objective) - or as a significant objective (that is, the objective is just one of several important ones) - may be marked and reported accordingly. In its reflections on participatory development, the DAC takes a rather utilitarian approach. Participatory development is regarded as essential for two major reasons: first, it is expected to strengthen civil society which in turn should provide a check on the power of government; second, it is thought to enhance the efficiency, effectiveness and sustainability of aid projects (DAC 1995:8). Moreover, while 'empowerment' is emphasized as vital, the concrete examples 'at local level' seem like concessions granted at development planners' discretion rather than rights beneficiaries are entitled to: "consultation on a particular issue, involvement in delivery of a service or implementation of an activity up to full decision-making where aid is given in support of a local initiative" (DAC 1995:9). The authors of the guidelines, however, admit that insights on participation are preliminary and further experience, commitment and research is needed. They also remark self-critically that development administrators often prefer to 'get things done' and are unwilling to engage in time-consuming democratic processes. Throughout most of the text, however, the authors remain confined to a one-sided donor and planner perspective. They are also not troubled by hierarchic or undemocratic decision-making processes in aid co-operation, nor do they consider participation to be a fundamental right of beneficiaries in development endeavours. Instead, they observe somewhat naively that "beneficiaries do not always participate in the way development agencies would like them to" (DAC 1995:9). In a report on "Participatory Development and Good Governance" published in two parts in 1997, the issue of participation in project implementation is not addressed at all - instead, the agenda is occupied by 'good governance' issues. The topics accordingly focus on the following issues: the role of donors in democratization processes; civil society and democratization; human rights and development co-operation; legal system reform; and finally, decentralisation and democratic local government (DAC 1997). While all of these are relevant points, none of them explicitly deals with the challenges of participatory programme implementation or with the democratization of aid relationships in general.

The World Bank, a leading voice in development discourse that prides itself as "the knowledge bank" adopted participatory approaches in various spheres of activities, especially in social development and rural sector programmes. In recent years, participatory approaches became essential in the preparation of country participatory poverty assessments (Francis 2001:85). The "World Bank Participation Sourcebook", published in 1996, documents corresponding endeavours. By the end of the 1990s, the voluminous research and documentation project "Voices of the Poor" was undertaken by World Bank staff relying on participatory research methods. More than 60,000 women and men from 60 countries were consulted. The results were published in three volumes between 2000 and 2002, with Robert Chambers being one of several co-editors involved (Narayan et al 2000a, 2000b, 2002). The ambitious text illustrates the capacity of the Bank to engage in research and public relations on a scale that most governments, research institutions and development organizations, especially those from developing countries, can not keep up with. At the same time, it also illustrates the limited will and ability of large organizations for substantial change. While a great number of people gave their opinion, their recorded 'voices' were edited and analyzed by researchers. Unfortunately, the main function of the publication is one of providing legitimacy to a range of World Bank policies rather than providing a genuine basis for policy change in the interest of the poor.

Evaluative studies of the World Bank's achievements in participatory development from the end of the 1990s come to the conclusion that the label 'participatory' is often generously attached, while the contents of programmes and projects remain largely unaffected. A comprehensive analysis of social factors (gender, social class, etc.) during preparation of projects for programmes remains the exception rather than the rule. While personal attitudes and procedural routines may at times have changed towards more inclusive patterns, organizational structures and hierarchies usually remained untouched (Francis 2001:87). This institutional instrumentalization of egalitarian concepts has become a common occurrence in development networks world-wide and has resulted in participation and gender becoming empty buzzwords, largely drained of their transformatory potential. As a result, many critics today demand a return to a more radical and political understanding of participation (Cooke and Kothari 2001:13; Hickey and Mohan 2005:238).

In agriculture, participatory concepts have led to a critical review of the longstanding 'Research and Extension' approach. Even in the large development organizations, the dominant discourse now holds that the distinction between 'agricultural experts' and 'knowledge consumers' is obsolete, as there are many "agents engaged in continuous processes of learning. [...] Thus the traditional 'pipeline' approach to promoting development, in which researchers develop new technologies, and pass them to extension agents who in turn are meant to persuade farmers to adopt them, must be abandoned in favour of a more inclusive and holistic approach" (Jones 2005:48). In practice, this does not necessarily lead to substantial support for smallholder producers. Agricultural policy often enough does not prioritize small-scale farmers. For example, in Kenya, large-scale commercial farm production for export and the emerging market of local supermarket chains is promoted and acclaimed as a recent model success story for African agriculture. Small-scale farmers, who cannot afford the necessary investment in packing, cool chains and food processing facilities are largely excluded from this development. While jobs are created by the boom in commercial farm horticulture and floriculture, many of them are temporary, low-paid and informal; with insecure workers who are highly vulnerable to poverty, often "women who juggle their reproductive role with that of a wage earner" (Barrientos et al 2005:74).

Intricate rural–urban as well as farm and non-farm interdependencies have been asserted and confirmed by integrated livelihood research. However, respective findings are still largely ignored in mainstream development planning. Public extension services have largely failed to address the implications of multiple livelihoods that combine farm and non-farm activities (Tripp 2001:484). As discussed in the previous chapter, a rise in agricultural output is usually due to investment from non-farm activities - yet PRSPs largely rely on the idea of "agriculture-led growth" (Bahiigwa et al 2005:120, Bryceson 2004:619). The complex trade-offs and many uncertainties African peasants face in their everyday existence are rarely taken into account in the established assumptions that usually guide mainstream agricultural policy. Sectoral and disciplinary perspectives are often narrow and reductionist, resulting in the prevalence of "beguiling assumptions and slick rhetoric of mainstream stances" that "have not delivered livelihoods for the poor" but have instead "made matters worse" (Scoones and Wolmer 2003:115).

In the last few years, rights-based approaches that originate in legal rights and empowerment strategies as well as in social movements claiming citizen's rights and democratization have gained importance in development co-operation. In particular, they have been promoted by advocacy NGOs who offer legal counselling and lobby for equitable legislation. With their commitment towards a more just society, they have added transformatory momentum to existing concepts of participation, empowerment and gender. The discourse of rights has a strong potential to challenge existing power structures; it "can sharpen the political edges of participation in the wake of instrumentalism produced by mainstreaming" (Cornwall and Nyamu-Musembi 2005:10). However, while NGOs have again pioneered the application of rights-based approaches in practical work, large bi- and multilateral agencies are taking time to incorporate and adapt the idea to their policy. As with other people-centred approaches, instrumentalism could become a problem. There are several reasons why rights-based approaches are attractive to donors - among other aspects, they emphasize the rights of beneficiaries and demand accountability from recipient governments. However, rights-based discourse is often adopted without considering its ramifications. Peter Uvin also argues: "The prime reason why development agencies adopt such language with its deliberate obfuscation is, of course, to benefit from the moral authority and political appeal of the human rights discourse. The development community is in constant need of regaining the high moral ground in order to fend criticism and mobilize resources" (Uvin 2002:4). In the same vein, Cornwall and Nyamu-Musembi ask "When a 'rights based approach' is deployed in the context of bilateral and multilateral assistance programmes, where do the obligations lie? [...] Does [the funding government] take responsibility for any negative human rights impact flowing from projects it has funded? None of these implications are explained clearly in any agency's policy" (2005:14). Neither of these authors deny that any change in rhetoric also contains a chance for naming injustices and demanding improvements, thereby paving the way for gradual improvement of aid practices. However, there is a strong case for not expecting too much from this latest 'cutting edge' trend in development discourse, as, like many other promising approaches before, it may be 'domesticated' in the course of being put into practice.

Finally, the question remains why established aid organizations, despite their progressive rhetoric, are so unlikely to implement participatory approaches? The lack of political will is often reflected in the conviction that certain established technocratic tools are indispensable in aid work. Commonly used management and planning tools, however, are often incompatible with participatory approaches. In order to gain further insight into the problem, two widely used tools of mainstream aid practice and their interdependency with participatory concepts will be presented here.

3.2. Are 'mainstream' planning tools compatible with participatory approaches?

> *Discourses are not only the way that things are said or written, but also concrete activities associated with them, such as LogFrames in a development setting (Hughes, Wheeler and Eyben 2005:67).*

At the same time that alternative concepts gained ground in social development, management approaches originating in business administration and psychology became standard requirements in many aid agencies. Contrary to participatory concepts in development that trust poor and powerless beneficiaries to be primary agents in development projects, mainstream planning tools accord this primary role to project management units. Thus, while actors are typically not named in management concepts, the leading role of planners, experts and managers is implicitly taken for granted. In everyday project communication, however, this role allocation becomes obvious even if allusion to participatory and emancipatory discourse is made: it is not unusual that development workers are said to 'empower' women, or planners said to 'allow' popular participation, etc. Ambitious and influential aid agencies strive to excel both in professional management and in cutting-edge development discourse, suggesting that they can deliver it all. Yet profound investigation reveals that management and participatory approaches are contradictory. It also shows that in most cases, management approaches are well established, while participatory principles are often reduced to more or less effective add-ons to mainstream aid practice.

3.2.1. Project Cycle Management (PCM)

The 'Project Cycle' refers to a planning approach the World Bank began to use in 1970, a period during which projects constituted the uncontested format of aid delivery (Biggs and Smith 2003:1743). As a management tool, the Project Cycle depicts projects as developing through a series of stages, starting from needs assessment through to evaluation. The modell of the 'Project Cycle' contains a strongly normative element, as it assumes all development projects should ideally follow similar sequences of activities. It is largely used in a prescriptive manner, namely as a model of how projects should be implemented. The underlying notion of development through project implementation was largely technical and economical (for a detailed description of the various models proposed see Potts 2002:12ff), leaving little concern for social processes (Robb 2004:26). At present, many organizations use the 'Project Cycle' as a planning tool, with the exact number of stages and descriptions varying slightly according to the specific organization. The following graphic illustration is taken from documents from the Commission of the European Community, which adopted the Project Cycle in this form in 1993 (Potts 2002:14).

3.2. Are 'mainstream' planning tools compatible with participatory approaches?

The concept of the Project Cycle includes several principles, namely that the phases should follow each other progressively, that decision-making criteria and procedures are defined at each phase, and that identification of new projects and its programming takes into account results of monitoring and evaluation processes of previous projects. Learning from past experience is an important principle that

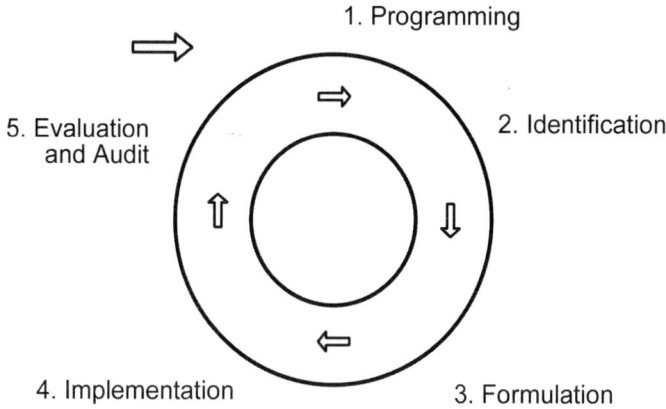

Figure 1: The Project Cycle (adapted from: European Commission 2004:16)

is also symbolised by the fact that a cycle is used to represent the project rather than a linear form. Adjustments to ongoing events are to be made at every stage in the cycle. The model of the Project Cycle has over the years become a core element of development discourse. For decades of aid co-operation, the idea that the project is the major unit of aid delivery, and that it evolves over clearly defined stages has become firmly established. The model, promoted by the World Bank, the OECD and other powerful players in aid co-operation, has become vital in the process of mainstreaming and enforcing standard formats and reliability. This does not only concern concrete project implementation, but also the larger framework of aid-co-operation. For example, when in 2002 the Austrian Ministry for Foreign Affairs began to enact the principle of "no project without evaluation" (OEZA 2006a:1), it justified this step by explicitly referring to the Project Cycle which includes evaluation as an indispensable part of project implementation.

In its original version, the Project Cycle had little consideration for participatory processes. The perspective taken in Project Cycle Management, while not explicitly naming actors, describes the activities coordinated by donors and Northern aid agencies. Recently, Project Cycle Management has been revised and readjusted, incorporating new approaches and concepts that broadened the scope for representation of beneficiaries' interests. "A whole new range of assessment criteria has been added to the original economic criteria, so that concerns such as the environment, poverty, gender, empowerment, human rights, capacity building, institutional development can be included in the assessments that take place at various points in the cycle" (Biggs and Smith 2003:1744). Additionally, planning tools such as the Logical Framework Analysis have been elaborated to fit into Project Cycle Management. Initially only relevant in the design phase, LogFrames are now used at all stages of the Project Cycle. Such trends towards combination and incorporation and their results in terms of aid practice will be discussed below. The Project Cycle has shaped more than 30 years of continuity in development co-operation, and present trends towards sector and programme support will not fundamentally change this: strategies and programmes still need concrete projects in implementation, and planning tools are used at all levels of strategy, programme or projects. Numerous 'best practice' guidelines continue to advocate Project Cycle Management despite disappointing experience in sustainability and popular participation. As Biggs and Smith (2003:1747) critically observe, the same recommendations and propositions are continuously repeated under the claim of 'learning from past mistakes'. While critical literature on the implementation of the Project Cycle model also exists, it seems to have little influence on mainstream practices. Most people working in aid co-operation take the terminology of the Project Cycle for granted, rarely questioning assumptions and implications of the dominant model. As Thomas Dichter, a senior US-American development practitioner and consultant self-critically observes, "we act as if development is a construction, a matter of planning and engineering. While we rarely use the term 'engineering', we regularly use an engineering lexicon: such words as 'plan', 'objective' and 'implement'. And we talk much about measurement and 'indicators'". Dichter also remarks that periods of 2-5 years constitute "wholly unreasonable time frames" for development to take place (2003:7). Similar to post-development thought, these remarks from 'within' the aid system remind us of how little, despite all the dramatic shifts in development discourse, has actually changed in the everyday routine of aid delivery.

3.2.2. The Logical Framework Approach (LFA)

Similar to Project Cycle Management, the Logical Framework Approach is a commonly used planning tool which has become part of the standard requirements of many bi- and multilateral donors (including the World Bank, DAC-OECD, EU, etc.). The first versions of the Logical Framework were developed for USAID in the late 1960s. They emerged from corporate and military internal planning involving centralized control and a dominant single objective (Dale 2003:57). It was subsequently adopted by CIDA in Canada and several of the UN Organizations, such as ILO and FAO. By the beginning of the 1980s, the German development agency GTZ (Deutsche Gesellschaft für Technische Zusammenarbeit) developed it further, adopting the concept under the name of ZOPP (Zielorientierte Projektplanung, in English: Objective-Oriented Project Planning [OOPP]). From there, the concept spread to the Scandinavian aid agencies, the British ODA and, by the 1990s, to the European Union (Hersoug 1996:380). In Austria, LFA terminology and principles have influenced project administration from the early 1990s onwards, even if it was only by the end of the decade that the governmental aid agency began to require all project documents from implementing organizations to correspond to the LFA format. As a major characteristic, current versions of LFA include a series of workshops that ideally include participatory sessions; as with other approaches, much depends on the facilitation skills of practitioners, and organizational constraints often impede participatory decision-making (Mutter 1995:166; GTZ 1997).

The Logical Framework Approach is primarily goal-oriented. It helps planners to establish a realistic objective, to check a project's internal logic, to create a basis for monitoring and evaluation, and become aware of underlying assumptions and expectations. It also focuses attention and helps to summarise key information into one brief document, providing a practical basis for donor-recipient communication (Aune 2000:687-688). Fig. 2, an illustration taken from European Union documents in 2006, lists the activities around the compilation of the Logical Framework Matrix. As the example shows, beneficiaries are included in the considerations under the heading of possible stakeholders. The description does

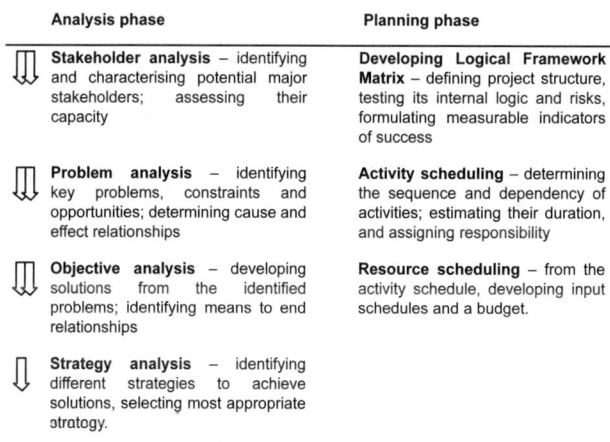

Figure 2: The Logical Framework Approach (Europe Aid Co-operation Office 2006)

not explicitly name actors, but as in the case of PCM, it takes the perspective of donors and experts, and their active and leading role, for granted.

As can be seen in the above description, the Logical Framework Approach in its present-day version includes mechanisms that allow for a regular adaptation to changing conditions. Fig. 3 shows the Logical Framework Matrix, the core document of the LFA. It requires the definition of one single overall objective, and while activities and their results may serve various purposes, they must all relate to the intended overall objective. At the same time, it is acknowledged that only activities (inputs) and results (outputs) are under full control of project management, while the level of purposes and overall objective can be determined only partly. The Matrix requires the setting of indicators (Objectively Verifiable Indicators, or OVI), as well as specifications on how the information is to be obtained, where, when and by whom (Means of Verification, or MOV). Finally, it provides an opportunity to discuss external factors important to project realization, and raises questions that help to reveal underlying assumptions as well as risks that may threaten projected outcomes.

The success of LFA – similarly to PCM, it is widely used not only in aid co-operation, but also prevalent in many other commercial and technical contexts – lies in its emphasis on rational precision and reflection. Proponents of LFA emphasize the following positive aspects: LFA elicits a range of perspectives and information at an early planning stage and helps to separate concrete achievements from more general objectives. It also prompts the identification of assumptions and expectations. A major emphasis is on a coherent 'means to the end' relationship between the various planning stages as they move from a lower to a higher level. In the process, different strategies are considered and unattainable goals can be eliminated. The orientation towards objectives introduces an optimistic and action-oriented perspective. The use of uniform terminology that is prescribed by

Project Description	Indicators	Source of Verification	Assumptions
Overall Objective – The project's contribution to policy or programme objectives (impact).	How the achievement of the overall objective is to be measured (Quantity, quality, time?)	How will the information be collected, when and by whom?	
Purpose – Direct benefits to the target group(s).	How the purpose is to be measured, including quantity, quality, time.	How will the information be collected, when and by whom?	If the purpose is achieved, what assumptions must hold true to achieve the overall objective?
Results – Tangible products or services delivered by the project.	How the purpose is to be measured, including quantity, quality, time.	How will the information be collected, when and by whom?	If the results are achieved, what assumptions must hold true to achieve the purpose?
Activities – Tasks that have to be undertaken to deliver the desired results			If activities are completed, what assumptions must hold true to deliver the results?

Figure 3: The Logical Framework Matrix (EuropeAid Co-operation Office 2006)

the LFA manual provides a common language in donor-recipient communication. Risks posed by the environment can be identified, resulting in the possibility of

3.2. Are 'mainstream' planning tools compatible with participatory approaches? 81

developing adequate strategies. Finally, the determination of indicators provides a basis for constant monitoring and evaluation.

Although LFA has been used for several decades now, there is little critical literature on the method. In reviews undertaken by USAID and ODA, the following problems with the implementation of the logical framework were noted:

> "A tendency for users to engage in mechanical box filling rather than thinking.
> A failure to allow targets to be adapted to changing circumstances.
> Unnecessary rigidity caused by projects designed to 'fit the framework'
> Overemphasis or misuse of quantitative targets.
> Difficulties in distinguishing between outputs and purposes. This problem also extended to problems with projects where the hierarchy of objectives did not fit neatly into the four-level structure.
> Difficulties in specifying the means of verification for the achievement of sector goals."
> (quoted from Potts 2002:35)

More general criticism remarks that LFA is not primarily concerned with economic efficiency and that it privileges aspects that can be measured quantitatively at the expense of others. Additionally, LFA does not offer advice on how to deal with conflicting goals, or bother much about how target groups can be involved in implementation (Hersoug 1996:383).

More fundamental criticism concerns the general perception of the planning process as rational activity, where objectives are established first, and a consideration of alternatives is followed by decision-making and finally corresponding action. As management literature has remarked some decades ago, the procedure may also be reversed, "first there is action, and then the goals are discovered, or [...] the goals are ascribed to action post factum, as a 'rationalization' or interpretation" (Hersoug 1996:386). Determination of goals at an early phase of project implementation may inhibit later adaptation to shifting circumstances or changing needs of target groups. Regarding the planning process, the stable and predictable environment assumed by the Logical Framework rarely captures the reality of development projects. Again, alternative understandings of planning processes could provide more useful insights. Contrary to the 'logic' of planning in LFA, means may not be selected according to objectives. Rather, objectives are often defined to suit the available means. Planning processes in many cases do not function in the linear way outlined in manuals. According to Weick, a plan is mainly a symbol of a joint effort to reach a common goal; in Weick's words, "any plan would do" (Weick 1979, quoted from Hersoug 1996:390). A plan would therefore principally provide a vision, a basis for a range of possibilities from which common activities can be developed, possibly also with the participation of beneficiaries.

Finally, it is the very advantages of LFA – the simplicity as well as the creation of a uniform standard – that also create problems. Both the language used and the planning mode is based on the perspective and needs of management units in aid and donor agencies. The pre-established squares do not leave much space for the consideration of target group heterogeneity or complex social conditions, neither do they ultimately bother about the extent of involvement of beneficiaries in decision-making: Although practitioners point to the fact that success depends on the incorporation of beneficiaries' and stakeholders' opinions into the process, any gaps are often filled by planners. Efficient management and precision is emphasized, while the attention given to group processes remains contingent on circumstances and individual preference. This bias towards administrative standards is a major reason why Robert Chambers and other PRA practitioners consider the use of LFA as incompatible with the use of PRA.

In everyday practice, organizations and aid workers are required to combine various methods, and to opportunistically ignore contradictions to satisfy various actors' requirements at the same time. In the process, LFA is typically accorded the role of shaping the general structure in the interests of donors' administrations, while PRA is reduced to local and community contexts to ensure maximum commitment of beneficiaries. "It is proposed that LFA and PRA be used in a complementary way. The LFA method is used to structure the overall planning process while PRA is used to identify local problems and to foster decision making at local level" (Aune 2000: 690). Such complementary eclecticism surely contributes to the tendency of creating 'toothless' understandings of PRA, that is, a practice where power differences are not challenged. Most aid agencies have adopted participation as a working principle without ever relinquishing their powerful positions in aid relationships. Practical experience shows that the inclusion of participatory exercises within the LFA routine tends to result in difficulties. The pre-set LFA 'boxes' constrain or completely prevent open debate. Formality, exclusive language use and time constraints are experienced as impediments that cannot easily be overcome during the course of the occasional workshop, as participatory processes require long-term co-operation (Marsden 2004:100).

LFA is too limited when multiple stakeholders with diverging interests are involved, or when flexibility and fundamental reorientation are required throughout a project's duration. From the point of view of evaluations, the use of the LogFrame privileges audit forms of establishing accountability at the expense of 'evaluation as learning' (Gasper 2000:27).

The process of adapting and elaborating management tools is a continuous one that has given rise to numerous approaches, formats and variations. Individual organizations often develop their own variants or combine their own choice of tools. Despite this apparent plurality, the basic components of these management tools are largely uniform, which gives them an important function as common points of reference. The development and use of tools such as PRA and 'Gender Planning' emanate from the desire to make qualitative concepts concrete and measurable. Yet qualitative principles tend to remain elusive, as reflected in everyday language use where policies and activities are often described in relative terms (for instance as more participatory, less gender sensitive, highly empowering). The combination of technical approaches with permanently changing qualitative principles - which, after all, originate from political demands - gives rise to ever new methods for practical application. Actors are keen to prove that they are aware of and experienced in all major cutting-edge trends. In order to be up to date, agencies periodically review their planning instruments, constantly adding new aspects to be considered. All this may make it rather difficult to exactly delineate and define a particular organization's policy. The following comment referring to the introduction of Project Cycle Management in GTZ in the mid-1990s illustrates the growing complexity: "The PCM concept incorporates the application of project planning and appraisal tools like ZOPP, PRA, gender analysis and others. These tools are not replaced by PCM but put into the flexible context of a planning cycle" (Nauheimer 1997:7-8). The vagueness created by this accumulation of approaches may be vital for the survival of organizations, as it opens up space for negotiation and compromise. For outsiders, for example, co-operation partners, however, it may become confusing or even frustrating, as organizations can justify accommodation and flexibility in one case just as well as arbitrary rejection in another.

3.2.3. LFA components: Stakeholder and SWOT Analysis as examples

PCM and LFA consist of a range of optional or routine components which have not been discussed in detail here. Just like PCM and LFA themselves, most of these supplementary concepts are well established in a range of domains from social psychology to business administration. In the following, the concepts of Stakeholder Analysis and SWOT Analysis (Strength-Weakness as well as Opportunities-Threats Analysis) will be briefly introduced. Stakeholder Analysis is the first stage in present models of LFA and a primary means of engaging with partners and beneficiaries. It is also the context within which LFA manuals explicitly recommend the use of participatory approaches.

SWOT is a concept for situational analysis and assessment which may be used by individuals or groups. It is of particular relevance to the empirical part of this study as it was regularly used in the SRAP (Sustainable Rural Agriculture Program) as a tool in planning sessions at village and team level[6]. In other programmes, SWOT is at times used as part of Stakeholder Analysis.

3.2.3.1. Stakeholder Analysis

The definition of stakeholders within LogFrame applications includes all those who affect or are affected by an aid project or programme (Overseas Development Administration1995:3, Narayan and Rietbergen-McCracken 1998:65, European

---

6 In the SRAP documents and recordings, the French abbreviation SEPO (Succèss, Echecs, Potentialités, Obstacles) is usually used, with key concepts and grids being translated to Swahili and English.

Commission 2004:61; Potts 2002:27). The first step in Stakeholder Analysis is compiling a list of individuals, organizations and groups who are relevant to the project. A differentiation of 'primary stakeholders', that is those who are primarily affected (including beneficiaries as well as those who may be negatively affected) on the one hand and 'secondary stakeholders', that is those who are involved in the delivery of the aid process, on the other hand, is made by some authors. In addition, all those who exercise significant influence over project implementation are often marked as 'key' stakeholders. The remarkable point about these categorisations is that possible negative consequences of a project are brought into consideration at an early planning stage, as the concept of stakeholders includes possible 'winners' and 'losers' who are to be considered in planning.

Next, each stakeholder's importance to project success and their relative power and influence is to be appraised. This includes a consideration of their interests, expectations, possible commitments and relationships to other stakeholders. Power and influence is assessed in terms of formal aspects such as position in organizational hierarchies, leadership functions, access to strategic resources, possession of knowledge and negotiation position; additional informal aspects include social status, degree of group organization, informal links, as well as influence or dependence on other stakeholders (Overseas Development Administration 1994:8). With a simple grid distinguishing individuals on the bases of importance and influence, four groups of stakeholders are identified. Standard recommendations of how to deal with the various groups are also provided.

As can be seen from the above summary, Stakeholder Analysis helps to identify power differentials and conflicts of interests between the various actors and beneficiaries involved. In contrast to the more radical transformatory participatory or empowering concepts, the ultimate objective of this analysis is not to address unequal social relations in order to change them into more egalitarian ones. Rather, planners are provided with a pragmatic tool to 'manage' their relationships with different individuals or groups in order to ensure effective project implementation. The consideration of various groups and individuals is expected to facilitate the identification of assumptions and risks, two points essential for the compilation of LFA frameworks. Moreover, while Stakeholder Analysis tools and exercises are recommended to be "used in a participatory fashion" (ODA 1995:4), this is framed in the sense of generous access to communicative events and information rather than joint decision-making. Even in this respect, however, caution is expressed, as the interests of some stakeholders can be covert, and there may be "few benefits in trying to uncover such agendas in public" (ODA 1995:4). Stakeholder Analysis requires planners to predetermine the extent of possible participation for all individuals, groups and organizations involved in a project. This encourages paternalistic relationships between aid agencies and recipient groups, especially as beneficiaries are considered as only one among various groups to be 'dealt with'.

3.2. Are 'mainstream' planning tools compatible with participatory approaches?   85

	high influence	low influence
high importance	Usually secondary or key stakeholders involved in aid delivery; the recommendation is to "construct good working relationships" and to "ensure an effective coalition of support for the project"	Usually primary stakeholders ('beneficiaries'). "They will require special initiatives if their interests are to be protected" and "they need to be kept informed"
low importance	Stakeholders not directly involved in aid delivery, possibly having interest divergent from project objectives. "May be a source of significant risk, and need careful monitoring or management"	Groups with little influence and interest in the project. "Unlikely to be subject of project activities or management"

Figure 4: Importance/influence analysis grid for Stakeholder Analysis (adapted from ODA 1995:10, Potts 2002:28)

3.2.3.2. SWOT Analysis (Strength-Weakness and Opportunities-Threats Analysis)

The SWOT concept is widely used in business administration for situational analysis and strategic planning. It is also commonly employed in psychological approaches to individual self-presentation and career planning in professional environments.

SWOT is a planning tool that combines an axis of time (past and future) with an axis of assessment (positive and negative). The resulting grid provides a simple framework for eliciting and writing up the various aspects of a concrete situation. In development work, the time axis is filled with reporting past activities and planning future ones, while the assessment axis give participants an opportunity to voice their own judgement of the issues at stake. The use of the SWOT concept in planning sessions means that participants are, in a first step, asked to identify strengths and weaknesses. This provides an opportunity to assess past achievements and failures and discuss their implications for the present situation. In a second step, interaction moves to future perspectives, focusing on opportunities and threats.

strength kupata uongozi bora (to obtain good leadership) ...	opportunities kuwa na uvuvi (to have fishing [activities]) ...
weakness (obstacles) kukosa soko la kufaa (absence of a suitable market) ...	threats wanachama kutohudhuria mikutano (members not attending meetings) ...

Figure 5: Example of SWOT-Analysis (Source: SRAP Programme Documents 1992, Swahili original with English translation)

The grid can be used for personal reflection and group discussion. The original concept does not address the issue of group processes around SWOT Analysis. As in other participatory group processes, some participants may be more influential than others, and the framework of possible topics and issues is likely to be circumscribed by aid workers. SWOT definitely has potential as an instrument in facilitating participatory processes, however, it does not per se ensure equal opportunities in decision-making. Rather, its qualities, such as those of other participatory tools, depend on previously established relations and on adequate implementation. Various points are important here. The principle of noting down all contributions by participants is important as it communicates respect and equality towards all participants present. The process of eliciting contributions can be further enhanced by dividing the participants into small groups, where some individual may be more likely to voice an opinion freely. With all these efforts, however, one should keep in mind that powerful group members are still likely to dominate the discussion. As examples from SRAP meetings illustrate in the empirical part of this study, the widespread tendency of aid workers to insist on the 'final word' manipulates the construction of consensus and constitutes an obstacle to genuine participatory processes.

3.2.4. Planning concepts and the 'reality of aid'

In everyday project implementation, PRA, RRA, PLA and other participatory concepts are widely used as planning tools with the intention of gaining popular acceptance, support and long-term sustainability for projects. However, they usually do not serve as main planning tools, but rather as a supplement to other methods that prioritize different objectives. Mainstream management approaches such as PCM and LFA, including their numerous supplementary components have absorbed and neutralised many of the innovative concepts including participation. Recent developments of 'scaling up' of participatory principles beyond the local community and the shift of donor support from projects towards programme and budget support have further enhanced the trend of using participatory approaches as superficial add-ons to otherwise strictly controlled planning processes of powerful aid administrations.

Realizing the limitations of rigidity that comes along with LFA and other planning tools, recent development discourse emphasizes the ideal of 'process' rather than 'blueprint' projects (Potts 2002:36). In process projects, planning is supposed to be indicative rather than fixed. Participatory processes are to be accorded the necessary flexibility in time schedules and planning. In practice, however, the distinction is often not clear-cut, and the final decision over acting 'flexibly' vs. 'rigidly' is often the prerogative of donors or Northern implementing agencies.

Finally, it is important to remember that long before LFA and PCM became mandatory in the various national and international development agencies, they had already shaped common perceptions of what constitutes projects and programmes and which roles the various actors in aid co-operation should take. At present, their importance in mainstream development discourse is ever growing. The rising demand for presentable political outcomes and comprehensible evaluation only enhances the popularity of uniform tools and methods. This includes the use of a specific language that is largely taken for granted. Actors in the North prominently figure in decisive activities of managing, planning, giving expert advice, or, more recently, facilitating. Their respective counterparts increasingly do the same, albeit under less comfortable working conditions. The actual subjects of development, however, are still referred to as targets, passive recipients and beneficiaries, or are managed as stakeholders – decades of participatory rhetoric notwithstanding.

3.3. Theoretical concerns: conceptual backgrounds and critical comments

Neither practitioners who developed participatory approaches nor the donors who adopted them into their mainstream programmes have shown much interest in their theoretical background. This is quite understandable as participatory methods were hardly ever intended or developed as theoretical paradigms. People-centred approaches to development constitute a conglomerate of different perspectives. Their strength lies in critical rather than programmatic positions. As there is no clearly circumscribed 'participatory' or 'alternative' development paradigm, in many cases, the 'alternative' is more or less defined as opposition to dominant development approaches. However, during recent decades, what was considered mainstream did not remain static but underwent major changes from a modernist state-centred to a neo-liberal model. In the process, policy-makers incorporated various 'alternative' ideas and added them onto their growth-oriented model. As mainstream development shifted its priorities, alternative concepts also broadened. "Over the years it [alternative development] has been reinforced by and associated with virtually any criticism of mainstream developmentalism, such as anti-capitalism, green thinking, feminism, eco-feminism, democratization, new social movements, Buddhist economics, cultural critiques, and post-structuralist analysis of development discourse" (Pieterse 1998:346). Alternative development and growing engagement of NGOs received a major boost together with political changes by the end of the 1980s and beginning of the 1990s. As outlined above, major donors, such as those organized in the OECD, had a range of motivations for adopting transformatory concepts in their development policy, as conventional top-down methods often failed, were inflexible and inefficient, and had paternalistic or neo-colonial connotations. Opportunistic motivation behind the use of the label 'participatory' has of course made the critical debate more complex, as opinions of what constitutes 'genuine' or 'rhetoric' use of the term are often controversial.

It is precisely through this engagement in a critical debate, and the fact that the promise of 'better' alternatives was frequently made, that the concept of participation has itself become the object of analytic scrutiny from different theoretical positions. Critical analysis on the basis of social, feminist, postcolonial and post-development theories have pointed to various conceptual flaws of PRA. They have also contributed some insights as to why some aspects of participatory approaches are difficult to realize in practice.

The following considerations do not aspire to discuss in detail the historic background of the various concepts and approaches relevant to participatory development (for introductory overviews, see Hickey and Mohan 2005; Miller, VeneKlasen and Clark 2005b:52; Pieterse 1998). They will instead concentrate on a few relevant approaches and their contributions to the critical debate around participation. The first point outlines some reflections on concepts of human relations and organizational development. This is followed by a discussion of Paulo Freire's 'Conscientization' as an early and influential contribution to participatory approaches in development. Thirdly, critical standpoints from development studies and related fields on PRA are addressed. Fourthly, relevant aspects of Postcolonial and Post-Development thought are presented. While these latter theoretical positions exhibit only limited concern with development practice, some of the issues they raise give essential insights into why participatory approaches have ultimately failed to significantly transform aid relationships.

3.3.1. Human relations and organizational development

Starting from the late 1930s, North American researchers began to study group dynamics to find ways of enhancing team effectiveness and human potential. In the 1950s, numerous approaches towards organizational settings were developed, including "sensitivity training, T-Groups, small group consensus-building (Delphi), role play, games and simulations, brainstorming, feedback, participant observation, values clarification and action research for improved planning" (Miller, VeneKlasen and Clark 2005b:52). While most of the concepts did not explicitly address unequal power relations, they nevertheless had the aspiration to contribute to more democratic forms of human interaction and were not limited to objectives of economic efficiency. They have, however, been used for a wide range of purposes and contexts, including military and commercial ones. Current uses often focus on management techniques and team building.

Concepts of group dynamics are important for understanding some of the problems of communities engaging in participatory development programmes. Cooke (2001:106 ff.) critically remarks that aid practice largely ignores the findings of organizational research. He discusses some of the group dynamics that are highly relevant to participatory community processes. The issues he raises include the fact that groups are more likely than individuals to take decisions involving risks (risky shift); group members may take certain decisions in order to please each other, falsely assuming that everyone else is in favour of a certain action, while in fact all are doubtful (Abilene paradox); closeness and solidarity among group members may lead to recklessness and lack of consideration towards outsiders, and decisions that adversely affect them (group-think). For example, in bureaucracies of large aid organizations, the prevailing 'group think' may affect individuals who "remain closed-minded, experience pressure towards uniformity, overestimate group power and consequently endorse self-censorship" (Hughes, Wheeler and Eyben 2005:66).

Finally, facilitators may also orchestrate processes of change where an initially created anxiety over an expected course of events is followed by the presentation of alternative action (coercive persuasion). Eyben also observes that, more recently, private sector organizations increasingly take into account evolving trends such as the complexity theory or the importance of improvisation, while in development planning, linear and unidimensional planning models continue to predominate (Eyben 2005:98).

3.3.2. Freire's 'Conscientization' and adult education

Paulo Freire's 'Pedagogy of the Oppressed' was developed from the late 1960s onwards. It radically criticized the unjust social relations between South and North and advocated social transformations that included the dismantling of powerful social institutions. Freire's approach was a pedagogic one, where naming[7] the world was instrumental in analysing and understanding it. His primary concern was with the poor, powerless and marginal people whom he termed the 'oppressed'. In his view, it was essential for the oppressed to find their own words for conditions and forces that shaped their everyday life: As they would become aware of their situation, they would see themselves as subjects and agents, and eventually begin to act and change their living conditions. Freire did not claim that the process of conscientization was in itself enough to achieve liberation; however, he considered a critical understanding of the oppressive situation as an essential precondition in working towards a just and free society. While he also regarded the 'oppressors' as caught up in constraints and in need of liberation, his vision for change was radical transformation and not step-by-step reform or negotiation. Addressing committed intellectuals and activists, he urged them to take sides. He argued against the illusion of objectivity as "Washing one's hands of the conflict between the powerful and the powerless means to side with the powerful, not to be neutral" (Freire 1985:102). As a method, 'conscientization' facilitated processes through which oppressed people were enabled to reflect critically on their lives. This in turn was intended to improve people's self-confidence, enhance solidarity in the community, strengthen their organizational basis and provide them with literacy and analytical skills.

Participatory approaches emerging out of NGOs' practice in development often refer to Freire's texts, however, most of them do not take into account its radical implications. Freire's uncompromising political attitude never abandoned the critical perspective on global injustice and inequality. On a theoretical level, Freire's

---

7 and writing – the concept was much used in literacy campaigns

idea that the oppressed did not question unjust power relations because of insufficient awareness of their situation did not remain unchallenged. While it was uncontested that dominant ideology shapes anyone's perspective of the social situation she or he is in, critics argued that poor and marginalized people often analyze their situation and the risks involved in change rather rationally. For the 'oppressed', acceptance of unfair social conditions may therefore be a measure of self-protection rather than ignorance.

However, development practitioners' primary concern was not with theoretical plausibility, but rather with practical application and tangible benefits. While Chambers correctly pointed out that "radical ideology [is not] a guarantee that teachers will abstain from didactic dominance" (1997a:62), most aid workers were more interested in simple and workable solutions than in complex ideological reflection. Their objective was to make development work more relevant by making it more pro-poor, more grass-root oriented, more practically relevant and more compatible with local conditions. Others, especially donors and Northern implementing agencies saw advantages in the fact that PRA approaches "were wrapped in a patina of radical politics" (Hailey 2001:99) because it helped them to overcome an at times paternalistic or authoritarian image. Reference to the concept of conscientization provided PRA with an image of progressive orientation. Mainstream reception at the same time remained ambivalent, as participation was being widely accepted as an "intrinsically good thing", which nevertheless was accompanied by the message that "considerations of power and politics on the whole should be avoided as divisive and obstructive" (Cleaver 2001:36).

3.3.3. Critical development studies: beyond good intentions

While PRA as a method has strong roots in practice, it also owes significant inputs to conceptual debates in the emerging field of development studies. Many researchers were initially keen to document the success of people-centred development approaches. With raised expectations and partly disappointing experiences, towards the end of the 1990s, a 'critical backlash' set in (Cooke and Kothari eds. 2001). Criticism on PRA focussed, for example, on Chambers' concept of power, his construct of the 'local' and his idea of knowledge.

3.3.3.1. Power

Chambers remains very vague about social inequality and concrete directions for change. As mentioned above, the frequent use of binary oppositions in his work inhibits differentiation and adequate appraisal of tangible situations. "'uppers' and 'lowers', North and South, professional knowledge and local knowledge […] are continuously evoked and rehearsed as popular slogans of participation and empowerment. […] It then becomes the main aim of participatory approaches to development to set about reversing them" (Kothari 2001:140) The dichotomies, however, are always imprecise and create the misleading impression that power is located at the centre, whereas considerations of power differences in social relations within communities or local organizations are made to seem irrelevant. Furthermore, the binary approach is unsuitable for an analysis of power that is exercised in processes and relationships. As Mosse remarks, "public participatory research methods are unlikely to prove good instruments for the analysis of local power relations since they are shaped by the very relations that are being investigated" (1995:29, quoted from Kothari 2001:143).

Instead of relying on generalizing oppositions, critical approaches in development studies increasingly base their analysis on an understanding of power that draws on Foucault's concepts of decentralized manifestations of power in all social relations. "Power must be analyzed as something that circulates, or rather as something which only functions in the form of a chain [...] It is never localized here or there. [...] Power is employed and exercised through a net-like organization" (Foucault 1980:98, quoted from Kothari 2001). As a result of differentiated analyses of power within aid relationships, much of the research concludes that PRA methods have promised but largely failed to overcome conventional hierarchies (Cooke and Kothari 2001:13, Hickey and Mohan 2004c:159, Mosse 2005). The reversal of the social relations between 'uppers' and 'lowers' is striven for, often some minor steps are taken in the right direction, but genuine progress towards egalitarian relationships is hardly ever realized. In short, participatory projects always operate under conditions of social inequality, and as long as this is not acknowledged by its practitioners, there will be misuse and a widening gap between rhetoric and reality.

3.3.3.2. Myths of local community and local knowledge

Another problematic generalization underlying PRA and other participatory approaches is the assumption of community homogeneity (Guijt and Shah 1998). Just as the analysis of power is difficult when complex relationships are reduced to binary oppositions, misconceptions and generalizations about beneficiaries abound when they are primarily identified as 'needy' groups in contrast to other, already developed ones. While some instruments such as wealth ranking exercises address social stratification, there is often only limited readiness to take into account the implications they have for development work. In many cases, conflict is avoided at the cost of the poor or otherwise marginalized within a village or group. In her work on agrarian transformation in South East Asia, Tania Li documents the instrumentalist use of the term 'community' in development discourse, concluding that in Indonesia, NGO practice may have made the concept advantageous for some social groups, for instance, ethnic minorities, but not necessarily for poorer people and women (1996:521). Li does not deny that by focusing essentially on a local community perspective some valuable insights may be gained. Like many other analysts, she, however, concludes that the primacy of the local community has often meant that the larger socio-political context is being shut out, and the social relevance of the project is limited (Hickey and Mohan

2004a:10). Chambers' own reflections deal extensively with problems of social exclusion on the grounds of poverty, gender, ethnicity as well as regional and climatic disadvantages. Nevertheless, PRA's frequent references to simple binary oppositions ('local vs. external' etc) tends to reinforce rather than to address the problem in its complexity (Cooke 2001:120).

Closely linked to the myth of the community is the concept of local knowledge, which is equally problematic. Scoones and Thompson sum up some of the doubtful but widespread assumptions underlying it: "farming communities in complex, diverse, risk-prone environments share common goals, access to resources (including information) and worldviews and that local knowledge is unitary, systematized and available for assimilation and incorporation with Western scientific knowledge (Scoones and Thompson 1994b:21). In reality, however, "knowledge is neither static nor simply 'local' but is situated within a dynamic setting which goes well beyond the farm gate and the rural household" (Scoones and Thompson 1994b:16).

3.3.3.3. Expert dominance and the construction of 'knowledge'

As mentioned in the first part of this chapter, participatory research and participatory action research are two of the sources from which PRA was developed. Scholars interested in the unequal power relations involved in knowledge generation in social science have developed various approaches in order to promote more equitable interaction throughout the research processes. These approaches challenge positivist epistemology including the notion of objective science and instead point to culturally and socially mediated processes of knowledge construction.[8]

The generation and use of knowledge in aid co-operation is intricately linked to issues of power and asymmetric relationships. For development planners, access to knowledge is important as it enables them to justify and legitimise their decisions and actions. Chambers repeatedly emphasized the primacy of attitudes over methods, yet, he was also ambivalent as he heavily relied on efficiency arguments to propagate his approach, frequently pointing out that PRA yielded faster and more useful information than other methods of social research (Chambers 1994a). Such reasoning certainly carried weight with development agencies and donors. In everyday development practice, such arguments have contributed to

---

[8] While approaches to participatory research originated in a variety of disciplines and research institutions, it should be noted here that in the 1970s, academics at the University of Dar-es-Salaam, Tanzania, made remarkable efforts in explicitly involving rural communities as partners and decision-makers in research undertakings (Miller, VeneKlasen and Clark 2005b:55; Shivji 2002:288, Mbilinyi 1974, Mapolu 1973). The 'International Participatory Research Network' that involved researchers such as Yussuf Kassam, Budd Hall, Rajesh Tandon, Marja Liisa Swantz and many others had some of its early origins in the 1970s at the University of Dar-es-Salaam in Tanzania (Hall 1997:2).

an extensive adoption of PRA methods; at the same time, they also led to a superficial and opportunistic use of the method. Having become part of what has generally been described as a process of 'convergence' in aid practices, PRA has turned into an increasingly standardised tool used on an international scale. This trend has disadvantages, as it privileges donor demands, reinforces organizational control and reduces recipients' flexibility in responding to challenges that arise in programme implementation. Because of prevailing power structures, PRA practice may result in the reinforcement rather than reversal of prevailing hierarchies. "a practitioner's enthusiasm for, and belief in, the utility and legitimacy of participation can obscure rather than reveal 'local knowledges'. [...] In fact the maps, matrixes, sensitively managed discussion groups and the famously 'relaxed approach' are already laden with the perspectives, logic, values and priorities of Western experts and these shape and determine the knowledge they produce" (Kesby 2003:4). Mosse, with regard to his above-mentioned study of a participatory agricultural project in India, concludes that the planning tools used did not facilitate a learning experience based on local knowledge, but rather constituted a process through which the farmers concerned acquired a new kind of planning knowledge and learned how to manipulate it (2005:95). As Mosse puts it, the farmers probably never became aware that their own knowledge was to be prioritized. Facilitators of PRA exercises usually enjoy a certain freedom in presenting methods according to their preference, and they are also in a position to assess the performance of those upon whom the technique is exercised. Beneficiaries rarely enjoy similar opportunities; they are usually neither in a position to negotiate PRA as a method nor to assess the performance of aid workers. In aid projects, the mere invitation to participate, the simple suggestion of inclusion in a process may be an attempt at exercising control over an individual or group. Pressure may be reinforced even by people who are opposed to or critical of certain practices. The very act of inclusion, instead of empowerment, may bring disadvantages for those concerned, and it may turn out to be difficult to challenge, as it comes with an assertion of democratic legitimacy, of common good and group advancement (Kothari 2001:142). Usually, there is no positive alternative for those who prefer not to take part in a participatory process induced through outside intervention. Moreover, PRA processes contain their own routines and fashions, giving community members who are experienced in the method an advantage when it comes to 'staging' successful 'performances'. As Kothari remarks, the "worrying aspect" is that such performances have widely come "to be accepted as reality" (2001:150).

3.3.4. Postcolonial perspectives

In theoretical debates, the critical engagement with the community versus global perspectives has in particular drawn on an emerging reception of postcolonial thought in development studies. PRA essentializes the 'local' as positive opposition to 'central/outside/foreign' and tends to ignore historic developments. For example, it pays little attention to the manipulated concept of the 'local' that was part of the ideology of colonial Indirect Rule or the South African apartheid regime. Postcolonialism challenges the dualistic notion of local versus central and offers a differentiated view of hegemony, resistance and 'hybridity' instead (Mohan 2001:163). It acknowledges the existence of power inequalities and dominance, but unlike PRA approaches, it does not suggest that these can be readily overcome by a mix of personal commitment, change in attitude and the correct choice of methods. Rather, postcolonialism contributes to recognizing forms of resistance and agency by poor and marginalized people, challenging the notion that they necessarily need to be empowered through outside initiative. PRA methods suggest largely technical solutions to what are often socio-political problems. Postcolonialism, on the other hand, brings in the wider political framework and points to the relevant domains of action. "Only by linking participatory approaches to wider, and more difficult processes of democratization, anti-imperialism and feminism, will long-term change occur" (Mohan 2001:163). Postcolonial thought can probably not fully resolve the core dilemma of participatory development work, which is about how processes of autonomous empowerment relate to outside intervention. However, the importance of a differentiated historic perspective on aid co-operation that includes the perspective of recipients must not be underestimated. It is only on the foundation of a respective contextualization that the potential for autonomous spaces can be explored, or that the requirements outside inputs need to fulfil can be determined.

In some respects, postcolonial authors have also faced criticism for using dichotomous concepts (for example, generalizing on "the West", etc.) on their part. Additionally, they have largely remained in the realm of an abstract cultural debate, showing little concern for material conditions. Nevertheless, postcolonial thought provides a worthwhile basis from which the often narrow perspectives of practical development can be examined and reviewed.

Such an exploration of possibilities should of course not gloss over the fact that in practice, postcolonial studies and development studies largely pursue disparate agendas – as Christine Sylvester puts it, "one field begins where the other refuses to look" (Sylvester 1999:704). Development studies on the one hand "do not pale at the idea of colonization" (Sylvester 1999:717) and show little concern about postcolonial hegemonies and continuity of foreign dominance. Postcolonial critics, on the other hand, have often neglected practical challenges of development work. Yet Sylvester convincingly argues that when compared to the capabilities of Western development agencies, postcolonial thinkers' potential input towards development practice is invaluable. The major contributions of postcolonial thought include the questioning of epistemologies privileging Western perspectives that have silenced the voice of the colonized other (Said 1978). Many scholars have also emphasized the implications of 'hybridity' under conditions of cultural domination (Bhabha 1994:296) and documented various forms of cultural and political resistance to foreign dominance. Postcolonial thought provides a basis for confronting racism in aid relationships, an issue that has hitherto been largely ignored both in theory and practice (Slater and Bell 2004:356). Feminist postcolonial authors have pointed to colonial continuities in gendered development discourse; their contribution will be discussed in detail in the following section on gender.

3.3.5. Post-developmentalism

Post-developmentalism refers to an approach that is uncompromising in its rejection of 'development' in all its forms, including 'alternative approaches'. Post-developmentalism has given rise to challenging and valuable critique. It has shown how development policies have in many respects become a pervasive mechanism of control that have effectively replaced colonial domination (Escobar 1994). However, the conclusions made by post-developmentalist authors are often generalizing, resulting in biased representations (Pieterse 2000:187). Instead of analysing complex socio-political backgrounds to development and modernity, an overall rejection of anything identified as 'Western' predominates. Post-developmentalists share romanticized illusions about the 'local' with some proponents of PRA. They tend to advocate a renunciation of modernity, and suggest engagement in autonomous and self-reliant projects that tend to be delimited and isolated from their environment. As Hickey and Mohan observe, this "seems very far from the intentions of those social movements on which post-development theorists claim to base their work" (2004b:61). Hickey and Mohan emphasize that social movements in countries of the South are multiple and diverse. A number of them work with the financial support of donors or development agencies from the North, often setting examples of how donor-recipient relationships can be reshaped on a more equitable basis. Much of post-development thought, however, gives little concrete attention to the active agency of the poor or marginalized when interacting with the aid system, but tends to portray them as helpless victims.

With respect to participation, post-developmentalists Esteva and Prakash argue that it has been "transformed into another sociological tool in populist or technocratic repertoires of ideological and political manipulation. It is still used to confer political legitimacy and technical elegance to developers' promotions and to governmental plans" (Esteva and Prakash 1998:283). Participation is regarded as inherently linked to the failed project of 'development' and therefore dismissed (Hickey and Mohan 2004b:61). Fals-Borda, one of the early advocates of alternative development, agrees that major points of the post-development critique of development are valid. His conclusion, however, is that "flexible concepts such as participation" (Fals-Borda 2000:632) must be deconstructed to separate problematic aspects, such as the tendency of development agencies to manipulate contents towards their own ends, from their positive empowering potential.

3.3.6. Donors and participation

Since the beginning of the 1990s, donor agencies have elaborated and diversified their policy in many domains. Taking up critical inputs from social movements and NGO practice donor organizations have come to incorporate principles of participation and partnership into mainstream policy. 'Minimum standards' have been established and can at least be appealed to.

It is however doubtful whether many of these 'good intentions' at policy level have 'trickled down' to aid practice. Evidence from projects and programmes indicates that changes are largely rhetorical and superficial. In concrete implementation, outside experts, including PRA facilitators, continue to dominate decision-making processes. Exclusion based on social class, gender or racist discrimination is not adequately addressed. Participation largely remains restricted to a few limited aspects of decision-making in community affairs, while the broader political and socio-economic context shaping peoples' lives remains unchanged.

In programmes funded by larger donors and international aid agencies, implementation is primarily structured through standard planning and reporting formats such as Project Cycle Management and Logical Framework Analysis. Throughout the last decade, these approaches have incorporated some participatory instruments. The problem is, however, that participatory processes within such programmes largely remain confined to marginal aspects. A practice of eclecticism prevails, with implementers facilitating participatory processes in decisions pertaining to 'local' affairs, but insisting on management approaches to satisfy donor demands for hard facts and figures. This tendency is certainly not conducive to an integrated democratic practice that would connect local with national and global perspectives.

Similarly, more recent trends in donor policy are unlikely to avoid what critics have called the 'simplicity trap'. Instead of taking into account complexity, ambiguity and the importance of improvisation, the "need for more strategies and coherent programming is emphasized. [...] this is like brandy as a cure for hangover" (Eyben 2005:98). Under the scrutiny of a critical electorate, public sector aid agencies in donor countries favour linear and unidimensional models of control and accountability. Results-Based Management (RBM), a recent approach that gives recipient countries a greater role in the administration of aid funds, is a case in point. It is again based more or less on a project/programme framework of implementing development, that is, on the assumption that problems can be solved within a limited time span and with a limited amount of resources, and that all actors involved in aid co-operation agree on the problem and its solution. Yet most 'problems' of the developing world are ambiguous, long-term and actors usually differ in their ideas on how improvements could be made (Eyben 2005:101).

Recent trends in donor co-ordination, such as alignment and harmonisation, have without doubt contributed to some extent to disciplining donors and reduced the transaction costs of recipient countries. However, they can also be problematic and possibly disempower recipients as donors may at the same time be "ganging up together" (Eyben 2005:102). Moreover, donors are more likely to get caught up in 'group think', as Hughes, Wheeler and Eyben (2005:66) put it, which means that they are encouraged to regard their perspective on development as the only relevant one.

Faced with disappointing evidence from practice, by the second half of the 1990s many researchers presented evidence in support of a 'critical backlash' against participatory approaches, with some critics rejecting the idea of participatory development altogether. Others have diligently assessed the achievements, failures and the changing framework of aid co-operation. Many have pointed out that failure of participatory methods such as PRA originates not only from difficulties in implementation, but also from conceptual shortcomings. These include the reduction of complex social relations to superficial, dichotomous polarities as well as the reliance on myths that portray communities as havens of mutual solidarity. The theoretical debate has raised numerous valuable points, which have, however, been largely ignored by the major donors and aid agencies - probably because they require addressing very real problems of inequality and dominance. Planning for agricultural development is, after all, "a highly ideological and political process, not a series of carefully planned and rational acts" (Scoones and Thompson 1994a:4).

3.4. Gender Planning: feminist concerns in development co-operation

> *There is and there must be a diversity of feminisms, responsive to the needs and concerns of different women, and defined by them for themselves (Sen and Grown 1987:18).*

This chapter has illustrated that, in the context of development work, the term 'participation' assumes a range of different meanings, depending on who is speaking, in which context and with what intention. Similarly, 'gender' and respective compounds such as 'gender equality', 'gender planning' and 'gender analysis' are used by actors in aid networks with a range of different intentions and connotations, reflecting both the divergent interests of speakers as well as the diversity in feminist approaches. The following considerations will focus on two aspects relevant to development co-operation: on the one hand, feminist approaches to development have resulted in manuals, guidelines and tools for practical implementation; on the other hand, they have also contributed to a critical theoretical debate. Some of the more influential practical concepts and tools include 'Women in Development', 'Gender Planning' and 'Gender Mainstreaming'. From the theoretical perspective, it is primarily 'postcolonial feminisms' and 'transnational feminisms' that have addressed challenges of South-North relations and development co-operation.

3.4.1. Gender discrimination, colonialism, and notions of development

African women's resistance to development imposed from outside is documented throughout the 20th century. For example, in South-Eastern Nigeria in 1930, women successfully protested against taxation, economic regulation and chiefs appointed by the colonial government, organizing what became known as the "Women's War" (Grau 1993:182 ff.) In Muranga in Kenya in 1948, women resisted coercive measures of environmental conservation. Women refused to be burdened with the rehabilitation of environmental degradation caused by expanding colonial settler agriculture (Kanogo 1992:15).

Development discourse after WWII was geared towards modernization and progress, and characterized by an explicit male bias. Rural development programmes targeted 'progressive farmers' or 'household heads', which meant that they primarily addressed men. Most programmes excluded women; some offered small and insignificant 'women's components' that did not reach beyond women's reproductive roles in nutrition and childcare. The involvement of African women in agriculture was largely ignored. From the 1960s onwards, population control became a major concern for some donors, for example, USAID. Population programmes usually addressed women rather than men, but they offered little to improve women's control over their lives. Rather, they promoted birth control methods that allowed little self-determination and were often detrimental to women's health: for example, sterilization, or, in later decades, three-months shots (also known under the brand name Depo-Provera) and hormone implants. Often, such methods were propagated while still being at trial stages. Many involved risky side effects and, frequently, the required medical supervision was not provided.

At the same time, the evolving discourses of development and progress did not miss the opportunity to emphasize the oppression of women in non-Western cultures and the advantages Western civilisation had to offer them. Moreover, while many African women participated in anti-colonial resistance, they also availed themselves of the opportunities the modern era had to offer, but not necessarily in the way envisaged by colonial authorities. Some migrated to urban centres, in defiance of colonial legislation and postcolonial ideology which preferred to keep women under the control of male authority in rural areas. They made use of whichever education and health facilities that were in their reach, even if the services available were poor and directed to the needs of boys and men rather than girls and women. In the first years of Independence, many African countries made remarkable advances in the provision of social services. As the South African sociologist Patricia McFadden puts it, African women took the first chance to "flee the backward constraints of patriarchal privatization and seclusion through the doors that are opened [...] by education and what is euphemistically called 'book learning'". Or, when this possibility was unavailable, they "worked themselves to the bone" so that their daughters and sons could experience the advantages offered by institutionally based knowledge (McFadden 2000:5).

3.4.2. 'Women in Development' and the role of the United Nations

In the early 1970s, women's interests were for the first time voiced within established development agencies, particularly within the United Nations (Kabeer 1994:2). Professional development experts pointed to the discrepancy between women's productive work roles and their relegation to reproductive contexts of nutrition, child-rearing and family planning. In 1970, Esther Boserup published her seminal study on "Women's economic role in development", arguing that development programmes had in many respects aggravated women's disadvantaged status. For instance, despite the fact that in Africa the majority of work in agriculture was done by women, agricultural programmes that introduced mechanisation as well as the use of fertilizers and improved seeds usually only targeted men. Women were 'left behind' in the production process. Based on Boserup's findings and other evidence of women's marginalization, some women experts in the United Nations began to demand policy changes so that women would also benefit from development programmes. Various arguments were put forward in support of this initiative: Liberal feminists tended to emphasize the ideal of equal rights for women and men. Development experts committed to the 'basic needs strategy' of the 1970s focussed on the key role of women in the provision of food and shelter. For economists, the financial return of investing in women was the primary argument; it continues to be used in present-day gender-mainstreaming discourse. Quantitative evidence was produced to prove that putting money in female education and health was the most efficient way to reach development objectives such as the reduction of fertility or the lowering of child mortality, etc. The respective discourse was instrumentalist: women, according to the analysis, had been excluded from development. They constituted a 'resource' that 'humanity' could not afford to leave 'untapped'. Such considerations, while addressing genuine biases, did not question mainstream development approaches in principle, but were often confined to rather superficial proposals for reform.

The emerging feminist discourse in the United Nations manifested itself in several international women's conferences that raised world-wide attention. Already the first conference in Mexico 1975 was accompanied by an NGO forum that facilitated encounters and exchanges between women's organizations and enabled NGOs to comment on policies and debates within the United Nations. There were considerable divisions over priorities that could be largely attributed to the geopolitics of the time: Women from the 'West' argued for equality, women from the 'East' for peace, while those from the 'South' were concerned with development. While the conference brought to the fore these differences, it also facilitated a pluralist discourse and awareness of the divergent concerns of women from different regions of the world. The conference in Mexico City resulted in a plan of action with the aim of equal access for women and men to education, political participation, health, housing, nutrition and birth control; this plan was to be implemented by 1980.

Within the United Nations, the conference led to the founding of the 'International Research and Training Institute for the Advancement of Women' (INSTRAW) and the 'United Nations Development Fund for Women' (UNIFEM), two organizations that established an institutional framework for training, research and operational activities. The period from 1976 to 1985 was proclaimed as the 'Women's Decade', and a second women's conference was prepared for Copenhagen in 1980. In 1979, the General Assembly adopted the *Convention for the Elimination of all Forms of Discrimination Against Women* (CEDAW), a document that was to safeguard the political, economic and social rights of women. CEDAW constituted an important step towards gender equality as it not only demanded the end of all forms of discrimination, but also compelled member states to implement measures of positive discrimination until all differences in women's and men's status were alleviated. The Convention has been ratified by 185 states (April 2008). However, the problem of implementation remains a major challenge, especially as some governments expressed substantial reservations to articles of fundamental importance. By facilitating women's conferences, founding special organizations and working out conventions and plans of actions, the United Nations laid the foundations for the evolution of development policy and practice in favour of gender equality. However, the adoption and implementation of the corresponding policies in donor countries took time and proved to be a challenging process.

3.4.3. Donors and the implementation of the 'Women in Development' (WID) approach

From the late 1970s onwards, NGOs and implementing organizations gained their first experience of co-operation pertaining to 'women's projects', and with time, some donors began to adapt their policy accordingly. By the mid-1980s, the UK and Sweden produced their first information booklet and policy guidelines on 'Women in Development'. Rosalind Eyben (2004:74) reports that in 1986, the British development agency ODA (Overseas Development Agency, renamed DfID - Department for International Development in 1997) published a policy paper titled 'Women in Development' (ODA 1986, quoted from Eyben 2004). The paper cautiously suggested that under certain circumstances, it was important to consider women's roles, but at the same time emphasized that no interference in cultural traditions was intended and that economic growth was the most important precondition for the improvement of women's situation. Despite the overcautious wording, these beginnings were remarkable as other donors took much longer to commit themselves in writing: Austria, for instance, produced the first respective documents in the mid-1990s. Countries like Sweden and the UK acted as pioneers by contributing their experience and knowledge within the Development Assistance Committee (DAC) of the OECD. In 1983, the DAC published its first 'Guidelines' for the implementation of WID in development co-operation. At the same time, it began to record and evaluate the respective performance of member states. In 1984, a consultative group on 'Women in Development' was formed whose membership was made up of WID experts from the aid agencies of the respective member states.

In 1985, the United Nations organized the third Women's World Conference in Nairobi. Delegates of the official conference adopted the *Forward Looking Strategies for the Advancement of Women* which were supposed to be implemented by 2000. The corresponding NGO forum was attended by numerous independent women's organizations, some of which used the opportunity to voice strong criticism of the WID approach in development co-operation. Members of DAWN (Development Alternatives with Women for a New Era), an organization of Southern women activists and scholars, presented a text that rejected WID's core idea of 'integrating women into development'. Analysing past development projects from various parts of the world, DAWN showed that women's interests were not accounted for in mainstream development co-operation. On the contrary, especially poor women often experienced a deterioration in their living conditions, for example, when large-scale agricultural projects were implemented in their area. This was due to the fact that women were usually excluded from the group of possible beneficiaries, and at the same time faced increasing competition in the use of resources such as land and water. In voicing their protest, representatives of DAWN used the metaphor of development as a cake, arguing that women had no interest in fighting for a bigger share when the whole cake was shrunk and poisoned. Rather, they preferred to bake one of their own - that is, reshape and reorganize the development process according to their own ideas and needs (Sen/ Grown 1987:20). DAWN presented its concept of 'empowerment' as an alternative to the WID-approach: women and men should determine themselves what development meant to them and be in full control of the planning and decision-making processes. DAWN's vision of empowerment also included a radical criticism of prevailing asymmetric donor-recipient relations.

Over the following years, the critical debate on WID eventually resulted in mainstream development organizations turning to the more elaborate approach of Gender Planning, the implications and details of which will be discussed below. Throughout the first half of the 1990s, the United Nations organized several international conferences which generated important momentum for the emerging debate on gender and development. Among these were the World Conference on Human Rights in Vienna in 1993, where feminist approaches contributed important new perspectives in international human rights' discourse. The International Conference on Population and Development in Cairo 1994, with its 'pro-choice' commitment as well as the focus on 'reproductive health' was another event that brought gender concerns to the fore. In 1995, the Fourth Women's World Conference took place in Beijing. It was accompanied by the most active NGO forum ever, with the slogan 'Women's rights are human rights' conveying a newly gained self-confidence. The official conference concluded with the Beijing Declaration and Platform of Action, setting an agenda of comprehensive social and political objectives. Additionally, the Platform of Action recommended the adoption of Gender Mainstreaming as a strategy that should ensure the realization of gender equality in all social and political domains.

3.4.4. 'Gender Planning' as a tool in development co-operation

By the 1980s, feminist scholars in development studies began to take the WID approach a step further. Reflecting the adoption of gender as an analytical category in feminist social science, more elaborate planning tools for development practice were devised. The fact that gender was recognized as a product of cultural and historical contingencies that could be deconstructed and reshaped in new ways opened new perspectives for working for women's interests in the development process. The most influential concept in this respect was developed by Caroline Moser, a British social anthropologist. Her approach of 'Gender Planning' (1993) was based on a comprehensive critique of previous WID approaches and their disappointing performance in development co-operation. Moser set out to develop simple, user-friendly planning tools that could easily be incorporated in the everyday planning routines of organizations.

The 'Gender Planning' approach is based on the assumption that women exercise a triple role in society. This triple role includes productive, reproductive and community-related activities (Moser 1993:15ff). For example, a woman could be found working in agriculture (productive), in household and childcare activities (reproductive) and volunteering in a local self-help initiative such as a nursery school (community-related). For Moser, an essential step in planning is finding out and making visible women's different roles as well as considering how any planned intervention would affect each of them. Another important notion in Moser's approach is recognizing that in development planning, women have both practical and strategic needs, and that both are equally important and legitimate. Typical examples of what she calls 'practical gender needs' would include improvements in nutrition, housing or access to clean water, while typical 'strategic gender needs' would be, for example, legal reforms to overcome gender biases in law.

Moser argued that WID approaches were bound to fail because they usually addressed only one of women's various roles. As a consequence, programmes often calculated unrealistic work schedules for women because they never took into account the sum of different tasks women accomplished. Moser also remarked that WID approaches often exclusively focussed on either practical or strategic interests of women and, as a result, were inflexible and unresponsive to the remaining domains. Furthermore, she pointed out that the WID concept was limited to technical solutions that could not resolve the socio-political conflict involved in asymmetric gender relations.

In contrast, her concept of 'Gender Planning' challenged unequal power relations: "Gender Planning is concerned with transformative processes that are highly political and can be assumed to involve conflict" (Moser 1993:83). 'Gender Planning' was to be based on careful analysis of ongoing activities and needs. The concept of the triple role and the practical and strategic gender needs was to facilitate a holistic approach to planning women's activity schedules. Programme planners had to enter into a dialogue with prospective communities to obtain the relevant information. However, control of this dialogue was still retained by planning experts: 'Gender Planning' was developed as a planning tool for aid agencies and their staff, not primarily as a method of conscientization or empowerment for local communities. In practical implementation, the ambition for social transformation through 'Gender Planning' could not be realized. Planning activities were usually limited to the objective of enabling equal participation of women and men in the community. 'Gender Planning' did not provide the means to question other asymmetric relations within the aid system, or to address gender relations beyond the community targeted through a particular programme. So, while Moser presented a highly differentiated critical analysis of previous WID approaches in development planning, she took a rather pragmatic stance in elaborating her own method, emphasising that simplicity and reduction of complex interrelationships were a precondition for ensuring broad application of the tool in development organizations. As a result, just as the preceding WID approaches Moser had so eloquently criticized, 'Gender Planning' did not provide answers to political challenges. Rather, it offered more sophisticated technical approaches to initiate and control social processes through outside intervention. 'Gender Planning' also failed to address power differences between women on the donor and recipient side of the aid relationship. As the Honduran feminist Breny Mendoza puts it, 'Gender Planning' is an "orchestrated process [...] conceived, directed, and even funded by First World women in which Third World women would learn to develop the capabilities they are missing to lead less oppressive and exploited lives. Thus, development becomes the grand equalizer between women [...]" (Mendoza 2002:301).

The widespread adoption of 'Gender Planning' as a tool in development co-operation ensured that the issue of women's exclusion and discrimination became a routine part of the agenda of aid organizations. Yet the changes aspired were often superficial, with their scope being limited to the local community perspective. It nevertheless took Northern development agencies some time until they incorporated 'Gender Planning' into policy papers and planning routines. The 'apolitical' position adopted by and large condoned the neoliberal development policy of the time. Structural adjustment programmes enforced austerity measures in education, health and public administration that often had particularly negative effects on women and girls. In many countries - including Tanzania - a large-scale deterioration of the welfare situation resulted, for which the good intentions of 'gender-planning' in aid programmes could hardly offer remedies.

3.4.5. Donor practice and the DAC (OECD) policy markers

In the implementation of 'Women in Development' (WID) and 'Gender Planning' strategies and the shaping of relevant discourses, multilateral agencies of the UN, the World Bank, as well as institutions of the European Union and the OECD played a vital role. For Northern donor countries, the efforts of the DAC in attaining common standards in aid practice were of particular importance. From the 1990s onwards, the DAC's policy requirements pertaining to 'WID' and 'Gender Planning' also shaped the relevant practice of the Austrian Development cooperation.

In 1983, the DAC published its first 'Guidelines' for supporting the integration of women in development; at the same time, it also started documenting the performance of member states in implementing WID policy. In 1984, a consultative group on WID was established within DAC in which WID experts from member states contributed to the policy debate. During the early years, countries like Sweden and the UK played a pioneering role by developing WID policies for their national agencies and sharing their experience within the DAC. In 1989, a first revision of the 'Guiding principles on WID' and of reporting practices on WID projects were undertaken.

The present gender policy marker system dates back to 1999, and is based on the Beijing policy objective of 'Mainstreaming Gender'. All projects and programmes are supposed to be critically reviewed with reference to specific 'gender equality policy markers', the outcome of which was to be reported to the DAC committee. The policy markers are defined as follows:

> "An activity can target gender equality either as a 'principal objective' or as a 'significant objective'. Principal (score "2") means gender equality was an explicit objective of the activity and fundamental in its design (i.e. the activity would not have been undertaken without this objective). Significant (score "1") means gender equality was an important, but secondary objective of the activity (i.e. not one of the principal reasons for undertaking the activity). Not targeted (score "0") means that the activity was screened for promoting gender equality, but was found to not be targeted to it. The reporting directives note also that activities which achieve a marker for gender equality as a principle objective are no 'better' than those with the significant objective score. If mainstreaming is practised, gender equality will often be a significant objective, integrated into projects, across the range of sectors" (OECD-DAC 2005:12).

The guidelines elaborate a number of additional criteria for assessing the quality of project proposals. Nevertheless, the classification into just three different categories - of which the 'significant' and 'principal' score are often collapsed into a general category of 'gender-relevant' projects, especially in reports - constitutes a problematic oversimplification. In a report published in 2005, the superficial nature of this bureaucratically induced mainstreaming effort becomes evident: for the period 1999-2003, 18 out of 23 member states marked more than 50% of their programmes as conducive to gender equality. Most of these programmes fell under the definition of having gender equality as a 'significant' objective, implying that gender issues are one of several programme targets. On a closer look, however, the contribution of these programmes towards gender equality remains unclear. Most of them are programmes in social development (sectors [if this refers to education, etc., it is not really required and would not be in this position in any case] education, health, population and water) that necessarily affect both women and men (DAC 2005:9). However, beyond the fact that the programmes target both women and men as beneficiaries, their ramifications for gender and other social relations remain largely unspecified, turning the whole exercise into more of a public relations effort than a convincing operative policy on gender equality. Classification depends primarily on self-assessment by programme applicants, as well as a brief desk examination of project documents by the funding agency. An in-depth analysis is hardly possible under these circumstances. Project performance is not examined at all. Even in cases where gender-relevant data is collected in the framework of an evaluation, this does not affect the prior scores on gender equality. What is measured is intentions and assessment is based on generalized past experience or preconceived assumptions rather than concrete empirical data. Gender policy markers function as a reminder of gender equality as a policy objective. They may help to avoid obvious cases of gender discrimination in project practice but they do not per se facilitate insights into complex and intertwined inequalities along social class, race and gender. Only an insignificant proportion of 'gender-marked' projects are truly committed to social change. The suggestion that more than half of the undertakings in bilateral aid in the 18 countries included in the report support social transformation towards equitable gender relations cannot be upheld by the statistical data presented. The DAC's gender markers may be helpful in encouraging donors' best intentions, but unfortunately they are inappropriate as a tool for radically transforming asymmetric gender relations (Maral-Hanak 2006b).

In Austria, the Ministry of Foreign Affairs by the early 1990s began to mark WID projects in its reports to the DAC. Over the years, the proportion of projects declared as WID-relevant rose steadily. For example in 1993, 23.76% of bilateral aid was reported as WID projects. However, principles according to which projects were assessed were often unprecise and in hindsight the criteria for classifying particular projects as WID are hard to trace (cf. Dick 1998:16). In 1994, participants in a gender training session commented that the Development Co-operation Department increasingly received project applications with WID orientation, as such projects allegedly had a better chance of being accorded priority and approval. However, in many cases WID-orientation of projects proved to be very superficial, often consisting of little more than an add-on paragraph (Krings, Neuhold and Perlaki 1994:22).

The current DAC policy markers were translated and adapted in 1999 (BMaA 1999). In 2003, 50% of the bilateral project and programme aid was reported as conducive to gender equality, the majority of which was classified as 'significant', that is, having gender equality as one of several project objectives (BMaA 2005).

As in the wider European context, this classification is based on very general criteria. For example, micro-credit programmes are always classified as gender-relevant because their commitment to equal gender relations is taken for granted - despite empirical studies that document problematic aspects such as, for example, that debt may exacerbate gender-related violence in households (Hanak 2000).

3.5. Feminist theory: intersectional analysis

As shown in the previous section, practical implementation of 'Gender Planning' in development work does not live up to the bold rhetoric of policy. This disappointing record is not only due to general problems of practice, but also to misinterpretations of concepts and theories. Feminist theory is relevant to development practice for several reasons. First, a deeper understanding of gender theories can help to avoid the superficial practices pervading much of present 'mainstreaming' activities. In particular, the intersectional analysis of racist, sexist and class discrimination usually neglected in development practice is of importance here. Second, based on intersectional analysis, some theories, notably postcolonial feminist approaches, have made invaluable critical contributions that offer very clear and practically relevant insights on 'aid relationships'. Third, a lively debate that links theoretical and practical challenges of development is currently ongoing, and this debate is increasingly between academics of the global South. The following sections will raise a few points around the concept of gender as a category for intersectional analysis, in particular from the perspective of postcolonial and transnational feminisms.

3.5.1. The emergence of gender studies

By the end of the 1980s, feminist social science changed its focus from 'women's studies' to a broader analytical perspective on 'gender relations'. The distinction between 'gender', which denotes a socio-cultural construct, and 'sex' as referring to biological differences between women and men had first been made by the British sociologist Ann Oakley (1972:16). The shift to gender analysis meant that instead of focusing attention on women's status or social role, the entire social relations between women and men became the object of feminist inquiry. Gendered social difference, instead of being regarded as determined by nature, was deconstructed and understood as open to change. 'Gender Studies' implied a more comprehensive approach than earlier feminist concepts: all social domains were to be regarded as possible objects of analysis, a broadening of perspectives that also reflected growing feminist self-confidence. The establishment of gender as a category in social science also meant that gender relations were increasingly analyzed in the context of other social parameters, such as social class or age, a perspective that was also partly taken up in feminist development studies. The commitment to gender analysis also meant that gender, understood as an intersected part of complex social relations, had to be studied separately in each social context, as generalizations and preconceived notions about the 'disadvantaged position of women in society' were criticized as containing little real information about concrete social conditions.

A differentiated analysis of gender relations in their social context not only creates a basis for investigating women as victims of gender bias and discrimination. It also helps to obtain information on women as agents and documents their options and achievements. In addition, it also provides a theoretical basis for the interrogation of asymmetric relations amongst women and research on how women subject other women to violence or exploit them. In recent decades, the analysis of gender relations was extended to include a perspective on women as perpetrators of crimes and victims in the context of slavery and racism (hooks 1981), colonialism (Mamozai 1989) and national-socialism (Thürmer-Rohr). Further topics of investigation included the unequal relations between women in patriarchal families (Kabeer 1994:129) and in exploitative labour relations (Mohanty 1997).

In development practice, from the mid-1980s onwards, Northern aid agency administrations began to adopt tools and methods that operate with reference to gender as an analytical category. However, as Regina Frey has shown in her study of gender manuals from various development agencies and authors, the reception of gender theories through the aid industry in many cases distorted the original idea (2003:138). First of all, the key terms of gender studies are often adopted without an explanation. Concepts such as the sex/gender differentiation are implicitly taken for granted, used in a sketchy way, with insufficient clarification and no reference to their origin. Second, in many cases, the use of terminology is misleading: for example, 'gender' is used interchangeably with 'women', or the difference between 'sex' and 'gender' is blurred by the undifferentiated use of compound terms such as 'sex roles' and 'gender roles' as well as 'sexual division or labour' and 'gender division of labour'. Third, some of the explanations offered for the concepts are reductionist or simply false, for instance, when biological ('sex') differences between women and men are presented as a 'reason' or 'basis' for the emergence of cultural ('gender') differences. In fact, many of the 'gender and development' manuals and policy papers do not adopt the gender concept for a differentiated analysis of complex gender relations. Rather, they convey a binary view of gender relations in which human beings are divided into two clear-cut groups, women and men, which are then qualified by superficial generalizations. Fourth, the complexity and richness of feminist approaches are rarely accounted for, with many ongoing feminist debates being ignored. In particular, 'Gender Planning' manuals of Western development organizations largely fail to acknowledge the insights of postcolonial and transnational feminisms, work that would be relevant as it explicitly deals with gender relations in developing societies.

3.5.2. Postcolonial feminism: deconstructing WID and nationalism

Postcolonial feminist scholars pointed to the importance of incorporating racism and colonialism into any analysis of culture and society. Investigating the complex intersections of class, race and gender, they critically deconstructed common assumptions underlying North-South relations, including the WID approach in development co-operation. While many postcolonial critics focussed on the cultural realm, some of the issues raised were of very concrete relevance to the development debate. In particular, Chandra Talpade Mohanty's work on 'discursive colonization' and on female solidarity as well as Gayatri Chakravorti Spivak's consideration of voice and representation are of importance here. In the African context, Anne McClintock and Amina Mama are among the scholars who have worked on nationalism and gender in colonial and postcolonial societies.

Chandra Mohanty's reflections on 'discursive colonization were based on the analysis of a number of books that had been published by ZED publications in a series entitled "Women and Development" in the 1980s, and came to the conclusion that most Western female authors depicted women in Third World countries as passive and dependent victims. Mohanty interpreted the creation of an ahistoric and stereotyped image of Third World women as a " discursive" colonization" that allowed Western female authors to adopt the role of liberated experts. She did not plead against research by Western scholars in general, citing, for example, Maria Mies' study of the lace-makers of Narsapur (Mies 1982) as a positive example of differentiated and action-oriented research. However, she had reservations about the idea that sustainable development could be initiated through external interventions and that Western feminists were a model for women worldwide (Mohanty 1988:61ff.).

In another paper, Mohanty addressed the issue of global solidarity amongst women which is taken for granted in some sections of feminist developmentalist literature, in particular in publications that supposedly give voice to women from different regional and cultural backgrounds. Rejecting the practice of diversity under Western control, she instead argued for carefully assessed coalitions in order to achieve feminist and anti-racist political objectives (Mohanty 1997:88).

Gayatri Spivak's work is similarly concerned with voice and representation. With her seminal paper "Can the subaltern speak?" (1988), she criticized the approaches taken by the Subaltern Studies Group in India. This group of social scientists, of which Spivak was a member, had concentrated on revealing voices of the poor and marginalized that had been excluded in mainstream history. Spivak widened the debate by questioning the conditions under which marginalized women could acquire voice at all. She also pointed to the role of patriarchal structures in the establishment of postcolonial states. Like other feminist postcolonial thought, Mohanty's work is primarily oriented towards a theoretical debate.

Postcolonial approaches also deal with the deconstruction of patriarchal nationalism. Anne McClintock's work focuses on patriarchal nationalist ideology in the South African context. It deconstructs ideologies of motherhood in Afrikaaner and African nationalisms in the 20th century (1997:107). Amina Mama's research focuses on the instrumentalization of women's politics by the military governments in Nigeria. Mama argues for the incorporation of the "postcolonial per-

spective" in feminist social science as it "offers a radically subversive agenda that goes against the grain of all imperial interests, as well as against the grain of mainstream national and African regional institutions. That means that boundaries must be pushed and people's deepest values overturned" (2002:7).
On the one hand, postcolonial feminisms are thus critical of the nationalisms in the independent African states. The establishment of male power in postcolonial states and the ideological mystification of the process - for example, the frequent use of metaphors such as the 'nation as mother' which conceal women's agency in liberation struggles - is critically interrogated. On the other hand, the dominance of Western feminist agendas is rejected and asymmetries between women are exposed. Divergent interests between women as well as the possibility of coalitions between them are diligently explored.

3.5.3. Transnational feminisms: working towards autonomous feminist practices

Relying on concepts of feminist postcolonialism on representation, diversity and coalition-building, some feminist scholars from Africa, Asia and Latin America have used the term 'transnational feminism' to describe their vision of an autonomous feminist practice (for example, Grewal 1998, Mendoza 2003). These authors differentiate 'transnational feminism' from 'global feminism', a term that is used to denote universalism and Western hegemony in feminist discourses on development. This terminology is unfortunately not very clear - after all, 'global' and 'transnational' are often used interchangeably in everyday language. What is important, however, is the difference between the two ideas which is definitely substantial: "Global feminism, that is, the hegemony of First World's women's groups to affect women's groups and women's lives world-wide by their interests and their policies" (Grewal 1998:518). As Inderpal Grewal argues, even progressive mainstream discourse, while using the language of pluralism and diversity, still promotes Western concepts as universal: "by ignoring history, contingency and context and addressing difference solely within a notion of non-conflictual pluralism, or of oppressions that can easily fit into a common framework rather than disrupt it" (Grewal 1998:518). Transnational feminisms, in contrast, are conceptualized as a plurality of non-Western, independent feminisms, represented through autonomous women's movements and feminist thought in Africa, Asia and Latin America. The challenge is whether these feminisms can be defined and practised in a way that avoids the instrumentalism and Western dominance of mainstream development discourse. In some cases, a clear-cut demarcation may not be obvious, especially as transnational feminisms are understood to comprise a plurality of approaches. Two aspects, however, are essential in making a difference: First, 'transnational feminism' as defined by the above-mentioned authors takes into account postcolonial realities, including the dependencies and inequalities of the aid relationship. Second, they rely on a practice of differentiated intersectional analysis of race, class and gender. Both aspects are regularly found lacking in the realizations of 'Gender Planning' as practised in development cooperation (Maral-Hanak 2004).

Reflecting on the political representation of women in Africa, Aili Mari Tripp illustrates the dimensions transnational feminisms may take in practice. Tripp documents how feminist transnational networks within the African continent emerged from the early 1990s onwards. National and regional organizations increasingly took up opportunities arising from the United Nations and other international initiatives. For example, the preparatory activities for the Beijing 1995 conference were widely used to promote and achieve objectives at a national and regional level. While "the forces driving many of the demands for changes in women's status were domestic, international pressures and norms clearly gave added impetus to these new demands" (Tripp 2005:2). In turn, African organizations, networks and institutions contributed significantly to the United Nations' activities towards gender equity. In the late 1970s, the 'All African Women's Conference' was one of the six organizations, and at the same time the only regional one, that participated in conceptualising CEDAW (Tripp 2005:1). From the 1990s onwards, significant activities have related to issues such as violence against women, women and conflict, the girl child, women's entrepreneurship, resistance against FGM, the role of governments and NGOs in service provision, as well as women and political representation. African women have also taken leading roles in international events, the most prominent example being the Tanzanian politician Gertrude Mongella, who chaired the 4th International Women's Conference in Beijing 1995; she currently holds the presidency of the Pan-African Parliament of the African Union.

On the African continent, too, women's achievements in the realm of political representation have been remarkable: In 2006, the first African woman president, Ellen Johnson-Sirleaf, was inaugurated in Liberia, being one of only approximately ten female leaders in the world. The average number of women legislators in Africa rose from just one percent in 1960 to 14.6 % in 2004, with the substantial increases taking place after 1990. In Rwanda, women have held 49% of the parliamentary seats since the 2003 elections; in South Africa, Mozambique and the Seychelles, they constituted one third of the legislators in 2005. Motivated by the Beijing Plan of Action, several countries have adopted quotas for women's representation in parliament, and 50/50 campaigns are active in South Africa, Namibia, Sierra Leone, Kenya, Uganda, Tanzania, Malawi, Zambia and Senegal. Within the African Union, women politicians' mobilisation and campaigning has resulted in five of the ten-person Commission of the African Union being women. As Tripp remarks, this success in 50/50 representation was preceded by long-lasting mobilisation and lobbying within continent-wide women's networks, and compares with just one-third of the members (8 out of 24) of the European Commission being women (2005:6).

One may of course argue that, on the whole, these are very limited achievements in women's political representation which moreover have little immediate relevance to the majority of women struggling for daily survival under desperate economic conditions. With widespread unreliable political conditions, there is a permanent danger that such progress, especially at national level, may be reversed any time. However, the prevalence of violence and economic hardship makes the commitment of democratic forces to social progress all the more important.

Academic and professional networks in Africa may serve as another example of transnational feminist movements. One of the first Pan-African independent academic women's networks was AAWORD, the Association of African Women for Research and Development. As early as 1982, AAWORD had voiced a critical position on the practice of WID in development co-operation. The main argument was that women did not need to be 'integrated' into development, as they had not been excluded, but rather had always been involved under disadvantageous conditions. In AAWORD's view, the WID approach did not address racism, sexism or discrimination based on social class. AAWORD scholars also critically reflected on the different conditions under which women in the South and North engaged in scientific research and were accorded respective expert status in the field of development studies (AAWORD 1982:106).

Throughout the following decades, autonomous research networks such as AAWORD gained importance as fora of independent intellectual debate. In many African countries, conditions for government-funded research and teaching have deteriorated, forcing academics into consultancies to make a living. As a result, feminist professional associations or NGO networks that channelled academic commitment towards women's movements have played an important role. Networks on national levels, such as the Tanzania Gender Networking Programme (TGNP), owe a good part of their personal and material resources to committed academics. The closeness of scholars to the challenges of everyday feminist practice has in turn influenced the academic debate. As can be followed up, for example, by feminist online journals from the Southern African region (Agenda, Feminist Africa, Jenda, Safere), national and regional feminist concerns as well as the challenges posed by the 'aid industry' are regular subjects of academic scrutiny, and the elaboration of a feminist epistemology relevant to the African contexts is a recurring issue. Despite adverse material circumstances, autonomous feminisms postulated by postcolonial scholars are becoming a reality through the work of numerous individuals, organizations, institutions and networks on the African continent.

3.5.4. Donors and Gender Planning

A closer investigation of donor policy and practice in terms of the implementation of 'Gender Planning' in development co-operation reveals a paradox: gender policy is well-established in aid discourse, but only a few programmes that effectively achieve just and balanced gender relations are implemented. This is due to a number of inter-related factors, but first and foremost to the opportunistic and superficial use of feminist concepts. In particular, donor's policy proves to be blind to postcolonial realities, such as linguistic, cultural and economic dependencies, as well as the necessity of intersectional analysis that gives due consideration to links between race, class and gender biases. Christine Sylvester's suggestion that postcolonial thought has much to contribute to the development debate marks an important point. Northern aid organizations still operate relying on the "firmly embedded notion of the originary status of Western feminism" (Alexander and Mohanty 1997:xx). Only a handful of African feminist organizations are established and courageous enough to insist on their own principles when negotiating local or international support. The majority of Africa-based feminist movements, experts and professional networks who engage in development work need to tune their programmes to the frameworks set by the powerful actors in the aid business when trying to secure a material base for their operations. The adoption of 'Gender Planning' into mainstream policy has not changed unequal power relations: 'Northern' aid agencies and experts continue to dominate processes of problem analysis and decision-making for projects and programmes that are implemented in the global 'South'.

3.6. Conclusion: Transforming relationships?

To provide a background for the empirical analysis of interpersonal communication in development networks, this chapter has looked at the scope and limitations of transformational concepts in aid co-operation. The discussion of origins and uses of 'PRA' and 'Gender Planning' has illustrated how international aid agencies instrumentalize alternative ideas in development discourse. As Schicho and Nöst argue, development co-operation is a sector of the economy in which "the powerful actors dispose of material means and information and control the 'product' development and its market. [...] The rapid replacement of contents and concepts makes it easy for the powerful actors to weaken the critical potential of the sector by taking over its concepts and ideas without renouncing their own objectives[9]"(Schicho/Nöst 2006:45). What becomes a cutting-edge trend is not necessarily what people need in particular social and historic circumstances, but what is convenient to the powerful. In most cases, newly-introduced concepts are not very innovative anyway, but rather newly dressed versions of well-known motifs and topics. Donors set criteria that enforce adherence to ever-changing cutting-edge trends, and 'partners' adapt and negotiate their plans accordingly. As we have seen, planning tools like 'Participatory Rural Appraisal' or 'Gender Planning' are contradictory and problematic in their own terms. The process of 'mainstreaming' these concepts into development practice has unfortunately not resulted in the transformation of aid relationships. One could rather say that if anything has been transformed, it is the originally radical concepts that have become meaningless add-ons to neo-liberal policy. The need for compliance towards donors leads to discrepancies and contradictions in implementation, which

---

9   Translation from German by Irmi Maral-Hanak

become most visible in interpersonal communication. It is the analysis of linguistic communication around the implementation of transformatory concepts which makes up the main empirical part of this study, which will be presented in the following chapters.

4. Sociolinguistic background: Participation and language use

4.1. Multilingualism, colonialism, racism

> "The term 'expatriate' itself is an interesting one, on the one hand distinguishing a certain group of people clearly from 'immigrants' and other dark-skinned arrivals, and on the other locating their identity not as 'foreigners' or 'outsiders' in a host community [...] but rather as people whose identity is defined a decontextualized English/American etc. person overseas. Being an 'expatriate' locates one not as an outsider in a particular community but a permanent insider who happens for the moment to be elsewhere. The very use of this term puts into play a host of significant discourses" (Pennycook 1994:219, endnote to chapter one).

Sociolinguistic enquiry focuses on variants in speech and the association of these variants with social factors. A sociolinguistic approach is promising where insights on the implications of language use in society are at stake, such as why 'development experts' or 'beneficiaries' choose to communicate in one language or variety rather than another, and how the use of a particular language is related to social discrimination and exclusion. From the linguistic vantage point, the object of investigation is the plurality of languages and variations, while from the perspective of social categories it is age, sex and social class (constituted by factors such as education, profession, housing, and others). Sociolinguistic analysis relates code choice, that is, the practices of using one particular language in a particular communicative situation, to the social characteristics of the speakers involved (Chambers 1995:14). Yet conventions on the use of linguistic varieties are not "solid social facts", but themselves "stakes in and outcomes of struggle between social forces" (Fairclough 1995:248). Language use does not merely reflect social stratification. Instead, it is part of the social formation, possessing a dynamic force that shapes society (Pennycook 2001:53). This chapter begins by tracing stereotypical attitudes towards languages in today's Tanzania to their colonial origins. It continues by discussing challenges to the sociolinguistic analysis of development, inequality and language use in the East African context. It then proceeds to analyze the data that was obtained in interviews on the social background and language practices of development workers and beneficiaries in two Tanzanian development networks.

In Sub-Saharan Africa, the relationship between language and society – issues such as who speaks which language to whom in what situation – is to a considerable extent shaped by the continent's recent history of colonial occupation. Foreign domination, including massive interference in linguistic practices, took place only a few decades ago and problems created by the prevalence of ex-colonial languages continues to pervade all aspects of life. Both colonial and mandatory rule were primarily interested in ensuring the smooth running of political administration and economic transactions. Consequently, controversies over the language of instruction in schools – in the case of Tanganyika the options were English, Swahili or other African languages of the 'territory' – mainly reflected "different views of how best to run a colony" (Pennycook 1998:20) and were rarely guided by pedagogical considerations. As Louis-Jean Calvet (1978:104) has argued, the colonial discourse on language relied on the notion that African languages were inferior to those of the European rulers, and it created a peculiar mix of stereotypical assertions and circular arguments that nevertheless claimed to have scientific validity. African languages were 'dialects' that were spoken by 'tribes' – both terms invoking a myriad of assumptions about the political structures and linguistic expression of colonized people that had little to do with the communicative, social and political realities in which Africans lived. The fact that many of the African languages were not written was taken as evidence that it was not possible to write in these languages. In the case of the languages that had developed or adopted an alphabet (some African languages including Swahili used the Arab script), respective orthographies were often dismissed as disfunctional. With regard to language structures, it was maintained that inflecting languages (a structure that Indo-European languages possess) were more 'advanced' than agglutinating or isolating languages. (All languages of the world belong to one of the three types, as do the languages spoken on the African continent. While this structural division is still a standard tool of modern linguistic description, there is no real evidence to support a respective hierarchy of language types). As African languages borrowed terms from European languages when naming technical innovations (for example, in Swahili 'baiskeli' = 'bicycle'), this was taken as proof that African languages could not express modern concepts. It was conveniently ignored that African languages were productive in coining their own terms (for example, in Swahili 'gari la moshi' [lit. 'steam wagon' = 'train'). Calvet (1978:104) also remarks that the "short memory of ideology" chose to overlook the fact that European languages like Spanish and French had borrowed terms from Arabic, and that, of course, all languages in contact exhibit such borrowing processes. In the case of Swahili, a language that acquired exceptional status and functionality even before the colonial occupation of East Africa, the myth of the "mixed language" played an additional role (a term that makes little sense from a modern linguistic viewpoint). Because of the high percentage of Arabic loanwords in Swahili, it was claimed that Swahili was not really a language of the Bantu group, but rather a 'mixed' Arab-African idiom (Whiteley 1969:7; Mazrui and Mazrui 1998:161). It mattered little that linguistic evidence pointed to the contrary. The grammatical structure of Swahili is clearly that of a Bantu language, and the influence of other languages at the lexical level is irrelevant for linguistic genetic classification. By comparison, English has one of the highest proportions of terms borrowed from other (mostly Romance) languages. These many borrowings into English have given rise to a richness of synonyms and expressions in the language – an attribute that is highly appreciated by its users. To some, this quality is one 'reason' why English has become such a successful world language. Yet English has always been classified a Germanic language, while Swahili, which has a lower proportion of borrowings, was in colonial times often presented as a so-called 'mixed' language, especially in popular descriptions. The implications of this perception were twofold: The first was that the use of 'mixed' suggested that there existed a 'pure' language (another, of course, unsuitable term to describe any language); the second was that this alleged Arab-African 'mix' placed an emphasis on the influence of Middle Eastern languages and cultures which, in the eyes of the colonizer, 'distinguished' Swahili from other African languages. In the first implication, 'mixed' assumed a meaning similar to 'contaminated'. Assumptions about the 'mixed' origins of languages were often coupled with the expectation that such languages were functionally reduced or degenerated versions of their supposedly 'pure' counterparts – a stereotype that creole languages continue to be confronted with today. A language thus disqualified could be presented as acceptable for the purposes of trade, lower education and administration, and at the same time be excluded from the more sophisticated tasks reserved for European languages. In accordance with the second implication, the British administration in Zanzibar, for example, institutionalized a racist hierarchy that placed Europeans at the top, Africans at the bottom and Arabs and Indians in between. In this context, asserting an Arab component in Swahili provided a pretext for giving Swahili a privilege over other African languages, while at the same time sustaining the colonial idea of ethnic hierarchy in the larger East African context.

This should only serve as a brief outline of arguments that can be pursued in greater depth. The colonial discourses on language provided a conglomeration of ideas and strategies that allowed the instrumentalization of languages for establishing hierarchies and control. It is important to note that, despite the systematic devaluation of African languages, they were not necessarily excluded from consideration for promotion and development, especially for primary education and lower administration. For example, a conference on education in the colonies sponsored by the British Government in 1925 proclaimed the importance of what it termed 'native languages' (Webb 2004:105). In British colonial discourses on Asia, the 'orientalist' stance supporting education in 'native' languages was no less articulate than the 'anglicist' one that argued for English only. The two positions resulted in "an apparently balanced educational policy, promoting the spread of European knowledge via English in higher education and via vernacular languages in primary education" (Pennycook 2000:57). In Africa, the Phelps-Stokes Commission Report of 1925 recommended the use of African languages in education, arguing that "All peoples have an inherent right to their own language. It is the means of expressing their own personality, however primitive they may be." (Jones 1925:19, quoted from Roy-Campbell 2001a:51). African languages were therefore not necessarily excluded from use in schools, but they were disqualified as primitive and space conceded to them was clearly circumscribed. Notably, they were assumed to be incapable of conveying any concepts relating to advanced science, technology and higher levels of government. These domains, which were at the heart of colonialism's 'civilizing' mission, and at the same time also the domains on which the emerging discourse of progress and development relied, were to be reserved for the English language. The report expressed reservations about using Swahili in education, concerned that it would endanger the position of English and other African languages. The colonial administration, however, continued to rely on Swahili as a language of instruction of elementary education for Africans. Higher education continued to be provided in English, but Africans' access to English-speaking education was limited. In 1955, the Binn's Mission Report took a similarly critical position on Swahili, again arguing in favour of other African languages and English (Roy-Campbell 2001a:54). Facing a rising anti-colonial movement that relied on Swahili as its primary medium of communication, attempts were made to discredit the language. It was argued that the use of Swahili was factionalist as it favoured Islam, or that it had been the language of the slave trade. As a result of the Binn's Mission Report, Swahili was able to retain its position in basic education, but not replace English in higher education.

Educational institutions were instrumental in planting the notion of the supremacy of European languages in the minds of the subjugated peoples. One notorious practice in schools all over colonial Africa was the use of the 'symbol', an object used to shame and punish anyone who dared to speak any language other than those of the colonial masters in class. Inequality was enacted and communicated in many other subtle ways, as Pennycook observes: "It is not so much that colonialism produces unique behaviours, words and ideas but rather it makes a set of practices and discursive frames more available, more acceptable" (Pennycook 1998:25). Ngugı wa Thiong'o has eloquently described how colonial education in Kenya not only forced the English language on pupils, but along with it a British cultural and geographical orientation that had no reference to Kenyan children's everyday experience (Ngugı wa Thiong'o 1993:34).

After Independence, the majority of African countries continued to use the ex-colonial languages as their official languages. It was only hesitantly that some countries eventually committed themselves to the promotion of African languages. At the national and regional level, conferences took place, declarations were made and action plans were adopted. Nevertheless, very little changed in day-to-day linguistic practice. In most countries, European languages continued to be used as the languages of education and official communication, excluding the majority of the population who had no knowledge of these idioms. Reflecting on the persistent dominance of ex-colonial languages, Vic Webb identifies three major reasons why the ambitious plans for linguistic change were so ineffective. First, as mentioned above, colonialism as a century-long "process of subjugation and domination led to the inferiorisation of indigenous cultural values, beliefs, patterns of behaviour" (Webb 2004:112), a development that could not be reversed in a few years or even decades. Second, globalisation, and in particular the dominance of Western transnational corporations and technologisation, has contributed to a continuous process of marginalization of African languages. Third, most governing elites in Africa have an interest in the exclusive function of ex-colonial languages: As long as politics and government are inaccessible to the majority of the population who have no access to these languages, it remains easier for the powerful to retain their privileges. "English is thus used as a gatekeeper, a separator, an exclusionary mechanism, and instrument to protect own interests" (Webb 2004:113). In development co-operation, the gate-keeping function of English may have far-reaching consequences, as Rose-Marie Beck has indicated in her description of a participatory project in Namibia. She observed that participants who were very articulate as long as their language, Herero, was used, became passive listeners when the exercise required them to write down notes, with the facilitator insisting that these notes be taken down in English (Beck 2006:310).

To summarize the effects of colonial educational and language policies, it is worth considering the fact that in East Africa, even today, having a good education is still popularly equated to knowing English well. With regard to the contemporary situation in Tanzania, the publisher Walter Bgoya concludes that the continued adherence to English in secondary education has meant that the country as a whole has "ended up with neither English nor education" (Bgoya 2001:289).

4.2. Sociolinguistic approaches and postcolonial challenges

Sociolinguistic descriptions of the coexistence of languages in plurilingual societies have only been partly able to capture the realities of postcolonial societies. Sociolinguists have developed models to account for the coexistence of language in society, with 'variation', 'diglossia' and 'bilingualism' serving as essential concepts. They have analyzed factors in individual speaker's linguistic choices, investigating notions of 'appropriateness' and 'attitudes'. The scope of action for political decision-makers is explored in work on 'language planning'. Finally, the expression of social inequality through language, including the divide between countries of the global South and North, have been accounted for in reflections on 'linguistic imperialism', 'linguicism' and 'linguistic human rights'.

Sociolinguists can be credited with broadening the field of linguistic inquiry – which prior to the 1950s was largely limited to prescriptive, comparative and historical approaches – to include social contexts. However, depending on the underlying social science perspective, sociolinguistic approaches have varied greatly. As Alastair Pennycook (2001:49) points out, sociolinguists have often relied on static and consensual models of social organization. In the following, a selection of approaches and concepts and their relevance for sociolinguistic research in East Africa will be briefly discussed.

Variation theory focuses on understanding the evolution and coexistence of linguistic varieties (sociolects, dialects[10], languages). Based on the empirical study of language use, variation theory has provided insights into social motivations for the use of nonstandard forms (for example, as a means of expressing group solidarity), and, most importantly, it has demonstrated the functional equality of all languages and varieties: All information relevant to human beings can be expressed in all natural languages or varieties that exist. On the base of variation theory, Labov (1970) and other sociolinguists have explicitly rejected racist disqualifications of particular languages or varieties, such as, for example, claims about alleged structural deficits in American 'Black English'.

Diglossia is defined as any linguistic situation where more than one language or variety is spoken and "clear functional differences between the codes" is involved (Wardhaugh 1992:86). In addition, the term often implies a hierarchical relationship between the varieties, as one is usually regarded as more prestigious.
Charles Ferguson's (1959) work has introduced 'diglossia' as a term referring to the complementary use of 'classical' or standard varieties of a language in conjunction with their dialectal counterparts, such as the use of Standard Arabic and Arabic regional dialects in present-day Arab speaking countries. Ferguson argued that standard (in Ferguson's terms 'high') varieties are used for communicative domains of greater prestige, while the latter pertain to informal functions of little esteem ('low').[11] Ferguson emphasized that speakers express social hierarchies and values through language use, as the 'high' variety is invariably related to more prestigious domains. However, in his model the coexistence of languages is primarily constructed in terms of a complementary and stable division of functions. Ferguson's concept explains how two different varieties may coexist in harmonious, static ways; he is less concerned about unequal social relations that underlie respective linguistic divisions and the possible dynamics of change involved.
Joshua Fishman (1967) extended the concept to account for functional divisions in the use of two or more distinct languages. Introducing the issue of individual linguistic competence to the debate, he asked whether those living in diglossic situations had the possibility to communicate in both 'high' and 'low' contexts, or possibly remained excluded from eminent domains. Fishman showed that it made a difference whether speakers in a diglossic situation were individually bilingual

---

10 Common linguistic definitions of dialect imply mutual intelligibility, or sharing a lexical base of at least 75%.
11 It has been remarked before that two of the varieties specified by Ferguson, namely French and Haitian Creole, do not fit the pattern of standard – dialect opposition, but rather constitute two distinct languages.

or not (diglossia with or without bilingualism). He also argued that it was possible to have widespread individual bilingualism without a functional division in language use (bilingualism with or without diglossia).
Sociolinguists like Labov, Ferguson and Fishman demonstrated the functionality and 'normality' of multilingualism in an era in which the supremacy of monolingualism and standard varieties was still taken for granted. They showed that nonstandard varieties were as complex and sophisticated as standard ones, that the presence of more than one language in a society did not necessarily lead to chaos, and that individuals could speak more than one language without necessarily performing inadequately in any of them. While these merits are unquestioned, the liberal approach in sociolinguistics has been critiqued as it "wishes for equality where there is none" (Pennycook 2001:49). In short, the above-quoted authors hardly dealt with the question of how varieties become 'high', 'low' or 'standard' in the first place, or why some varieties are the focus of racist slurs. In liberal sociolinguistic work, social inequality is described – usually in terms of stratification – rather than questioned. The underlying model is one of a harmonious society, in which it is assumed that every member works for the common good. Such an approach neither considers the conflictual nature of social relations nor does it account for the fact that language plays an important role in the negotiation of social inequality. Sociolinguistic enquiry based on a static model of society remains caught up in the question of how language mirrors the existence of social groupings: A person's social background, so the assumption, largely determines how she or he speaks. Such approaches ignore how social class, gender and race intersect and are linked to social dominance and struggle. They therefore fail to account for more complex manifestations of social difference. Contemporary poststructuralist, feminist and postcolonial approaches, in contrast, have demonstrated how gender, race, class and identity are constructs which themselves require explanation. Instead of limiting themselves to description, these approaches have encouraged critical enquiry into agency. A critical sociolinguistic approach that takes up this challenge would therefore focus on the question of how people use language to negotiate, interact and deal with manifestations of inequality – as language use "is about producing and not just reflecting realities" (Pennycook 2001:53).
In his reinterpretation of the sociolinguistic concept of diglossia in several African countries, Louis-Jean Calvet (1987:47) has adopted a critical stance towards linguistic description. He points out that, as in many countries of Sub-Saharan Africa the majority of the population does not speak the 'high' variety (in most cases an ex-colonial language), prevailing language policies continue to serve the elites and exclude the majority. The reality is that languages not understood by the majority enjoy the highest social prestige and are used in administration and politics. Policies privileging former colonial languages not only enforce a eurocentric cultural orientation, but they are of course also incompatible with any form of inclusive or participatory development communication. In order to

describe the hierarchy between ex-colonial, regional and minority languages in some African countries, linguists have also used terms like 'embedded diglossia' (Calvet 1987:47).

'**Appropriateness**' has become another key term in sociolinguistic description, relating to the choices speakers have in linguistic variety, style, register, strategy, etc. 'Appropriateness' is, for example, indispensable to the concept of communicative competence as developed by Dell Hymes (1972). He argued that in order to communicate successfully, speakers cannot simply apply the grammatical rules of a language; they must also know what is 'appropriate' and how to express it in a given social context. The concept of communicative competence has helped second language teaching reflect on the socio-economic and cultural context in which a language is used.

While the observation of social norms determining the appropriateness of language use can provide useful information for language learners, it also raises many questions about the societies in which these norms apply: Who determines the relevant linguistic standard, and why are speakers of some varieties discriminated against? Why is deference or mitigation expressed along the lines of social class, gender, age or ethnicity? The use of 'appropriateness' as a linguistic concept often leads to the unquestioned acceptance of an issue rather than the facilitation of critical analysis. In politeness studies, 'appropriateness' is at times invoked when deference is expressed by one speaker towards another on account of difference in social status, for example from a younger person towards an older one, or from an illiterate towards a an educated person. Instead of analysing and questioning cultural norms that create and maintain social inequality, hierarchies are reinforced.

A similarly veiling notion of appropriateness often appears in the debate on the medium of instruction in educational institutions. The UNESCO Position Paper on "Education in a multilingual world" of 2003 finds clear points of orientation in this regard. First, it argues that the mother tongue should be used in initial instruction and continue to be used as late as possible in education. Second, where the mother tongue is different from the official or national language, communication in the official or national as well as one or more foreign languages should be encouraged, particularly through the early acquisition of a second language. Third, measures are recommended to ensure the elimination of any form of discrimination in education, to further the rights of linguistic minorities, and to raise awareness of the positive value of cultural and linguistic diversity (UNESCO 2003:30-32). However, this clear theoretical commitment towards additive bilingualism – that is, the provision of mother tongue education *as well as* access to regional and international languages – encounters both material and ideological obstacles in its implementation.

The "truism that learning in a language which is not one's own provides a double set of challenges" (UNESCO 2003:15) is "obvious but not generally recognized".

Concerns for offering literacy or primary schooling in a child's first language often become secondary when the official or standard language is argued to be the more 'appropriate' idiom for educational institutions. As Fairclough has argued, "portraying standard English and other languages or varieties as differing in conditions of appropriateness, is dressing up inequality as diversity: Standard English is 'appropriate' in situations that carry social clout, while other varieties are 'appropriate' at the margin" (Fairclough 1995:225). While there are certainly pragmatic reasons for teaching standard language in education, Fairclough points out that this should not prevent teachers from exposing students to critical views about standard varieties.

More often than not, notions of what is 'appropriate' are shaped by prevailing power relations. With its appeal to common sense, 'appropriateness' provides comfortable answers when other explanations would require a more differentiated analysis and possibly bring to light unsettling facts. In development co-operation, prevailing notions about what languages are 'appropriate' often hold that English is indispensable in working for progress and technological innovation. Yet even a superficial survey of linguistic conditions shows that the objective of broad popular participation and transparency requires the active support of African languages that are widely understood, and that this may include languages with both minority and official status.

Language attitudes constitute another eminent concept in sociolinguistic description which should not only be considered, but also subjected to further analysis. Language attitudes are the result of historic developments; they are not merely determined by economic and pragmatic factors. For example, in Namibia, English is only spoken by a small minority of the population, yet it enjoys high acceptance as an official language because it is associated with the liberation from South African rule.

The example of South Africa also shows how the history of colonial domination and apartheid rule has shaped deeply ambivalent language attitudes. The Freedom Charter, adopted by the ANC in 1955, proclaimed that "All people shall have equal right to use their own languages" (ANC 1955, Beukes 2004:6). During apartheid rule, however, the policy of 'Bantu Education' coupled racist discrimination in education with mother tongue instruction at the primary school level. In 1976 protests against the introduction of Afrikaans as a language of instruction in secondary schools led to the Soweto student uprising which became the most outspoken political protest against the apartheid state. At the end of the apartheid era, popular resentment of any linguistic policy that did not favour English in education was widespread. "Amongst speakers of African languages [...] liberation was imagined in English" (Heugh 2003:130). The democratic constitution of 1994 affirmed its commitment to official multilingualism and recognized eleven official languages. However, the implementation of these ambitious policies was sluggish, the result being that little was done to ensure the equity of African languages. There is still unequal access to government services and information (Beukes 2004:15). Public domains and work environments remain dominated by the English language. Parents continue to opt for English language instruction for their children. Yet despite the socioeconomic pressures in favour of English, some observers have also pointed to the concerns speakers of African languages have voiced about the lack of recognition given to their languages in education and public contexts (Banda 2004:272). It is therefore highly problematic to regard linguistic attitudes as static, or to instrumentalize them in justification of hegemonic linguistic policy and practices.

Part of the problem is that the debate on languages of instruction in Sub-Saharan Africa is often framed in terms of an exclusive 'either – or' scenario (Qorro 2003:188). It is either the ex-colonial language or the African language, English or Swahili. At the same time, language attitudes are often complex and ambivalent, as they mirror a history of deep social inequalities. In Tanzania, the demand for English language instruction is primarily motivated by an interest in good education and access to an international language (Rugemalira 2005:70). However, as Qorro (2003:188) has pointed out, many countries in the world successfully offer their students both quality education in the first language <u>and</u> access to English as a foreign language.

Language planning is a domain that focuses on the scope of action for political leadership in language use. Within this domain, 'status planning' refers to the official recognition granted a language, while 'corpus planning' involves concrete measures for language development, such as the expansion of the lexical base of a particular language. Given the political sensitivity of the subject, linguists have often sought to assume a particularly detached and 'objective' position. A number of categorisations have been suggested in this context. These include the division between 'endoglossic' and 'exoglossic' (Heine 1979:31ff) language situations, distinguishing those countries which have put foreign languages in the position of official language (exoglossic) from those which use indigenous languages (endoglossic). Other classifications have focussed on the number of languages possibly involved in diglossic language coexistence. Using game theory to develop a model that accounts for language use in the multilingual countries of Sub-Saharan Africa, David Laitin finds a '3 ± 1 outcome' to be the most common language pattern of language use (1992). This means that most speakers use their first language, which is likely to be a minority language, and/or an African language of wider communication, an ex-colonial language and, contingently, an additional language if the individual's first language is different from the minority language used locally in primary education. An individual's motivation in language choice is seen as largely determined by economic considerations: "People only use a second, third or fourth language if they need to for socioeconomic and political mobility" (Eastman 1991:140). This approach explains tendencies towards rationalization. It points to the discrepancy between the formal official

4.2. Sociolinguistic approaches and postcolonial challenges 125

recognition that is often readily granted to African languages and the practical reality that language use remains tied to ex-colonial languages. However, it also portrays linguistic developments as predetermined by socioeconomic constraints: "Language change follows social change, and social change moves in the direction of perceived power and prestige" (Eastman 1991:147). Unfortunately, this approach lacks the historic depth to account for the formation of social inequalities and future perspectives of change. As such, it discredits any promotion of African languages and merely serves as an apology for an "English only" policy in the continuation of colonial language policies. Beneath these arguments lies a descriptive concept of sociolinguistic epistemology that fails to critically examine linguistic practices in postcolonial contexts. While claiming to refrain from explicit political commitment by asserting 'objective' sociolinguistic description, such an approach is in fact highly political, as it supports ongoing practices of linguistic domination (Pennycook 2001:49, Tollefson 2006:57). Clearly, the example of Swahili in Tanzania in many ways illustrates the possibilities of an alternative policy of language planning, a proposition that will be explored in greater depth in the next section (Abdulaziz 1971, 1980; Polomé 1980, O'Barr 1976).

In direct opposition to the use of ex-colonial languages in Africa, the concept of **linguistic imperialism** describes the powerlessness of those marginalized and excluded by present-day linguistic policies in Africa. In the late 1970s, the Kenyan author Ngugi wa Thiong'o, at that time already an acclaimed English language novelist, began writing and publishing his works in both his mother tongue, Kikuyu, and English. Committed to the facilitation of the political participation of poor peasants, Ngugi became highly critical of the dominant role of English in present-day Kenya. Robert Philippson (2001:185) has presented a profound critique of the past and present worldwide hegemony of English which he calls "linguistic imperialism". In addition to documenting the historical developments which led to the dominant position of English in the world, this approach examines the practices of social exclusion and repression that speakers of minority languages face. It names grievances and demands change in linguistic policies. However, Philippson's approach has been criticized for its failure to account for the agency of those described as oppressed. Those who experience neo-colonial linguistic policies have developed a number of ways of resisting, subverting and appropriating the languages they are confronted with (Blommaert 2005b:410, Pennycook 2001). The dictum of the 'empire writing back' has come to refer to the ways in which writers in all parts of the former British Empire have appropriated and shaped 'New Englishes' in their own work (for example Canagarajah 2000:127, 1999:187). Arguments within the postcolonial framework have shown that there are different strategies for tackling the challenge created by linguistic hegemonies. However, in most African countries the majority of the population has neither access to a secondary education nor proficiency in ex-colonial languages. This is one reason why these aspects of the postcolonial debate faced the criticism of remaining elitist and less relevant.

One concept related to the debate on linguistic imperialism is that of **linguistic human rights**, which proclaims that every person has the right to education and other social services in her or his language. For the African context, this entails a challenging agenda, such as providing access to literacy in every living African language, promoting of the use of African languages in secondary and tertiary education, and raising African languages to the status of official languages (Philippson and Skuttnab-Kangas 1995:344-345). But linguistic human rights were also identified beyond the development and provision of services in a person's mother tongue. The UNESCO declaration includes both "the provision of schooling in their languages, if so desired" as well as the access to regional, national and international languages, and the creation of "positive attitudes to minority [...] languages and the cultures they express" (2003:16) in its listing of the linguistic rights of minority groups.

Reviewing the practical experience of mother-tongue education based on the concept of linguistic human rights, Christopher Stroud instead proposes an approach based on **linguistic citizenship**. Discussing the poor performance of many mother tongue education programmes, Stroud (2001:341) points out how the 'rights discourse' fails to adequately address the way speakers of minority languages are socially marginalized. In order to achieve transformative development, he argues, empowerment of and active participation by the speakers of minority languages is a key factor. Kathleen Heugh likewise identifies the importance of an "empowering sense of linguistic citizenship" (2003:142).

This short review of sociolinguistic approaches has made frequent references to the work of Alastair Pennycook, as his consideration of postcolonial perspectives and his critical position towards linguistics are particularly useful in identifying issues relevant to development work in postcolonial Africa. Alastair Pennycook advocates a 'postcolonial performative view of language', some aspects of which are listed here:

> - The need for a critical social theory capable of analysing social inequality.
>
> - An approach to language that goes beyond description and moves toward critique.
>
> - An understanding of the shortcomings of a model that emphasizes appropriateness.
>
> - A view of language as both productive and reflective of social relations.
>
> - A need for a historical understanding of language use.

> A view of culture, identity, and global politics that avoids essentialism and instead looks at forms of resistance and appropriation.

> The need to always work contextually (Pennycook 2001:72).

While the above outline constitutes a broader critical approach to sociolinguistics, it is of particular value when approaching linguistic challenges in the context of development work. The challenges of linguistic choice have largely been ignored in aid co-operation. Even authors who focus specifically on development communication have directed comparatively little attention to the challenges of multilingual environments (see for example Melkote and Steeves 2001:340). The next section will focus on the sociolinguistic situation in Tanzania, while examining the linguistic dimension of aid co-operation.

4.3. Tanzania: a critical perspective on linguistic choice

The most remarkable aspect of the linguistic situation in Tanzania is the strong position of Swahili, which is an official language spoken by more than 90% of the population (Roy-Campbell 2001b:272). Most other Sub-Saharan African countries rely on ex-colonial languages for communication at the national level, languages that often only 5-20% of the population are familiar with. In Tanzania, although English continues to be a prestigious language of secondary and higher education, professionalism and international communication, Swahili is the primary language of interaction at the national level, being firmly established in such domains as basic education, administration, political debate and a significant portion of development communication. The functions of the remaining more than 120 African languages of Tanzania are usually described as being restricted to the domain of the home, village, local informal contexts and cultural performances. Multilingualism in Tanzania is therefore not a neutral expression of linguistic plurality, but rather a reflection of the history of colonialism in a distinct pattern of social inequality – a constituent feature of the postcolonial predicament. In the following, some aspects of the historic background of this development will be discussed, with a particular focus on the exceptional position of Swahili.

Swahili is a language of the Northeastern Bantu subgroup whose speakers settled in the area between the Webi Shebelle and Tana rivers in Southern Somalia and Northern Kenya in the first millenium AD. The language is particularly close to the neighbouring Sabaki languages. By the end of the first millenium AD, Swahili speakers, who were originally a fishing and agricultural people, turned to trading and navigation, subsequently establishing settlements on the East African coast that extended to Northern Mozambique. Between 1000 and 1500 AD, those independent city states on the East African coast which had acquired wealth through trade in gold and other items included, for example, Lamu, Malindi, Gedi, Mombasa, Bagamoyo, Unguja (Zanzibar) and Kilwa. Their trading routes linked the East African inland to the Persian Gulf. An urban culture developed, with Islam becoming the dominant religion. The Portuguese conquest from the 16th century onwards resulted in destruction (in particular in Mombasa and Kilwa) and stagnation in many of the cities. The Portuguese, however, did not manage to establish a continuous presence on the coast. In the 18th century, political leaders in Mombasa entered an alliance with the Busaidi, the ruling family of Oman, to get rid of the Portuguese. While the Portuguese were successfully driven away, Omani rulers took control of the coast, establishing themselves in Zanzibar. Their economic base at that time relied very much on trade, which followed the century-old inland routes. Towards the end of the 19th century, Germany took control of the Tanzanian mainland, and Britain established itself in Kenya, Uganda and Zanzibar. By this time, Swahili had already spread into many parts of today's mainland Tanzania. German colonial rule relied on African employees in lower levels of administration. The language used was Swahili, an option that helped to keep costs low. Disregarding the existing Arabic orthography, the Germans developed a Latin orthography for writing Swahili and forced the literate speech community to adopt it (Legère 2006a:387).

The British mandatory administration that took over mainland Tanzania after the collapse of the German colonial empire restricted Swahili to lower levels of education and administration, while higher levels of education and government were reserved English. This ensured that Africans were largely excluded from the higher positions of power for which English was needed – education, if available at all, was mostly carried out in Swahili and allowed only a few men to become low-level government employees. Within the greater colonial context, the use of one African language at a country-wide level was nevertheless exceptional. Swahili was present in domains in which few other African languages were used. Economic, cultural and social developments such as migrant wage labour, urbanisation, growing mobility, emerging media and popular culture were important factors in the spread of the language (Mulokozi 2002:1). In 1930, an Interterritorial Language Committee was established to promote the use of a standardized form of Swahili. Despite the fact that other varieties such as the Kimvita dialect of Mombasa had a longer literary tradition, the committee decided to adopt the Unguja variety as "Standard Swahili", as it was already widely used in trading, administration and schools (Khamisi 1991:207). The committee also standardized the orthography – from the turn of the century onwards, the Latin alphabet had begun to replace the Arabic one – in addition to the grammar, lexicon and process of accommodating borrowings from other languages. Dictionaries, teaching materials and a journal served as a body of reference for language users. The committee monitored language teaching, and the production of literary texts and translations. Within a two-tier system in which English had primary status and Swahili secondary status, a limited effort was made to adapt the language for use in lower educational and administrative domains. At the same time, the policy of having Swahili and not English as a language of instruction in primary schools remained an issue of controversy until the end of the colonial era (Puja

2003:118). In particular, when the use of Swahili became a unifiying factor for the anticolonial movement, the British authorities resorted to a policy of divide and rule, endorsing other African languages and English as languages of instruction in primary education (Legère 2006a:387).

In the 1950s, the Tanganyika African National Union (TANU) recognized the potential of Swahili for the anticolonial movement and further promoted it by using it as its preferred means of communication. Swahili embodied the unity of Africans vis à vis the foreign colonial power. In the first years of Independence, the new government further extended the use of Swahili to include internal administration, the courts, primary education and politics. The Interterritorial Language Committee was transformed into the Institute of Kiswahili Research in 1964. Two years later, the Tanzania Publishing House was established. In 1967 the National Swahili Council was founded and in 1970 the Department of Kiswahili was founded at the University of Dar-es-Salaam (Mulokozi 2002:2). Both institutions were to enhance language development, mainly through terminological expansion, but also through linguistic and literary research. In 1967, Swahili was adopted as the official language of government. The use of Swahili in public contexts became a core element of the implementation of Ujamaa ideology. While English was associated with colonial oppression and the other Tanzanian languages with ethnic factionalism, Swahili stood for a commitment to socialist values. As Blommaert puts it, "the 'better' or 'purer' one's Swahili would be, the better a socialist Tanzanian patriot one would be" (Blommaert 2006:247). In 1968, the government declared its policy of 'Education for Self-Reliance'. Swahili was introduced as a language of instruction throughout primary school. At the same time, promoting access to primary education became an important objective, with levels of primary school enrolment rising to 93% of the age cohort towards the end of the 1970s.

In 1969, a plan was adopted to introduce Swahili as language of instruction in secondary and tertiary education. As a first step, the subject of 'Politics' (Siasa) was taught in Swahili in secondary schools. In the following years, manuscripts for school textbooks for other subjects were prepared in Swahili, but the planned shift of the language of instruction in secondary schools continued to be delayed. The Tanzanian Government ultimately lacked the decisive momentum and backed down from the plan, although experts still advocated the shift to Swahili. The efforts of educators and linguists to implement a change in the medium of instruction were disappointed in 1984, when a strategy paper on education announced a stronger role of English in the educational system (Legère 2006b:177). The move to favour English came at a time of political and economic crisis when the Tanzanian government was keen on gaining international recognition, and the "need for foreign aid went hand in hand with the renewed acceptability of English" (Blommart 1992:59).

It took 14 years before the issue of having Swahili as a medium of secondary school instruction was brought back on the agenda. In its 1997 'Sera ya Utamaduni' (Cultural Policy) document, the government of Benjamin Mkapa once more alluded to the long-term goal of having Swahili as a language of instruction at all levels of education. It argued that the much-needed knowledge and technology provided in English would only benefit the small elite who understood that language, and announced a plan that was to prepare the use of Swahili as language of instruction at all levels of the education system (MEC 1997:19, Mulokozi 2002:4, Brock-Utne 2002:28). To date, this plan has not been implemented. As Mulokozi observes, president Benjamin Mkapa "cleverly evaded the language question by directing that the debate should continue. And so it continues!" (2002:3). Official policy stops short of introducing Swahili in secondary and higher education and thereby also inhibits its use in professional and technical contexts.

Retaining English as a language of secondary education has created a problematic situation: Pupils have to study in English, a language which they often have not adequately mastered, while Swahili is not fully acquired for use in technical and professional domains. English medium instruction assumes that 'submerging' students in English in school enables them to learn the language effectively. In Tanzania, this approach has shown poor results. In the last two decades, several reports came to the conclusion that "levels of English were too low in most schools for effective learning to take place" (Brock-Utne 2002:27). Despite the implementation of the 'English Language Teaching Support Project' (ELTSP), a ten year programme of co-operation between the Tanzanian and British government initiated in 1986, the situation continued to deteriorate (Qorro and Roy-Campbell 1997:47; Malekela 2003:106-107). A large number of students fail simply because they do not comprehend classes taught in a language of instruction that is irrelevant to most Tanzanians' everyday experience. Research in Tanzanian classrooms shows that secondary school students do far better when the language of instruction is Swahili (Roy-Campbell 2001b:273, Mwinsheikhe 2003:143). In many cases, the English language proficiency of teachers has been found to be insufficient. Observers argue that the job of English language teachers is not aided but rather made difficult by teachers of other subjects who communicate with the students in poor English. But while the deteriorating status of English is partly due to the lack of relevance the language has in society at large, the teaching of Swahili in secondary schools is equally neglected. In research carried out by the Institute of Kiswahili Research (IKR) in 2003/4, Swahili teachers mentioned the following problems: insufficient time allocated for the teaching of Swahili (only three periods per week compared to six for English); occasional lack of qualified teachers, with teachers of other subjects being called in to fill the gaps; absence of any follow-up training or seminars for graduated Swahili teachers (Msanjila 2005:216, 217). For a long-term perspective of the educational system in Tanzania, substantial improvements will have to be made in the teaching of both languages. Changing the medium of instruction to Swahili and at the same time supporting the teaching of English as a foreign language is an option favoured by linguists familiar with the situation (Qorro 2003:188). Its implementation, however, depends on not only making a principal decision, but also supplying the right material conditions. In this context, the "pathetic state of government schools" (Mulokozi 2002:4) constitutes an eminent challenge. As Rugemalira reports, even better-endowed primary schools in Dar-es-Salaam are found to have eighty children in their smallest classes, with half of the children sitting on the floor and hardly any textbooks available (2005:67). Under such circumstances, educational achievements of any kind are virtually impossible to attain, and most children who leave primary school are ill-prepared for secondary education.

In a long term perspective, the issue of having or not having a functioning "language of instruction" matters not only to the educational system itself, but also to the country's social development. Education plays an important role in making information accessible. "If formal education and other worthwhile information such as research findings were disseminated in languages that the majority of the people understood, this would go a long way towards educating and informing the general public and enable them to bring about their own development" (Qorro 2003:192). Language policy in the educational sector affects other key domains. It is only when Swahili is introduced in secondary and higher education that it will also become relevant for high-level professional, scientific and administrative domains. The development of Swahili in recent decades shows that claims about the language being inadequate for technical contexts are not only untenable from a theoretical point of view, but have also been refuted in practice: The language is already functioning in a number of social, cultural and technical domains. It is the language in which most Tanzanian newspapers and journals are produced and it is very much present in audiovisual media. Remarkable works of literature have been written and published in the language. Swahili is also being used in technical contexts, with the presentation of a Swahili version of Microsoft's text processing programmes in 2005 serving as a recent case in point. A number of textbooks and dictionaries for teaching science subjects in Swahili have been written and published (Mutasa 2003:201). Ultimately, of course, "like an inventory of technical terms, Kiswahili teaching materials can only be accumulated through a process of actually using the language and thereby creating a need for such materials" (Rugemalira et al 1990:30).

Despite the progress Tanzania has made in promoting Swahili, the country faces the same predicament as other African nations: As long as African languages are barred from most contexts of social eminence and prestige, speakers will suspect that these languages are deficient in some way, and that by learning them they are wasting their time (Desai 2001:338). After 1995, when private schools were allowed to operate, primary schools using English as a language of instruction mushroomed, reflecting parental preference for education in English (Rubagumya 2003:156). The majority of Tanzanian secondary and university students have problems following classes in English, but still favour English as a language of instruction, assuming that a Swahili-language education would carry less prestige (Mwinsheikhe 2003:141; Puja 2003:123). Those Tanzanian politicians who decide on language policy belong to the elite minority who have successfully negotiated their way through English language higher education, and who are not necessarily sensitive to the difficulties of the majority (Roy-Campbell 2001b:271). Against this background, linguists' efforts to promote the use of Swahili or other African languages in English language domains are often derided by administrators or officials who themselves do not have any linguistic qualifications (Legère 2004:37).

Compared to Swahili, Tanzania's more than 120 other African languages play a marginal social role. For these languages, the term 'minority languages' has been proposed, as this accounts for the fact that all Tanzanian languages apart from Swahili are marginalized and excluded from public domains (Legère 2002:169). Minority status in this sense does not refer to the number of speakers – they may be 3-5 million, as in the case of Sukuma, or just a few hundred; rather, it refers to the lack of official recognition these languages experience. Often, the derogatory attitude towards these languages is already explicit in the terms used to describe them. Karsten Legère draws attention to the fact that the term vernacular is still used, although it is "derived from the Latin *vernaculus*, 'domestic, native' and in turn from *verna*, 'home born slave'" (Legère 2002:167). Expressions like 'local' or 'ethnic' language are problematic as they suggest that these languages carry intrinsic properties that prevent them from functioning beyond certain places or groups. Legère notes that the term 'national languages' would be preferable, if understood as denoting languages that have evolved in the area of what today constitutes Tanzania. However, as in the past the term 'national language' has been reserved for Swahili, presently this is not an option.

The relationship between Swahili and the 120 Tanzanian minority languages is a difficult one, as the growth and spread of one African language has partly taken place at the expense of the others. In the decades after Independence, official policy did not support the development of minority languages. It was argued that this would only lead to ethnic cleavage and that the problematic economic situation forced the country to set priorities (Blommaert 2006:247, Legère 2002:170; 1992:107). Only in the 1990s, at a time when multipartism was introduced, did the promotion of minority language development become acceptable in public discourse. The "Sera ya Utamaduni" (Cultural Policy) document from 1997 gave official recognition to activities supporting the development of minority languages, and the publication of grammars, dictionaries and all types of texts was encouraged. The "Sera ya Utamaduni" document, however, did not really break with longstanding stereotyped attitudes towards minority languages. Again, minority languages have either been instrumentalized as sources for the lexical expansion of Swahili, or reduced to being a "treasury of culture and tradition". 'Preservation' and 'sustainment' rather than dynamic action has been associated with minority languages. Limiting the scope of Tanzanian languages to these domains not only represents a very narrow view of language, but is also based on a problematic view of culture. As Bgoya says, "the erroneous notion that African culture is only its folklore, including its oral tradition, music, dance, rites of passage and their rituals, frozen in a kind of static idealised time and space, is not helpful" (Bgoya 2001:290). The idea that creativity on a high level, "using but not limited to traditional props and genres" (Bgoya 2001:290) might be realized using a minority language seems just as inconceivable to the policy makers as the use of these language in science and technology.

Assimilation processes affecting speakers of minority language have been intense on the coast as well as in urban areas. Children whose parents still spoke one of the minority languages often grow up with Swahili as their first language (Puja 2003:120). Minority languages with 20,000 and fewer speakers are under greater pressure of assimilation than those of more populous speech communities. Speakers of such languages also assimilate into other minority languages with greater numbers of speakers (Batibo 1992:88). In remote areas, children who have grown up monolingual in one of the minority languages have difficulties following classes that are taught in Swahili. In the case of speakers of non-Bantu languages, pupils have been found to have an inadequate command of Swahili even after years of schooling (Legère 2002:170). In monolingual environments, mother-tongue-based bilingual education would probably be the most promising option for present-day Tanzanian primary schools (Batibo 2006:279).

Tanzania's co-operation partners have shown limited concern about the linguistic challenges of carrying out development work in a multilingual society. The problem of bias against African languages is unfortunately not limited to nations where the systematic deprivation in social and cultural domains has led to a biased perception of potentials. It is also widespread in development organizations and networks where professionals would have ample opportunity to acquire more balanced information on linguistic and cultural conditions. However, in most aid agencies there is little sensitivity or consideration of the pressures that lead to decisions such as the one to continue the use of English as a language of education for official use. As a result, "education donors in Africa have mostly worked to strengthen ex-colonial languages" (Brock-Utne 2002:34). Development practice during the 1960s and 1970s, with modernization's emphasis on human capital and education, continued the colonial practices of providing specialized and technical knowledge in European languages. For example, the textbooks given to African students were originally created in Europe for European students. However, the practice of supplying inadequate Eurocentric textbooks did not cease with the end of the colonial era. In Tanzania, in its initial years after 1986, the English Language Teaching Support Project ELTSP provided textbooks produced in Britain for British students which were irrelevant to the Tanzanian context, but had been supplied for free. At a later stage, books authored by Tanzanians were also used, but again, the economic interests of the donor nation took precedence: Printing was assigned to British publishers instead of Tanzanian publishers (Brock-Utne 2002:36).

Many development experts regard the use of English in former British colonies as neutral or even beneficial. "There is a failure to problematize the notion of choice, and therefore an assumption that individuals and countries are somehow free of economic, political and and ideological constraints when they apparently freely opt for English" (Pennycook 1994:12). Development planners are often not aware of the problematic nature of asymmetric linguistic situations and do not inform themselves about policy measures that could help participants overcome language barriers. "'Development' researchers, including those specialising in education, seldom focus on language issues" (Philippson 2001:187). If language is addressed at all, it is usually relegated to the process of implementation rather than considered in long-term planning (Robinson 1996:30). The assistance of interpreters is taken for granted, but their work is not considered worthy of much attention or support. As Thomas Bearth and Diomandé Fan have pointed out, the translation process itself poses numerous problems for development work. It reinforces perceived social and cultural asymmetry, as development messages inevitably originate from outside language. It dichotomizes the processing of inferences, because listeners are forced to follow the translator's interpretation of the original message. It carries an anti-dialogical bias, as the activity of translation inevitably takes control of the agenda and hinders free negotiation of topics. Finally, it imposes constraints on utterability and face regulation. Critique or discussion of past negative experience with development organizations are likely to be avoided, as they carry a risk for those uttering them (Bearth and Fan 2006:280-283). Western experts are often ignorant of both the implications of complex linguistic situations and the languages involved. In many cases, they hide their incompetence behind a set of stereotypical negative attitudes that tend to take the shape of pseudo-academic arguments – many of which bear striking similaritiy to those used in colonial discourse more than half a century ago. These include, for example, anachronistic concerns about the alleged purity or impurity of languages and speculations about mysterious structural or lexical deficiencies in possibly all languages that are not part of the Western European school curricula. In addition to resulting from ignorance, the donors' arguments are also often motivated by tangible national interests. While there is no substantial lobby behind African languages, European languages continue to be promoted through respective donor nations. For example, funding for the English Language Teaching Support Project ELTSP was granted by the British government on the condition that English would be retained as a language of instruction in secondary schools (Roy-Campbell 2001a:153).

The continued dominance of ex-colonial languages is particularly worrying when considered from the perspective of democratization and popular participation (Mazrui and Mazrui 1998:99). As Birgit Brock-Utne points out, donors appear to be preoccupied with good governance and decentralisation but choose to ignore the fact that "some 90% of the people of Africa have no knowledge of the official language of their country, even though it is presumed to be the vehicle of communication between the government and its citizens" (Brock-Utne 2002:17). As a matter of fact, these are also the same languages donors use when communicating with the political leadership of African countries, a practice that has kept development co-operation intransparent to the majority of the population.

This historic perspective on the language situation in Tanzania has focussed on the exceptional status of Swahili. Although instrumentalized for colonial administration, it eventually became a powerful medium for the anti-colonial movement. After Independence, the postcolonial state turned Swahili into a symbol of socialist transformation. Ultimately, the language project turned out to be more successful than the political ideology of Ujamaa that had promoted it in the first place (Blommaert 2006:249). Swahili successfully replaced English in a number of public domains – however, the decisive step of making Swahili the language of instruction in secondary schools remains to be implemented. At the same time, the example of Swahili also illustrates the complex relationships between African official languages and minority languages. The postcolonial ideology of promoting Swahili in Tanzania has been coupled with a policy of actively discouraging the use of all other Tanzanian languages in all public contexts. Speaking minority languages has been considered equal to holding conservative and factionalist attitudes, whereas Swahili has symbolized progress and national unity. Just as there has been no status envisaged for any language apart from English or Swahili, neither have there been efforts made towards corpus planning for these languages, such as creating an orthography or working towards lexical expansion. The challenge is therefore to open spaces that go beyond the domain of 'home and traditional culture' for minority languages.

In Tanzania, as in other countries of Sub-Saharan Africa, a multilingual language policy and practice is often thought to be too costly. It is also frequently argued that African countries have more pressing problems. While both arguments seem convincing at first, empirical evidence opens up a different perspective. The actual cost of corpus planning, that is for example the expansion of the lexical base or the creation of text books, may be comparatively moderate, especially in light of the overall cost of the educational system. At the same time, there is ample evidence that education in a child's first language is by far the most effective form of learning, not only in the achievement of basic literacy and numeracy, but in the acquisition of all sorts of academic skills (Legère 2004:38; Brock-Utne 2002:7; Desai 2001:337). In contrast, learning in a language with which a child is unfamiliar poses numerous obstacles. Many of Africa's pressing problems are indeed closely related to these pervasive mechanisms of linguistic social exclusion (Webb 2004:111).

In development co-operation, there is little critical awareness of the problematic nature of discriminatory language policies and practices. This may be due to several factors. First, while there exist – admittedly often inadequate – instruments to deal with discrimination on grounds of gender or ethnicity, there are no established mechanisms for dealing with racism and its implications in practices of linguistic exclusion. Consequently, the problem of linguistic hegemony in aid networks is rarely addressed. Second, linguistic arguments have often been belittled when economic or technological progress is at stake. Third, the contributions of the academic debate have often been problematic, as these are not free of stereotypical perceptions of languages. As Saida Yahya-Othman critically remarks, multilingualism in itself has often been assumed to be problematic, with Africa being described as "the epitome of both underdevelopment and multilingualism" (1990:45). The task of linguistic corpus and status planning is therefore not only to develop and adapt languages, but also, to break through the cycle of negative stereotypes. Material deprivation and negative attitudes have effectively prevented most African languages from functioning in domains beyond the home and the local arena. There are exceptions, however, with Swahili presenting a notable example.

4.4. Language use and inequality in two agricultural development programmes

The particular sociolinguistic situation in Tanzania, as delineated above, creates specific opportunities and challenges for development communication. Without a doubt, the fact that one language is understood by more than 90% of the population constitutes an exceptional achievement by a language policy committed to broad popular participation in social, economic and political domains. However, some communicative bottlenecks typical of the postcolonial situation remain to be addressed. One major problem lies in the fact that programmes often rely on academic or technical knowledge – for example, improved seeds that require specific planting methods which are primarily available in English rather than Swahili. This fact in itself raises a number of issues, each of which probably needs to be addressed separately. First, despite several decades of "Farmer First" policy, RRA and PRA, knowledge and innovation originating in rural areas often still lacks recognition and acceptance. Second, there are few networks that facilitate the exchange of knowledge among rural farmers. Instead, if information is considered relevant by outsiders, it is then often documented in urban centres and in languages inaccessible to the peasant population. Third, even participatory programmes are to a large extent designed externally. Fourth, formal institutions of higher learning and research in Africa continue to rely on ex-colonial languages. As a consequence, farmers are rarely in a position to directly access information on innovative approaches, depending instead on aid workers' mediation. This poses several interrelating challenges for agricultural extension workers. First, there is the pedagogical aspect of getting ideas across in an intelligible and convincing manner. Second, processes of cultural adaption may be required. Third, there is a need for translation, a task for which aid workers are rarely specifically prepared or rewarded.

Another problem relates to the hierarchical nature of languages use in aid networks. Thus, it is presently rather unthinkable for Tanzanian development NGOs to forward applications or reports written in Swahili to donors and Northern aid agencies. Northern donors and development organizations usually accommodate the fact that they might need to use a language of wider communication rather than their own national language – a development that has been promoted by processes of integration among donors such as those co-ordinated by DAC-OECD. But this disposition seems strictly limited to *European* languages of wider communication. Tanzanian development NGOs co-operating with foreign partners have to forward all relevant documents in English. This, however, means that beneficiaries have no opportunity to review information which is passed on about them, or to obtain information on those parts of the aid network beyond the national framework. Again, their knowledge depends entirely on Tanzanian aid workers' willingness to share information with them. Additionally, even Tanzanian aid workers' knowledge about the organizational structures, objectives and self-image of their Northern counterparts often remains fragmentary, as information on the up-to-date state of policies and relationships between the ministry, donor agency and possibly development organization of the Northern co-operation country may not be accessible even in the English language. At times, Northern partners may consciously prefer to remain secretive about some issues, and use the linguistic cleavage to keep matters obscure. More often, however, the intrinsic bias is not consciously enhanced, but simply taken for granted. Northern aid workers gain experience by travelling and meeting partners from various backgrounds, whom they visit, support, monitor and evaluate. Their Southern counterparts have far less opportunity to travel in their jobs, and when these visit their Northern counterparts, they are rarely invited to assess their performance. Their lack of knowledge about the entirety of the aid system is in turn often an impediment to their gaining status as development experts. As these few examples show, linguistic obstacles and donor-recipient inequality are closely intertwined.

In the following, interviews conducted with aid workers and beneficiaries of two Tanzanian agricultural programmes will be discussed. The open qualitative interviews provide an idea of the diverse individual linguistic backgrounds involved. They also illustrate how complex attitudes towards languages are formed and contradictions accommodated. Finally, they also anticipate some of the deeper social rifts that emerge more conspicuously in the text analysis sections of the following chapters.

4.4.1. The Sustainable Rural Agriculture Programme (SRAP)

The SRAP was established as a Tanzanian-Austrian co-operation programme to promote rural development through a focus on improved organic farming techniques. Initiated in 1992, the programme targeted village youth in three places in North-Western Tanzania, offering them training as well as access to tools and implements. At the beginning of the research in 1994, groups of about 15-20 members had formed in two villages; in a third village, operations had been suspended after an unresolved theft of the programme's agricultural tools. The programme initially reached out mainly to men, who had undergone a year of training in agriculture and skills of various trades, such as masonry and carpentry. They formed a core group within the programme and were continuing common activities as the "Follow-up Group". At the time of research, efforts had been made to iniatiate a separate Women's Group, as the initial programme had failed to attract them. Additionally, a Youth Group had recently formed, with whom another cycle of year-long training had begun.

The SRAP was run by a team of three aid workers: two of them Tanzanians employed by the local Catholic Diocese, which functioned as project holder; one of them an Austrian employed by the Austrian implementing organization. The Diocese provided the administrative infrastructure, office space and supervision. The concept and design of the programme had been laid out by experts of the Austrian implementing organization, which also ran similar programmes in two other areas in Tanzania as well as in Zambia. The organization secured funding from the Austrian Government, paid the Austrian development workers, carried out monitoring and provided short-time experts. Its ideas of participatory development included the following:

> Planning: target group and local project holders contribute their models, visions and needs and we our possibilities and conditions of funding. This ensures that programmes are negotiated with the people concerned without pressure of time (IIZ 1994:1).

The above statement by the Austrian implementing organization rationalizes an asymmetric process of decision-making. It suggests that the actions of partners on both sides are determined by practical constraints. The target group and project holder have 'needs', while the Austrian organization has 'possibilities. The opportunity of actively shaping the programme is assumed to be primarily with the Tanzanian partners, as only they are seen to "contribute [...] models and visions". However, by referring very generally to "conditions of funding", a rationale for ultimate control of the Austrian organization is retained. Finally, the notion of "negotiating without pressure of time" suggests equality among the co-operation partners, where in fact there is none.

In everyday implementation, the Project Team had a pragmatic view of participation similar to that which prevails in many participatory programmes (cf Kelsall and Mercer 2003, Green 2000). The emphasis was on getting group members to take part in the programme's offers. A lot of effort was put into organizing and holding meetings in which beneficiaries and stakeholders were made familiar with the programme's objectives and activities. The limited scope of the programme – two groups of no more than 20 people each – and the commitment of the three aid workers attending to them meant that communication and activities were frequent and well-organized. As a result, there was intense participation in the sense that a stable group of people regularly took part in meetings and activities. However,

decision-making on important and principal issues remained largely in the realm of the team or the implementing organization; the extremely limited nature of participation in decision-making will be discussed in the next chapter.
Regarding the composition of the group, male farmers in their thirties were well represented from the beginning, whereas efforts to take women and younger men on board had been made rather recently, which meant that they also had little say in issues concerning the group as a whole.
Another challenge to participatory practice was inequality within the team which mainly reflected organizational affiliation to the respective 'donor' or 'recipient' side of the programme. The Austrian Agricultural Advisor had close contact with the implementing organization, which meant that he had more information and a greater influence on financial decisions within the programme. The Tanzanian Programme director was theoretically his superior in the Project Team, but in practice had less influence on the way the programme was implemented. The third member of the team was a Tanzanian Social Worker. She had only recently started working there, and was still coming to terms with the often contradictory patterns of decision-making and implementation. Inequality also manifested itself in the respective contracts and salaries team members received: The Agricultural Advisor was paid according to Austrian standards, whereas his Tanzanian colleagues received Tanzanian salaries.
As the Tanzanian project holder, the Catholic Diocese had a hierarchical organizational culture, which did not help much to encourage egalitarian communication. Additionally, interference such as the Bishop diverting the use of the project car for other undertakings of the Diocese were not uncommon, especially when representatives of the Austrian implementing organization were absent. The team occasionally considered operating independently of the Diocese by setting up a separate NGO as project holder. This plan was carried out by the end of the 1990s.

4.4.2. Linguistic preferences of individual actors (SRAP)

Beneficiaries: Members of the village groups are women and men aged between 20 and 40 years. Of the 18 villagers participating in various meetings in village M., 17 were interviewed, and of the 15 participating in the meetings in village T., 12 were interviewed. Most of them earned their living in agriculture, in addition to some minor activities in fishing, masonry, carpentry or blacksmithing. More than half of them stated that they lived in thatched brick houses, only a few had aluminium roofs, and fewer than half of the households involved owned radios. Yet they were not necessarily the poorest farmers in the village; the programme explicitly addressed those with initiative and a will to improve conditions in the village.
Both the women and men stated that they had completed 'Standard 7', that is, seven years of primary schooling. All 29 women and men interviewed stated

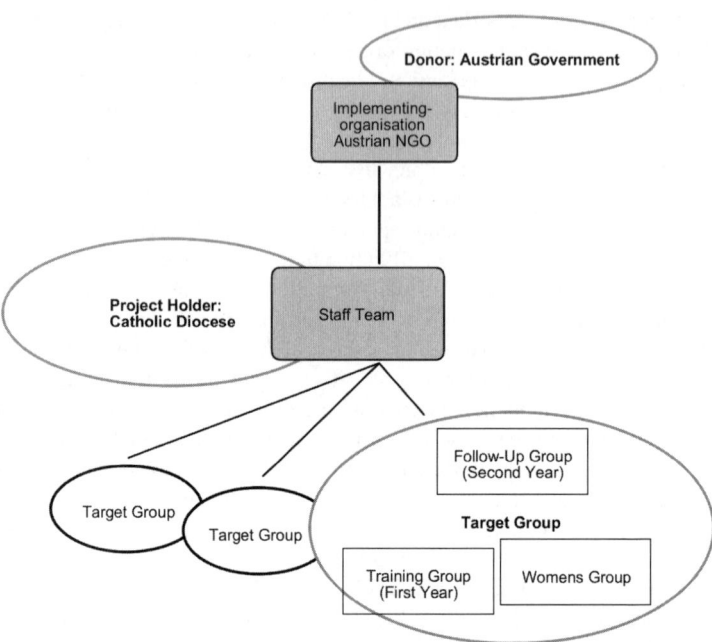

Figure 6: SRAP: Organizational Network

that they had had seven years of primary schooling, with the exception of two representatives of the village government who were in their fifties and sixties respectively, and had received only two years of schooling. Accordingly, all were at least bilingual, being fluent in their first language (Kwaya in the first village, Jita in the second) and Swahili. Of the two project groups, one woman and two men had received training outside the village after their primary education (typing, mechanics). However, due to financial constraints they had not completed their courses and had come back to the village. A few members stated that they had a little knowledge of English. Some said that, because of the similarities between Kwaya and Jita, it was also possible to understand a little of the respective other language. One mentioned that he understood some Luo, while another said he also understood Kabwa and Kerewe. Two group members said that because of the similarities between the languages they could understand some of the neighbouring languages, but not speak them.

The two languages Kwaya and Jita both belong to the Haya-Jita language subgroup (Bantoid, Southern, Narrow Bantu, Central, J, Haya-Jita [J.20]). Thanks to a high proportion of lexical similarities between the two languages, partial mutual intelligibility may be assumed. Figures on the number of speakers of minority languages in Tanzania are generally difficult to obtain, as Tanzanian cen-

4.4. Language use and inequality in two agricultural development programmes 141

sus data do not include information on linguistic or ethnic affiliation. The only source available, the Ethnologue, reports 217,000 speakers for Jita, and 102,000 for Kwaya. As Legère (2002) cautions, however, these numbers are the result of speculative projections of long outdated census figures, and therefore highly unreliable.

When asked about their linguistic competence, most people emphasized their first language and Swahili, but also mentioned – often partial – knowledge of other languages. Personal language competence was, for example, described in the following way:

> "I use Swahili, Jita and a little Luo. If a person speaks English I can recognize some of the words, a little." (Mimi natumia lugha ya Kiswahili, Kijita na Kijaluo kidogo. Kama mtu akiongea naweza nikatambua na baadhi ya maneno ya Kiingereza, kidogo) (Mr. B. Kasawe, farmer, 22/2/94).

> "The first language is Jita, the second Swahili, the third English – just reading it." (Lugha ya kwanza ni Kijita, ya pili Kiswahili, na ya tatu Kiingereza - kukisoma tu) (Mr. C. Mtaki, farmer, 22/2/94).

When asked about the use of these languages in everyday interaction, people mentioned a range of purposes for using both their first language, either Kwaya or Jita, and Swahili. Some described using the languages in separate domains. These usually coincided with those outlined in the official Tanzanian discourse, in which minority languages are designated as belonging to the realm of the home and culture, while Swahili is considered the language of work committed to progress and development, as well as official contexts.

> "When at home I use the home language – that is Kwaya." (Nikiwa nyumbani natumia lugha ya nyumbani - yaani Kikwaya) (Mr. R. Mbuna, farmer, 21/2/94).

> "If it is at home I use the indigenous language, Jita, but if it is at work we use Swahili." (Kama ni nyumbani natumia lugha ya kienyeji, ya Kijita; lakini kama ni kazini tunatumia lugha ya Kiswahili) (Mr. M. Kigeli, farmer, 22/2/94).

Many group members, however, point out that this separation is not a rigid one. If necessary or desired, languages other than Swahili may also be used in work contexts.

> "Of the languages, we use more Swahili. But if necessary you can also use the indigenous language, dialect. You can just use it, at work." (Zaidi kwa lugha tunatumia Kiswahili. Lakini inapobidi unaweza ukatumia hata lugha ya kienyeji, kilugha. Unaweza ukatumia tu, kwa kazi) (Mr. B. Kasawe, farmer, 22/2/94).

A pragmatic attitude predominates, where intelligibility is obviously the primary concern.

> "Yeah if I work, I mostly use Swahili language and Kikwaya for those who don't understand Swahili well." (Eeh nikifanya kazi / sana sana natumia lugha ya Kiswahili / na ya Kikwaya kwa wale wasioelewa Kiswahili vizuri) (Mr. R. Mbuna, farmer, 21/2/94).

"Not understanding Swahili well" refers in particular to problems some group members might have with unfamiliar technical language. Explanations in Kwaya or Jita are often preferred when new concepts are introduced – despite the fact that such concepts are often named by borrowing words from English or Swahili.

However, in meetings that address a wider public in the village, Swahili is likely to be used exclusively, especially when administrative or political village functionaries are involved. This is due to the legacy of the early decades after Independence when speaking minority languages in public was associated with factionalism. The Chair of the village government in village T., who was also involved in the SRAP programme, would only use Swahili for activities within the group.

> "If I work in the group, I use Swahili." (Nikifanya kazi kwenye kikundi natumia Kiswahili) (Mr. M. Ngoka, farmer, 2/3/94).

Other group members reported that they were more flexible, especially in situations where all participants had the same linguistic background – that is, they all spoke Jita or Kwaya.

> "(At) work, like farming, I use Kwaya, or at times Swahili, both languages." (Kazi, kama ya kilimo, natumia Kikwaya, au wakati mwingine natumia Kiswahili, lugha zote mbili) (Mr. M. Kilanya, farmer, 21/2/94).

> "Yeah, as here we work with one ethnic group only, we very much use our home language if at work. But if foreigners, who do not know our home language Jita, turn up, we use Swahili." (Eeh, kwa vile sisi huku tunafanya kazi kulingana na kabila moja tunatumia sana sana lugha ya kinyumbani tukiwa kazini. Lakini wakitokea watu wageni ambao hawajui lugha ya kinyumbani ya Kijita, tunatumia Kiswahili) (Mr. C. Lukolo, farmer 18/2/94)

But a flexible attitude to language choice does not only relate to the use of Kwaya and Jita at work. Some villagers also mentioned that Swahili is an option for them at home and within the family.

> "When I am with my family, I use two languages, Swahili and Kwaya." (Nikiwa na familia yangu, natumia lugha mbili, Kiswahili na Kikwaya) (Mr. M Ngoka, farmer, 2/3/94).

Asked which language he used at home, one group member said that he spoke Jita at home, but also Swahili in order to teach his children.

> "I use Jita. And Swahili for teaching the children." (Natumia Kijita. Na Kiswahili kwa kufundisha watoto) (Mr. C. Lukolo, farmer 18/2/94).

A closer look at the statements on language use reveals that, in fact, many speakers say that they use both languages in a variety of situations. Any view based on clearly separated domains for minority languages and Swahili, as expressed for example in the official "cultural policy" document, is obviously at odds with the far more complex patterns of overlapping language use that emerges here. What is consistent with the official language policy, however, is the way in which the use of the two languages is framed discursively. The use of Swahili is taken for granted and often presented as the first choice in communicative situations per-

4.4. Language use and inequality in two agricultural development programmes 143

taining to the development programme. In contrast, the use of Jita and Kwaya is seen as requiring explanation. Some of the arguments presented in this context include: Not all people may understand everything in Swahili; or the fact that the programme group is linguistically homogenous, so that nobody is excluded as a result of the use of Jita or Kwaya. Reference is also made to the informal nature of the work done within the programme, implying that the 'official' language Kiswahili is not necessarily required when doing ordinary farm work. In the same vein, it may also be noted that Swahili is simply referred to as 'lugha' (language), but Jita and Kwaya are furnished with attributes that emphasize the official view of their limited function. The most commonly used of these phrases is 'lugha ya nyumbani', (language of the home) and a similar idea is expressed in the term 'lugha ya kienyeji' (indigenous/local language). Finally, the expression 'kilugha' (dialect, slang) has a derogatory connotation. Despite this consistency with the present day political discourse in Tanzania, the women and men interviewed sketch out a pragmatic attitude to linguistic choice, in which the use of all languages at their disposal is conceivable in a wide range of contexts. Considering the complex interplay of factors mentioned – formality, situation, topic, competence of interactive partner and individual preferences – parallel use of both languages, as well as frequent language switching, must be anticipated. The exclusive use of one language, such as the restriction to Swahili in the context of formal meetings, is thus the exception rather than the rule.

<u>Staff:</u> Members of the project team use Swahili as their official working language. They also use English, especially when interacting with foreign co-operation partners, or when preparing written documents for them. In addition, English terms are frequently used for technical specifics, a practice that will be discussed in greater detail in the next chapter. As is common among qualified professionals in many fields in Tanzania, knowledge of Swahili and English is an indispensable precondition for the job. At the time of research, the Programme Team consisted of three people, the Programme Director, the Agricultural Adviser, and the Social Worker.

The Programme Director was a former teacher and church youth leader with additional training in community development. At the time of research he was 36 years old and employed as a development worker by the Diocese. When asked about his knowledge of languages, he named his first language, then Swahili and English:

> "First, I know my mother tongue, Luo, then I know Swahili, and I have a fair knowledge of English." (Najua lugha ya mama kwanza, Kijaluo, halafu najua Kiswahili, najua na Kiingereza kiasi) (Mr. L. Nyange, Programme Director, 28/2/94).

Excellent knowledge of Swahili was taken for granted in the context of the programme. And indeed, many Tanzanian professionals who grew up speaking one of the minority languages de facto use Swahili like a first language, especially if they live and work away from their home area. Some hardly use the language they grew up with, speaking Swahili both in public and private contexts. Usually, their children grow up with Swahili as their major language, resulting in a growing number of Swahili first-language speakers in Tanzanian urban areas. The mobility of educated professionals all over Tanzania has significantly contributed to the spread of Standard Swahili all over the country. Although the Programme Director's home area is not far from M. town where he lives now, and his wife also has Luo as her mother tongue, they state that they primarily speak Swahili with their children.

With regard to English, the Programme Director has a good working knowledge – he easily communicates in the language in the various situations needed, whether in the weekly planning meeting, in interaction with foreign project partners, or on trips abroad. Yet he grades his knowledge as 'kiasi' (fair) and has readily participated in English courses as part of his on-the-job-training. He has some of his letters going overseas corrected by people with a better command of the language. This importance given to the correct use of the English language is due to the fact that in development co-operation, career opportunities depend very much on competence in English. Improving proficiency is always an advantage.

As became evident later in the interview, he also has some knowledge of Jita and Haya, the languages spoken in the programme area, as well as Kurya. He acquired these languages in the village where he grew up.

> "There are other languages which I understand well, for example Kurya; if a person speaks Kurya, I understand and answer her/him. And then I can understand Kwaya, because I was born there, therefore I can also speak a little Kwaya. I also understand Jita, if a person speaks, I can answer. I understand about half of the words in Jita." (Kuna lugha nyingine ninazoweza nikazisikia vizuri kwa mfano Kikurya; mtu akisema Kikurya namwelewa na nitamjibu. Halafu na Kikwaya naweza nikaelewa kwa sababu nimezaliwa huko, kwa hiyo naweza nikasema na Kikwaya kidogo. Kijita pia nasikia - mtu akisema naweza nikamjibu. Karibu nusu ya maneno ya Kijita naweza nikayasema) (Mr. L. Nyange, Programme Director, 28/2/94)..

Knowledge of minority languages is valued, as it may help to establish contact with people in the village who have difficulties with Swahili.

> "When I am in the villages I use more Swahili, and sometimes I can mix it with indigenous languages, especially when talking to the elderly." (Ninapokuwa vijijini ninatumia Kiswahili zaidi na wakati mwingine naweza nikachanganya na lugha ya kienyeji hasa ninapoongea na wazee) (Mr. L. Nyange, Programme Director, 28/2/94).

Villagers certainly appreciate the fact that an outsider makes an effort to speak their language, and development organizations are aware that this can be an important factor in establishing trust. But this is as far as it goes: Knowledge of these minority languages is not a precondition for the job, nor are there incentives to reward it, and the organization makes no effort to improve its staff's knowledge in that respect. In Tanzania, efforts to develop languages and enhance peoples's competence go towards Swahili and English, and development organizations are no exception. It is therefore not surprising that the Programme Director, who knows several Tanzanian languages, makes little effort to pass on this knowledge to his children, instead speaking Swahili with them.

The Agricultural Adviser is an Austrian development worker who was employed on an international contract by the Austrian partner organization. He was 32 years old, had trained as a teacher and acquired a specialisation in organic agriculture. In addition to his first language German, he was fluent in English and had a fair knowledge of Kiswahili. Having formerly worked in Papua New Guinea, he also spoke Papua New Guinean Pidgin. Additionally, he mentioned some passive knowledge of French and Spanish.

> "O.K., concerning languages, first of all there is German, my mother tongue, English, I know Pidgin, Pidgin-English and Swahili. I have also learnt but forgotten French, and I once began to speak Spanish." (Okay, Sprachen, das ist einmal Deutsch, meine Muttersprache, Englisch, Pidgin kann ich, Pigdin-Englisch und Kiswahili, vergessen aber gelernt habe ich Französisch und Spanisch habe ich auch einmal angefangen zu reden) (Mr. R. Fischer, Agricultural Advisor, 3/1/94).

Commenting on his everyday use of these languages in the working environment of the programme, he said that he spoke Swahili when in the villages, and Swahili and English in the working environment of the Diocese. In staff discussions, he used Swahili as far as his ability went, switching to English when having difficulties expressing himself.

> "Here in M. I mainly speak two languages, that is Swahili, which I mainly use in the villages, I speak only Swahili in the villages, and I use English and Swahili at the level of the Diocese. [...] In the office we mainly speak Swahili, when I find it difficult, I change to English" (Da in M. spreche im hauptsächlich zwei Sprachen, das ist Kiswahili und das hauptsächlich in den Dörfern, ich rede nur Kiswahili in den Dörfern und Englisch und Kiswahili auf dem Diözesanlevel [...] Im Office (= im Team I.M.) reden wir hauptsächlich Kiswahili, wenn ich mir schwer tue, dann wechsle ich ins Englische (Mr. R. Fischer, Agricultural Advisor, 3/1/94).

It is obvious that Fischer has made efforts to master Swahili and communicate in this language, the main working language of development in Tanzania. As is not unusual for foreign aid workers, the organization employing him had arranged for a Swahili course at the beginning of his work period in Tanzania. Fischer actually spent a lot of time with the farmers on the fields, and he was able to communicate his ideas without an interpreter. Despite all the readiness he shows about adapting to the linguistic situation, his statement is not free from a common bias foreign learners tend to have about Swahili and its communicative potential. On the one hand, he admits that his Swahili competence is limited, as he says that he switches to English when he encounters difficulties in the team. On the other hand, he implies that he knows enough Swahili to discuss all relevant issues in the village in Swahili. One possible implication is that in rural or informal contexts, the language does not need to be much elaborated, and that the expression of more sophisticated ideas in urban or professional contexts is adequately done by switching to English. But such assumptions, which are commonly voiced by many European or North American speakers of Swahili, may actually be a misunderstanding. For Tanzanian professionals, switching from Swahili to English usually constitutes one of several options, and the incidence of switches varies with audience and context. In contrast, in the case of foreign learners, code-switches to English are mostly triggered by their linguistic incompetence in Swahili. Yet instead of being regarded as an individual's lack of competence, this is considered adequate practice which everybody seems to follow, and is even popularly explained away with alleged intrinsic deficiencies of the language. Practices of language use that are experienced in everyday interaction are taken as given and unchangeable, their historic and political contingencies ignored. So although foreign learners of Swahili, especially those working in development co-operation, often express a positive attitude towards strengthening the position of Swahili or minority languages, they are rarely aware of underlying social and cultural hierarchies created and maintained by prevalent patterns of language use.

The third member of the team, the Social Worker, had joined the team only recently. At the time of the research she was in her mid-twenties and employed by the Diocese. Her first language is Chagga. As in the case of the Programme Director, Swahili was the language she mainly used in work contexts. Although her English was good and she received all her secondary and tertiary education in English, she views her ability rather modestly: "Kiingereza kidogo" (a little English).

> "I understand Swahili, and then I understand a little English and the mother tongue – Chagga. When I am at work, I use Swahili." (Nafahamu Kiswahili halafu nafahamu Kiingereza kidogo na mother tongue - Kichagga. Nikiwa kazini natumia Kiswahili) (Ms. A. Msemwa, Social Worker, 17/2/94).

Like the Programme Director, she has completed an English course as part of her on the job training. In fact, she uses a lot of English at work, too, especially in team meetings, when interacting with Austrian project partners and when writing up protocols or reports. However, she expresses reservations about her English language skills, implying they could be insufficient. She is obviously not concerned about her Swahili competence, which she considers sufficient.

Because their two major working languages are second languages, all three project team members have a principal interest in improving their language skills by learning from each other. Thus, there may be several factors at work that motivate the use of English or Swahili in the interaction among team members. At the same time, this reflects asymmetrical North-South relations in which, despite the prominent role of Swahili in Tanzania, development organizations primarily support their staff in improving their English competence. Despite being the official working language, Swahili does not enjoy a similar effort, for example in the form of advanced courses or terminology development. Usually, aid workers are left to fend for themselves with knowledge acquired from primary education or, in the case of foreigners, short-term courses, experience gained on the job and the occasionally available publication in Swahili. Finally, one can also say that the lack of recognition given to minority languages by the government is mirrored in development organizations: While there may be individual awareness or commitment to using these languages, no formal recognition is given to those staff members who apply these languages in development work.

4.4.3. The Rice Cultivation Mechanization Programme (RCMP)

The RCMP was initiated in 1985 and based on co-operation between the Ministry of Agriculture in Zanzibar with the Food and Agricultural Organization (FAO) and the African Development Bank (ADB) as financial donors. The programme focussed on rainfed rice cultivation which has a long tradition on the islands of Zanzibar and Pemba. Rice is a highly valued staple food that is in great demand, especially in urban areas. It is not difficult to find a market for locally-produced rice – the challenge is to compete with cheap imports. The programme aimed at increasing production by making modern technology accessible to farmers. Know-how, improved seed, fertilizer and mechanical implements were to be made available for sale or rent at subsidized prices. The programme was designed to reach out to peasant farmers in four rural areas (Muanda, Kilombero, Cheju and Pemba).

148   4. Sociolinguistic background: Participation and language use

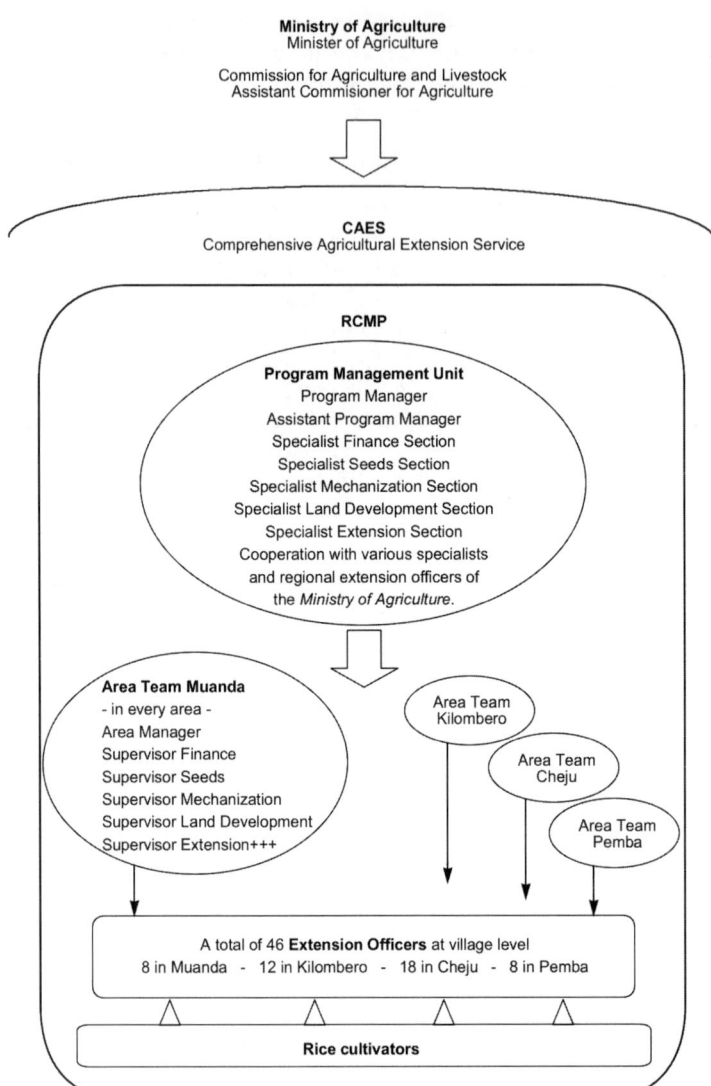

Figure 7: RCMP - Organizational Network

In its organizational set-up, the RCMP was part of the Ministry of Agriculture, its staff being regular employees of the Ministry who had been assigned to the programme. Regarding financial planning and technical implementation, the programme primarily answered to the donors, as it was largely independent of the

4.4. Language use and inequality in two agricultural development programmes 149

Ministry. RCMP management had financial resources and implements such as vehicles, motorbikes, tractors and other agricultural machinery at its disposal to which other sections of the Ministry had no access. The programme's staff included a 'Management Unit' comprising 'specialists' in several fields, as well as four subordinate 'Area Teams' with a comparable allocation of professionals, most of whom were university graduates. On a third level, the programme relied on Extension Officers for its everyday implementation. Extension Officers were usually local farmers who had undergone short-term agricultural training. They provided an essential communicative link between the rice cultivators and the technicians.

During the initial programme phase from 1985 to 1990, a team of four engineers from a British consulting firm for agricultural development, comprising a project manager, an extension specialist, an agricultural engineer and a service manager, provided technical assistance. From the beginning onwards, Tanzanian counterparts worked together with them. When the foreign technicians left in 1990, they took over the management of the programme which was to last until 1995. Apart from the central Project Management Unit, the programme had area teams in each of the four fields in which it operated.

At the beginning of the 1990s, the Comprehensive Agricultural Extension Service (CAES) of the Ministry of Agriculture had undergone organizational restructuring as part of an FAO project (Nöst 1997:239). One aspect of the restructuring effort had been to co-ordinate all foreign-funded programmes working with extension agents (Hanak, Nöst and Schicho 1995:33). At the time of research, the process of integrating various programmes working with extension agents was still ongoing. In general, working conditions within the CAES could be characterized by low pay, lack of incentives and scarce means of transport. One major motivation for employees to retain their jobs was the offer of advanced training, which, however, resulted in frequent study leaves that interfered with work efficiency. Despite their often limited experience with conditions relevant to agriculture in Zanzibar, foreign technicians working with the CAES often received salaries that exceeded those of their Tanzanian colleagues and usually had more attractive working conditions (transport, benefits). At the time of research, monthly salaries for the Tanzanian staff of the RCMP's Programme Management Unit amounted to approximately 40 US$. In interviews, staff members reported that they made their living through their own farming activities rather than their official job.

As pointed out in Chapter 2, participartory approaches such as the PRA have emerged in search of alternatives to the inflexible and hierarchical bureaucracies of agricultural extension common to the state-centred development policy of the 1960s and 1970s. By the 1990s, the Ministry of Agriculture in Zanzibar, like other governmental bodies in recipient countries, had officially adopted participatory approaches in its interaction with peasant farmers. The British consulting firm it worked with proclaimed that its principle was to assist with the design and implementation of locally-owned and delivered development strategies. However, despite this formal commitment, and despite the reforms the Comprehensive Agricultural Extension Service had undergone in the early 1990s, implementing people-centred development within the bureaucratic structure of the Ministry remained a challenge. In particular, discouraging material conditions led to a situation where at times "rather than providing services for clients, [activities] merely serve[d] the reproduction of the bureaucratic system" (Nöst 1997:238).

Due to its specific task and independent funding, the RCMP had developed a separate infrastructure, including its own office space, cars and motorcycles – a vital resource in the working environment of the CAES where "the better part of the [staff's] working hours is spent negotiating transport needed to visit the villages and to attend to planned events"[12] (Hanak, Nöst and Schicho 1995:33). Outside funding had also facilitated the core element of programme activities: the supply of know-how, improved seed, fertilizer and tractor services to the farmers at subsidized rates.

Administering its own budget had given the RCMP a certain autonomy in planning and implementing its activities, and had contributed to a dynamic organizational culture. Frequent interaction with the rice cultivators, such as eliciting their opinions and feeding them back into the planning process, was part of the organizational self-concept. The RCMP was more effective in realizing the Ministry's commitment to participatory approaches than other programmes or units. At the time of research, the programme was in its final phase. The phasing out of funding, scheduled for 1995, was imminent. For the programme's staff this meant that they would eventually return to the usual difficult working conditions within the Ministry. Regarding the programme itself, the perspective of having to do without external finance raised the question of long-term sustainability. In interviews, rice farmers complained about poverty and harsh living conditions, stressing the importance of government support. They argued that they often did not have the money to buy inputs even at subsidized rates. The issue repeatedly featured in the recorded management team meetings: Would the farmers be able to afford the advanced technology even if they had to pay market rates, and would they be able to maintain higher levels of production? In this critical phase, actors in the Project Management Unit frequently made reference to opinions voiced by rice cultivators in order to emphasize their arguments in management meetings.

In commenting on the everyday implementation of participatory practices within the programme, staff members argued that regular meetings with beneficiaries were essential. Technicians assumed that the opportunity to assess and evaluate was available to programme staff and beneficiaries alike, and that the "[the meetings'] intention [...] was to examine and consider how we performed in the past season, maybe where we did not do well so that we could adjust ourselves and

---

12   Der Großteil der Arbeitszeit wird der Tätigkeit gewidmet, die Verfügung über ein Transportmittel zu verhandeln, das notwendig ist um die Dörfer aufzusuchen und die geplanten Veranstaltungen abzuhalten.

4.4. Language use and inequality in two agricultural development programmes 151

where we did well, to be able to congratulate ourselves" (madhumuni yake [...] ilikuwa ni kutafakari na kuzingatia huu msimu uliomalizika tumekwenda vipi labda wapi hatukufanya vizuri ili tuweze kujirekebisha na wapi tumefanya vizuri kuweza kujipongeza) (Mr M. Ramadhani, 27/7/94). Listening to the peasants' opinion and taking note of their needs was repeatedly emphasized. However, there was no intention of enabling beneficiaries to take part in the planning and decision-making on programme activities.

When asked about the programme's interaction with the Ministry, the Programme Manager emphasized his unrestricted access to high-level meetings. "The Ministry [...] usually just calls, invites a large number of actors to these meetings. As a result, you will find that there is a smooth, very good exchange of information in the Ministry" (wizara, [...] huwa inawaita, inawaalika watendaji wengi wengi tu katika vikao hivi. Kwa hivyo utakuta mtiririko wa taarifa ni mwepesi sana ni mzuri katika wizara) (Mr. K. Salum, Programme Manager, 25/07/94). As an autonomous part of Tanzania, Zanzibar has a separate Ministry of Agriculture, whose scope of activities is limited to the islands of Unguja and Pemba. As a result, both formal and informal communication is intense and actors tend to be familiar with each other.

Apart from meetings, formal communication emanates from the Programme Management's duty to report to senior administrators in the Ministry. Activity reports and documents on meetings among the team and with beneficiaries are regularly forwarded. Direct contact between representatives of the Ministry and farmers may also be established in the form of occasional visits by the former in villages.

> "Even the minutes of the meetings we hold with the villagers are forwarded to the Ministry. [...] Now they get to understand exactly what we talk with these farmers, which opinions they hold, they get it directly. It is therefore easy for them, if they have a programme of visiting agricultural areas, and talking to the farmers, they already have information about the affairs of the farmers there". (Mr. K. Salum, Programme Manager, 25/07/94).

> (Hata dondoo, minutes za mikutano tunayofanya na wakulima tunazipeleka wizarani. [...] Sasa wanapata kuelewa hasa, sisi tunazungumza nini na wakulima hawa, wao mawazo yao yako vipi, wanapata moja kwa moja. Kwahivyo ni rahisi wao kama wanakuwa na programme kutembelea maeneo ya kilimo, na kuzungumza na wakulima, wanakuwa tayari wamekuwa na taarifa kuhusu mambo ya wakulima wale pale)

While the quantity of information provided may be substantial, communicative channels generally follow top-down hierarchies. Managers give out assignments and directives, and expect progress reports in return. As the following quotation from one of the extension supervisors shows, 'up' and 'down' are common notions in describing relationships in the network:

> "Well our usual job is to instruct our Extension Officers, we brief them about the kind of work and how we proceed [...] we receive directions from our superiors, they give them to us, and we pass them on to the Extension Officers. And the Extension Officers, [information about] their activities in the fields, their usual work, reaches us in the office, and we send it up. [...]

Our section manager there receives [the information] from above, passes it on to us, and we hand it down. (L. Yusufu, Area Extension Supervisor, 11/8/1994).

(Aaa kwa kweli kazi zetu za kawaida ni kuwaongoza wale Mabwana Shamba wetu wale tunawafahamisha jinsi ya kazi na utaratibu wetu unavyoenda [...] tunapata maagizo kutokana na wakuu wetu pale wanatupa sisi halafu sisi tunapeleka pale kwa Mabwana Shamba. Na Mabwana Shamba shughuli zao wanazofanya kule mabondeni sasa kazi za kawaida zinatufikia sisi ofisini tunazipeleka juu. [...] Mkuu wetu pale kwenye section yetu pale ambaye yeye ndiyo anapewa kutoka juu halafu anatupa sisi tunaziteremsha chini)

4.4.4. Linguistic preferences of individual actors in the RCMP

The analysis of interviews and meetings for this study focuses on data obtained from the RCMP Project Management Unit (for data on other sections of the Ministry of Agriculture see Hanak 1998, Nöst 1997, Hanak, Nöst and Schicho 1995). No questions on language use were included in the interviews carried out with extension officers and peasant farmers, as they seemed to operate in a monolingual Swahili environment. Of the eight staff members in the Programme Management Unit of the RCMP, five were interviewed. These were highly trained specialists in agriculture, project management and the fields of their respective sections (finance, mechanics etc). Most had worked with the Ministry of Agriculture for decades, participating in various short courses or post-graduate courses in the country and abroad. The first language of all members of the Programme Management Unit was Swahili. English was their second language, acquired mainly through secondary and tertiary education as well as on the job training.

"I understand English, but the mother tongue is Swahili. Then English and Russian. I studied in Russia for 6 years. And a little Arabic." (Ninaelewa Kiingereza, lakini mother tongue ni Kiswahili. Halafu Kiingereza, Kirusi. Nimesoma Urusi 6 years, na Kiarabu kidogo kidogo) (Mr. M. Chumbe, Senior Mechanic, 27/7/94).

"My original language is Swahili, and I get on with English very well." (Lugha yangu original ni Kiswahili, na Kiingereza ninakipata vizuri sana) (Mr. L. Musa, Accountant, 28/7/94).

The official working language was Swahili. When working with foreigners, English was spoken. Moreover, English was widely used in reports and in communication with the financial donor, the African Development Bank. Reports to the Ministry of Agriculture could also be made in Swahili. As made explicit by the assistant manager, there was an awareness that, even when Swahili was spoken, one or the other English word might be inserted.

"The official working language here is Swahili, but as we work with foreigners here sometimes we use English. If we are amongst ourselves we do not use English. Except that we know that in conversation it just happens that we insert some words in English." (Lugha rasmi hapa ya kufanyia kazi ni Kiswahili, lakini kwa vile tunafanya kazi na wageni kwahivyo baadhi ya wakati tunatumia lugha ya Kiingereza. Tukiwa kati yetu hatutumii Kiingereza. Isipokuwa tunajua katika mazungumzo tu hutokezea tena tukaingiza neno moja moja kwa Kiingereza) (Mr. O Ramadhani, Assistant Manager, 27/7/94).

The Accountant described how the official working language changed to English when the British experts were present during the first five years of the programme.

> "Right now, since these foreign experts from the technical assistance, those who came from England, left, we do not use English. When they were here, the language was English only, in the meetings, up to the meetings we used English." (Kwa sasa hivi toka kuondoka wale wataalamu wa kigeni wa technical assistance wale ambao walitoka Uingereza, hatutumii Kiingereza. Walipokuwapo wao ilikuwa lugha yetu ni Kiingereza tu, kwenye mikutano, mpaka kwenye mikutano tulitumia Kiingereza) (Mr. L Musa, Accountant, 28/7/94).

While the official language was Swahili, one engineer pointed out how, de facto, the job required constant switching between Swahili and English. The notion of 'mixing' the two languages frequently occurred in comments on language use.

> "At work I use two languages, I mix [...] Swahili and at times English, because often when you work you deal with some foreigners, for example at the project we had technical assistance from England. So, some don't know Swahili, so we speak English with them. And writing reports, we mix Swahili and English reports. So we mix, depending on whom you talk with and where." (Kwenye kazi natumia lugha mbili nachanganya [...] Kiswahili na mara nyingine Kiingereza, kwa sababu mara nyingi unapofanya kazi unashughulika na watu wengine wa kigeni kwa mfano katika mradi sisi tulikuwa na technical assistance kutoka Uingereza. Kwa hiyo wengine hawajui Kiswahili kwa hiyo tuzungumza nao Kiingereza. Na kuandika ripoti tunachanganya ripoti ya Kiswahili na ripoti ya Kiingereza. Kwa hiyo tunachanganya kutegemea nani unaongea naye na wapi.) (Mr. M Vuai, agricultural engineer, 7/7/1994).

Zanzibar is one of the original areas of the Swahili people, and all staff members stated that Swahili was their mother tongue. The issue of Tanzanian minority languages was therefore not relevant to the RCMP programme.

4.4.5. Conclusion: Language competence and training in the working environment

The challenge of analyzing statements about linguistic preferences and language use is that speakers do not constantly reflect on the linguistic varieties they use. As a result, there may be considerable differences between what people think or say they do and what they actually do. It is therefore important to supplement the information provided in the interviews with data on concrete interaction, which will be the focus of the following two chapters. The following issues emerge when one makes a preliminary assessment of the statements made in the interviews:

In the SRAP programme, development workers were offered language courses paid for by the employer which could be attended during working hours. The Tanzanian employees attended advanced courses in English, and the Austrian development worker, who had primarily been employed to work directly with peasants in the villages, completed an extensive basic course in Swahili. Within the team, the Austrian expert stated that he could always resort to English when he felt that his competence in Swahili was insufficient, a practice his Tanzanian colleagues readily accommodated. During short-term visits by foreign experts who usually did not know Swahili, Tanzanian team members were expected to translate for them. No measures, such as, for example, courses, were considered to promote the use of Swahili in higher-level management or technical domains. Nor were there any formal incentives to motivate employees to acquire Kwaya or Jita – efforts in these respects depended entirely on the initiative of individual staff members.

In the RCMP, the British experts who were present during the initial phase of the project relied exclusively on English as their working language. Theirs was a position of higher-level management, and their Tanzanian counterparts in the management section were expected to speak English with them, as well as help out with translations when this was required. The Tanzanian members of the project management unit were university graduates who had received their secondary and at least part of their higher education in English. After the departure of the British experts Swahili became the primary language of interaction in meetings, however staff members commented that they often 'mixed' English and Swahili. Again, there were no measures to promote Swahili in high-level technical or managerial contexts. Given that Zanzibar is one of the home areas of the Swahili people, it would probably not have taken much effort to develop an adequate terminology.

The organizational policies and cultures in the two development networks offer two examples of how, in different ways, linguistic hierarchies are reinforced and English continues to be unduly privileged. This can not primarily be explained by the fact that development co-operation involves international relations, a domain where the use of English could be expected. Foreign correspondence, reports and interaction with short-term visitors obviously has to be handled in English. But the larger part of work takes place in a Tanzanian, Swahili-speaking environment. Despite the fact that Swahili is the official working language in both the Catholic Diocese of M. and the Ministry of Agriculture in Zanzibar, the dominant position of English seems uncontested – particularly in two aspects.

The first is that Tanzanian development workers communicating among themselves in Swahili report that frequent use of English technical terms is common, a practice that is of course rooted in the Tanzanian educational system. The prominent role of English is, however, also linked to the idea that high-level technological and social progress is the domain of English rather than Swahili. This becomes clear in a widely practiced dual approach: Swahili and to a very limited extent even minority languages may play a role as a means of communication in reaching out and informing beneficiaries, but Swahili is not promoted at the higher levels of development management. This is a pity, as a unique possibility of making higher levels of development management transparent and accessible to popular participation is lost. While staff members are supported in improving their competence in English, no comparable input is given to facilitate the use of Swahili in high-level domains. Blaming the situation entirely on the education sector is problematic, as students and their parents can only be motivated to learn a language they experience as functional in important domains. The development sector could serve as a model in this respect.

The second point concerns the presence of foreign development workers with long-term contracts. A decreasing number of those who work at the 'grass roots' level are encouraged to learn Swahili, however the majority of 'experts' working at higher levels are not required to adapt to their linguistic environment. Instead, Tanzanians are expected to adapt to the needs of (mostly European or North-American) colleagues, whether this means switching to English or acting as interpreters. Tanzania has gone a long way toward establishing an African language in a number of formal working domains. Yet Western experts, who operate in English all over former 'anglophone' Africa, expect to do the same in Tanzania, where English still has the status of an official language. This raises the question of whether a postcolonial 'recipient state' has any other option than to comply with such expectations. Development experts are a substantial part of the aid industry in which the donors, and not the recipients, determine conditionalities.

Code choice in development programmes works to maintain hierarchies: By preserving English in a high-level position, management units and teams effectively prevent beneficiaries from having access to flows of information and decision-making. The adoption of participatory principles through development organizations has not affected these practices. As pointed out in chapter three, participatory principles are mostly about improving outreach and raising the commitment of target groups, which includes using their language(s) in development interaction. It does not mean that hierarchies and management practices are remodelled, which would entail more innovative linguistic politics than merely retaining colonial patterns of using African languages in rural areas and using English in technological matters and high-level administration.

The issue of minority languages only features in the SRAP programme set in Western Tanzania. The RCMP Zanzibar is in one of the few settings in Tanzania where the the population's first language is Swahili, which also enjoys official status. Some staff members and beneficiaries state that they have made individual efforts to acquire neighbouring minority languages apart from their first languages. In the case of development workers, however, this aspect of their qualification receives informal recognition at best. Fluency in Kwaya and Jita is acknowledged as a means of establishing trust between beneficiaries and staff. There is, however, little consideration of the possibility that using these languages in programme activities might encourage the participation of villagers who would otherwise remain excluded

5. Swahili-English codeswitching in development communication in Tanzania – an obstacle for participatory development?

5.1. Introduction

Practical considerations seem to determine the norms of language use in development networks. In Tanzania, the use of Swahili is taken for granted for communication in rural areas. At grass-root level, using English is not a viable option, as peasant farmers are not proficient in the language. In development organization's staff meetings Swahili is the working language together with occasional codeswitching to English. In communication with donors, English is used. However, many of the taken-for-granted rules about language use in development networks are a result of the dominant role of English in the country. In addition, donors and Northern implementing agencies enforce the use of English in several ways. For example, in the SRAP programme in Musoma, staff meetings were usually conducted in Swahili, including occasional codeswitching to English. Written records of these meetings were, however, kept in English. This facilitated accountability towards the donor, but precluded a similar openness towards rural target groups. More examples could be added: It was usual for target group members and aid workers to accommodate the linguistic needs of foreign partners, either by switching to their preferred language or through providing a translation. The reverse rarely happened: project applications, annual reports and other essential programme documents were rarely compiled or translated into a language that would make them accessible to the target group. Likewise, beneficiaries had little say in the way their voices were edited and represented in and beyond the development network.

In short, one could generalize that in development work in Tanzania the use of Swahili is in the interest of beneficiaries, while the use of English excludes them. In contrast, foreign donors benefit from the use of English, as it gives them access to programme information. But how about the case for Swahili-English codeswitching, where lexical material from English is embedded in Swahili discourse? Is this just an expression of creative language use in which the dominance of English is widely resisted except for a few decorative elements one could easily do without? After all, Standard Swahili is widely used in public and official domains in Tanzania. Or is codeswitching a strategy of exclusion, an expression of higher status and a factor aggravating hierarchies? Or is it evidence of a deficiency in individual linguistic competence, prompted by lexical gaps in Swahili that are filled with English? In view of the present educational system in Tanzania, where Swahili is neglected in higher education, this would not be surprising. Or does the myth that African languages are inappropriate for communicating technical innovations still play a role here (Neke 2003:186)? While such popular interpretations have fortunately been discarded in sociolinguistics since the 1960s, they still pervade donor and Western expert circles, whose members are rarely sufficiently informed about or competent in languages that are not part of European school curriculars.

Codeswitching is a complex phenomenon that has been a major focus of sociolinguistic inquiry. Starting from the realization that codeswitching is an expression of bilingual competence and of speakers' ability to creatively draw on a variety of linguistic resources at their disposal (Gumperz 1982), detailed studies on the meaning and structural properties of codeswitching in a variety of contexts have been carried out, a number of them in East Africa (Eastman 1992, Blommaert 1992, Myers-Scotton 2002, 1993a, 1993b). Documenting Swahili-English codeswitiching patterns in a variety of informal situations, Myers-Scotton argues that Kenyans competent in English use Swahili-English codeswitching to convey both peer solidarity as well as higher education and professionalism. In Tanzania, codeswitching has been found to be a common practice in formal contexts such as teaching and learning. In secondary-school classrooms, some teachers who lack adequate competence to explain subject matters in English switch to Swahili – a reasonable alternative to confronting students with inadequately understood ideas in an often incomprehensible variety of English. But teachers who are proficient in both languages use codeswitching, too: a common strategy is to present a topic in English and repeat every sentence in Swahili to make sure that students follow. In her research in secondary schools, Halima Mwinsheikhe found that 89% of the teachers she interviewed 'admitted' using Swahili in class, primarily to explain key concepts (Mwinsheikhe 2003:138). Swahili was also used in order to encourage participation of students who would not dare to contribute or ask questions in English (Brock-Utne 2002:42). Additionally, teachers often used Swahili when handing out assignments, admonishing students or engaging in other aspects of classroom management. Yet the change to Swahili did not prevent students or teachers from inserting technical terms in English. On the contrary, there was usually little effort made to integrate Swahili technical vocabulary. As Mwinsheikhe observes, "they [teachers and students] seemed not to be searching in their memories for a Kiswahili translation" (Mwinsheikhe 2003:138). As Blommaert (1992:58ff) documented, frequent codeswitching is a typical part of 'Campus Swahili' spoken by staff and students at the University of Dar-es-Salaam. "English elements in a Swahili matrix flow of speech bear a potenial for marking importance, newness of relevance in an utterance. [...] More relevant chunks of information, such as topic, may therefore be marked by means of borrowing or codeswitching" (Blommart 1992:62). As the examples from secondary schools and university show, codeswitching is commonly used both by proficient bilinguals and by speakers who are not fully competent in the two languages involved. In organizational contexts, codeswitching may serve various functions: it may mark a change in topic, or the arrival or departure of participants in a conversation. It may be used as a means of emphasising an aspect, or strategy of conveying authority. At the same time, it may also be prompted by a perceived or real lexical gap in a speaker's linguistic competence (Winford 2003:108). Individual lexical gaps in Swahili technical vocabulary in Tanzania can be attributed to the educational policy of having secondary and higher education in English rather than Swahili. For this research, it is important to maintain a principal distinction between codeswitching as a means of expressing stylistic virtuosity or as a strategy of compensating lexicals gaps, as they have different implications for linguistic policy. Specifically, the empirical analysis in this chapter will focus on differences of language use by aid workers in staff meetings and in meetings with beneficiaries, as what may be an 'inclusive' language use in a professional context may work out to be 'exclusive' in meetings where peasant farmers constitute the main target group.

5.2. Theorising codeswitching in the East African context: the work of Carol Myers-Scotton

The work of Carol Myers-Scotton constitutes a major contribution to the study of codeswitching both from a linguistic and social perspective (Myers-Scotton 1993a; 1993b; 2002). Myers-Scotton has not only developed a linguistic modell of codeswitching patterns, but also worked systematically to investigate the reasons why speakers choose to switch languages under certain social and situational conditions. In her empirical research, she has concentrated on Kenya and Zimbabwe. Reflecting on the social motivation for codeswitching between Swahili and English by Kenyan workers, she argues:

> "In the work situation, the most salient attribute of English is without doubt 'plus education', especially in those white-collar jobs where expertise acquired via education is at a premium. Any worker would be glad to index his or her expertise via use of English. But the problem is that English has other attributes which may or may not be equally salient when the qualification 'interactions with peers' is added to 'work situation'. English has the additional attributes of 'plus authority' (through its association with anglophone Africa's colonial heritage as well as through the language-use patterns of those Africans who are now in authority). It also has the attribute 'plus formal' (via its use in public and/or formal settings or for formal topics). These other attributes mark English as a device for increasing social distance among participants, or emphasizing a power differential. The typical worker who knows English well does not want to give up the image of being well-educated, but neither does he or she wish to be pretentious with peers. [...]
>
> What to do? Many urban African workers take the middle course and use combinations of linguistic varieties in such an interaction type; i.e. they engage in a switching pattern between the variety which makes their expertise salient and a variety which indexes high solidarity. [...] (The fact that both varieties are relatively neutral in regard to 'ethnicity', is of much additional importance)" (Myers-Scotton 1993a:72-73).

The social context described here explains why codeswitching may be considered a neutral linguistic choice in many African urban settings. "Far from violating norms of linguistic behaviour, codeswitching can be the norm itself, the only appropriate mode of speech in many common situations" (Swigart 1989:84). Yet the situation varies in the different East African countries: In Tanzania, the use of Swahili and English in some respects carries other connotations than it does in Kenya. In Kenya, English is more widely used and Swahili may in some contexts be associated with a derogatory meaning, as it is "the language spoken in a downward fashion by a superior to the wananchi, 'the masses' or to any subordinate individual" (Myers-Scotton 1993a:86) – obviously a legacy of colonial linguistic practice. By contrast, in Tanzania, the status of Swahili has been promoted to an extent that it has become the preferred choice in many formal contexts. Still, many parallels can be drawn on the sociolinguistic situation of the two countries, such as the primary role of English in higher education, science and technology.

Investigating codeswitching as a widespread communicative practice in urban areas in Africa, Myers-Scotton has developed the "markedness modell" to account for social motivations behind patterns of codeswitching. Assuming that language choice conveys a message about the communicative situation it takes place in, she defines those instances where societal norms on the expected code for a particular communicative event are met as "unmarked", and those where these norms are violated as "marked". For example, the general social expectation for university students in informal situations at Nairobi campus is to use Swahili and English. Swahili-English codeswitching is thus a neutral or unmarked choice for interaction in such cases. However, two students who decide instead to speak to each other in Kikamba, which happens to be their first language, are perceived as excluding others who do not know the language. Would the students change for example to English, they would be regarded as elitist, distant or formal. In both cases the switches would be regarded as marked choice.

Analysing empirical material from data in Nairobi and Harare, Myers-Scotton documented the widespread use of codeswitching as an unmarked choice. She argues that codeswitching in many urban African contexts is a strategy of neutrality, in which "it is the overall pattern of codeswitching which provides the social message, not any single individual switch. [...] Individual switches in unmarked codeswitching may have specific rhetorical functions within the conversational text, of course; it is just that each one does not index a new social message" (Myers-Scotton 1993a:149). In contrast, with marked switching, "it is the point of the switch itself (and what follows) which has social import (Myers-Scotton 1993a:149)." In regard to marked switching, the model is particularly revealing as to why some instances of codeswitching carry the potential of communicating conflict and discord: Violating social norms on language use potentially conveys social distance, contempt or excludes participants.

Illustrating the normality of codeswitching in everyday interaction, the "markedness model" significantly extends the work of Gumperz (1982:55, 75-81) and

5.2. Theorising codeswitching in the East African context: the work of Carol Myers-Scotton

other sociolinguists who had already pointed to the creative use of codeswitching and discussed a number of its social functions.

Altogether, the markedness modell comprises four related types of codeswitching: 1) codeswitching as a sequence of unmarked choices 2) codeswitching itself as the unmarked choice 3) codeswitching as a marked choice and finally 4) codeswitching as an exploratory choice; this classification is supplemented by the 'virtuosity' and 'deference' maxims, additional tenets that account for the influence of language proficiency and politeness considerations (Myers-Scotton 2002:16ff).

The modell has its merits in drawing attention to the fact that codeswitching is a strategy used primarily by competent bilingual speakers. It shows how in multilingual environments, codeswitching is often an expected (unmarked) choice, while in some instances, it can also fulfil distinct (marked) interactive functions. These are important insights, not the least because popular opinion continues to associate codeswitching primarily with individual linguistic incompetence.

From the perspective of critical applied linguistics, the model's major weakness lies in its approach towards social norms on code choice. While the author emphasizes that code choice is socially contested, the underlying sociological model assumes a static situation. In particular, there are summary descriptions of speakers' attitudes to code choice that suggest a homogenous outlook rather than conflicting interests. The fact that in Kenya and Zimbabwe, African languages are largely excluded from professional contexts, is presented as given rather than questioned in its historic and political implications. Consequently, Myers-Scotton locates codeswitching largely in informal settings, taking for granted the primacy of English in formal, professional and technical contexts. In Tanzania, where from the 1970s onwards a committed policy in favour of Swahili challenged the postcolonial linguistic order, historic contingencies differ. To account for the Tanzanian linguistic situation, a more differentiated approach is required, even though it may not conveniently feed into a binary (marked/unmarked) model. However, instead of unduly simplifying the range of motivations behind linguistic choice, this could open a perspective on the range of personal and social objectives negotiated through code choice.

Regarding language structures, linguists widely agree that codeswitching is never an arbitrary mix of two languages, but governed by grammatical rules like any other form of speech. What is contested, however, is the extent to which rules pertaining to the languages involved play a role in various forms of codeswitching. In order to account for the structural aspects of intra-sentential codeswitching, Myers-Scotton developed the Matrix Language Frame Model (Myers-Scotton 1993b) that sees one language as determining the morpho-syntactic properties of the utterance. The role of the other language is restricted to providing certain lexical categories. The Matrix Language Frame Model differentiates between dominant language, i.e. the matrix language and the embedded language.

There are three types of codeswitching constituents under the model:

➢ mixed constituents which consist of morphemes of both participating languages, the matrix language and the embedded language;

➢ matrix language islands, constituents consisting of only matrix language morphemes; and

➢ embedded language islands, constituents consisting of only embedded language morphemes (Myers-Scotton 2000:205)

The matrix language is usually the one the speaker is more proficient in, often, but not necessarily her of his first language. It is also the language that in a certain social setting is the expected (or "unmarked") choice for a communicative event. In many cases, the matrix language is also dominant in the society at large. But as Myers-Scotton remarks, "any discussion of the nature of the matrix language is complicated by the fact that matrix language assignment is dynamic. [...] a change within the same conversation is possible" (Myers-Scotton 1993b:70). At any given point in a conversation, however, there can be only one matrix language.

In regard to her Swahili data from Nairobi, Myers-Scotton remarks that in the case of "multiple groups (with different first languages) engaging in codeswitching, not everyone's first language can be the matrix language; only one language must surface as the matrix language" (Myers-Scotton 1993b:218). Swahili in this context is regarded as a "neutral solution" between speakers of different other first languages.

The Matrix Language Frame Model predicts that morphosyntactic constraints pertaining to the matrix language will structure mixed constituents that combine the matrix and embedded language. For example, the System Morpheme Hypothesis claims that if system morphemes are required in mixed constituents to signal system relations, they will be matrix language system morphemes (Myers-Scotton 1993b:70). In a sociolinguistic environment where Swahili is established as a matrix language, we could thus expect that English bound morphemes are not used with Swahili stems. In her Nairobi data, Myers-Scotton found no Swahili or English nouns or verbs inflected with English affixes in Swahili-English mixed constituents (Myers-Scotton 1993b:109).

Myers-Scotton's models on the linguistic and social implications codeswitching have been widely discussed and critiqued, especially in regard to their validity in other social and linguistic environments (for example, Boussofara-Omar 1999, Muysken 2000). This brief overview over some of the relevant concept does not aspire to enter the details of that debate. Its main intention is to shortly present some aspects of Myers-Scotton's work this study draws on, such as the notion that codeswitching may surface as a neutral, expected choice, and that it may be used to express certain interactive messages such as emphasis or authority. In regard to structural aspects of codeswitching, the study follows Myers-Scotton's approach of not making a principal distinction between single-lexeme and other

forms of intra- and intersentential codeswitching (Myers-Scotton 1993a; 1993b; 2002).
Going beyond Myers-Scotton's approach to codeswitching as a phenomenon of urban informal communication, this study also anticipates that codeswitching may be used as a strategy to fill lexical gaps in individual speaker's competence in workplace interaction. The next section focuses on Tanzania's efforts at extending Swahili's lexical base to adapt the language for use in professional environments, and to the social challenges involved in such an undertaking.

5.3. Lexical borrowing and terminology development

"Borrowing" lexical material is a common language contact phenomen, especially in languages of wider communication. More than 75% of the words in present-day English are borrowed from other languages (Winford 2003:29). Borrowings 'enrich' the recipient language with material from other languages and expand speakers' choices of lexical and stylistic expression. Technical innovation is often accompanied by specific vocabulary, and speakers can display their learning and expertise by resorting to specific expressions (Winford 2003:35). Borrowings from other languages can be used by monolingual speakers without any knowledge of the "donor" languages involved. Borrowings are often, but not necessarily, integrated into the morphology and phonology of the matrix language. While there are principal differences between borrowing and codeswitching, concrete examples at times prove difficult to classify. Myers-Scotton asserts that "a continuum exists between borrowing and all forms of codeswitching material so that codeswitching and borrowing are not distinct phenomena" (Myers-Scotton 1992:21, cf also Eastman 1992:1). Part of the difficulty of distinguishing borrowing and code-switching is related to the fact that in multilingual societies, there are often no clear-cut boundaries between monolingual and bilingual speakers. It is widely held that monolinguals can engage in borrowing, but not in codeswitching. However, concrete examples show that it may be difficult to establish whether a particular speaker is bilingual or not. Myers-Scotton illustrates this problem with the example of a Malawian peasant farmer in conversation with a visitor whose mother originated from the same village. The conversation was in Chitumbuka, until the visitor revealed that he is a university lecturer by profession. On this point, the peasant started to insert English expressions into the conversation. As Myers-Scotton argues, it makes little sense to enter "the quandary of defining the speaker as bilingual or monolingual" (Myers-Scotton 1993b:193; incident reported by Lupenga Mphande from the University of Malawi). The prevalence of codeswitiching in a society and the individual habit of participating in this practice are of greater importance than proficiency in the languages involved. Standard seven school leavers or secondary school drop outs have some knowledge of English, and patterns of language use may individually differ.

Languages integrate or 'borrow' lexical material from other languages following various patterns. These include morphological and phonological adaption and loan translations (calques), blends with borrowed lexical stems or morphemes. Often, lexical material is borrowed when new concepts or items are introduced into a speech community. Alternatively, innovations may be named through creative processes such as the coining of neologisms or the extension of the meaning of existing concepts (Winford 2003:45). All these phenomena of lexical extension occur naturally among languages in contact. They may, however, be systematically advanced as part of language planning efforts.

Recognizing the importance of accessible linguistic resources in education, Swahili terminology development has been one of the priorities in language planning activities in Tanzania (Senkoro 2004:15). Activities included the compilation of terminological lists, translations of scientific texts, and the preparation of text books for primary and secondary education (Legère 2004:41). Initially the National Swahili Council (Baraza la Kiswahili la Taifa - BAKITA), an institution founded in 1967, was instrumental in corpus planning activities. During the eighties, the role of BAKITA was largley taken over by the Institute of Swahili Research (Taasisi ya Uchunguzi wa Kiswahili – TUKI). Language planning activities for Swahili resulted in a "dynamic lexical development" (Legère 2004:40) including the development of particular terminologies and the standardization of the language.

In lexical development, various approaches and procedures have been used over the last decades. In the following, a short summary of the methods for lexical expansion is given (cf Ohly 1987, Samsom 1988, Legère 2004, Kiango 2004).

> In coining neologism, lexicographers may attribute a distinct semantic value to any syllabic formation that conforms to the phonological criteria of the target language, although this is rarely done arbitrarily. Usually, lexemes used in the process are more or less descriptive, referring to shape, characteristic or use of the object to be named. For more complex concepts, various lexemes representing different aspects of meaning are put together in verbal or nominal phrases or compounds. For example mzizi-pau = aereal roots and stems (mzizi = root, pau = rafters, poles carrying the roof) (Akida 1973, quoted from Kiango 2004:6).

> Deletion of morphological elements as well as clipping or omission of lexical constituents may be used to avoid clumsy or lengthy expressions (Ohly 1987:225ff) in neologisms and derivations. For example kiua + wadudu = kiuwadudu (insecticide) (Kiango 2004:12).

> Semantic extension of existing terms. This is a common strategy in colloquial language use. For example ndege = aeroplane (extended from the original meaning bird) (Kiango 2004:11).

- ➢ Derivation: Much of Swahilis conceptual richness and subtlety is expressed through derivation. Verbal and nominal derivation is a particularly productive and important source in lexical development (Mochiwa 2004). For example: sumaku (magnet), usumaku (magnetism), sumakisha (magnetise), jisumakisha (auto magnetise), usumakishaji (magnetisation) (Mtesigwa 2004:4, Ohly 1987:226).

- ➢ Borrowings from Swahili dialects, Bantu languages and other African languages. As part of language planning efforts, such "internal" borrowings have received much support as a laudable effort to preserve the "African" character of the language. In practice, however, the number of newly introduced internal borrowings in Swahili is rather limited. In some cases, meanings are extended to introduce new aspects into existing concepts. For example Ikulu (in Gogo: House of elders in charge) -> state house (Ohly 1987:242).

- ➢ External borrowings are mostly from Arabic, English or Latin. Historically, borrowings in Swahili mostly originated from Arabic, but also from other languages such as Persian, Hindi, Portugese, German and Turkish. At present, English borrowings dominate contexts of scientific and international terminology. Borrowings are adapted phonologically and morphologically, with Swahili orthography following pronounciation. For example "baiskeli" from English bicycle, "ikweta" from English equator (TUKI 2001).

- ➢ Loan translations (calques) are a specific form of borrowings. For example "kiwavi jeshi" from English "armyworm". In some cases, loan tranlations communicate another than the intended meaning; in this case they are better replaced by free descriptive coining.

Corpus planning activities are an attempt to accelerate, optimize and standardize language contact phenomena. For corpus planning to be successful, it has to be linked with respective status planning, to insure dissemination and implementation in institutions of learning, workplaces and public institutions. The most important test all terminology needs to pass is the acceptability by the user. A terminology list that is not distributed and put into practical use will fail to have an impact on language development. Educational institutions have a primary role here – one major reason why the use of Swahili in higher education would be so important. In short, one could say that Swahili successfully became an official language in Tanzania due to its being the language of instruction in primary education countrywide. Similarly, the lack of political will to introduce Swahili at the level of secondary and university education undermines the use of Swahili to the remaining social domains.

At present, the neologisms originating from various sources result in at times confusing synonyms for one and the same concept. The inaccuracy in turn alienates speakers and feeds into existing prejudices against Swahili and other African languages not being adequate for use in science and technology. Lack of regional co-ordination also poses a problem here; but as pointed out above, the more important factor is the language of instruction used in the educational system.

For the rural agricultural context, there are specific actors who are important in the dissemination of standardized terminology: Apart from schools, these include the agricultural extension service, media such as journals or radio, as well as development agencies. The acceptance of the new terms is a complex process that is both dependent on existing communicative structures as well as instrumental for enhancing them. In recent years, some of the Tanzanian advocacy organizations have made remarkable efforts to support Swahili lexical development in the domain of their primary activities. For example, the Tanzania Gender Networking Programme (TGNP) provides an explanatory list of key concepts in gender and feminist activism in Swahili (www.tgnp.co.tz). Some policy papers relevant to the PRSP process have been translated to Swahili. Acceptance and negotiation of terminology is obviously a major challenge: after all, development communication should not only consist of a 'reach out' to the target group, but also facilitate dialogic encounter.

5.4. Bilingualism and codeswitching in formal meetings: attitudes and language use

To gain an overview over codeswitching practices in development networks, a first outline of opinions expressed in interviews as well as evidence from recorded conversations was compiled. This overview raised further questions, which guided the analysis of the text examples.

In short, the following statements on attitude and motivation for language choice were made in the interviews: Aid workers preferred to use Swahili because it was their official working language, everybody could understand it and it was the expected language in interaction with the rural target groups. They also said that they spoke it better than any other language. Aid workers expressed commitment to promoting Swahili as a participatory means of communication in development work. As to the reasons for speaking English, they stated that is was the language of higher learning and of technical knowledge. Moreover, it was indispensable in communicating with their foreign colleagues. In both networks, Tanzanian aid workers had collaborated with foreign aid workers, and both had mentioned that this had made them use English in formal meetings. Some aid workers also commented on codeswitching, explicitly stating that they mixed Swahili and English in everyday interaction. Repeatedly, technical terminology was mentioned as a major reason for using English as well as for codeswitching to English.

5.4. Bilingualism and codeswitching in formal meetings: attitudes and language use

Regarding the cursory analysis of the recorded conversations, the following initial picture was obtained: Generally, codeswitching was a regular but not too frequent occurrence. By far the largest part of grass-root level meetings and staff meetings were conducted in Standard Swahili. In staff meetings, Swahili was used as the main language of interaction, with Swahili and Swahili-English codeswitching representing unmarked choices. In grass-root level meetings, Swahili was used. Codeswitching to English occasionally occurred but often represented a marked choice: as peasant farmers hardly spoke any English, codeswitching to this language had to be accounted for, otherwise it was likely to cause offence. The usual pattern of codeswitching in staff meetings was intrasentential codeswitching, where an occasional single-lexeme switch was embedded into an otherwise Swahili matrix text. Intersentential codeswitching, in contrast, was rare, occurring only in two meetings within the whole data sample. The respective two meetings had themselves been exceptional as during the course of these meetings, English had been extensively used by a foreign aid worker. In sum, this initial assessment of attitudes and language use raised the following additional questions:

- ➢ What is the relationship between the use of technical language and codeswitching to English?
- ➢ How are technical matters communicated at grass-root level?
- ➢ What is the relationship between the communication with foreign colleagues and codeswitching to English?
- ➢ How do individual speakers adapt to different communicative situations?
- ➢ Which role do language competence and lexical gaps play in codeswitching?

In the following, seven text passages will be discussed in detail to find some answers to these questions. They were selected to illustrate different aspects of language use in stakeholder and staff meetings.

5.4.1. Rural development communication as a Swahili domain

The first example was taken from a rural meeting. Although this passage did not include any instances of codeswitching, it was included into the analysis to illustrate the use of technical terms at grass-root level. The text itself is a summary of a group discussion on resources, problems and possible solutions in agricultural work. The results of the discussion were noted down in a protocol, which the group's Chairperson, Mr. Kasawe, read out at the subsequent meeting. Being part of a written document, the wording is more carefully chosen than in oral spontaneous speech, which would rarely contain such dense listings of abstract and technical concepts.

Example 1

Kasawe:[1] [...] baada ya maswali hayo wajumbe walianza kujadili kila swali na kutoa majibu yake xx na kutoa majibu ya kila swali / kuhusu nyenzo wajumbe walisema kwamba / nyenzo walizonazo ni kama ifuatavyo: maji, mashamba ya kutosha, watu, virutubisho, mashamba mapya, pembejeo, mbegu / xxx / utaalamu, juhudi, ushirikiano /
baada ya kumaliza hilo waliingia katika swali la pili / katika swali hili wajumbe walianza kutoa matatizo yanayowakabili ili kupata jibu hatua zipi zichukuliwe / walisema matatizo hayo ni kama yafuatavyo• / ukame, wanyama waharibifu, ukosefu wa nyenzo rahisi za umwagiliaji, ugonjwa katika mimea, mashamba yaliyochoka, ukosefu wa virutubisho, wizi /
wajumbe walisema kwamba hayo ndiyo matatizo yanayowakabili / kwa hali hiyo — / kwa hali hiyo waliona kwamba hatua za kuchukuliwa ni hizi / kilimo cha umwagiliaji kwa kutumia nyenzo rahisi, ushirikiano katika — xxx, ushirikiano — kupambana na wanyama waharibifu, utumiaji wa utaalamu katika kilimo hasa kupambana na magonjwa yanayoshambulia mimea, kama vile kupumzisha ardhi, kubadilisha mazao, kuchanganya mazao, +++ kilimo cha mseto, utumiaji wa mboji, kilimo cha matuta, uchaguzi mzuri wa mbegu bora zinazostahimili ukame na za muda mfupi /
M4-SRAP:1

Kasawe: [...] after these questions the delegates started discussing each question and (possible) answers xx and giving answers to each question / concerning the resources the delegates said that / the resources they have are as follows: water, enough farmland, people, fertilizers, new fields, agricultural supplies, seed / xxx / expertise, zeal, co-operation /
after finishing this one they entered the second question / in this question the delegates started to give the problems they face in order to get the answers as to which steps should be taken / they said that the problems are as follows / drought, pests, lack of cheap implements for irrigation, plant diseases, depleted soil, lack of fertilizers, theft /
the delegates said that these are indeed the problems they face / because of this - / because of this the steps to be taken are as follows / irrigation farming with cheap implements, co-operation in xxx / co-operation – fighting pests, using expertise in farming especially in fighting plant diseases, such as letting land lie fallow, mixing crops, +++ mixed farming, use of compost, contour farming, fine selection of excellent seed that is drought-resistant as well as fast-growing [varieties]/

Most of the technical terms occurring in this passage were nouns that represented one of the multiple patterns of coining, derivation, semantic extension or borrowing typical for lexical formation in Swahili: "Nyenzo" originally denotes "raw materials"; its meaning in contemporary usage is extended to "resources" and "means of production". "Pembejeo" (agricultural supplies) is a specific coining. Derivations such as "virutubisho" (nutrients/fertilizers) [abstract noun derived from "rutuba" (fertility) and verb "rutubisha" (make fertile) with causative verbal extension plus class 8 prefix] are particularly common, another example being "umwagiliaji" (irrigation) [abstract noun derived from verb "–mwaga" plus applicative verb extension, with class 11 prefix]. Another frequently used pattern is the noun group with connective: "Kilimo cha mseto" (mixed farming) [noun group; noun kilimo derived from "–lima" (dig) and prefix class 7, noun "mseto" derived from verb "–seta" (mash) and prefix class 3], "kilimo cha matuta" (contour farming) [noun group; noun "tuta" indicating a raised bed for planting, the meaning in agricultural contexts is extended to contour farming]. These examples illustrated that technical terms for agriculture were widely available and in use. Some terms are realized as descriptive relative clauses, for example "mbegu bora zinazostahimili ukame" (quality drought-resistant seed) "mashamba yaliyochoka" (depleted soil) or "magonjwa yanayoshambulia mimea" (diseases that affect plants / plant diseases). "Ugonjwa katika mimea" (diseases in plants / plant diseases) is an alternative to the latter term. "Utaalamu" is a borrowing from Arabic, integrated into noun class 11, denoting an abstract. Some of the paraphrases used here obviously originated in the intention to use simple wording for effective communication. Understandable language is as much a product of common effort as the results of the discussion it is used to convey.

This first example illustrates that technical discussion in standard Swahili is an everyday occurrence in target group meetings: Both aid workers and members of the target group discussed technical issues in Swahili.

Table 1: Analysis of Swahili technical terms in Example 1

Swahili technical terminology	
nyenzo (resources)	semantic extension "raw materials" -> "resources, inputs"
virutubisho (fertilizer)	derivation "rutuba" (9/10) -> v. "rutubisha" (causative) -> noun class 8
pembejeo (agricultural supplies)	specific coining
utaalamu (expertise)	borrowing of Arabic origin -> Integration into noun class 11 to denote an abstract concept
umwagiliaji (irrigation)	derivation from verb "–mwagilia" -> integration into noun class 11
kilimo cha mseto (mixed farming)	noun group; noun "kilimo" derived from "–lima" (dig) and prefix of noun class 7, noun "mseto" derived from verb "–seta" (mash) and prefix of noun class 3
kilimo cha matuta (contour farming)	noun group; noun "tuta" indicating a raised bed for planting, the meaning is extended to contour farming
mbegu bora zinazostahimili ukame (quality drought-resistant seed)	descriptive relative clause
mashamba yaliyochoka (depleted soil)	descriptive relative clause
magonjwa yanayoshambulia mimea (plant deseases)	descriptive relative clause

5.4.2. Negotiating language use and activities for the week

The second example was taken from a SRAP staff meeting. The focus of conversation was on formalities of the programme director's working contract. The linguistic pattern in this meeting can be summed up as "usually mostly Swahili, but at this point in time with an unusually large share of English". In particular, Mr. Fischer, the Austrian aid worker, used English extensively. The other team members responded either in English, Swahili, or, as Mr. Nyange, the programme director, by intersentential codeswitching between the two languages.

Example 2:

Nyange[2]: ya / they will do it this week / nijaribu kumwuliza M. **if he has a chance this week** kati ya Alhamisi na Ijumaa **at least to report also this** / *(kimya)* / sababu mimi kwa kweli **I feel I need to go to Dar es Salaam because** last week nilikutana na mtu wa S. / ananiambia / inaweza ikanipata mimi / **its two month they don't know whether I am working here or I am where** / **because I don't have a permission of** serikali / **so I am not happy to work** / xx / sifurahi: kufanya kazi / **I need to go** /
Fischer: so / unapendekeza nini? / **but it depends when you want to go** / **when I know that you want to go on a certain day** / sawa / then tell me +++ /
M8-SRAP:31

Nyange:[3] *ya / they will do it this week* / I should try to ask M. *if he has a chance this week* between Thursday and Friday *at least to report also this / (silence)* / because me seriously *I feel I need to go to Dar es Salaam because* / last week I met a person from S. / he told me / it can get me / *its two month they don't know whether I am working here or I am where* / because I don't *have a permission of* the government / *so I am not happy to work* / xx / I am not happy at work / *I need to go* /
Fischer: *so* / what do you suggest / *but it depends when you want to go* / *when I know that you want to go on a certain day* / OK / *then tell me* +++ /

In the above example, codeswitching was not in any way motivated by considerations of an adequate technical terminology. Codeswitching at the level of the clause, as mentioned in the introduction, was a rare occurrence in the whole data sample. In the example here, Nyange used it in response to a contribution by Fischer, the foreign aid worker, that was entirely in English. By using intersentential codeswitching, Nyange negotiated language use: by shifting freely between Swahili and English at the clause level, he signaled that he had no problem to continue the conversation in English; at the same time, he also invited his conversational partner to shift back to Swahili. Codeswitching often has echoic aspects, and code choices that find the acceptance of other participants are mirrored. Intersentential codeswitching is an expression of professional in-group identity – only development workers, but neither beneficiaries nor foreign co-operation partners have a good enough command of both languages to participate in this free shifting between languages. Individual switches may also serve the function of emphasis, the occasional repetition further emphasizing the importance given to an assertion, for example as in "I am not happy to work / xx / sifurahi: kufanya kazi".

Table 2: Overview Swahili-English codeswitching in Example 2

Swahili-English Codeswitching	
they will do it this week	intersentential
if he has a chance this week	intersentential
I feel I need to go to Dar	intersentential
because last week nilikutana na mtu wa S.	intersentential + intrasentential
because I don't have a permission of serikali	intersentential + intrasentential
Etc.	

5.4.3. Personal style, technical terms and development jargon

The next example was taken from a weekly staff meeting in the RCMP in Zanzibar. The conversation was about planning activities within the program: testing ploughs for the preparation of land for rice cultivation. Mr. Salum, the manager of the programme, had a habit of frequently switching to English for single lexemes. The following example, which contains an English expression in about every other line, was typical for his language use in team meetings.

Example 3:

Salum: Ni sahihi / hilo wazo zuri / hasa Mferejini kule / zile *plot* ndogondogo / ni vizuri kidogo kuendelea na hizi *trial* / ni *testing* tu ya majembe / nafikiri bora kufanya hivyo / nani Z. kuliko kuendelea na kupanda / kitu muhimu zaidi ni kujua / ni kupata taarifa kuhusu uzuri wa jembe katika kutenda ile kazi yenyewe / tusiende katika suala la kupanda na kuna mambo ambayo huko hii *team* iliyopo haiwezi kufanya lolote zaidi / kwa hiyo twende hapa hapa kwenye mambo yetu ya ku*test* jembe, wakati, xxx nini *time,* pengine hata wakati wa kulima una umuhimu wake kwa upande wa jembe / ukiangalia *moisture content* ya ardhi yenyewe kwa nyakati tofauti inawezekana kuna tofauti /
Nakusudia kusema kwamba / bora tuendelee na hii **testing** kama tulivyoiandaa mwanzo, tusiende kwenye kupanda / jengine, kulikuwa na mambo matatu muhimu hapa / habari ya mbegu hasa kwa Pemba, haya mawasiliano na bara bora tuyafanye mapema mapema, kwa sababu kama tutafanikiwa kupata mbegu basi, kwa ajili ya Pemba ni **source** hiyo tu, kwa sababu hawa jamaa wanavuna kuanzia **August,** sasa hatujui utaratibu wao na upi wa kuuza lakini, kwa kuwa tushawasiliana mwanzo, kwamba tutakuwa na haja kubwa ya mbegu huenda pengine wakakubali kutupatia **between August September,** kwa Pemba itakuwa hatujachelewa / kidogo **at least** tutawahi /
M21 RMP:8

Salum: This is correct / that is a good idea / especially there in Mferejini / these rather small *plots* / it is good to continue these *trials* / it is just *testing* the ploughs / I think it is best to do that / who Z. instead of continuing to plant / it is more important to know / to get information concerning the quality of the plough in doing the job itself / we should not go into the issue of planting while there are things that this *team* there can do nothing much about / so lets go right here into our affairs of *testing* ploughs / the time xxx what, *time,* maybe even the time (timing) of digging is of importance for the plough / if you look at the *moisture content* of the soil at different times it can be different /
I mean to say that it is best to continue with this *testing* of ploughs / lets not go into planting / otherwise, there were three important things here / the issue of seeds especially for Pemba / it is better to have this communication with the mainland rather early / because if we manage to obtain seed / for Pemba there is only this *source* / because these people harvest starting from *August,* now we don't know their plan and which one to sell / but because we have already communicated in the beginning / that we will require large amounts of seeds / maybe its possible that they will agree to provide us *between August September* / for Pemba we will not be late / somehow, *at least,* we will be in time /

In this passage, Swahili was the dominant 'matrix' language into which English terms were embedded. Many of the switches concerned technical terms, for instance the expression „moisture content". As mentioned before, the use of English originates from the fact that most technical literature or training on the subject is in English. English terms are available as alternative expressions – and their knowledge was shared by all participants present. A closer look at the terms occurring in the sample reveals that these were concepts for which Swahili equivalent terms were in everyday use – such as for example *plot, trial, testing, team, time* and *source*. Considerations of style were more important here than the need to fill lexical gaps. In the passage where Salum actually paused to search for an English word, this did not concern a technical term but the everyday notion of "time": "wakati, xxx nini time, pengine hata wakati wa kulima una umuhimu .... " (time, what, *time,* maybe even the time of digging is important …). The repetition of the term in English merely served to highlight this aspect as important; neither the use of an English term, nor its repetition in Swahili, is caused by a lexical gap or an individual lack in linguistic competence.

Verbal stems of English origin are frequently inflected with Swahili tenses and aspects in processes of borrowing and codeswitching (Petzell 2005:92). Combinations of foreign word stems with Swahili affixes as in "kutest" (to test, to experiment) could also be interpreted as loanblends rather than codeswitching; however, our text corpus does not show a repeated use of them.

The names of the months like August and September are established borrowings in Swahili; however, while they are usually phonologically adapted to Swahili (and orthographically represented as Agosti, Septemba) in the example here they were pronounced according to the phonological rules of English. As there is a tendency of educated bilinguals to pronounce "loans as close to the original as possible" (Myers-Scotton 1992:31), the issue of whether these two words constitute a borrowing or a switch remains open.

The last of the embedded switches was the discourse marker "at least". Because of their importance in structuring discourse, discourse markers are frequently codeswitched or borrowed in language contact situations (Myers-Scotton 1992:36). In our example, "at least" was an instance of codeswitching that re-occurred only twice in the rest of the text.

To sum up the analysis of this passage, codeswitching cannot be accounted for by the need to use technical terms. Rather, expression of emphasis and professional status emerge as the main motivation for codeswitching.

Table 3: Overview over Swahili-English codeswitching in Example 3

Swahili-English intrasentential codeswitching	
plot	single lexeme, noun
trial	single lexeme, noun, occurring twice
testing	single lexeme, noun
team	single lexeme, noun
kutest	single lexeme, verb, morphological integration
time	single lexeme, noun
moisture content	compound noun
source	single lexeme, noun
August, September	nominal phrase, borrowing; English pronounciation

Swahili-English intrasentential codeswitching	
at least	discourse particle

5.4.4. Rendering technical information

In the next example, Mr. Luwamba, the Development Director of the Diocese of Musoma, reported about an official journey he undertook to visit an NGO active in water development in Western Kenya. In the passage quoted here, Luwamba accounted for the visit and provided information about the NGO's work. In this situation, he frequently switched to English, while during the rest of the meeting, he mostly used Standard Swahili.

Example 4:

Luwamba: Tuliondoka hapa tarehe tatu kwenda Kenya kwenda kuangalia kazi wanayofanya watu wa KWAHO / ambayo yanahusu mpango wa maji provision of water halafu kuna mambo ya health and sanitation halafu kuna community organization mobilization na income generating activities ndizo wanazozifanya watu wa KWAHO /

Luwamba: We left here on the third going to Kenya going to look at the work the KWAHO people are doing / which concern the plan for water / provision of water / then there is the issue of health and sanitation and then there is the issue of community organization mobilization and income generating activities / these are the things the KWAHO people are doing /

There were several factors that contributed to the frequent occurrence of codeswitching here. First, the technical details reproduced in this passage were originally presented by KWAHO staff in English. As a result, the relevant technical terms readily came to mind in English while an equivalent Swahili terminology would have had to be researched on first. It may also play a role that this was an account of a trip to Western Kenya, where it was even more likely that English rather than Swahili was used in both formal and informal contexts. Second, switching to English as well as using borrowings to discuss technical details conveyed professional status on the speaker, as usually only those with a secondary or higher education have a command of the language.

Taking a closer look at the words appearing in English in the text, some of them may be summarized as 'development jargon', such as the words appearing in the initial sentences: *provision of water, health and sanitation, community organization, mobilization, income generating activities, site* ya *project, based, some activities, programmes*. All these terms occur frequently in texts pertaining to development programmes such as proposals or reports. Then, there are the more specific technical terms, all of them nouns, referring to concepts or items relevant to the water technology used by KWAHO: *shallow wells, rig, hand pump, spring protection, natural springs, catchment, concrete*. There is a third group of words, comprising mostly verbs and adjectives, which refers to processes related to the use of technology in water programmes. This group includes everyday notions for which Swahili words are widely in use: *drawn, seal, contaminated, sealed, open, flow*. Finally, with *"and then"*, there was also an English discourse marker which was used twice in the short passage.

Codeswitching to English in the whole passage includes both rare technical as well as everyday familiar terms. It may be interesting to consider context and processes here: training and information acquired in English is reproduced in Swahili with codeswitching to English. While ignorance of some technical terms is the reason for some of the codeswitching, many more English words than 'necessary' by this criterion appear in the text. Many of the English terms used are accompanied by adjacent Swahili equivalents: *health / afya, kuhamasisha / mobilization, spring / chemchem, hand pump /pampu ya mkono*. Most of the instances of switches concern single or compound lexemes; only few of them are integrated into Swahili morphology. Some English nouns are joined by connective, such as *"site* ya *program"*, or *"catchment* ya ile *spring"*, some verbs take an infinitive prefix ku- such as "ku*seal"* and "ku*flow"*.

While Luwamba usually did not engage into such frequent codeswitching in representative board meetings, frequent switches can be considered a neutral choice in reporting activities. Codeswitching in this example served the function of emphasizing important aspects of the message, of conveying linguistic and technical competence, of constructing authenticity in reporting. It was also motivated by greater familiarity with some of the English rather than the Swahili terminology.

It seems that the necessity to switch because of terminological requirements at some points 'engenders' even more switches into English. For instance, when explaining about spring protection, Luwamba used the Swahili term "chemchem" (spring) alongside with the English term "spring", but subsequently refrained from using the Swahili term with the English adjective "natural" or the noun "catchment": "kwa hiyo kunakuwa chemchem ambayo inakuweko *natural, natural springs* sasa wanachofanya ni kwamba wanakwenda kwenye *catchment* ya ile *spring"*

Table 4 Overview over Swahili-English codeswitching in Example 4

Swahili-English intrasentential codeswitching	
provision of water	nominal phrase
mambo ya health and sanitation	nominal phrase, morphological integration into Swahili
community organization, mobilisation	nominal phrase, compound noun
income generating activities	compound noun
site ya project	compound noun, morphological integration into Swahili
based	participle
some activities	nominal phrase
provision of water	compound noun
programmes	single lexeme
shallow well	compound noun
rig	single lexeme
hand pump	compound noun
spring protection	compound noun
natural springs	single lexeme, compound noun
catchment	single lexeme, noun
concrete	single lexeme, noun
drawn	single lexeme, verb
and then	discourse particle
kuseal	single lexeme, verb, morphological integration

5.4.5. Rural contexts - mitigating codeswitches by translation

The following examples illustrate aid workers' language use in meetings with peasant farmers. In this context, the anticipated choice was to use Standard Swahili. Aid workers by and large conformed to this expectation. When working in a rural area, they consciously avoided codeswitching from Swahili to English, as peasant farmers had none or only a very limited knowledge of this language. For most cases, aid workers had no problem in adapting to their linguistic environment and replacing potential instances of codeswitching with Swahili terms. Yet, a few instances of switches still occurred. Such switches violated expected norms of language use. They were therefore often accompanied by mitigating elements, such as an apology, explanation or translation, so as not to cause offence.

The examples were taken from a meeting of Ms. Msemwa, the Advisor of the Women's Groups, with the women's group in one of the villages of the SRAP network. Msemwa's topic was a course on nutrition including a practical session on cooking.

Example 5 A:

Msemwa: sasa tutakuwa tunajifunza hayo tu kila mara mpaka mwezi uishe / xxx / au tutakuwa - / na katika hii kozi ya afya na lishe / kwa sababu baadaye tutakuwa na kufanya *kwa vitendo* / tutakuwa tunafanya *practical*, *kwa vitendo* / eeh / sasa / labda tungeangalia vitu ambavyo tutavihitaji wakati huo wa kufanya *kwa vitendo* / ili tu— kusudi tutakaposema tutakuwa na hii afya na lishe tutakuwa tunahitaji vitu gani gani / vikapate kununuliwa kufuatana na malengo / xx / lazima tutahitaji sufuria. M01-SRAP:9

Msemwa: now we will just be learning this every time until the end of the month / xxx / or we will be - / and in this course about health and nutrition / because later we will be and doing it in practice / we will do a *practical*, in practice / eeh / now / maybe we should look at the things we need at the time we do the practical / so that in order when we will be saying / we will be with this health and nutrition / what are the things that we will need / they should be available and bought according to the objectives / xx / at least we will need a cooking pot.

Table 5 Overview over codeswitching and technical terminology in Example 5.A

Swahili-English intrasentential codeswitching	
practical	single lexeme, noun; specification

Swahili technical terminology	
kwa vitendo	adverbial expression

Msemwa introduced the idea of having a practical as part of the nutrition course with the Swahili expression "kwa vitendo". Then, in the next clause, she used the English expression "practical", and immediately again added the Swahili equivalent to explain the concept to those who did not understand the English word: "Sasa tutakuwa tunafanya practical, kwa vitendo /" (we will also be doing it practical, in practice). This translation was important both for comprehension as well as in a symbolic sense: using an English term was seen to create a social distance or even affront the audience. In the course of the meeting, she used the Swahili term "kwa vitendo" more than ten times, adding the English term "practical" only twice altogether.

For comparison, one could consider the example below, taken from a staff meeting that took place two days later. While discussing the same topic in a staff meeting, Mwemwa again switched to the English term "practical" in a Swahili-language discussion; but in interaction with other Swahili-English bilingual aid workers, she did not bother to provide a Swahili equivalent.

Example 5.B:

Nyange: umepangaje?
Msemwa: ni: / tuna mipango miwili ya kuendelea na haya mafunzo tu / halafu pia tuliona kwamba ni — / kwa sababu ya haya mafunzo

Nyange: how did you plan it?
Msemwa: it is / we have two plans of just continuing with this training / and then we also thought that it is - / because of these training

5.4. Bilingualism and codeswitching in formal meetings: attitudes and language use

itafikia siku tutafanya practical / sasa niliwauliza sasa tutakapofanya practical / kitu kama mboga hivi / tutaenda kununua mjini wakati sisi tunaweza tukalima? M02-SRAP:11

there will come a day where we will do a practical / so I asked them when we do the practical / things like vegetables and the like / will we go to buy them in town while we can cultivate them?

Throughout this staff meeting, Msemwa switched to the word "practical" four times without using the Swahili equivalent "kwa vitendo". The comparison shows that on the one hand, codeswitching practices were carefully adapted to suit the respective communicative context; on the other hand, it also shows that in rare cases, single lexeme codeswitching, paired by Swahili equivalents, occurred in contexts where they were considered inappropriate.

This practice left target group members with ambivalent feelings. It may have given them an opportunity to become familiar with English terms aid workers considered important in everyday activities. The pattern of repeating core terms in two languages is very much used in bilingual teaching and learning contexts, where content is taught along with terminology and language. Such codeswitching practices are, of course, inappropriate for a context where the teaching of English is not at stake. In the above-quoted meeting, they left the listeners with the disturbing impression that Standard Swahili, the language they knew, was somehow deficient for communicating development. The fact that aid workers are in many ways regarded as role models merely adds to the problem here.

5.4.6. Lost for words - the dominance of English in teaching and learning contexts

The following examples continue to illustrate the difficulties that aid workers may face when they try to implement knowledge acquired in the English-medium education system into an everyday rural context. In a training session on sewing, Msemwa was suddenly lost for words when she started to explain the parts of the sewing machine in Swahili. While she generally described her own competence in English in rather modest terms, "Nafahamu Kiswahili halafu nafahamu Kingereza kidogo" (I understand Swahili and then I understand a little English), during the training session she found out that in this domain, it was her knowledge of Swahili rather than English that was limited. As she explained later during the event, like most of her education, she had had her instruction on sewing in English.

The excerpts discussed here were taken from a training session that was conducted by Msemwa for the women's group of one of the villages of the SRAP programme. Msemwa began by showing the machine and its use, explaining the different parts and their names in Swahili. One of the group members, Ms. Salome Madilu, had gone to get her notebook. When she came back, Msemwa repeated the main parts of the machine:

Example 6.A

Msemwa: Salome, nimeanza, nimesema ina sehemu kuu nne /
Madilu: Sawa /
Msemwa:
Hapa ni mkono, hapa niliposhika hapa ni mkono, hapa ni kichwa, hapa ni shingo, hapa ni bamba / M15- SRAP:4

Msemwa: Salome, I have started, I said that it has four main parts /
Madilu: OK. /
Msemwa: This here is the arm, this here where I am holding it is the arm, here is the head, this is the neck, and this is the table /

While some group members took notes, Msemwa went on with explaining the hand wheel. Generalizing her own experience, she claimed that often, English terms rather than Swahili ones were used for the machine parts. "mara nyingi wanapenda kutumia Kiingereza" (many times, they like to use English). Prompted by this remark, one of the group members, Ms. Mkongwa, asked for the English term.

Example 6.B

Msemwa: ... nini hii gurudumu dogo, gurudumu dogo / katika mashine gurudumu dogo linasaidia - / kuna majina mengi - sasa nikitumia Kiswahili / mara nyingi wanapenda kutumia Kiingereza / lakini ni gurudumu dogo
Mkongwa: Na Kiingereza ?
Msemwa: Kwa Kiingereza linaitwa ni **hand wheel** /
Wote: hand wheel (kucheka) M15- SRAP:4

Msemwa: ... this is what, the hand wheel, the hand wheel / on the machine the hand wheel serves to - / there are many names - now if I use Kiswahili / but many times, they like to use English / but this is the hand wheel /
Mkongwa: And English?
Msemwa: In English it is called *hand wheel* /
All: *hand wheel* (laughter)

Msemwa mentioned it to her and the group members repeated it amongst laughter. While the new term was of little practical value to group members, they nevertheless used the opportunity to participate in this learning experience initiated by a member who knew some English.

Msemwa then went on to explain further parts of the machine. Discussing the stitch regulator, the spool pin and the bobbin, she found that she was unable to name these parts in Swahili. Struggling to make herself understood, she tried to illustrate and explain.

Example 6.C

Msemwa: ... hapa, hapa ni sehemu ya xx / wakati unaposhona kama unataka vionekane vi-**stitch** vidogo vidogo ndiyo unarekebisha hapa hivi unaweka hapa / M15- SRAP:4

Msemwa: ... here, here there is a part of xx / when you are sewing if you want very small *stitches* to appear then you adjust it here and you put it here /

Describing the stitch regulators function in Swahili, she used of the term "stitch" in English, integrating it into Swahili morphology with a prefix from noun class 8 signifying smallness and plural. While she explained "regulator" with the Swahili verb "rekebisha" (correct, regulate), the use of the term "stitch" made the explanation incomprehensible for most of her audience. She then tried to come up with an equivalent of "stitch regulator" in Swahili; this, however, only resulted in a long pause: „sasa inaitwa ni xxx" (now this is called xxx) and a switch to English „kwa Kiingereza (anacheka) stitch regulator, stitch regulator" (in English <laughing> its stitch regulator, stitch regulator /) She then continued to introduce a Swahili term (mabandi)[13] for "stitches" for further explanation "inarekebisha maba:::, kwa Kiswahili ni maba::::::ndi" (it regulates the sti::::, in Swahili it is sti:::::tches), at the same time again showing the respective item. One of the group members who was busy writing tried to see it and Msemwa repeated: "inarekebisha mabandi" (it regulates the stitches).

Example 6.D

Msemwa: ... sasa inaitwa ni xxx (wengine wanacheka) / kwa Kiingereza (anacheka) **stitch regulator, stitch regulator** / inarekebisha maba:::, kwa Kiswahili ni maba::::::ndi /	**Msemwa:** ... now this is called xxx (the others laugh) / in English (she laughs) stitch regulator, it adjusts the sti:::::tches, in Swahili it is sti::::tches /
Madilu: mbele hapo	**Madilu:** in front here
Msemwa: inarekebisha mabandi	**Msemwa:** it adjusts stitches
Madilu: Inaitwaje?	**Madilu:** what is it called?
Msemwa: Ee, kwa Kiingereza ni stitch regulator. Lakini kwa Kiswahili ni nini, ni nini xxx kifaa kinachorekebisha mabandi, mabandi / ukubwa wa mabandi au udogo wa mabandi / M15- SRAP:4	**Msemwa:** Well, in English it is stitch regulator. But in Swahili it's what, it's a device to adjust the stitches, the stitches / the length or shortness of the stitches /

When Madilu asked for a repetition to take notes, Msemwa finally came up with an explanatory paraphrase in Swahili „kifaa kinachorekebisha mabandi" (instrument regulating stitch length). Her inability to name an equivalent in Swahili rendered her visibly nervous. The group members took it with irony: ignorance on the part of the teacher comes as a relief to the learner struggling to grasp new information. After all, it may be possible to use the machine without remembering detailed names for all its parts.

Msemwa however continued to strain herself with the new items coming up, remaining very concerned about providing adequate terms or at least explanations in Swahili. In the next example, she showed how to place the thread on the machine. While searching for a Swahili paraphrase for the spool pin[14], she again first switched to an English word in the explanation: "Kifaa cha ku*direct*", then trying Swahili "kuonyesha" (showing) and finally arriving at the term "ongoza" (lead,

---

13 TUKI 2001 renders "bandi" with "baste" or "tack" and "piga bandi" with to "baste" or "tack". TUKI 1981 renders "bandi" with "mshono wa mkono ambao ni wa kushikiza tu" = hand-made stitch for basting/tacking only.

14 Ohly 1987 renders "spool" with „kibiringo", and spool-pin with "pini kibiringo". TUKI 1996 renders spool with „kidonge/kigurudumu cha uzi"

direct). Madilu was obviously irritated by this word search, understanding "kinaunguza" (it burns) instead of "kinaongoza" (it directs), but this misunderstanding was easily clarified. Msemwa then gave the English term "hii inaitwa nini kwa Kiingereza inaitwa ni spool pins" (it is called what / in English it is called spool pins), then searched for a Swahili alternative: "Kiswahili chake / ni kama ka xx, kau xxx pin kadogo" Prefixing ka-, a noun class not existing in Standard Swahili but in many other Bantu languages and colloquial Swahili, she indicated a small item, hesitated, repeated and then just filled in the English term "pin". As "ka-" is mainly used pejoratively in colloquial Swahili, its use to indicate smallness is likely to constitute an interference form other Bantu languages.

Realizing that her explanation is not very precise, Msemwa resigned to an apology, saying that she had had her instruction on sewing machines in English and therefore was not familiar with the Swahili terms. But it was important for her to point out that the Swahili terminology definitely existed, and that she was going find out and provide it: "Kipo Kiswahili chake nitawapa majina yote" (There are Swahili words for this and I will give you all the names).

Coming to the next item to be explained, she gave the term in English without any further comment, "kuna kifaa fulani kinaingia hapa / kinaitwa *bobbin*[15]" (there is a certain item which enters here / it is called *bobbin*). Not bothering any longer for an adequate Swahili word, she just continued to explain the function of the parts of the machine.

Example 6.E:

Msemwa: na hii hapa ni / kifaa hichi ni kifaa cha ku**direct**, kuonyesha, kinaonyesha, kinaongoza uzi kuingia kwenye sindano / kwa sababu uzi wetu tutakuwa tumeuweka hapa / tumeuweka hapa, kinaongoza uzi /
Madilu: kinaungu:::za?
Msemwa: Kinaongo::::za / ni kifaa kinchoongo::::za uzi kuingia katika nini / ninajaribu kueleza ngoja baadaye nitawapa majina yake / hicho ni kifaa kinachoongoza uzi kuingia kwenye sindano / uzi unakaa hapa / hii inaitwa nini kwa Kiingereza inaitwa ni spool pins / lakini ina Kiswahili chake / ni kama ka xx, kau **xxx pin** kadogo / kama sehemu / kuna jina nitawapa majina bado sijui Kiswahili chake vizuri / (anacheka) nilijifunza kwa Kiingereza lakini kipo Kiswahili chake nitawapa majina yote / halafu hapa / hapa ni sehemu ya / kuna kifaa fulani kinaingia hapa / kinaitwa **bobbin** / sasa kile kifaa kinachoingia hapa kinakuwa na uzi mdogo /
M15- SRAP:44

Msemwa: and this here is / this device is for directing, showing, is shows, it leads the thread to enter into the needle / because we will have to put our thread here / put it here, it leads the thread /
Madilu: it burns?
Msemwa: it leads / it is a device that leads the thread into what / I am trying to explain wait later I will give you its names / this here is the device that leads the thread to enter the needle / the thread stays here / what is this called, in English it is called *spool pins* / but there is a Swahili word for this / it is like as small *pin* / like a part / it has a name I will give you the names I don't yet know its Swahili words well / (she laughs) I learnt it in English but there are Swahili words for this / I will give you all the names / then here / here is the part of / a certain utensil enters here / it is called *bobbin* / now the utensil that enters here has the small thread /

---

15 Ohly 1987 renders both "bobbin" and "spool" with „kibiringo". TUKI 1996 renders "bobbin" with „kibiringo" and spool with „kidonge/kigurudumu cha uzi".

The above quotations of the training session illustrate that codeswitching prompted by the speaker's lexical gaps in the matrix language actually occurred. For this training session on the function of the sewing machine, Msemwa prepared to explain the function and maintenance of the machine, probably not bothering to go through all the names of its individual parts. After all, the objective was using the machine and not talking about it. However, after beginning her instruction, and especially as some group members ask for more detailed information on the machine, she discovered that she was somehow stuck with English terms. Being dedicated to offering understandable, practical training and at the same time being committed to the use of Swahili, she was quite disturbed by her limited knowledge.

While in the examples given, Msemwa acknowledged the problem and promises to remedy it, there are probably other situations where trainers just proceed using English terms, unwilling to admit their own ignorance.

Table 6: Overview over Swahili-English codeswitching in Example 6.A - 6.E

Swahili-English codeswitching	
hand-wheel	single lexeme, compound noun
vistitch vidogo	single lexeme morphological integration noun class 8
kudirect	single lexeme, verb, morphological integration
spool pin	single lexeme, compound noun
bobbin	single lexeme, noun

5.4.7. Searching for words – preparing Swahili terminology for rural outreach

The following example is from a staff meeting in which the challenge of finding standard Swahili terms for communication in the village was taken up. The debate was about a 'seed risk insurance' the team wanted to offer to the peasant farmers. The objective was to encourage peasant farmers to use eco-farming methods and to plant early. Some of the farmers were reluctant to try new approaches, wary to lose seed in such experiments. Some feared that if they planted early and the rains were late, seed was going to be lost. A 'seed risk insurance' by the project team would replace seed lost in such endeavors.

Aware that this concept would have to be communicated to the peasants in Swahili, the programme director brought up the question of an adequate Swahili term for "risk". Note that the whole discussion, except for the term "risk", was in Swahili.

Example 7:

Fischer: wanaweza ku— tunaweza kuangalia kama risk /	**Fischer:** they can – we can regard it as a *risk* /
Nyange: risk	**Nyange:** *risk*
Fischer: risk za mbegu	**Fischer:** seed *risk*
Nyange: risk ni nini kwa Kiswahili ?	**Nyange:** what is *risk* in Swahili?
Fischer: nadhani —	**Fischer:** I think -
Msemwa: ni - kama kuna hasara itakayojitokeza	**Msemwa:** it is - if there is a damage that may occur
Nyange: hasara itakayojitokeza +++	**Nyange:** a damage that may occur +++
Fischer: hasara /	**Fischer:** a damage /
M02-SRAP:3	

While nobody has the exact term readily in mind, Msemwa offers a paraphrase: "kama kuna hasara itakayojitokeza" (if there is a loss that will occur).[16] The strategy of taking the closely matching term "hasara" (damage) and representing "risk" with a conditional and a descriptive relative clause got rather close to the concept, but was cumbersome. Nyange and Fischer shortened the paraphrase, but then proceeded to another related topic before arriving at a more satisfying solution. While no exact term was established in this case, the important fact was that the issue was raised and taken serious in the team. A word that is consciously searched for will sooner or later be obtained from relevant literature, training, colleagues or dictionaries, or it may even be specifically coined for the programme context.

Table 7: Overview over Codeswitching and Swahili technical terms in Example Seven

Swahili-English codeswitching	
risk	single lexeme, noun

Swahili technical terminology	
kama kuna hasara itakayojitokeza	conditional and descriptive relative clause

5.4.8. Discussion of results

Regarding the questions the examples were approached with, the following results can be summed up:

The first point concerns the complex relationship between the use of technical language and codeswitching to English. In interviews aid workers had asserted that they used codeswitching to English primarily in order to communicate technical issues, giving several reasons why the respective Swahili terminology was less accessible to them. Evidence from the examples analyzed produces a signifi-

---

16 TUKI 1996 gives "hatari" for the noun "risk" and several possibilities for the verb; "hatari" has primarily the meaning of "danger".

cantly different picture: Some of the codeswitched material indeed involves technical expressions. But the larger share of instances of codeswitching cannot be accounted for by the alleged unavailability of technical terms in Swahili. Most of the terms in question are in popular and widespread use in Swahili. Moreover, in the passages analyzed, many English codeswitched expressions are accompanied by an adjacent Swahili equivalent.

Table 8: Codeswitching to English for which Swahili equivalent is used by the speaker in the same utterance

Example	Codeswitching to English	Swahili equivalent
2	I am not happy to work	sifurahi kufanya kazi
3	time	wakati
4	health	afya
4	mobilization	kuhamsisha
4	hand pump	pampu ya maji
4	spring	chemchem
5	practical	kwa vitendo
6	hand wheel	gurudumo dogo
6	kudirect	kuongoza
6	stitch	~ bandi (= baste, tack)

While this table just lists repetitions by the same speaker that occur in the immediate contexts of the original utterance, many more of the codeswitched terms are actually in common use in Swahili within the respective communicative events. Thus, lack of availability of technical terms is not the primary reason for most instances of codeswitching. The examples discussed give evidence of a number of alternative motivations for codeswitching: Single lexeme codeswitching to English in a matrix Swahili text is used to express individual style, emphasis, quotations, expertise and authority. Only a small proportion of the respective terms is used because there is a lexical gap in the speaker's Swahili language competence – the implications of which will be discussed below.

The second point was about the communication of technical matters at grassroot level. Aid workers and beneficiaries express technical concepts in Standard Swahili, with the terminology originating from specific coining processes, loan translations, borrowings, derivations and semantic extensions. Some of the arising lexical gaps are filled with English, but these are exceptions and speakers use strategies of mitigation (translations, explanations or excuses) so as not to offend their audience with the use of a language that is incomprehensible to them.

The third point concerned patterns of communication with foreign colleagues. In staff meetings, foreign aid workers at times prefer to speak English even if they are fairly competent in Swahili. Responding to English utterances with Swahili-English intersentential codeswitching, Tanzanian aid workers indicate that they do not necessarily consider the use of English their own preferred choice. English may provide a safer ground for the foreign aid worker to develop his arguments. For Tanzanians, intersentential codeswitching offers a way of responding foreign counterparts in their language as well as maintaining the connection to their own linguistic preference.

The fourth point concerned speakers' individual flexibility in multilingual environments. The comparison of speech of the same speaker on the same topic in staff and target group meetings provides evidence of a distinct ability to adjust to a variety of communicative environments. In staff meetings, aid workers use single-lexeme codeswitching which is part of the expected repertoire. In stakeholder meetings, they translate the respective English terms into Swahili, largely suppressing codeswitching to English. In case codeswitching still occurs, its inappropriateness is acknowledged by various strategies of mitigation.

The fifth point was about lexical gaps as a cause for codeswitching. Examples analyzed show that instances of codeswitching are motivated by a variety of reasons such as considerations of status, style, quotation, emphasis etc. Only in few cases codeswitches is caused by lexical gaps. These, however, may lead to communicative problems, especially at grass-root level. Among the staff members of development organizations, efforts are made to enhance the common competence in time before lexical gaps become a problem. Without institutional support, these individual efforts are, however, insufficient to meet the challenge.

5.5. Conclusion

There is no simple answer to this inquiry into the interdependence of codeswitching practices and participatory development. The phenomenon remains ambivalent: on the one hand, prevailing codeswitching patterns are part of an exclusive language of staff in development organizations that exacerbates hierarchies and distanced expert status; on the other hand, codeswitching is a creative and autonomous practice that makes maximum use of given language resources. For a conclusion, both negative and positive aspects are summed up here:

Among the negative aspects of Swahili-English codeswitching there is the fact that development professionals do - and have to - resort to English when drawing on their knowledge and experience. It is one of the disturbing realities of postcolonial societies that skills and technology are still largely acquired and communicated in English rather than Swahili. Evidence from the examples analyzed confirms that the relationship between the English language and expertise develops dynamics of its own. Even in domains where Swahili terminology is well advanced, aid workers codeswitch to English to enhance their individual expert status and the importance of their argument. In this way, a language barrier is maintained between aid workers and beneficiaries. This makes it difficult for beneficiaries to gain information about development organizations, their policy, and their processes of decision-making. The findings of this research confirm that switching to the ex-colonial languages is used to secure status and maintain hierarchies in development networks. They also suggest that codeswitching is an obstacle for beneficiaries in gaining ground and participating. As linguistic barriers often remain unquestioned, these findings create an important starting point for future research on the role of language in participatory development.

Apart from these general findings, there is one thing the examples analyzed show very clearly: Codeswitching motivated by lexical gaps, especially if occurring in the speech of aid workers in rural contexts, are symptomatic of structural sociolinguistic challenges. Like with the proverbial iceberg, seemingly minor deficiencies in linguistic competence are easily underestimated and likely to cause extensive communicative problems. With an audience that does not speak English, even a few lexical gaps in individual Swahili proficiency interfere and effectively prevent a serious discussion of the topic at stake. Filling these gaps with English is problematic, as this alienates and excludes peasant farmers who constitute the target group of the programme. Even if translations, explanations and apologies are offered, the message that implicitly looms large remains problematic: English, a language that is incomprehensible and beyond reach for beneficiaries, is indispensable in development.

There is awareness of this problem among aid workers, but it is approached rather indirectly. Interestingly enough, staff members rather tend to problematize their perceived lack of proficiency in English. With the exception of the Austrian aid worker, none of them had reservations about her or his knowledge of Swahili. This is not surprising, as Swahili is a first or quasi-first language to all of them. Ignorance about Swahili technical terms has its roots in the educational policy. As a consequence, popular perception tends to associate terminological limitations with the language rather than with the individual speaker. Development organizations largely seem to share this view, not being particularly concerned about improving the Swahili proficiency of their staff.

Among the positive aspects of prevalent patterns of Swahili-English codeswitching in development work there is the fact that despite the pro-English bias in higher education and the limited access to technical information in Swahili, English has not replaced Swahili in formal contexts in development networks. Instead, communication in Swahili, together with Swahili-English codeswitching, is the norm. This makes interaction at least partly accessibly to beneficiaries. For example, it is easier to translate an occasional English switch into Swahili instead of translating an entire conversation. Intrasentential codeswitching between English and Swahili is also used as a strategy to change the language of communication with bilingual foreign aid workers from English to Swahili, and therefore employed as a means to negotiate national versus foreign linguistic preferences.

Regular codeswitching taps the resources of a rich terminology in English and creates awareness for differentiated expression. As the respective domains are often equally relevant for the Swahili speaking rural context, aid workers face the challenge to enhance their Swahili competence accordingly. Tanzanians can rely on the continuous work of institutions such as BAKITA (National Swahili Council) and TUKI (Institute of Swahili Research) who foster Swahili language development on a national level (Kiango 2004, Mtesigwa 2004). These institutions compile technical word lists and dictionaries, but in turn depend on practitioners who put their work into use. In regard to dissemination and implementation a lot remains to be done. At the same time, the widespread use of Swahili at grassroot level communication in development confirms the importance of the task at hand.

Summing up, one could say that both the consideration of positive as well as negative aspects points to the need to generally enhance Swahili language development as well as supporting individual speakers in improving their competence. Codeswitching does not in itself pose a problem for participatory communication. Speakers usually adapt their language and use the appropriate code depending on their conversational partners. While codeswitching may be used as a means of excluding less educated speakers, there are other instances where it is employed to challenge donor-recipient power relations. The issue constituting a major problem, however, is the gaps in individual Swahili competence, caused by the bias towards English in aid workers' education and everyday professional routine. In order to open communicative channels for beneficiaries, and to make information and decision-making processes more accessible, the vital role of Swahili must not be limited to the domain of outreach in rural areas, but has to be taken serious at organizational level, too. In Tanzania, rhetoric support for the use of Swahili at public functions is part of the political and social culture. Development organizations are no exception. They regard the widespread use of Swahili as an asset in participatory development, as a communicative channel with the potential to facilitate bottom-up communication and transparency. However, the image of Swahili as a medium in development communication is somewhat biased: often, Swahili is regarded as an effective medium for simple-style grass-root communication, but as insufficient for technical debates on middle or higher organizational levels.

So what should development organizations do? It is obvious that development organizations can not make up for structural biases that originate in having English and not Swahili as a medium of instruction in secondary and tertiary education. But development organizations can make a change by balancing instead of aggravating a problematic situation.

In concrete programme implementation, however, organizations rather support their staff in "on the job" competence development in English instead of Swahili. In the SRAP network, the organization offered its staff technical courses which were held in English, and it also paid for intensive English courses in Nairobi that should enhance the staff's communicative competence. Only foreign aid workers were trained in Swahili, but the aim of this was mainly to enable them to communicate with beneficiaries in the village. In the Ministry of Agriculture in Zanzibar, a main incentive in work was the prospect of regular overseas postgraduate training which takes place in English or other foreign languages. Training and information disseminated in Swahili concentrated on reaching peasants and village level Extension Officers. Swahili being the first language of a large majority of Zanzibaris, support for Swahili lexical expansion would no doubt have been particularly effective.

Despite such shortcomings, Tanzania has a unique chance by having a language that is already used in so many social domains. On the part of the beneficiaries, any minor initiative in support of Swahili (such as individual efforts by foreigners to learn the language) is usually received enthusiastically. Development organizations should thus consider some of the following measures:

First, they should produce important project documents in both Swahili and English. Secondly, they should provide explanatory dictionaries and time for an adequate linguistic preparation of programme activities in rural contexts ("What is risk in Kiswahili?"). In this context, the enlisting of professional linguistic help in rendering essential programme concepts into Swahili would probably be helpful. Third, organizations should consider further measures that enhance the use of Swahili in higher-level technical and organizational contexts, such as language training offers for staff members or commissioning translations of relevant technical literature.

Aware that this concept would have to be communicated to the peasants in Swahili, the programme director brought up the question of an adequate Swahili term for "risk". Note that the whole discussion, except for the term "risk", was in Swahili.

6. Discourses on participation: negotiating programme implementation

6.1. Donor dominance in development discourse

Linguistic interaction in development co-operation is in many ways shaped by asymmetric relationships between donors, implementing organizations and recipients. Both sides, donor and recipient, regard development co-operation as a means to pursue economic, political and strategic objectives – but the concrete agendas and priorities usually differ considerably. The term "donor-driven" has come to denote the fact that, in case of conflicting interests, those disposing of the financial means are usually in a far better position to assert their agenda, while recipients in the long run have to comply with whatever is offered.

"Donor dominance" or "Donor-drivenness" are of course imprecise terms, as they include a range of attributes and behaviours, from explicit conditionality in international relations to subliminal persuasion on the interpersonal level. The mainstreaming of participatory approaches (Hickey and Mohan 2004a:5) in recent years has meant that the principle of participation, partnership and ownership has in many cases replaced hierarchical top-down communication. Inequality within aid relationships, however, has not disappeared. Instead, control and disciplinary measures are exercised in more subtle ways. As pointed out in Chapter 3, uniform instruments of documentation and control such as the Logical Framework Approach have become standard throughout the development industry. These instruments are primarily orientated towards fulfilling the donor's need to enhance accountability. The fact that they are supplemented here and there with elements informed by participatory and other "alternative" approaches may facilitate instances of egalitarian dialogue and open spaces for ecological or gender considerations. However, amendments of this sort also add to the complexity of the process. Recipients are invariably confronted with ever more elaborated requirements in planning and reporting on development programmes.

The issue is further complicated by the fact that patterns of respective donor-recipient behaviour not only concern donors and recipients at the imaginary 'beginning' and 'end' of the aid relationship, but are reproduced at any intermediate level in between. Every institution or individual who has influence on the distribution of aid money, from the Northern ministerial bureaucrat to the village extension officer in the recipient country, may assume a 'donor' role in the sense that powers derived from the control of financial resources are used to impose conditions and exercise power over those to whom the money is handed. It is, for example, not uncommon that Northern implementing organizations may assume 'donor' behaviour when interacting with their Tanzanian counterparts. Here, proximity to the governmental donor agency may be unduly emphasized or conditionality be imposed or justified in its name. Pretensions of this sort are often explained away by Northern development workers as inevitable structural constraints of the business (Baaz 2005:125). However, recipients hardly share this view. Instead, they will often feel that demands by donors exceed the scope of what would be reasonable or fair. Nevertheless, the recipients are rarely in a position to question details of the process. Of course, the implications of financial dependency vary from one organization to another. For example, well-connected international NGOs, politically motivated advocacy groups and small voluntary initiatives may experience dependency in fundamentally different ways. Some may always have additional options, for example working with other donors or specifying their own preferences. But many will lack the necessary resources and instead comply with counter-productive demands even if they put the programme's objectives at risk. Apart from this, tuning project documents and keeping communication up to date with the latest trends in the aid business requires access to information and resources. A good administrative infrastructure may help some organizations attend to bureaucratic requirements, and at times even iron out minor irregularities. At the same time, small or grass-roots-orientated initiatives may fail to afford the most basic material requirements for maintaining communication with potential co-operation partners. Their proposals or reports may be disqualified on formal grounds, or simply lose out in competition with more sophisticated offers.

In order to analyze the phenomenon of "donor dominance" as it extends to all areas of the aid network, this part of the research focusses on the spoken and written interaction of various actors in the process of development planning. In order to gain an understanding of the decentred "microphysics of power" (Foucault 1976:32,33), research will not be limited to a small group of people situated at the "top", but focus on two agricultural programmes in Tanzania. In the following, the theoretical and methodological framework for such an undertaking will be discussed. Critical Discourse Analysis and Critical Linguistics provide the main points of reference for this section.

6.1.1. Critical Discourse Analysis – an influential 'school' in critical linguistics

"Perhaps this is my main criticism. The position argued by CDA is not new at all. It has been debated since Plato and Aristotle" (Stubbs 1997:109).

Critical Discourse Analysis as a distinct field of linguistic enquiry emerged in the late 1980s and early 1990s (Blommaert 2005a; Fairclough 2003, 2001, 1995; Jäger 2001a und 2001b; Menz 2000; Titscher et al. 2000, van Dijk 2007, 2001; Wodak and Martin 2003, Wodak 2001a, 2001b). Situated at the interface between (poststructural) social science, history and critical linguistics, CDA bears potential for research on interpersonal development communication that is particularly relevant to this study of interpersonal communication in development networks.

Discourse analytic approaches have been widely used in critical works on development, including work relating to participatory approaches (Mosse 2005; Hickey and Mohan eds. 2004; Cooke and Kothari eds. 2001; see Baaz 2005 and Ziai 2006 for a broader overview and critique on Foucauldian discourse analytic approaches in postcolonial, post-development and development studies). What is particular to Critical Discourse Analysis and lacking in most of the above mentioned work, however, is the focus on language use as a primary field of inquiry. CDA refers to a broader framework of linguistic analysis and relies on a wide range of linguistic approaches and methods which are combined with inputs from other disciplines, such as the social sciences and cultural studies. While CDA does not prescribe or advocate a single method of analysis, its emergence has rendered a range of linguistic methods more systematically accessible for social and cultural analysis. In order to explore the potential of Critical Discourse Analysis for research on development communication, the major tenets of the CDA "school" will be briefly discussed here (Blommaert 2005a:21; Wodak and Martin 2003:5, Wodak 2001a, Titscher et al 2000, Fairclough and Wodak 1997). As Wodak and Martin (2003:5) caution, "the studies in CDA are multifold, derived from quite different theoretical backgrounds, oriented towards very different data and methodologies. Researchers in CDA also rely on various grammatical approaches. The definitions of the terms 'discourse', 'critical', 'ideology' and 'power' are also manifold". In order to take into account at least some of the heterogeneity of CDA approaches, the general introduction will be followed by brief accounts of work by the so-called 'Viennese School' around Ruth Wodak and the work of the British linguist Norman Fairclough.

Much of CDA scholarship claims an explicit commitment in favour of marginalized and discriminated groups, and the term 'critical' is mainly adopted to characterize attitudes towards processes of research and analysis. Within CDA, self-reflexivity of one's own scholarly work and the creation of critical awareness about social inequalities, power and language use are important objectives (Wodak 2001a.2). CDA's effort to politicize the study of language has attracted criticism from linguists who focus on a descriptive perspective (cf Schegloff 1997, Stubbs 1997).

Apart from this, the term 'critical' is also used to express an affinity to other scholarly traditions, such as Critical Theory in social science and Critical Linguistics (Wodak 2001a:2, Bluhm et al 2000:4, Titscher et al 1998:178, Mills 1997:8, van Dijk 1993:251). This includes the neo-Marxist social theory of the Frankfurt School, and in particular the work of Jürgen Habermas (1970, 1971, 1986). Several authors also refer to the work of Antonio Gramsci (1971), in particular his concept of hegemony which explains how dominant forces achieve popular acceptance and maintain control by manufacturing consensus on their interpretation of reality (Fairclough 1995). CDA scholars have also drawn on the work of Michel Foucault, such as his idea of power relations as omnipresent in social networks, the role of discourse in the creation of fluid power relations, and the interrelatedness of power relations with the production of knowledge (Foucault 1976). The concept of difference(s) as elaborated in Cultural Studies and Gender Studies (Hall 1996, Butler 1990) has also been essential.

Linguistic description and analysis in CDA is often carried out in reference to Michael Halliday's Systemic Functional Linguistics and the emerging 'Critical Linguistics' based on this approach (Wodak and Martin 2003:2). "As early as 1970 M.A.K. Halliday had stressed the relationship between the grammatical system and the social and personal needs that language is required to serve" (Wodak 2001a:8, referring to Halliday 1970:142). Based on Halliday's work, a critical approach towards the use of language for the exercise of social power and control evolved (Fowler and Kress 1979:185). The continuing significance of Systemic Functional Linguistics lies in the fact that "it offers clear and rigorous linguistic categories for analyzing the relations between discourse and social meaning" (Blommaert 2005a:25). For example, by exploring the use of language in the negotiation of class interests, grammatical features relevant to the study of language and power were identified (Fowler 1985:69).

Linguistic description and analysis in CDA has evolved in critical dialogue with emerging fields of linguistic enquiry that have shared CDA's principal focus on 'text and talk'; these include classical rhetoric, pragmatics, semantics, applied linguistics, conversation analysis, discourse analysis and text linguistics. CDA is multidisciplinary in its outlook, with various scholars focussing on different issues and adopting rather heterogeneous theoretical approaches. "CDA, and discourse analysis in general [...] are not methods that can simply be applied in the study of social problems. Discourse studies is a cross-discipline with many sub-disciplines and areas, each with its own theories, descriptive instruments or methods of inquiry" (van Dijk 2001:98). At the centre of linguistic analysis lies "the role of discourse in the (re)production and challenge of social dominance" (van Dijk 1993:249). The focus is primarily on social issues rather than on "words as such, as linguistic objects" (Wood and Kroger 2000:9). CDA authors share an interest in making transparent processes of social hierarchization, subordination, discrimination and exclusion. Gender relations, racism, institutional and mass media communication as well as identity research are primary concerns. Discourse is understood as a social practice, and defined as "a complex bundle of simultaneous and sequential interrelated linguistic acts, which manifest themselves [...] as texts, that belong to specific semiotic types, that is genres. The most salient feature in the definition of a discourse is the macro-topic, like 'unemployment'" (Wodak 2001b:66). Discursive entities are conceived as open systems, with each macro-topic relating to various sub-topics, and as hybrid inter-discursive relations.

6.1.2. Theoretical and methodological diversity in CDA

Methodologically, "operationalization is problem oriented and implies linguistic expertise" (Meyer 2001:30) in a broad 'structural-functional' sense (van Dijk

2001:97). Most authors use a qualitative-hermeneutic approach. In the analytical process, any detail at any level of linguistic structure may be considered relevant. In practice, however, the analysis has often been limited to a few select items that are chosen according to research interest. As Meyer (2001:16) observes, a rather "small range of linguistic devices" prominently features in critical discourse analytical work. Linguistic analysis of an extensive text corpus is always limited to particular features, as it is simply infeasible to include all possible aspects (van Dijk 1993, Stubbs 1997). As the realization of form, function, and meaning in any text is multilayered and complex, the selection of linguistic features analyzed is an essential factor in the research process. Interpretation, which follows in the next step, depends on the availability of contextual information. As Siegfried Jäger cautions, discourse analysis can provide no more than the description of facts (2001a:222); it does not necessarily lead to definite and clear-cut results. The analytical process in CDA is understood as open-ended: if additional information on text or context is obtained, the results may have to be revised accordingly. The collection and interpretation of data are often ongoing and simultaneous processes, and insights from one part are often used to optimize the realization of the other. In order to be comprehensible and transparent, a clear explanatory description of the interpretative process is vital. Consultations with social groups on whom the research is carried out are given importance, especially if these are marginalized and discriminated persons. However, interaction is limited to obtaining information and cross-checking results, while the act of interpretation is reserved to the researcher. There are usually no attempts to give other persons an active role in the interpretive process.

Scholars of the 'Viennese School' around Ruth Wodak have focussed a good part of their work on the analysis of popular opinion and public discourses on Austria's past. Relying on the discourse-historic method, they have investigated the way patterns of argumentation and intertextual links have evolved over time (Benke and Wodak 2003, Menz 2003, Wodak et al 1990). Studies have focussed on the National Socialist past (Wodak et al 1990), the experience of Rumanian asylum seekers in Austria (Wodak and Matouschek 1993) and perceptions of national identity (Wodak et al 1998). The discourse-historic approach has in particular contributed to the investigation of implicit forms of language use, such as hidden hints, metaphors, and presuppositions; here, the extensive study of empirical material is of primary importance. Research work carried out by the Viennese School of CDA also includes studies on institutional and organizational interaction, such as doctor-patient relationships and business communication (Menz 1991, 2000).

Concrete steps have been suggested for the organization of research work: First, the specific context is to be recorded, as discourse should be understood within a context. Second, the propositional contents of the texts are to be analyzed in relation to historic facts. Third, a textual interpretation by scholars from the disciplines in question (history, sociology, psychology) may be requested. Fourth, the texts are extensively described at all levels (Titscher et al, 1998:194). Analysis is understood as three-dimensional, including contents, discourse strategies, and concrete linguistic realizations at the level of text, clause or word (Wodak 2001b:72).

Norman Fairclough has been credited with having developed the most elaborate theoretical model in Critical Discourse Analysis (Menz 2000:43ff). Fairclough focusses on the relationship between socio-political change and discursive change. Arguing that "the language element [...] has in certain key respects become [...] a crucial aspect of the social transformations which are going on" (Fairclough 2003:203), he has developed an elaborate framework for the analysis of text as a sociocultural practice, in which discourse practice plays a mediating role.

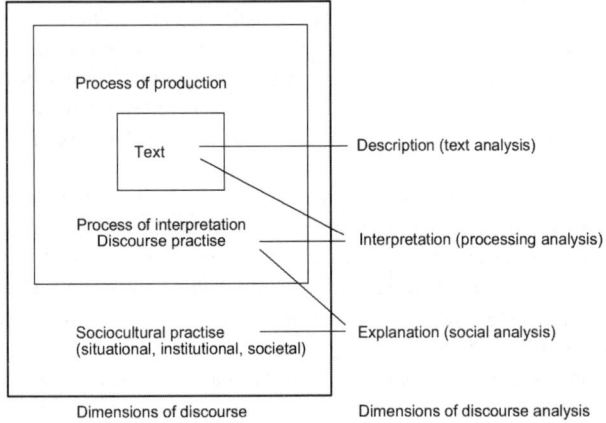

Figure 8: Fairclough's model of discourse (1995:98)

Fairclough relates three aspects of analysis (description, interpretation and explanation) to the various aspects of his concept of discourse. At the level of text analysis, attention is focussed on aspects of lexicon, grammar, cohesion and argumentative structures (Menz 2000:43). With regard to the functions of texts, Fairclough adapts a perspective from systemic functional linguistics (Halliday 1994), focussing on three 'types of meanings' of texts, which pertain to action, representation, and the constitution of identity (Fairclough 2003:27). To these types of meanings, he relates genre, discourse and style as forms of linguistic expression. Genres are realized as actional meanings and forms of a text, discourses are manifest in representation, and styles can be observed in identification (Fairclough 2003:206).

In relation to discursive practices, Fairclough draws attention to processes of production, distribution and consumption of texts (1995:9). Analysis at this level includes illocution, coherence and intertextuality. In his work on discursive and social change, Fairclough concentrates on intertexuality, which investigates the way distinct genres merge into each other under changing socio-economic conditions. Genres as text types "are important in sustaining the institutional structure of contemporary society – structural relations between (local) government, business, university, the media, etc" (Fairclough 2003:32). He points out that for each social situation there are texts which more conventionally conform to a particular genre and others that are more creative; and he identifies 'orders of discourse' (a term adapted from Foucault) as sets of discursive practices that are conventionalised for particular social situations (1995:10). The analysis of the dimension of discursive practices is of particular importance in Fairclough's approach, as it provides the interface between the micro-perspective of the texts and the macro-perspective of the larger social contexts.

Regarding the third dimension of socio-cultural practices, Fairclough invokes Gramsci's (1971) concept of hegemony to explicate his view of social relations as a permanent struggle between social forces. Social domination is expressed in discursive formations, with linguistic interaction constituting an essential field of social encounter. Fairclough is committed to a multidisciplinary approach that closely connects with contemporary approaches in social sciences.

In his analytical work, he frequently addresses global socio-economic developments, reflecting, for example, on "the sort of language which constitutes 'teamwork', 'consultation', 'partnerships', or 'appraisal'), [...] internationally disseminated and imposed by organizations like the International Monetary Fund and the World Trade Organization" (Fairclough 2001:128).

Discussing the merits of Fairclough's theoretical model, Florian Menz (2000:43ff) points to its comprehensive conception, its commitment to the investigation of dominance relations, and its contributions towards an interdisciplinary perspective for sociology and linguistics. From a more critical perspective, Menz observes the following issues: First, there are inconsistencies in the differentiation of the dimension of text and discursive practice. In particular, Fairclough's approach implies that genres or text types can be clearly defined, while they may actually be subject to continuous variation and adaptation – which in turn makes it difficult to differentiate specific instances of normative and creative language use. Second, he notes the subsumption of situational, institutional and social perspectives in the socio-cultural dimension, which may lead to a neglect of institutional perspectives. Third, Menz points to inconsistencies in the integration of Gramsci's concept of hegemony, which would imply the production of social consensus, rather than social struggle, as Fairclough sees it. Fourth, Menz also remarks that the empirical basis of Fairclough's work is comparatively limited.

Referring to Critical Discourse Analysis as a whole, Ruth Wodak lists some "open questions and perspectives". Many of these issues have figured in critical remarks on CDA, raised, for example, by representatives of conversational analysis (Schegloff 1997) discourse analysis (Stubbs 1997) or literary criticism (Widdowson 1995). They include: problems in the operationalization of theory;

a lack of theoretical foundation in the selection of linguistic indicators; unprecise notions of context; political commitment leading to bias; and failure to realize true interdisciplinarity and transdisciplinarity (Wodak 2001a:12).

6.1.3. CDA and poststructural critics

From another perspective, Alastair Pennycook (2001:80) has pointed out how CDA research has only partly been able to account for the agency of marginalized or discriminated persons. He argues that, despite a professed interest in the decentral, grass-roots enactment of power relations, much of CDA research continues to understand the process of exercise of power through language as a largely top-down process. For example, language use by political elites and the media have a prominent place in CDA research (Bluhm et al 2000:5).

In this regard, insights from postcolonial discourse analysis may point to viable alternatives (for an overview, see Mills 1997:105). For example, concepts of hybridity (Bhabha 1994: 173) and intersecting identities (Mohanty 1997:83) have opened new perspectives on postcolonial North-South relations. As Pennycook critically observes, however, postcolonial perspectives in discourse analysis have largely been ignored by linguistic approaches to discourse analysis, including CDA, which he terms "narrowly Eurocentric" (Pennycook 2001:80). This leads Pennycook to conclude that CDA has meanwhile become established "as another form of 'mainstream critical work' that closes down the possibility for thinking about critical text analysis in different ways" (2001:79). A combined poststructuralist and postcolonial stance, so Pennycook's argument, may result in a reconceptualisation that "allows for a move away from the frequent clumsiness of a model that works with ideologies produced by dominant groups" (2001:108) and facilitate more complex and subtle analysis. As Terry Threadgold has pointed out, there exists "more than one form of critical reading practice", as concrete empirical analysis provided by CDA and more abstract forms of poststructural theory need to exist side by side in order to allow for continuous critical engagement (Threadgold 2003:24). This is certainly not promising to bias analysis and conclusions in favour of tangible linguistic evidence. After all, as Blommaert reminds us, discourse analysis has to incorporate more than just linguistic features. "To the extent that we still believe that discourse is a linguistic object, the meaning of which can be fully tapped by deploying linguistic analysis, we shall never get there" (Blommaert 2005a:235). Creatively connecting relevant social theory to linguistic analysis is a practice anticipated in the CDA framework (Meyer 2001:19). For the context of development co-operation, postcolonialist approaches offer invaluable perspectives on linguistic and cultural dominance as well as related counter-strategies. In regard to the analysis presented here, linking the analysis of speech to the major insights of the preceding chapters is important: This concerns first of all the background of historic experience Tanzanians have with participatory approaches in development. Secondly, it is important to bear in mind the way PRA, Gender Planning and other 'tools' used in the delivery of aid programmes are biased to serve the interest of donors and Northern implementing agencies. Third, linguistic analysis needs to be aware ot the way the hegemony of English in Tanzania tends to reinforce the dominance of Northern actors and concepts in development (and vice versa). However, situating the analysis within the respective historical and socio-economic context is only a fist step in approaching the substantial challenge of incorporating poststructural critique into Critical Discourse Analysis.

6.1.4. Research issues and approaches to analysis

The empirical research on which this part of the study is based was initially guided by an interest in the role of communication in social development. This soon led to an enquiry into motivations and concepts that had formed communicative norms and behaviour in the two programmes studied. Participation, which by the 1990s had become popular in ever growing sections of the development industry, was soon found to be an essential idea that shaped communicative encounters.

For this chapter, the analysis of data corpus (transliterated meetings, interviews and field notes from participant observation) pertaining to the RCMP and SRAP programmes focussed on questions about the relationship between participatory approaches and programme implementation. Of particular interest were the ways beneficiaries and development workers conceived of and realized participation in the framework of the programme. A related objective was to gain an understanding of how they negotiated their often divergent perspectives in the process.

The interaction of participatory approaches and asymmetric power relationships emerged as particularly relevant in this context: Could participatory approaches contribute to the establishment of more egalitarian relationships between development workers and beneficiaries? And how did an actor's position in an asymmetric "aid relationship" influence her or his vision of participation? A critical discourse analytic approach was chosen in order to obtain both an understanding of relevant social and discursive manifestations of participatory development.

Information was gathered for a comparison of the targeted and actual condition of each programme, with a focus on respective participatory practices. This included brief organizational histories, organigrams, and basic data on programme objectives and performance, as well as a rough idea about the challenges and problems the programmes faced (cf Chapter 4). The relevant information was also linked to the recent history of Tanzania (Chapter 2) and current practices and discourses of participatory approaches in development co-operation (Chapter 3).

In a subsequent step, the data corpus was used to extract more detailed information on discourse and practices surrounding participation. The transliterated data from recorded meetings and interviews was examined for instances where the concept of participation was implicitly or explicitly referred to. This search for discourse passages relevant to participatory approaches in development co-operation was informed by recent theoretical work on the subject, in particular

by the debate on "tyranny" vs "transformation" (Cooke and Kothari eds 2001; Hickey and Mohan eds 2004; Mosse 2005)
From the analysis of interviews and meetings, three aspects of participation emerged as salient. In Swahili, 'participation' was usually translated with the verb 'shiriki' [co-operate, participate, share in, take part in- TUKI 2001] or the noun 'ushirikiano' which is derived from it. Both the development workers' and peasant farmers' understanding of participation primarily denoted shared communicative events, at least partly inspired by PRA, ZOPP, SEPO and similar approaches (cf Chapter 3). Apart from this, the term was also understood to mean co-operation, which comprised contributions by beneficiaries in labour and kind, as well as the expectation of benefits in material terms. In short, the analysis mainly focussed on the practice of alleged participatory communication; on the development workers' efforts to get the peasant farmers to 'do' or contribute their part, as well as on the beneficiaries' endeavours to gain access to the material goods offered by the programme. Negotiating the mutual process of 'give and take' was an essential part of the communicative interaction recorded and analyzed.
The linguistic analysis of the selected text passages on participation followed three related approaches. An initial consideration of various linguistic phenomena was limited to Fowler's (1985:78) list of linguistic features relevant to the analysis of power. These include lexicalisation, transitivity, syntax, modality, speech acts, implications, turn-taking, address forms and phonology. In particular, the notion of strategic use of linguistic forms in interaction was considered (cf Wodak und Martin 2003).
A second perspective of analysis focussed on the perceptions that actors in the aid relationship had of each other. In particular, the often stereotyped images that development workers have of beneficiaries were explored. Discourse-historic studies (e.g. Wodak et al 1990) offer a broad spectrum of methodological approaches here.
A third perspective considered the role of genres and inter-textual or inter-discursive references. In their propositions, actors in the two networks related prevailing ideas and concepts of development both implicitly and explicitly. Samples of various genres of text emanating from one network of organizations allow the analysis of "genre chains", in which a particular topic can be traced throughout various communicative events, but is reformulated to suit the organizational context (cf Fairclough 2003:31, Iedema 1999). As a result, information created at one point of the network traversed a variety of genres and organizational contexts, taking different shapes depending on the respective context.
The analysis of data was based on a hermeneutic-qualitative interpretation of the discourse samples against their historic and social background, with the intention of opening a detailed perspective on some of the "realities of aid" recorded throughout the research. In the following, the main arguments around the selected topics will be illustrated with quotations and discussed; linguistic considerations relating to the respective quotations will be attached in small print. The main

objective of the analytical process is a critical understanding of the various meanings the different actors in the development process attach to "participation" and the implications this has for development theory and practice. It should be noted at this point that even short text passages quoted to illustrate a particular point are often multilayered and therefore repeatedly lead to cross-references and connecting remarks.

6.2. Participation as dialogic exchange

Peasant farmers and development workers alike agreed that communication, and in particular dialogic exchange, was of fundamental importance to participatory approaches. Throughout the recorded meetings and interviews, numerous remarks were made to the effect that beneficiaries and development workers should meet and exchange ideas on a regular basis, that everybody should be able to take the floor and contribute, and that the voice of all concerned was important. Development workers made an effort to get into contact with peasant farmers and listen to them. They also critically reflected on their own role, reflecting the core tenet of PRA approaches that demands personal ethical commitment from development workers (cf Chambers 1997b).

Positive attitudes towards participatory communication as such were thus widespread. However, participatory observation of the recorded meetings documented the following tendencies which put some of these good intentions into question. In particular:

➢ Relationships between actors in development were, as in other development programmes, of an asymmetric nature. In many cases beneficiaries tried to anticipate what donors and development workers wanted to hear and donors and development workers exercised control via conditionality.

➢ The development workers' intention to 'listen' to the beneficiaries' concerns may have proved difficult to realize, as there were often considerably diverging interests within the groups. Leaders speaking for a group of beneficiaries often represented only a part of those present, and controversial issues tended to be suppressed in communication with outsiders. As a result, marginalized persons within the beneficiaries' groups had little chance of making themselves heard.

➢ Rural peasants often worked under time constraints, and committing time for meetings possibly resulted in other important activities being neglected. Some of the intended beneficiaries did not find the time to attend meetings and represent their interests (women with young children being a case in point, cf Hanak 1998).

In the following, various examples will be presented to illustrate the commitment expressed towards participatory communication as well as strategies to deal with its inherent contradictions.

6.2.1. The importance accorded to meetings in development work

Openness and collective empowerment: Numerous text passages from both within the SRAP and RCMP networks document that, for peasant farmers, assertiveness and openness to sharing thoughts and experiences seemed a matter of course. Freire has emphasized the role of the community in processes of learning and creation of knowledge: "no one can say a true word alone - nor can she or he say it for another, in a prescriptive act which robs others of their words" (Freire 1970:69)"). His charismatic words have aptly described and at the same time motivated people in many parts of the world – those whom he termed the "oppressed" – to work collectively for their own liberation. The next example, quoted from an interview with L. Mkongwa, a female peasant farmer from the village T. of the SRAP, emphasized the importance of sharing ideas with others.

> **Nijumuike** na wenzangu kuingia mawazo [...] kumbe yule mtu amechangia pale mawazo umesikia lile wazo limekuwa zuri **linakusaidia katika maisha yako** ehe (Int. Ms. L. Mkongwa, 7/2/94:1)

> Mkongwa emphasizes the importance of organizing: "nijumuike" (I should become part of a group) and the advantages of exchanging thoughts, as "kumbe [...] lile wazo [...] linakusaidia katika maisha yako" (actually [...] that thought [...] helps you in your life).

Statements of this kind reflect positive experiences with the communicative processes in the SRAP. Of course, activities of other development organizations, the local government or church similarly emphasized values of co-operation and mutual learning. However, within the SRAP network, the formation of a close-knit community of beneficiaries constituted an objective in itself, which was regarded as vital for processes of empowerment of individuals and strengthening of communities. Communicative events involving beneficiaries were organized in weekly intervals. In the RCMP, less effort was put into building beneficiaries' groups. All the same, in the RCMP as well, peasant farmer's organizations were entrusted with various responsibilities, such as channelling information and feedback and co-operation in organizational issues. Meetings took place at monthly intervals. Although the intensity of meetings varied, both programmes emphasized the importance of communication.

Attendance and intensity of meetings as indicators of success: From the point of view of the development organization's staff, regular meetings of beneficiaries reflected the programme's vitality. In addition, opinions voiced by beneficiaries in meetings played an important role in legitimising the programme's policy and decision-making. Claims that programme activities had been designed in response to beneficiaries' needs and suggestions were often made, especially in texts that presented the programmes' achievements to outsiders.

The following example is an excerpt from the presentation of an annual report within a monthly staff meeting in the RCMP network. The importance of finding out the farmers' needs through regular meetings with their representatives was emphasized.

> **Ramadhani** (assistant manager): (reading out the yearly report) [...] Kwa kutaka kuhakikisha kuwa huduma zetu tumetoa kwa mujibu wa **mahitaji ya wakulima wenyewe** / tumekuwa tukifanya vikao vya mara kwa mara na **viongozi** wa **jumuiya za wakulima** / mara ya mwisho viongozi wa RBA wamekutana na viongozi wa jumuia hizi **kutafakari kazi za msimu uliopita** kama ifuatavyo / *(an enumeration of groups, places and dates of meetings follows)* / (M20 RRDP:1-4)
>
> In this introductory passage of the report, reference was made to several terms that are constituent of participatory development discourse. This included the mentioning of **"mahitaji ya wakulima wenyewe"** (needs of the farmers themselves), of **"jumuiya za wakulima"** (farmers' communities) and their leaders **"viongozi"**. Again, the mere quotation of these terms carried important implications, including the assumption that farmers necessarily formed communities, and that their needs could summarily be learnt through meeting their leaders. The discourse of participatory development shaped strategies of programme representation in significant ways: both in the documentation of achievements and in the legitimisation of organizational decisions, reference to the allegedly "authentic" voice of the beneficiary seemed essential. **"Kutafakari kazi za msimu uliopita"** (**reflecting on last season's work**) alludes to expectations on the beneficiaries' role in appraising and evaluating programme achievements and demonstrates the extent to which participatory approaches have been internalized: Assessment, in this understanding, is no longer the prerogative of the experts, but supposedly based on an initial rating carried out by the beneficiaries themselves.

One must, however, bear in mind that, of the multi-faceted, contradictory and inconsistent voices of the beneficiaries, only few were taken up and discussed in staff meetings or reports. The variety of – often contradictory – opinions discussed in meetings at the grass-roots level was often edited and reduced to one or two major points, decided on by the consensus of staff members.

<u>Absence as failure:</u> Just as successfully conducted meetings were valued as an achievement per se, lack of attendance at meetings or training sessions often provided a starting point for critical reflections. The following example is from an SRAP staff meeting. The Advisor of the Women's Group reported on her demonstration of the use of compost in village T. While she was cautiously positive on the issue, the Agricultural Advisor assessed the event in negative terms. He critically remarked that only few people attended the event which was supposed to be an exemplary demonstration for all.

> **Fischer** (Agricultural Advisor): **Samahani!** / **I have** some problem with that / because **the participation is not good** / it was not good /
>
> **Msemwa** (Advisor of the Women's Group): Mhm /
>
> **Fischer: I don't think** it was a good example for other things / (M08 SRAP:3)

"Samahani" (excuse me) constitutes a discourse particle that introduced the confrontational remark, carrying additional emphasis through the use of Swahili in an otherwise English utterance. Fischer partly mitigated the face-threatening act at the personal level through an excuse, and through taking responsibility for his own feelings. ("I have some problem with that" and "I do not think..."). Yet at the same time the factual claim for objectivity is undaunted: "the participation was not good".

In this instance, as in other staff meetings, the beneficiaries' participation became an indicator used to assess the performance of the programme. The ensuing discussion focussed on how staff members could improve villagers' attendance by being more punctual and having activities at a time of the day that was more convenient for those less likely to attend (for example, women), so that more villagers would find the time to come. It was also decided to work more closely with some of the more promising leaders who, it was hoped, would encourage others.

Expectations and rules on communicative participation: Interactional routines and the production of written minutes and reports were to a large extent subject to the development organizations' need to account for their work, and to their expectations of group 'participation'.

In the following example, staff of the SRAP programme discussed the weak performance of the project group in one of the villages. The fact that the group functionaries did not meet on their own to prepare themselves for the monthly board meeting was identified as a major reason for the group's poor performance.

Msemwa (Advisor of the Women's Group): The third thing is I think they have problems again to **meet** /

Nyange (Programme Director): Ya /

Fischer (Agricultural Advisor): Walikutana kabla ya **jopo**?

Nyange: Nina mashaka / we tried to ask some questions / it seemed nobody knows /

Msemwa: Mhm /

Nyange: They don't even meet.

Msemwa: Wanaform agenda ndiyo wanapotuona kwamba tumekuja kwenye jopo / katika **kipindi** cha kufanya jopo ndiyo wanaform **ajenda** / inabidi tuzidiscuss tena kama sisi ndio **wapangaji** wa ajenda /

Fischer: Ndani ya kutengeneza **katiba** / mliweza kuangalia <+++> wanakutana?

Nyange: Katiba inaonyesha lazima wakutane kabla ya jopo / (M11 SRAP:3)

In this text passage, reference was made to familiar concepts of group formation, meetings and participatory planning. These references to principles of participatory development work were primarily made using technical terms such as "jopo" (board meeting), "kipindi" (set time, period) and "ajenda" (agenda) which referred to time schedules and processes of preparation. Mentioning the "katiba" (constitution) of the group served as a reminder of the group functionaries' duties: As they wrote the constitution themselves, it was they who volunteered to take care of preparations for meetings. This obligation was later made explicit through the modal expression "lazima wakutane" (they have to meet). Nominalizations such as "wapangaji" (planners) often carry implicit meanings. Here, the term alluded to the desirability of beneficiaries' active role in planning processes, which was then contrasted with their disappointing performance. Of course, conceptual references of this kind do not necessarily carry uniform meanings. But as the example shows, they enabled three like-minded staff members to arrive at a congruent assessment of a problematic situation within a few brief conversational turns: The fault was found in the beneficiaries' lack of initiative. In the everyday practice of programme implementation, the demands involved in participatory planning processes were not questioned: The time-consuming nature of the process and the peasants' general time constraints did not feature in the debate.

Significantly, staff did not question whether there had been any rational reasons why some beneficiaries preferred not to spend their time in lengthy meetings in preparation of other lengthy meetings, or whether patterns working in village M might not have been adequate in village T.
Normative demands in relation to communicative practices were not limited to development workers. In following example taken from a meeting in the SRAP network, X, a male farmer of the senior follow-up group, gladly took the opportunity to lecture members of the newly-founded women's group on how to organize their meetings properly.

> **Lukolo:** [...] kwa sababu wanachukua kipindi kirefu **bila kukutana** [...] hata kama **ukiwa** na ushirika ni **lazima muwe** mnakaa kikao / vile vikao vinaweza kuwa vinawaamsha nguvu / wanafanya kazi [...] hasa **bila vikao** - kusema• jamani **tukae** kwa pamoja **tufanye** kwa pamoja, **hawana** / [...] **kama** watakuwa wanakaa kwa pamoja wanafanya kazi kwa pamoja baada ya kuwa wameelewa umuhimu wa kuwa wanakaa pamoja / **basi watafanya kazi bila matatizo yoyote** / kwanza **waelewe** umuhimu wa kufanya kazi kwa pamoja / ni vikao ndivyo **vinafanya** mtu anaelewa umuhimu / **wawe na vikao** vyao bila kuingiliwa na wanaume / wanakaa wao wenyewe / kama kuna wewe mshauri unawashauri / kama watahitaji mwingine kuweza kupata mawazo yake basi wanamwita lakini siyo kwamba ni lazima aingie kwenye kikao chao kutatua matatizo yao (M04 SRAP:22)

> Lukolo's account on the one hand contained negative forms to illustrate what he regarded as the main deficiency "bila kukutana" (without coming together), "bila kikao" (without meeting), "hawana" (they don't have it). In order to elaborate on the ideal state in contrast to this, modal forms were used: the conditional "ukiwa na ushirika" (if you have a co-operative), "kama watakuwa wanakaa" (if they sit together); nouns expressing modality: "lazima" (it is necessary); the subjunctive "muwe na" (you should have), "tukae" (we should sit), "tufanye" (we should do), "wawe na vikao" (they should have meetings), "waelewe" (they should understand). In order to emphasize general assertions on the positive impact of having meetings, the future tense "watafanya kazi bila matatizo yoyote" (they will work without problems) and present tense "vikao ndivyo vinafanya mtu anaelewa" (meetings make a person understand) were used. The unmitigated assertions phrased in the indicative tense made this statement forceful and self-assured. Advice was expressed in modal forms of conditionality and necessity.

The above statement was based on several assumptions which by and large reflected the discursive consensus among beneficiaries and development workers within the programme. It includes the notion that meetings are a precondition for any type of common activity, that they foster understanding and help reduce and resolve problems, and that they make participants take their own work more seriously. Apart from this, it is also implied that meetings empower participants to meet on their own without outside interference, with outside advice only given when group members explicitly request it.

While several valuable experiences were expressed here, the core aspect was lost in the process: Although well-intentioned, Lukolo's contribution amounted to nothing more than one of the unsolicited impositions from outside that he so eloquently criticized. As shown above, the practice of turning alternative approaches into sets of rules is one that is primarily induced by the administrative necessities of development organizations. But it is also part of some group members' effort to demonstrate their knowledge and experience. The implications of participatory approaches for gender relations will be discussed in greater detail in a later section of this chapter.

Communication and asymmetry: With respect to the interaction between the development workers and peasant farmers, differences in various actors' abilities to influence practices within the network were occasionally brought up. Peasant farmers – in many cases rather politely and indirectly – implied that they depended in many regards on the development workers' benevolence, and that there was little they themselves could do to change practices that they perceived as working to their disadvantage. In the following example from the RCMP, a representative of the rice farmers illustrated the extent to which he saw co-operation depending on the government's good-will.

> **Machano** (Chair of rice farmers in V.) Jambo langu la kwanza natoa shukrani kubwa kuhusu utaratibu huu wa sasa kwani **tulizoea** tangu zamani **kutembelewa** lakini kwa muda mkubwa **hatutembelewi na kuulizwa shida** za wakulima sasa tunashukuru kwamba **serikali imekaa na kufikiri** kwamba **kurejea tena utaratibu wa kushauriana** baina ya walimiwa na wale maofisa wa serikali waliohusu kazi za ukulima hilo tunalishukuru. (M19 RCMP:5)

> In his contribution, Machano initially expressed his appreciation of regular and organized communicative exchange, which he construed as the 'usual' state of the relationship between farmers and extension workers: "tulizoea kutembelewa" (we were used to being visited). However, he then went on to point out the failure of the extension service to live up to this expectation. In this, he portrayed the farmers as passive and dependent: "hatutembelewi na kuulizwa shida" (we are not visited and asked about our concerns). He did not, however, explicitly name the actors who could be blamed for this. Instead, the government was stylized as a person-like singular actor: "serikali imekaa na kufikiri" (the government has sat down and thought). Note that when the speaker proceeded to comment on the recently improved state of affairs, he used verbal forms that emphasized reciprocity, such as "kushauriana" (mutual counselling), and explicitly named the communicative partners. Yet, by referring to the role of the policy framework "serikali [...] kurejea tena utaratibu wa kushauriana" (the government [...] re-introducing the pattern of mutual counselling), he made it clear that he put the responsibility primarily with the (governmental) development organization. His contribution is thus a clear reminder that the option of farmers unilaterally engaging in participatory communication is not promising.

Parts of this statement sounded submissive and reminiscent of clientilist relationships. Portraying oneself as dependent and passive in this case served as a strategy of reminding the powerful partner of the unequal relationship and the responsibility he or she has. Yet, although communication was far from being egalitarian here, the appeal to an ideal at least opened a perspective beyond the mere expression of powerlessness. Asymmetries of power or status among peasant farmers, which were rarely explicitly addressed in meetings of both networks, will be discussed in the next part of this section.

6.2.2. Access and organization: Who participates where, when and how?

Engaging in organizational processes: The SRAP's understanding of participation demanded a considerable commitment of time to different types of meetings and training courses which took place regularly. In order to organize these meetings, beneficiaries were expected to form groups and elect functionaries such as chairpersons, secretaries and treasurers. These functionaries played a key role in the realization of meetings, as they were expected to communicate the programme's principles to motivate their fellow group members.

> **Kasawe** (Chair village M.): e: / **Ndugu Wajumbe** / napenda nichukue nafasi hii fupi / niweze kuwashukuru kwa muda ambao tumeshirikiana / tangu asubuhi nafikiri **tuko pamoja** kwa kufanya shughuli mbalimbali / (M4 SRAP:1)

> The above example was taken from a meeting of a village group with project staff. The words of encouragement were uttered by the group's Chairman at the point of closing one section of the meeting and opening the next. With the words "Ndugu wajumbe" (comrade delegates) the Chairperson addressed all participants, development workers and peasant farmers alike. In fact, retaining the address form "ndugu" (comrade/brother) in rural development long after the dismantling of Tanzanian socialism was a typical example of the use of egalitarian forms in development communication. Additionally, in the examples "tumeshirikiana" (we co-operate) and "tuko pamoja" (we are together) an inclusive "we" was used to refer to development workers and peasant farmers attending the meeting.

Here, the village Chairman made an effort to communicate a message of appreciation for those present. At the same time, however, he glossed over underlying asymmetries· All present could voice their opinion, yet peasant farmers ultimately had a very limited influence on decision-making, and women even less of an influence than men. Development workers attended meetings as part of their paid jobs, while peasants could not count on an immediate compensation for their presence. Placing meetings and their entire organization at the hands of beneficiaries was an important part of ensuring commitment, common consensus and shared discourse – not necessarily despite the persistance of the many asymmetries of the aid relationship, but because of them.

Within the RCMP programme, procedures of village level group meetings were not necessarily equally concerned with formally handing over responsibilities of interactional management. In the SRAP, an effort was made to ensure that meetings between development workers and beneficiaries were managed by the functionaries of beneficiary groups. In the more hierarchical structure of the Ministry of Agriculture, of which the RCMP staff was after all a part, it was often a senior extension staff member who would chair respective meetings. The extension staff were generally less concerned with adapting to the communicative routines of the groups they worked with (cf Hanak 1997). The scope of the programme was a major reason for extension agents to be less concerned about individual group arrangements. Yet the principle that everyone present at a meeting should have an equal opportunity to be heard could always be relied on.

> **Hamis** (Chair in village J): **Bosi** na mie **nilikuwa na mchangio**, lakini mgongo wako huku unakoweka
>
> **Mnali** (district manager D): Haya basi **ungekuja mbele** nikakuona. (M19 RCMP:14)
>
> For Hamis, one of many farmers' representatives present at the meeting, "Bosi" (boss) served as a form of address to the district manager that was both ironic and respectful, as well as a discourse marker initiating a contribution from a person who was not in the addressee's visual field. "Nilikuwa na mchangio" (I had a contribution) was phrased in the indicative past tense, the propositional content actually being "I want to make a contribution". The specification "lakini mgongo wako huku unakoweka" (but there what you turn your back on) criticizes the the manager for ignoring his presence. Mnali's response was a respectful encouragement to speak "ungekuja mbele" (would you come forward).

In this case, an experienced farmers' representative had no problems making himself heard, as the communicative framework was based on democratic principles of interaction.

Participation vs exclusion: Organizational policy was a primary factor determining who was admitted as participant and who not. In both the SRAP and RCMP programmes, the benficiary group was primarily composed of male peasants with some basic resources and innovative ambitions. In the case of the SRAP, beneficiaries had to commit a considerable amount of time to training activities, while in the RCMP programme fees for the mechanized services had to be afforded. Both programmes were set in rural communities where the people lived in very modest or even precarious conditions. Neither of the programmes made an effort to specifically include the poorest sections of the respective communities. The few women who could benefit from an equal footing with the men were often the heads of households or disposed of some minimal independent financial resources – conditions which did not apply to the majority of female peasant farmers in the respective areas. For some of these women, participation was based on their being married to male group members and taking part in a separate 'women's group in some limited capacity. And while young unmarried men had begun to form a youth group, there was no comparable offer for young unmarried women. Despite the fact the gender equality was emphasized in the implementing organization's policy outline, the programme in many ways exacerbated rather than balanced existing asymmetries (Hanak 1998). Women were expected to participate in the programme, but not in a way that would challenge the men's position. Interestingly enough, the very discourse on the importance of women in development in many ways served to confirm their subordinate position. Consider the following remarks made by the Chairman of the group in village M., which was part of a closing statement in a planning meeting:

> **Kasawe:** (Chair village M): [...] kitu kingine ambacho nakisema ambacho nilikiongea, ambacho nakisisitiza zaidi ni kuhusu wanawake / wanawake tunawasahau katika maendeleo / na **ukiangalia idadi ya wanawake katika Mkoa mzima wa Mara ndiyo wazalishaji wakubwa wa uchumi** / kwa hiyo **nawahusia wenzangu / wale tulioko na wanawake nyumban**i / tujaribu kuwasukuma kwenye maswala ya namna hii / maswala ya namna hii ni maswala ya kimaendeleo / kwa hiyo tusiendelee na mtindo ule wa zamani ambao babu **zetu walikuwa wanawakataza akina mama kula Kamongo** / hii wanakula wanaume tu si ya wanawake / huu mtindo tuache / kama inavyoonekana sasa hivi tunaendelea sisi **tunasahau wanawake nyuma** / sasa wao **nani atakayewainua** / kama ndiyo **muda wetu huu wa kuweza kuwashirikisha**, kama niliyosema kwamba siri ya maendeleo ni ushirikiano / mkiwa na ushirikiano mzuri mnaleta maendeleo / bila ushirikiano hakuna maendeleo katika nchi hii na katika kijiji hiki na katika familia unayotoka / (M4 SRAP:32)

> The Chairman began his argument with an emphasis on the economic dimension of women's work, a common trope of the "Women in Development" rhetoric: "ukiangalia idadi ya wanawake katika Mkoa mzima wa Mara ndiyo wazalishaji wakubwa wa uchumi" (if you look at the number of women in the whole Region of Mara, they are major economic producers). The argument of women's importance in agricultural production was also widely used in public political discourse in Tanzania throughout the 1980s and 1990s. Furthermore, the speaker marked a break with a perceivedly discriminatory past "babu zetu walikuwa wanawakataza akina mama kula Kamongo" (our forefathers did not allow women to eat lungfish). While the Chairman thus pledged his good intentions for an emancipatory agenda, he continued to exclude and treat women as objects on a communicative level. Throughout his statement, he commented on the men's responsibility for the women of their families, but he ignored the women present: "tunawasahau wanawake" (we forget the women), "nani atakayewainua" (who will lift them up), "muda wetu wa kuweza kuwashirikisha" (our time and ability to make them participate). Finally, while addressing gender imbalances, the speaker located women in the domestic realm, and addressed his mixed audience as if it were only male "kwa hiyo nawahusia wenzangu / wale tulioko na wanawake nyumbani..." (so I ask you my friends / those of us who have women at home...).

The Chair's statements came at the end of a two-hour meeting in which the two women of a village target group who were present contributed only one turn each. (For a discussion of gender-specific processes of silencing and exclusion in the network, see Hanak 1997). The Chairman blended paternalistic, neo-liberal and gender-equity arguments in his appeal. At the very least, he used the opportunity to claim the status of men as facilitators helping women. As Mosse aptly observed: "Making women the prime targets, the ones who need developing, allows men to deny their negative beneficiary status" (Mosse 2005:170).

Time, place and 'authority': Regarding the setting of time and place for meetings, practical considerations, such as the work schedules of the development workers and peasant farmers, were significant. Within both programmes, it was understood that the development workers had to get into contact with peasant farmers in the rural areas they were living in, and that this was best accomplished by attending meetings on a regular basis. However, transport was often a problem, so that reliability or punctuality was not always granted.

In the mid-1990s, public transport in rural Tanzania was unreliable and insufficient, and continues to be so in most areas. The SRAP and RCMP had cars, motorbikes and bicycles at their disposal, but these were often not plentiful enough to cover all staff transport needs. As Nöst (1997) has pointed out, negotiations on access to transport in the Agricultural Extension Service in Zanzibar could take up a large part of the working time of the higher levels of extension staff. Distribution of these means of transport often reflected status differences among staff members. For example, a meeting of (village level) Block Extension Officers and their superiors from the Ministry that was held in rural Zanzibar meant that all participants had to travel up to 30 kilometers to arrive at the meeting place. The ministerial staff used cars or motorbikes, while Block Extension Officers had only poorly maintained bicycles to cover the distance. Yet it was usually the village-based Block Extension Officers who waited for the Extension Officers from the capital – in one observed example the wait took four hours. In the SRAP team, the Tanzanian Programme Director used a motorbike, the (foreign) Agricultural Advisor drove the car, while the Advisor of the Women's Groups travelled by bicycle.

Whether a group would wait for latecomers often depended on the status of the persons in question (cf. Meier 1997:55). At the meetings observed for this study, there were also instances where obligations towards higher-ranking authorities disrupted long-term planning at short notice. In the following example, the Manager of the RCMP programme informed his colleagues at the beginning of a staff meeting that he had less than on hour to attend to the scheduled meeting which could normally take up to two hours. His excuse was that he had been informed on short notice of a meeting with the Assistant Minister for Agriculture.

Salum (programme manager): **Karibu / tusipoteze wakati sana** tuna masuala mengine yanatusubiri / naona **nimeambiwa kuna kikao na Naibu saa nne** / kwa hivyo tuanze tu moja kwa moja / **tuanze hapo pa mechanization** / (M21 RRDP:1)

A shortish "Karibu" (welcome) served as an introductory greeting to the colleagues attending the staff meeting. With "tusipoteze wakati sana" (we should not lose much time) the manager then admonished himself and the others to proceed swiftly. It was nine o'clock in the morning and the explanation for the time pressure was given rather casually: "kuna kikao na Naibu saa nne" (there is a meeting with the deputy [minister] at ten). The implication was that he as manager had to attend this meeting. This information was preceded by the discourse particle "naona" (I see / I think) and the passive form "nimeambiwa" (I have been told) – both clear indications that the manager regarded himself as bound by an obligation towards the ministry rather than his commitment to his fellow colleagues. There was no further excuse given; instead, the manager used hortative forms to get staff members to continue business without further discussion. With "tuanze tu moja kwa moja" (Let's just begin straight away) he opened the meeting and passed it on to the representative of the mechanisation section: "tuanze hapo pa mechanization" (let's begin with mechanisation).

The priority given to the Assistant Minister and his agenda was taken for granted and not questioned at any point. Organizational routines that linked the value of an individual's time to her or his position in a hierarchy pervaded participatory meetings on several levels.

Turn and topic control: In accordance with political and organizational culture in rural Tanzania, active involvement in development activities also entailed assuming functions in the respective organizational settings. In the SRAP, meetings between development workers and beneficiaries were usually conducted by functionaries of the beneficiaries' groups. This also meant that these groups had to meet independently in order to set the agenda and prepare topics for discussion. Being responsible for the 'management' of communicative events ensured that beneficiaries played an active role in meetings: Barriers on the way to the "floor" were certainly reduced for participants who had developed a habit of taking extensive turns as group functionaries. The following example illustrate that the 'correct' allocation of these formal roles could not easily be ignored.

> **Ndutu:** [...] / hapo ndipo nilikuwa na maana yangu kabla Robert hajafunga.
>
> **Kilanya** (secretary of the village group): Hajafunga - anayefunga ni Mwenyekiti si Robert ! (M13 SRAP:21)
>
> In this example, a group member attempted to introduce a new topic at the end of a long debate. The speaker pointed out that he needed to make his point before the Agricultural Advisor, who had just made a longer presentation, closed the meeting. However, he was immediately corrected by the group's secretary: The Agricultural Advisor did not have a mandate to close the meeting, as this was the prerogative of the Chairperson.

Putting peasant farmers formally in charge of conducting communicative events had a strong symbolic effect. Apart from this, it encouraged them to regularly comment on and summarize developments from their point of view. However, this did not necessarily mean that they could effectively influence decision-making processes.

The 'diplomatic' move of allocating interactional roles in an effort to balance asymmetric relations was also observed in other parts of the network, for example, in a meeting that had mainly been intended as an act of good will between the SRAP team and the Diocese, which acted as the Tanzanian counterpart organization in the network. This organizational set-up meant that, in practice, Tanzanian staff members were employees of the Diocese, and that the Team was formally under the supervision of the Development Director of the Diocese. At the time of research, there was a background of strained relations. On the one hand, the team had occasionally acted rather autonomously. Given the financial independence it had through foreign funding, it had also felt that it could afford to do so. The Diocese, on the other hand, with its rather hierarchical organizational structures, felt that it had been left out of important developments.

The meeting had been called in order to improve the flow of information between the team and the Diocese. It brought together the team members M., H. and S. and Luwamba, the Diocese's Development Director, a person who was very sympathetic towards the team's concerns. At the beginning of the meeting, Nyange, the Tanzanian Team Leader, invited Luwamba to preside over the meeting. That said, he told Hörmannseder, the Austrian development worker, to read out last week's protocol, at the same time appointing him to the position of Secretary.

Luwamba: Nani Mwenyekiti (pause) **rasmi** ...

Nyange: Ni wewe

Luwamba: Kumbe. (anacheka) Oooh wajumbe kikao kimefunguliwa, karibuni.

Nyange, Msemwa: Asante sana.

[...]

Luwamba: Minutes, minutes zilizopita ?

Nyange: Anazo hapo Robert atasomea / **Robert ndiyo katibu leo**

Fischer: Ooh!

Luwamba: Ongeza michango basi katibu

Fischer: Asante Mzee. Sawa, tulikutana tarehe ishirini na tatu, mwezi wa tatu / ni nani alihudhuria, ni wewe mwenyekiti .../ (M14 SRAP:1-2)

Luwamba's question "Nani Mwenyekiti (pause) rasmi ... " (who is the [pause] official chair) concluded a short phase of small talk that took place as the four participants gathered in the room. Nyange took charge of the team: His "Ni wewe" (it's you) was both determined and reassuring. Luwamba then took up the Chair's role by enquiring about the last meeting's protocol. Nyange assigned the task of Secretary to Fischer, again in no uncertain terms: "Robert ndiyo katibu leo" (Robert has got them here / Robert is the Secretary today). Fischer is caught by surprise, as this tedious task is usually left to Msemwa, the junior female Social Worker. Yet he is quick to comply, and while his "Asante, Mzee" (Thank you, Elder) may sound clumsy in a working context, it is appreciated as part of Fischer's effort to negotiate Tanzanian language and culture.

Given Fischer's dominant position in the programme – the Northern implementing NGO expected him, like other foreign development workers or experts, albeit informally, to retain control over finances and major decisions in the programme – this move partly reversed the factual hierarchy in the team. Fischer, understanding the symbolic implication, was quick to cope with the challenge of reading out and later writing up the protocol in Swahili. Just as contemporary development discourse combines partnership with asymmetry, a development worker's job involves seemingly contradictory tasks: enacting partnership when this is called for, and retaining control where core issues are at stake.

6.2.3. Egalitarian communication and democratic decision-making

Participatory communication is partly understood as an end in itself, and partly as a means of preparing participatory decision-making processes. However, both in the SRAP and the RCMP, the peasant farmers had only a very limited opportunity to influence decision-making. Instead, the social prestige of decision-making by majority vote was used to legitimise decisions made elsewhere. This also applied to the use of more elaborate communicative tools to elicit opinions and preferences.

<u>A share in decision-making: limited to trifling issues?</u> It is important to consider which decisions are submitted to voting by beneficiaries. In development co-operation, some decisions always remain the prerogative of the donor, such as the amounts released. Programme design and practice are necessarily the domain of the implementing organization, with donors having a major say in the overall policy framework. With participartory approaches in social development programmes, their voice has gained recognition and importance, while consultations have become routine. Nevertheless, consultative processes are usually limited to a mere forum where concerns can be voiced.

In many cases, the available choices can thus be summed up in terms of 'take it or leave it'. That is, instead of having the opportunity to vote 'by hand', beneficiaries have the option of voting 'on foot' – of walking or opting out of a programme. Beneficiaries can thus decide whether to participate in a programme or not, but the possibility to influence a programme's implementation is limited. Depending on the programme, there might be some leeway in details concerning concrete work, timing and individual preferences in implementation. These are the areas where democratic processes can be found at work. But the line between what is negotiable and what is not is often communicated implicitly and taken as a matter of course.

In both the SRAP and the RCMP, the programmes were largely designed from outside. This did not mean that the importance of democratic decision-making processes was ignored. However, they remained restricted to a circumscribed number of occasions. These concerned, for example, the choice between two alternatives within an otherwise fixed framwork or, as in the following example, the proposal of making an additional effort under difficult conditions.

In the following example, the Agricultural Advisor of the SRAP programme wanted to convince the group in village M. to make an extra effort to promote organic agriculture in the village. He suggested that they organize a competition among farmers who implemented the following practices: "having contours, having terraces, using fertilizer of manure or compost, and mixing crops". He started by praising them for efforts he had previously seen. He mentioned that "even" the group in village T. was going to have a competition of this kind, challenging his audience not to lag behind the other group. Next, he constructed the moral challenge of dealing with the prevailing drought, claiming that "ukame una—unaamsha akili ya mtu kabisa" (drought completely wakes up a person's mind). He compared the farmers who make an effort to "kupigana na ukame" (fight with drought) to the villagers who "wameshakata tamaa" (have given up already) [M04 Chumwi 10-02-94:12]. He also promised that the team was going to bring in a water expert who would look at the possibility of irrigation in fields around the lake, an issue the group had shown interest in earlier. After these introductory remarks, he made his proposal, not without naming the difficulties the undertaking might encounter:

> **Fischer** (Agricultural Advisor):... na mimi nataka kupendekeza hii mashindano hapa pia / kama mnaweza kukubali / mashindano madogo / [...] kama ni ngumu bado acheni ni pendekezo ambalo lina:: kazi nyingi / kazi nyingi inaingia / ninajua / lakini kama ni ngumu bado **acheni** / tungeiacha / kwa sababu hali ya hewa ni ngumu, nini / ninajua kama uharakishi kitika kilimo huwezi kupata nyingi labda / **nani anajua** / lakini pia ni kwa **kuona mbali kidogo** inaweza kusaidia / na hii ni sababu / kwa hii naweza kupendekeza hii / Mwenyekiti, nafikiri **ni vizuri kujadiliana** au **ni rahisi ku / kukataa au kukubali, sijui** / ni mawazo yangu juu ya hali ya kilimo na juu ya — ya mbali kidogo. (M04 SRAP:12)

> After having presented his idea, he hedged his proposal by telling them „acheni" (leave it) it if it is too hard; he also mentioned the disadvantages it could have: „lina: kazi nyingi" (it means a lot of work) offering again the alternative „tungeliacha" (we should leave it) adding „hali ya hewa ni ngumu" (the weather is difficult) „nani anajua" (who knows). In a last plea for the proposal, he used strategies to mitigate and relativise: „kuona mbali kidogo" (some foresight), „ni mawazo yangu" (it is my opinion), „ni vizuri kujadiliana" (it's good to discuss) „ni rahisi kukataa au kukubali" (it is easy to object or agree).

The proposal was subsequently discussed, and after three supportive statements by other group members it was decided to vote on the issue. All present raised their hands in agreement; there was no voice of objection.

<u>Brainstorming: Don't copy from your neighbour</u> The political culture of majority consensus also played a vital role in group discussions led by the development workers. Techniques of "brainstorming", working in small groups, or visualising contributions on cards were occasionally used in the RCMP programme to facilitate communication on important issues.

The following quotation was part of the discussion on income-generating projects within the SRAP project. Several members of the women's group had proposed opening a coffee shop. Following the programme policy, Msemwa explained that staff could not support income-generating projects, but it could offer training on related issues. The group had already discussed the option of providing a course on nutrition and health. In order to widen the debate on this issue, Msemwa invited the group members to think about other issues for which training could be helpful – and to write them down on a piece of paper.

> **Msemwa** (Advisor of the Women's Group): sasa nilitoa haya madaftari / **naomba** tu nigawie karatasi / kila mtu andike kabla hatujafanya lolote / **nafikiri kila mtu ana mawazo tofauti** / **utaandika** — unaandika mawazo ambayo wewe unafikiri kwamba hii hali ya kuamua kuji-

funza haya mambo ya lishe na afya na baadaye kufungua mkahawa huo unatazamia kujifunza nini / **naomba kila mtu aandike** / unaandika tu / **unataja hata mambo sita hivi** / kila mtu anaandika / yeye anatazamia kujifunza nini kwenye hii tutaita kama semina au kama mlolongo tu / mfululizo wa masomo / utakuwa hauna mwisho / unaendelea tu / xxx / unaandika kwenye hii karatasi / halafu baadaye unakuja kuna nini / kalamu hiyo hapo / sijui tumeelewana / **kama kuna mtu ana swali aniulize** / **unaandika jina lako juu tafadhali** / xxx / ikiwa hujaelewa hatujaelewana unaweza ukauliza swali / xxx / kuna watu unaweza ukawauliza / wavulana wengine waliobaki kuna instructor amekaa pale / naye unaweza ukamwona ukamwulize yeye na anaweza akakushauri / *(wanacheka)* xxx

[…] mimi ambacho naona ndiyo vizuri ni ukijifunza unaandika tu / unatazamia kujifunza nini / **usifanye kazi inayofanana na mwenzako tafadhali** / kila mtu anataja vyake / mi nataja vya kwangu pia (M01 SRAP:4)

Msemwa presented her concern as a polite request, e.g. "naomba tu nigawie karatasi" (I ask you that I may distribute the paper). She was expressing her appreciation of everyone's contribution with an assertion: "nafikiri kila mtu ana mawazo tofauti" (I think everybody has a different opinion). She gave detailed instructions when it came to how the brainstorming was going to be done: "Utaandika" (you will write), "naomba kila mtu aandike" (everybody should write please) "unataja hata mambo sita hivi" (you mention up to about six items), "kama kuna mtu ana swali aniulize" (if anyone has a question she should ask me) "unaandika jina lako juu tafadhali" (you write your name on top please). The extent to which the process was understood as an outside-mediated learning experience was obvious from the last half-ironic admonition: "Usifanye kazi inayofanana na mwenzako" (Don't copy from your neighbour).

In this workshop-like interaction guided by Msemwa group members shared their ideas and expectations. Writing proposals on cards and discussing them was supposed to ensure that all present received equal attention. The exercise successfully prepared a common planning and decision-making process. It also confirmed Msemwa in her expert position, as she facilitated the process and made group members familiar with brainstorming activities. It is, however, important not to ignore the context: Msemwa had just explained to the group that its aspirations to open a coffee-house would not be supported by programme staff. The offer to have courses on nutrition, calculation and other issues relating to the original plan presented a very limited alternative. The means by which this was discussed lent legitimacy to the whole process, yet, as Beck (2006:210) found in her study on a moderated discussion process in a rural project in Namibia, the use of participatory approaches in the moderation of communicative encounters does not necessarily lead to egalitarian communication. In the above example, the process was primarily used to motivate a group after its proposal had been flatly turned down.

6.3. Participation as an obligation to contribute: Time, labour and user fees

Participatory programmes depend on the potential beneficiaries' willingness to co-operate. With the spread of neo-liberal ideology throughout the 1980s, social development programmes increasingly emphasized the need for initiative and contributions on the part of target groups. The role of the state was increasingly curtailed in favour of market-oriented approaches. This also influenced the reception of alternative approaches such as participation and empowerment, as they eventually found their way into mainstream policies.

Demands on common people to make efforts towards community advancement date back to concepts of community development from the colonial period (Hickey and Mohan 2005:239). Cases where a majority of poor people came under pressure to contribute to projects which benefited only a small elite have been documented (Kelsall and Mercer 2003; Crewe and Harrison 1998:162). Several studies have found that beneficiaries perceive participatory approaches primarily in terms of the obligations they imply, as demands on time and other resources may be considerable (Mosse 2005). Hickey and Bracking conclude that especially "the poorest may view direct participation as a risky and time-consuming strategy" (2005:852).

The SRAP and RCMP each depended on the peasants' readiness to commit their time and labour (for example in the training offers of the SRAP program), as well as financial resources (for user fees in the RCMP program). This corresponded to a policy environment in which the initiative and economic contributions of beneficiaries were increasingly emphasized as a prerequisite for attaining sustainable development.

6.3.1. Communicating obligations: The framework set by organizational policy

General principles: The SRAP and RCMP had various ways of communicating both the principal and concrete expectations they had about the ways peasant farmers should co-operate. This was not limited to internal planning meetings but included public presentations, and in the case of the RCMP the opportunity to disseminate information through the Ministry of Agriculture's radio broadcast or journal. In the SRAP network, great effort was made to communicate the programme's underlying concept of development. The following example is taken from a public meeting in the village, in which this vision of development was presented and discussed.

> **Msemwa** (Advisor of the Women's Group): [Vijana] **waanze** kutumia nguvu zao kushughulika **hapa kijijini** [...] maendeleo yale ya mjini yakija huku kijijini watu [ha]watakuwa na hamu tena ya kukimbilia **mjini**. (M13 SRAP:5)
>
> Msemwa used the subjunctive to express the normative expectation the programme had about the village youth: "waanze kutumia nguvu zao kushughulika hapa kijijini" (they should use their strength to get busy here in the village). Eventually, so the argument went, this would bring development to the village, and in turn people would no longer feel the urge to "kukimbilia mjini" (run off to town).

This vision of development, which emphasized the welfare of the village community, originated from the Austrian partner NGO and partly stood in conflict with the more individual-oriented ideas on development the farmers themselves had – an aspect that will be discussed in detail in the following section.

Another related example of a principal policy matter was the fact that the SRAP primarily offered training – in order to improve the beneficiaries' ability to improve their lives on their own. Training session involved different kinds of practical demonstrations and work on both common and individual fields. The benefits peasant farmers obtained from taking part in these trainings were often of a long-term rather than immediate nature. They ranged from technology acquired (for example ox-plowing), to benefits for the wider community (the major motivation for planting trees, for instance). The organization made training available for free, having been able to establish a group who had internalized the concept: "tuko watu wa mafunzo" (we are people of learning), one of them commented (Lukolo M09 SRAP:9). Nevertheless, attendance of training activities could not always be taken for granted. At the time of research, beneficiaries increasingly suggested activities with tangible material outcomes which will be discussed in the following section as "income generating projects".

Adapting principles in implementation: Within the RCMP programme, a comparable matter of axiomatic policy was the fact that farmers had to pay user fees for ploughing, harrowing and weeding services. Actual implementation had varied throughout the programme. Initially, the RCMP's tractors would begin to plough the fields, leaving the collection of the fees to the farmers' associations However, many farmers did not pay and debts accumulated. It was then decided that only those farmers who paid cash would be served. This did not solve all the practical problems involved in implementation, but it made certain that beneficiaries could not avoid paying, as M. Vuai, the head of the mechanisation section, explained in an interview:

> .../ halafu na then **inaamuliwa kwamba** [...] **watu walimiwe kwa cash walipe** / tena ndo matatizo yameanza / mpaka sasa **kila mmoja** anakuwa **anakwenda anapotaka**, (Interview MZ Vuai Specialist/M 27/07/94:21)

> Vuai portrays the decision taken by the RCMP management in a depersonalized and passive way: "inaamuliwa kwamba" (It is [was] decided that): Normative expectations are expressed in the subjunctive: "watu walimiwe kwa cash walipe" (people should pay cash so that [their fields] are ploughed). However, sidelining the farmers' associations in the process created new problems, as the farmers' willingness to pay did not correspond with pre-planned schedules. "Mpaka sasa kila mmoja anakuwa anakwenda anapotaka" (even now, each one of them just comes when she /he wants).

Insisting on fees meant that some poorer peasants were excluded from the programme. Although the fees collected covered less than 20% of the actual cost of the services offered, farmers did complain about the financial burden, and staff debated its implications. Abolishing fees was dismissed as impossible, just as the era of Ujamaa development was regarded as irretrievably past. If ploughing services had been offered for free, so the argument goes, it would not have been possible to meet demand. Some staff members nevertheless regretted the bias against poorer peasants. Demanding payment in advance meant that those who could command more resources were in an advantageous position. As Vuai put it, "mwenye kuleta pesa ndio tunamfanya zaidi" (we do most for the one with ready cash) (Interview Bw MZ Vuai Specialist/M 27/07/94:21)

Other staff members were cautiously positive about collecting user fees, arguing that this rewarded those who were sincere and committed: "tutanza kulima mahala ambapo wakulima wamelipa / na wao wenyewe kama wanaona umuhimu wa kufanya mapema, watalipa mapema (Bw. MA Chumbe M20 RCMP:7) (We will start to plough in the places where the farmers have paid/ and if they themselves realize the importance of doing it early, they will pay early).

Despite these mixed experiences, the possibility of grading fees according to the social situations of the farmers was not considered. In general, extension staff felt that it was enough of a challenge to provide good service to those who paid. Activities such as ploughing had to be carried out in consideration of rainfall, soil conditions in each area, and farmers' individual practices and preferences. Securing the maintenance of tractors and setting up time schedules in accordance with the farmers was a major task.

Working morale - the virtues of participating: When development organizations and their staff verbalised expectations on beneficiaries' behaviour, elements of a work ethic or morale were often part of the message. For example, in one of the previous examples, migrating to town was branded as "kukimbilia mjini" (running off to town), while in another it was implied that those who did not pay also did not take the work seriously. In meetings, value judgements of this kind were often expressed indirectly, while more straightforward remarks were typical of informal contexts.

The following passage is quoted from a semi-formal discussion between Fischer, the Agricultural Advisor and Kigeli, the Instructor of the group in village M. "Instructor" denoted one of the functions village group members could take on. It entailed the ability to share technical knowledge with other group members, and it was the only function a group member was paid to do for a small fee. The objective of their exchange was to prepare Kigeli's visit in T., officially to facilitate communication between the groups in the two villages. It was obviously hoped that a visit by one of the leaders of village M. would have a positive effect on the work morale of the group in village T. Informally, staff had fostered a competitive attitude between the two villages. They occasionally made comparisons in which the role model character of the group in village M. was emphasized, while an attitude of carelessness was said to prevail among members of the group in village T. In preparation for his visit, the Agricultural Adviser emphasized a need for orderly planning and regular work.

6.3. Participation as an obligation to contribute: Time, labour and user fees   217

> **Fischer:** Pia Manuel na hili ni muhimu sana ni kuangalia upande wa kupanga kazi. Wao wanafanya kazi lakini mpango wao wanapanga sio kazi nyingi, kidogo sana, labda masaa mawili asubuhi na jioni **mara nyingi hawafanyi kazi** kwa mfano, **huwa wanachelewa mara nyingi katika kilimo** wanachelewa mara nyingi na baadaye wanalalamika 'Ah, bado hatujapanda na mvua imeshanyesha'. Mara nyingi hii inatokea. Sio kwamba wewe unawasukuma sasa lakini labda unaweza kuwaonyesha njia nzuri kidogo. […]
>
> **Pia kuamka mapema ni kitu ambacho hawajaelewa**. Kwa kawaida, wanaenda kulima kama saa mbili, labda saa moja na nusu kama mmoja anaamka mapema.
>
> **Kigeli** (Instructor village M.): **Wako jirani na mjini ndio sababu.** (M07 SRAP:1)
>
> Fischer insinuates that peasants in T. work too little and too late. "Mara nyingi hawafanyi kazi" (often they do not work at all); "huwa wanachelewa mara nyingi katika kilimo" (often, they are late with farming) "kuamka mapema ni kitu ambacho hawajaelewa" (getting up early is a thing they do not yet understand). Kigeli responds by blaming the allegedly demoralizing influence of the town: "Wako jirani na mjini ndio sababu" (They are close to town that's why).

The main reason for the poor performance of the project group in village T. is identified in their failure to plan properly. It implied that planning practices as advocated by the SRAP would be an essential solution to the 'habitual laziness' portrayed above.

6.3.2. The need to plan

As far as concrete activities were concerned, staff members of both programmes would communicate their organization's concepts during the ongoing planning process. First of all, the participatory planning process was in itself a requirement that originated from the development organizations rather than the beneficiaries. Involving all those concerned in the planning process, it was to ensure greater efficiency and better attendance of activities. Yet, despite the fact that the choice of activities was negotiated and schedules were not dictated from outside, the outcomes were not necessarily satisfactory.

<u>The planning routine as an end it itself:</u> Problems partly arose as a result of a planning process that was designed to involve all those concerned, yet did not really originate in their initiative and priorities. In many respects, tools that were used to ensure participatory planning developed dynamics of their own. Meetings were held to prepare the agendas of other meetings, and activities were put on the agenda because weekly or monthly plans had to be presented.

The following example was taken from a meeting from the women's group in village T. Msemwa asked the members of the group to make up their mind about common activities for the following few weeks. She explained to the group that a board meeting would take place in two days, at which some activities of the women's group would have to be presented.

> **Msemwa: sijui tunapendekeza nini, jamani** / tumalize tu mambo ya jopo ya kesho kutwa / kuna jopo / sasa unajua tena kwenye jopo wale wanaohudhuria **lazima kusoma shughuli zinazoendelea na akina mama** / kutakuwa ni hiyo kuendelea na **mafunzo ya nani ya afya**

> **na lishe** / sasa tutaendelea nayo tu kwa maneno tu au kutakuwa na vitendo / pamoja na vitendo nafikiri / halafu sasa tutakuwa na kazi nyingine zaidi ya nini? / **tuwe na** kazi gani zaidi? (M01 SRAP:9).
>
> Msemwa began with an open question "sijui tunapendekeza nini" (I don't know what to suggest) and an emotional interjection "jamani" (my goodness). She then continued with a modal expression of necessity "lazima kusoma shughuli zinazoendelea na akina mama" ([they] must read out the activities of the women's group) that left little alternative but to come up with a suggestion. Additionally, she pointed to an activity which had previously been put on the planning agenda, "mafunzo [...]· ya afya na lishe" (a course on health and nutrition), and suggested that it was time to implement it into practice. A hortative "we" could be traced throughout the statement: tunapendekeza (we suggest) tumalize (we should finish) tunaendelea (we continue) tuwe na (we should have).

Communicative routines – in this case, the fact that a plan had been undertaken and recorded in a past meeting – were referred to in order to vest the suggestion with urgency. At the time of research, the newly-founded women's group had yet to be familiar with the program's routines. In a staff meeting, Msemwa had called this process "stabilising the co-operation of women" (M08:19). As the elected functionaries of the group did not yet feel confident enough to chair the group or represent it at board meetings, Msemwa did this for them. Thus, an important part of "organizing" the group was actually about getting to know the organizational routines of the programme, especially the meetings. For obvious reasons, it was important to Msemwa that women's activities and opinions would acquire a tangible presence at board meetings. 'Learning' the communicative routines of an organization or network in that case had become an objective of its own. However, what happened was largely a process of integrating the group into existing structures. There was little room for questioning or adapting established procedures to their needs. This may very well have resulted in planning decisions towards which participants felt little affinity.

<u>Planning and negotiations</u> In the SRAP, farmers could propose common activities for which they sought the programme's support. The advisors would then specify the conditions under which such undertakings could be realized. These were guided by the general framework of the programme, as well as concerns of everyday implementation. Approval in regard to one issue was therefore often linked to demands in regard to another, as the following example shows. Members of the project group had requested the acquisition of a pit saw. They were wary of the rising price of wood planks and hoped to learn basic carpentry work. In the meeting with the advisors, their proposal was read out and discussed:

> **Ngoka** (Chair village T.): pia wajumbe walitaka kupata msumeno wa kupasulia mbao **kwa ajili ya mafunzo** / (M03 SRAP:8)

The qualification "kwa ajili ya mafunzo" (for training purposes) reflects the farmers' awareness of the programme's focus on training. In the ensuing discussion, the Agricultural Advisor, who was positive about the plan, brought up two things he wanted group members to do before he would go about buying the saw: They should first acquire some basic knowledge about carpentry from experienced people in the village and start planting trees.

> **Fischer:** na pia Mwenyekiti / sisi **tunajua** na nafikiri wote **tumeshaelewa** / kama **tunakata** miti **tunahitaji** kupanda miti pia / kabla ya kutumia ule msumeno inaitwa *pit saw* / ndiyo **lazima kupanga** — **kupanga kazi ya kupanda** / kazi ya kitalu cha miti / nafikiri **ni vizuri zaidi** / hein?! / kazi hizi mbili zinaenda paoja / sisi wote tumeshaelewa / hata kama tunachukua miti ya — miti ya nje / haitegemei / hein?! / ni sawa / ni sawa ya xx kukata hapa / sisi tunataka — sisi wote tunataka tupate miti hapa hapa, miti ya kukata / au hapana ?
>
> **Group members:** Ndiyo
>
> **Fischer: Unaweza kukubali, Mkufunzi ?**
>
> **Mbuna** (Instructor village T.): Ni vizuri tu (M03 SRAP:9)
>
> In his bid to convince the group members, Fischer used a hortative "we" as in "tunajua" (we know), "tumeshaelewa" (we have already understood), "tunataka" (we want), "tunahitaji" (we need) "tunachukua" (we take). The modal form of necessity was combined with impersonal forms "lazima kupanga kazi ya kupanda" (the job of planting trees must be planned) "ni vizuri zaidi" (it is better). Additionally, volume and pitch of voice played a role in emphasizing persuasive intentions. The request for a confirmation from Mbuna "Unaweza kukubali, Mkufunzi" (can you agree, Instructor) is an attempt to secure agreement, a reminder that assertions made with a hortative "we" could not be taken for granted.

In the mutual 'give and take', agreements on beneficiaries' obligations thus evolved through a process of negotiation. With more or less explicit pressure exerted by development workers, some group activities found their way onto the planning agenda without much enthusiasm on the beneficiaries' side. The development workers had their own ideas about how development work in various domains should be carried out, and it was only rarely that beneficiaries questioned their specifications.

6.3.3. Beneficiaries' contributions as an indicator of programme success

In both programmes, the peasant farmers' contribution of time, resources and labour was taken as a key indicator of programme success, as it reflected their acceptance and appreciation of the respective intervention.

Monitoring progress: Playing a key role in organizing activities, keeping track of the target group's work and intervening when deemed necessary was a primary occupation of the development workers in both programmes. In the SRAP programme, for example, both Tanzanian and foreign development workers were referred to as advisors (washauri) rather than volunteers, experts or development workers. However, "advising" did not mean that development workers waited for beneficiaries to come and seek their opinion. Instead, development workers often set the initial framework of possible activities, initiated and supervised planning processes and subsequently monitored the group's activities and achievements.

This was done by following up formal sessions of reporting in meetings, and taking part in ongoing work in the field or in the workshop.

In village T. the group had agreed that each group member would plant five tree seedlings around the project's compound. In their monthly report at a meeting with the advisors, the farmers stated that work had begun and was ongoing. The Programme Director then cautiously asked for more precise information.

> **Nyange** (Programme Director): **mimi ningependa**, [...] kuelewa ni wangapi wameanza / kwa sababu tutabaki nalo hivi hivi [...]
>
> **Mbuna** (instructor village T) naona ni mmoja tu, Instructor tu, ndiye ameanza / wengine naona wote bado hawajaanza *(kimya)*
>
> **Nyange:** sasa ningependekeza huenda sisi **wajumbe wa kamati tumwunge mkono Instructor ili wengine waige** kutoka kwetu
>
> (M03 SRAP:5)
>
> Nyange posed his question in a very polite and indirect way: "ningependa kuelewa" (I would like to understand). The reply to this was somewhat disenchanting: It turned out that only the person reporting had started planting trees. After a short pause, the Programme Director responded with a hortative "we": "sisi wajumbe wa kamati tumwunge mkono ... wengine waige" (we, the committee members, should support him... so that others can imitate him).

With this relatively restrained admonition from the director the meeting proceeded to other points of the agenda. However, depending on circumstances and personal dispositions of those involved, peasant farmers who defaulted were in many cases reprimanded in a more direct language.

Development workers' frustration For some development workers, discrepancies between their organization's expectations and the beneficiaries' responses were obviously stressful. Casting their experience in general instead of individual terms was a means of coming to terms with some of the tensions they experienced.

In the following example, Nyange, Director of SRAP, told other members of his team about his encounter with an extension agent from the government's Agricultural Extension Service. He reported that the Extension Officers shared his discouraging experiences with peasant farmers who remained indifferent to efforts and advice.

> **Nyange:** / it seems some problems which we face / he also faces them / like late planting / people are not planting on time / so we try to find ways of making people plant in time / like using manure / he says — he mentioned that out of one hundred and something farmers he is working with / only three of them use manure / he is trying to find ways of making them use manure but he don't get ways of making them use at all / (M08 SRAP:8)

The implicit message was that, if other professionals and organizations also failed to achieve their intended results, the fault was possibly not to be found with individual development workers or organizations. Instead, the comparison suggested that farmers generally behaved irrationally (planting late, not using ma-

6.3. Participation as an obligation to contribute: Time, labour and user fees 221

nure) and that this was why development workers (both from the SRAP and the government's Extension Service) remained unsuccessful.

Peasant farmers' response: silence, indirectness, constructive criticism Peasant farmers' statements in regard to their own readiness to participate varied greatly. They ranged form defenceless silence to enthusiastic agreement with or explicit criticism of the programmes' practices. Obviously, those who were unable to meet demands opted out in the long run. Others, who were only just coming to terms with the programmes' practices, exhibited moments of defenceless silence. For example, the representative of the newly-founded women's group in village M. was criticized in a board meeting for the group's poor performance. As her argument was derided by other (male) group members present, she subsequently preferred to remain silent (cf. Hanak 1998). Those who had come to understand the programme's intentions and routines and were positive about being part of them usually expressed their readiness to engage. If they found the conditions too demanding, they were likely to reassure staff about their efforts to catch up. However, when their own expectations were not met in the long run, some farmers occasionally resorted to depicting themselves as the passive objects of more powerful forces, such as the government or development organizations. Trust in the participatory qualities of the programme obviously had its limits, and communicating powerlessness was a way of expressing this.

Apart from this tendency towards indirect forms of communication, which in one or another way reflected relations of dependency, peasant farmers also voiced explicit criticism of the programme's setup. The following two examples were selected because they allude to conflicts of interests among the farmers themselves, an aspect which the development organizations were often unable to sufficiently take into account.

In the next example, a representative of the rice farmers complained to the RCMP's management about problems with the implementation of ploughing schedules:

> **Machano** (Chair farmers' group in V): Majembe tunayopata kama kuna utaratibu yanaweza yakatosheleza / lakini utaratibu hakuna / na **utaratibu** huo **unavunjwa** [...] / kwa sababu leo **jembe linapangiwa** siku tatu lilime hapa, lakini siku tatu **halijamalizika** kesho utalikuta wapi / (M19 RRDP:5)

> Through the use of impersonal forms (passive and resultative) such as "utaratibu unavunjwa" (the schedule is not adhered to) and "jembe linapangiwa" (the plough is assigned) "halijamalizika" (it has not completed) the speaker avoids naming the persons responsible. The complaint was kept in general terms, leaving it to the management to infer who was responsible for the irregularities.

The complaint which was phrased rather openly left various issues unresolved: Who is responsible for the unreliability in planning? Are some farmers able to divert resources to their own benefit? A tendency to remain impersonal was also found in other cases. In the following example, which was taken from an interview, it is other, fellow farmers who do not pay punctually, thereby creating a problematic bottleneck. As fees had to be paid in advance, a failure to raise money in time not only delayed work on the field belonging to the farmer in question, but also affected others around her or him.

> **Sisi wenyewe** wakulima time nyingine huwa **tunachelewa** kuweka pesa za kulimia / **kwa maana ulete fedha kwanza ndio upate kulimiwa** / kwa sababu time nyingine utakuwa wewe unazo pesa hizo za kutaka kulimia / **mwenzio bado hajapata pesa za kulimia** / sasa ndio **kidogo** ikawa **inafanya kukawia kupata kufanya ile kazi yako** (Int Ms. K. Omar 2/9/94:2)
>
> The farmer mitigates her complaint with self-blame: "sisi wenyewe [...] tunachelewa" (we farmers [] are late ourselves). Awareness of the programme's rules is expressed in the subjunctive and passive "kwa maana ulete fedha kwanza ndio upate kulimiwa" (because you need to bring money first before, so that you can get [your field] ploughed). Despite all mitigations, for example "kidogo" (a little), the point is clear: "mwenzio bado hajapata pesa za kulimia / [ ] inafanya kukawia kupata kufanya ile kazi yako" (your friend who has not got the money for ploughing / [] causes a delay in getting that work of yours getting done).

Presenting the problems as more than just individual failures was an important factor in getting the development workers' attention. In the SRAP network, farmers repeatedly complained that they could not afford to spend their time in training sessions when they had to worry about basic material necessities, examples of which will be discussed in the section on 'material benefits'.

6.4. Participation as entitlement to material benefits

Equitably sharing the fruits of development was the third major aspect of participation that featured in meetings and interviews. The following section is about peasant farmers' expectations and their ways of negotiating their needs and objectives in everyday programme implementation. Development workers used different approaches to respond. On an organizational level, feedback from beneficiaries occasionally led to reviews of policy and practice. It should be noted that a major part of communication between development workers and farmers concerned the logistic details of the delivery of goods and services, such as planning when and where to engage in ploughing, weeding, and training courses. The focus in this section, however, will not be on these sorts of planning arrangements. Instead, controversial issues will be looked at, such as what happened when peasant farmers' requests and organizational policy did not match, how regulations were negotiated, and to what extent participatory approaches made the organizations more flexible in responding to peasants' needs?

6.4.1. Individual expectations and the wider policy context

Peasant farmers' expectations: Like other participatory programmes in social development, both the SRAP and the RCMP programmes professed that they paid particular attention to the beneficiaries' needs and priorities. Material interests were of primary importance here; in fact, for most of the peasant farmers inter-

6.4. Participation as entitlement to material benefits

viewed, they constituted the primary motivation for participating in the programme.

In the interviews conducted, the peasant farmers who were beneficiaries of the SRAP and RCMP programmes were on the whole positive about receiving aid in order to improve their everyday living – even if their own idea of development and how it could be achieved often differed from the two programme's agendas. Being able to afford basic necessities such as food, clothes and housing as well as medical services and education was a primary concern for many. In light of the deprivations they had had to cope with, they felt entitled to whichever form of support the organizations had to offer, many even stated that they expected the government and other actors do more for them in terms of material support.

When asked which expectations they had of the respective development programmes, many peasant farmers talked about attaining a life free of poverty and want. They knew malnutrition, poverty-related disease and problems in accessing basic education from their own experience. As Green found in her research in Southern Tanzania, peasant farmers' idea of development focuses on "*maendeleo ya mtu binafsi*" (personal development) which "encompasses a range of lifestyle aspiration" including the ability to provide for one's familiy (2000:68). Individual peasant farmers did not necessarily see development in terms of community advancement. Within the SRAP network, farmers defined development in the following terms:

> "maisha mazuri [...] kama nina -eeh pata chakula cha kutosha au pata hela ya kununua nguo na kusomesha watoto" (Int Mr. J. Mkongwa 23/2/94:3) (a good life [...] if I get enough food or money to buy clothes and educate the children)

> "kuepukana na umasikini (Int Mr. M. Ngoka 3/2/94:12) (avoiding poverty)

> "pengine ulikuwa na nyumba mbovu na sasa umepata nyumba nzuri / ulikuwa pengine chakula chako ni kidogo sasa umepata chakula kingi / pengine ulikuwa umeshindwa kusomesha watoto sasa unawasomesha vizuri (Int Mr. M. Kilanya, 21/2/94:8) (maybe you had a dilapidated house and now you have got a good house / maybe you had little food and now you have a lot / maybe you failed to educate the children and now you educate them well)

> "Nisiwe na maisha duni kabisa / hata mtu asipate yale mahitaji ya lazima ya mwanadamu" (Int Mr. R.Mbuna 21/2/94:6) (I should not have a completely miserable life, so that a person can not even get the basic human needs)

> "kufanya kazi na kupata riziki yangu / kwa mfano chakula, pesa pamoja na matumizi" (Interview Mr. M. Salu 2/3/94:3) (working and making my living / for example, food, money and [household] expenses)

> "nikiwa na mji wangu / nikifanya kitu changu kinachonisaidia nyumbani kwangu" (Int Mr. B. Mbozi 22/2/94:2) (if I am on my homestead / if I do something that helps me in my home)

As one of the farmers summed it up, basic human needs were the main concern: obtaining housing, food, clothes for family members, education for the children. Some also specified the need to improve their monetary income.

"labda tuongezee miradi mbalimbali [...] ili tuwe tunapata [...] hela". (Int Ms. L. Mkongwa 7/2/94:2) (maybe we should add various projects [...] in order to get [...] money)

"kupata mradi wa kupata fedha" (Int Ms. T. Nabaki 2/3/94:2) (getting a project to get money)

Within the RCMP programme, similar answers were given: Food security was a primary concern. Beyond subsistence, many peasants mentioned the need to improve cash incomes. Other concerns included buying supplementary food and clothes, and attending to their children's needs.

"Ukisha kulima vyakula unavyovitaka / unapata manufaa ya kula wewe na watoto wako" (Int Mr. K. Suleiman 3/8/94:3) (If you have cultivated the food you want / you get the benefit of eating, you and your children)

"Kwanza kuweza kuondoa wasi wasi wako wa muhangaiko wa vyakula [...] Eee unapata sehemu mbili / wewe unapata benki nyumbani mwako ya chakula na huku unapata pesa za kuweza kujisaidia na kuweza kutafuta kitoweo na viguo guo vya watoto na wewe mwenyewe" (Int Mr. K. Mcha 8/8/94:2) (First, to be able to put away worries about food / [...] well you get two advantages / you get a food bank at home and at the same time you get money with which to help yourselves / to be able to get the side dish and some small amount of clothing for the children and for yourself)

Kwanza kupata chakula / na ukiwa unapata mazao mengi / wenzio wakibahatika wanauza / sasa kama anauza anapata huduma za mama watoto na watoto wenyewe / eee inakuwa maisha yake yanakwenda vizuri (Interview Bw. Mjaka Haji Juma, mkulima mpunga na dereva (Int Mr. M. Bakari 9/8/1994:4).(first to get food / and if you get other products / some of your colleagues are lucky enough to sell / now if he manages to sell something, he gets something to provide for the needs of his wife and the children / yes, his life goes on well /

Kupata chakula chako mwenyewe / ule na watoto wako / kama kinakuwa kingi unauza / ili upate kivazi nyumbani / hii ndiyo maendeleo (Int Mr. O. Juma 6/7/1994:3) (Getting your own food / so that you may eat with your children / if it is a lot you sell / to get something to wear at home / that is development)

The concern for better living conditions featured in most of the recorded interviews. Individual considerations dominated, while community advancement was secondary. The SRAP and RCMP were ambivalent in their responses. On the one hand, they regularly solicited the peasant farmers' opinions in ongoing planing processes, so that some concerns were actually accommodated. On the other hand, their insistence on peasant farmers' commitment of time and financial resources meant that those most in need of material support were probably excluded, and that some of the concerns considered primary by peasant farmers remained unattended to.

Both programmes offered the farmers access to material goods they would not have obtained otherwise: In the SRAP, group members shared a range of tools, as well as training in technical skills relevant to organic farming and rural crafts. In the RCMP, ploughing and conventional farm implements were offered at reasonable fees. Farmers in both cases appreciated the offers, yet they also made regular attempts to negotiate their own needs when they differed. For example,

6.4. Participation as entitlement to material benefits 225

farmers in M. emphasized the need to attain tangible monetary incomes, while those in Zanzibar pointed out that the fees charged were a difficult burden to bear for rural households. As programme implementation proceeded, farmers in both networks explored possibilities and limitations of influencing programmes in their own interest.

<u>Hakuna bure:</u> Some farmers and development workers expressed regrets about the fact that, by the 1990s, the government's policy had irrevocably turned away from the idea of free social service provision or subsidies for agricultural implements. In social development programmes, goods and services were no longer offered without some kind of reciprocity. Instead, demands for the active commitment of beneficiaries, such as labour, user fees or otherwise, had become the rule. Development workers of the SRAP and RCMP network were at the same time well aware of and part of this wider tendency. Many felt that the welfare approach had outlived its service, arguing that it led to dependency and passivity. Others, however, were concerned about the implications of an approach that excluded the poorest.

The following example illustrates how the idea of charging nominal fees had become common practice. It is taken from an RCMP management meeting in which the discussion was about a training opportunity for mechanics offered by another development organization. While these offers had been free of charge in the past, in this case the inviting organization had asked for a monetary contribution from each organization sending trainees to the courses.

> **Vuai:** (Specialist Mechanization): **kuna nafasi ya kupeleka mechanics wawili katika xxx iliyoandaliwa na VALMET** / na mara nyingi hupeleka xxx inakuwa ni bure / lakini mara hii **wametaka tucontribute twenty thousand** /
>
> **Salum:** (Programme Manager) Twenty thousand shillings from kwa kila mmoja au kwa wote?
>
> **Vuai:** Kwa kila institution ni twenty thousand itakayoshiriki / kuna nafasi ya watu wawili kutoka kila institution xxx kwa wiki tatu /
>
> **Salum: Hakuna bure** sasa hivi / sawa / lakini ni juu ya kitu gani ?
>
> [...]
>
> **Salum:** Mimi nimekubali / au mna objection yoyote / twenty thousand kwa watu wawili kwa wiki tatu / hao **nafikiri wanachukua trainer anatoka bara / hiyo ni contribution ya kummaintain huyo** / (M21 RCMP:3)

Vuai informs the participants at the meeting: "kuna nafasi ya kupeleka mechanics wawili katika xxx (we have an opportunity to send two mechanics to [a course]). He then cautions that a fee is charged, using the subjunctive to express the expectation "wametaka tucontribute twenty thousand" (they want us to contribute twenty thousand). This information leads the manager to a dry conclusion: Hakuna bure sasa hivi (nothing is free nowadays). A few turns later, he offers an argument in justification: "hao nafikiri wanachukua trainer anatoka bara /

hiyo ni contribution ya kummaintain huyo" (I think they employ a trainer from the mainland / this is the contribution to "maintain" him)

In the ensuing discussion, the contents of the course, as well as the fact that facilitating training opportunities was an important incentive for staff members, were discussed. Considerations on whom to send followed. Finally, the manager expressed his approval, and justified the fee as fair and reasonable. Recognizing that "there is nothing for free nowadays" in this case served to appreciate an offer the programme could obviously well afford. Yet the remark also reflected the way neo-liberal policy changes on a macro-economic level affected everyday programme implementation. The withdrawal of government subsidies for a range of farm implements was another aspect, which will be discussed later in this section.

The message that development goods were not or no longer to be handed out for free was also communicated to the farmers. Ideas and plans brought forward by the beneficiaries at grass-roots level meetings in the SRAP network included a variety of income-generating projects. Women talked about their wish to start a coffee-house, men about a fishing boat or shop. At the time of research, staff members had repeatedly refused to support any such plans, as they did not regard them as economically sustainable. This was common knowledge, yet proposals continued to surface. Whenever demands or proposals for income-generating projects were made, they were often founded on arguments referring to material neediness and deprivation. In the following example from the SRAP programme, the women's group had requested to start a community coffee house (in a meeting that had preceded this research). The group's proposal implied that the initial capital to start the coffee-house should be provided by the programme. In a subsequent meeting, Msemwa, the development worker attending to the women's group, explained why the plan was unacceptable for the SRAP team:

> **Msemwa** (Advisor of the Women's Group): [...] waliokuwa kwenye jopo / tuliona kwamba ilijitokeza nani· moja / ajenda moja / kwamba akina mama kazi walizojipangia za mwezi wa kwanza / kwanza wangependekeza kuwa na mkahawa pia / sasa ilionekana / yaani unaposema unataka kuwa na gari ni wakati **halijaeleza sababu** ya kuwa na ile gari ni kwa nini? / na: utalipata **kwa njia gani**? / **haina msingi** / kama unataka kuwa na gari mpaka uelewe utakuwa na **shughuli gani** inavyokushughulisha ya kuweza kupatia **pesa ya kutosha** kununua ile gari / sasa sisi tuliona **mkahawa** kama **imekuja tu kutoka hewani** / (M01-SRAP:4)

> The proposal was dismissed in no uncertain terms: The argument was characterized as "**haina nguvu**" (having no strength)", and was compared to the desire for a car for which "**halijaeleza sababu**" (no reason has been given), and which was said to "**haina msingi**" ("have no base", and, above all, lacked "**pesa ya kutosha**" (sufficient money). In short, it was as if "**mkahawa imekuja tu kutoka hewani**" (the coffee shop had materialized from the air).

With a square reminder of the group members' poverty and limited capacity, Msemwa effectively discouraged any further insistence on the project. While the SRAP team turned down the proposal for a communal coffee house, it agreed to offer courses in nutrition and basic calculation which would improve the group members' ability to engage in such endeavours on an individual basis.

6.4.2. Requests in circumstances of need

Faced with the challenge of securing a precarious livelihood, the peasant farmers regularly turned to the development organizations with very specific requests for material goods. Knowledge of the organization's policy and past practices shaped the way they presented their appeals. Apart from this, reference was often made to the urgency of a particular situation. The development workers, who were confronted with these demands, were constrained by their organization's policies. In many cases, they had no option but to point to directives from superior levels of the network which opposed the issue at stake. In other cases, they had some freedom to interpret policy and rules. Occasionally, debates within the organization alse led to a review of policy or practice.

<u>Appealing to past practices:</u> Rice farmers in the RCMP programme were still only coming to terms with rising prices for fertilizer and pesticides, as the following two contributions by representatives of rice farmers illustrate. The first contribution emphasized the importance of fertilizer for rice farming in the area. It explained that the current harvest had been a failure, as many people could not afford to use fertilizers. The second contribution recalled the era in which fertilizer was readily available due to government subsidies.

> **Machano** (Chair Farmers' Group in V.): [...] **kwa upande wa serikali tunaomba itusaidie mbolea** / yaani mbolea imekuwa ghali / wakulima hawaimudu / na ikiwa hawapati mbolea mpunga haupatikani / (M19 RRDP:6)
>
> (we ask that the government help us with fertilizer / that is, fertilizer has become expensive / the farmers can not afford it / and if they do not get fertilizer there is no rice)
>
> **Hamis** (Chair Farmers' Group in J.): [...] jamani kwa ufupi mbolea ipo / lakini bado **bei ina ugumu wake** / [...] mbolea siku zote hizi / miaka yote / iliyokuwa tunaitumia kwa bei rahisi / ilikuwa inapata msaada / watoaji msaada sijui kama wamechoka au wameisha nguvu zao / hakuna sasa ile mbolea ya msaada / (M19 RRDP:17)
>
> (my goodness in short the fertilizer is there / but the price has its difficulty / [...] all these days / all these years / we have used fertilizer at a cheap price / it was subsidized / those giving aid I don't know whether they have become tired or whether their strength is gone / there is now no subsidized fertilizer /
>
> In the first instance, the farmers' representative from V. made a straightforward appeal to the government, arguing that farmers could not afford fertilizer at market rates, but desperately needed it for rice cultivation. His colleague from J in turn recalled past practices of the government subsidizing agricultural implements.

The programme staff present during this meeting acknowledged that the farmers experienced problems, but obviously had no possibility of granting the request, as the issue of agricultural subsidies was a matter of national (and international) policy and beyond the RCMP programme's decision-making scope. The withdrawal of subsidies from agricultural implements had been one of the conditions imposed by the IMF as part of its Structural Adjustment Programs in Tanzania and elsewhere.

The exception to the rule: In the follwing example from a village meeting in the SRAP network, one of the peasants asked the development workers for tick pesticide for his livestock. He underlined the urgency of the problem: "wana kupe wengi sana [...] wanaweza wakapata magonjwa" (they have many ticks [...] they may contact disease). He also referred to previous practice, mentioning that they had used this pesticide before, but now run out of it. However, using such pesticides against livestock parasites conflicted with the programme's orientation towards organic farming. It also went against the principle of providing training and knowledge rather than goods.

> **Kigeli:** asante Ndugu Mwenyekiti / miye mengineyo yangu nilikuwa tu **nawomba** e: **mshauri kama kuna uwezekano** wa dawa ya kupe kwa kweli ng'ombe wetu sasa hivi wana kupe wengi sana / baada ya dawa ile kuisha tuna wasiwasi / labda wanaweza wakapata magonjwa mabaya sana baada ya kuwa hawajazoea kuumwa na kupe / wana kupe wengi sana / **ninaomba tu labda kama kutakuwa na uwezekano** Alhamisi nasi tujaribu **kuiangalia** hiyo dawa tujaribu labda kuwazuiazuia
>
> **Fischer:** kwa kawaida mnajua **siyo rahisi kukuba— kukubali** / unajua, sawa / a: lakini tunakubali, nafikiri / lakini pia tunataka kuangalia uwezekano wa dawa mpya kabisa, dawa ya kienyeji, dawa za sehemu mbalimbali lakini dawa ambazo zinapatikana kwa rahisi na kwa bei nafuu, kwa rahisi, kama dawa ya mbegu au dawa ya majani ya marobaini / umesikia / inaweza kusaidia / pia dawa ya mti mmoja u:tupa, utupa / tunaweza kupanda ule miti, ni vizuri / tafadhali angalia — angalieni mbele kidogo **mara moja tunaweza kufanya, kuweza — tunaweza kununua dawa bado lakini ni mwisho kabisa** / sawa / baadaye tunasimama kweli / **tunasimama kweli miguu yetu kabisa** kwa kufanya utafiti wa dawa mbalimbali, dawa ya kienyeji na: — / pia kama haifanyi kazi dawa fulani sawa mna— mnanunua wenyewe / sawa (M04 SRAP:30)

The farmer phrases his request in a polite, restrained and indirect way. The verb –omba (ask, request, beg) features twice, as well as the conditional clause "kama kuna uwezekano" (if there is a possibility. "Labda" (maybe) is a way of hedging the proposal. Using the verb "kuangalia" (have a look into) instead of a concept like obtaining or providing contributes to the indirectness of the proposal.

The Agricultural Advisor hesitated and expressed his disapproval „siyo rahisi kukubali" (it is not easy to agree), but then agreed to solve the impending problem. However, he made it clear that this was an exception: „mara moja tunaweza kufanya, kuweza — tunaweza kununua dawa bado lakini ni mwisho kabisa" (we can do it once, we can buy pesticides once more, but that's absolutely the last time) He added that, in future, alternatives such as herbal remedies had to be sought out. Otherwise, the peasants would have to buy the pesticides themselves. At the same time, he portrayed the beneficiaries as immature children who had yet to learn to stand on their own feet, urging them to act more mature in the future. „baadaye [...] tunasimama kweli miguu yetu kabisa" (later [...] we really stand completely on our own feet).

The answer is long-winded, the conclusion is pragmatic. Answering the request with lengthy explanations on alternatives in the form of organic pesticides may in itself work as a deterrent for anyone planning to voice such a request in future. The Agricultural Advisor uses several paternalistic images in this passage. By asking the group members to be more far-sighted, he in fact asserts that any demand for support is equal to a lack of maturity. Insisting that "this is the last time", he assumes the role of the person who monitors the adherence to the rules, but in some way also stands above them. In this way, he stages himself as a benevolent superior who risks conflict with the programme's policy for the benefit of the group.

The authority to dispose of "development goods" was certainly a principal aspect in the asymmetric relationships of the development network. The staff of implementing organizations may have limited powers to take decisions at their discretion. However, the means at their disposal were frequently used to re-enact asymmetry in aid relations.

Adaptation to given frameworks: Invitations to reflect on one's needs created space for peasant farmers to develop their own initiatives as part of the ongoing participatory planning processes. In the following example from a planning meeting in the SRAP network, group members in village M. reflected on ways to combat the negative effects of the drought. One of the farmers proposed irrigating fields close to the lake (Victoria), pointing to the ability and potential of the group. Apart from this, a certain urgency was emphasized: The objective was "to save our lives", and part of the suggested strategy was to "rush out to the lakeside".

> **Lukolo:** Kwa vile tuko watu wa **mafunzo**, nami nilikuwa **nataka kuunga mkono wazo** ambalo umesema **tungeingia** ndani ya mafunzo ya kila namna - namna ya **umwagiliaji**, **labda** sasa hivi **tungekuwa tumevamia** maeneo ya ziwani kusudi **kuokoa maisha yetu**. 09 SRAP:9
>
> Knowing very well that the programme's policy was primarily to provide training in agriculture, he introduced his proposal by adapting it to this framework. Apart from emphasizing the training aspect, the proposal was carefully worded in modal forms: the conditional clauses "tungeingia" (we would have gone into) and "tungekuwa tumevamia" (we would have rushed) served as strategies of persuasion, "labda" (maybe) expressed restraint and hesitation. References to other speakers as in "I want to support [lit. join hands with] the idea ..." were rhetorical devices intended to facilitate group consensus: Referring to statements that were voiced earlier in the meetings enhanced the authority of the claims made.

The proposal for lakeside irrigation was soon accepted by staff members and put into practice a few weeks later. In this case, one group member successfully used his knowledge of the organizations' policy – i.e. the focus on training – to make his idea more acceptable. A similar trend could be observed in a number of other proposals from the beneficiaries' side (cf the proposal for the acquisition of a pit saw in the previous section). This did not necessarily mean that the focus on training per se was approved of under all circumstances, as a statement by another group member in the same meeting showed:

> Masami: Mtu anatoka nyumbani / ana **familia** yake / anakuja hapa kwenye mradi / anapofika hapa anakaa tu ni mafunzo / ni mafunzo / matokeo yake anakosa hata hela ya kununua sabuni /
>
> (M09 SRAP:4) (A person leaves her/his home / she/he has a family / she/he comes to the project / when she/he arrives she/he just sits and it's training / it's training / the outcome is that she/he lacks even the money to buy soap)

Dependency: In the bid to convince development workers, peasant farmers occasionally referred to their dependency on the organization's support. The following example, taken from the annual report as discussed in an RCMP management meeting, summed up some of the arguments made by farmers' representatives. In particular, farmers said that the use of agricultural implements had previously been progagated by the government to the extent that young farmers could no longer cope without them.

> Salum (Programme Manager): kwanza [wakulima] wanasema kuwa huko nyuma tunakotokea wazee wetu walikuwa wakulima bila ya kutumia mbolea au dawa. **Wizara imetuelimisha** vya kutosha juu ya matumizi ya pembejeo hizo. Na sasa wakulima hasa **vijana,** tayari wameshazoea. Leo wengi wao **hawako tayari kulima bila ya vitu hivyo**, […] Upatikanaji wa dawa au mbolea umekuwa mdogo msimu huu, hata bei zake nazo zimepanda sana. **Wanaomba wapunguziwe bei ya pembejeo.** (M20 RCMP:2)
>
> In the report, a narration of the experience of several generations of farmers is related, which is used to appeal to the government's sense of responsibility. "Wazee wetu walikuwa wakulima bila ya kutumia mbolea" (our parents farmed without using fertilizers). It is the government who changed this: "Wizara imetuelimisha juu ya matumizi ya pembejeo" (the ministry educated us on the use of implements). As a result "vijana … wengi … hawako tayari kulima bila ya vitu hivyo" (Many of the young people are not prepared to farm without these things). The report then concludes: "Wanaomba wapunguziwe bei ya pembejeo" (they ask to have the price of the implements reduced for them).

In short, the argument was that the Ministry's previous promotion of fertilizers had created a dependency among the farmers and that it should therefore reduce its price. While this part of the report recorded the way farmers perceived themselves as passive dependents of the government's actions, there was actually little that project staff or even superior employees of the Ministry could have done. Decisions of this issue were taken elsewhere, and for some members of the RCMP's management, painstakingly registering peasant farmers' difficulties with this part of macro-economic policy changes was a way of expressing their own critical view of it.

In other instances, dependency was expressed through imagery, for example relating to children's development. Another example from the SRAP, again concerning the issue of income generating projects, was based on the image of a child eventually "standing on his/her own feet". In this imagery, the farmers were

6.4. Participation as entitlement to material benefits

portrayed as children, while the development workers had the role of parents or teachers.

> **Silima**: Mradi wetu una mwelekeo mzuri, una utaratibu mzuri kwa sababu unamfundisha mtu angali bado ana- / **anakaa chini** kabla hajatembea baadae **anajiburuza kwa kutambaa** kwa mikono, **anasimama** baadaye **anatambaa kwa miguu** baadaye **anakimbia** ndiyo maana ya SRAP lakini katika utaratibu ule mimi nilikuwa naomba tu waangalie mambo / huyu mtu anakimbia sasa anahitaji avae viatu / kwa hiyo nilikuwa naomba tu m/kiti ni kwamba waangalie utaratibu mwingine wa uzalishaji / (M09 SRAP:6)

> Drawing on the analogy of a child's development and social development in the village, Silima concedes that development has to be made step by step and that no progress can be made without patience in learning processes. Yet at the point where the person in question is able to walk and run, he gives the story an unexpected turn, arguing that this was the time to think about shoes, or more precisely, other approaches towards productive undertakings.

This uncomfortably paternalistic metaphor again points to dependency experienced by the peasant farmers. Just as parents would provide their children with shoes, so the argument goes, a responsibly acting development organization would offer further support.

Powerlessness: The above examples illustrate how the peasant farmers explicitly pointed out their own dependency on the development organizations' benevolence. Resignation to what they perceived as a weaker position was also expressed in more indirect ways. At times, the peasant farmers' comments displayed an attitude towards development work which was conspicuously at odds with the image of participatory development that was promoted, for example, by the SRAP programme. This was particularly true when issues at stake were categorically rejected by staff members, as in the example of income-generating projects.

> **Mataluma**: Mimi naona mradi ni mzuri ila tu **tungetafutiwa** hii miradi ya uzalishaji
>
> (M09 SRAP:4)
>
> **Mataluma**: naona mradi ni mzuri ila tu **wangetuletea** mradi wa uzalishaji (M09 SRAP:4)
>
> **Mbala**: Hivyo labda **tungepewa** labda mradi mwingine wa **kusaidia** watu / inawezekana watu wangekuwa ni wengi zaidi ya hawa tulio nao sasa hivi / (M09 SRAP:4)
>
> [...]
>
> **Mbala**: Kama **tungepata** mradi mwingine wa uzalishaji / kusudi mwanachama anapotoka hapa tayari anapata nini? hela ya kutumia nyumbani pamoja na familia zake [...] / unakuta wanakikundi wote / asilimia kubwa ni watu / tuseme wanafamilia / kwa hiyo unakuta kwamba anapokuja hapa kufanya kazi / akikosa hela kwa kweli **familia yake inakuwa duni** / (M09 SRAP:5)

> Modal forms of possibility repeatedly occurred in the elaborations of the proposal. Mataluma expressed his request by using verbs that left all initiative and responsibility in the hands of the development workers, such as "tungetafutiwa" (they should find for us) and "wangetu-

letea"(they should bring us). Mbala asked for "mradi [...] wa kusaidia watu" (a project to help people), implying that the SRAP training offers did **not** effectively help group members. Verbs used include "tungepata" (we should receive) and "tungepewa" (we should be given). The neediness of group members is visualized through reference to their families: **familia yake inakuwa duni** (Her/his family remains in abject conditions) as their potentially productive members fail to make money.

For the SRAP – and in this respect it stood in line with other development-relevant participatory discourse – ideal participatory development fostered both empowerment and self-reliance. In everyday implementation, this often translated into step-by-step reciprocity: In order to gain access to development goods, beneficiaries were expected to commit their time and good will to community concerns, training and other issues the programme considered important. Mataluma and Mbala seemed strongly disappointed that, even after more than a year of training, there was still no prospect that the programme would support income-generating activities. They experienced themselves as unable to influence or negotiate programme policy in this realm, and felt dependent on the programme staff's good will. This experience of powerlessness was mirrored in linguistic forms expressing passivity and a choice of verbs expressing the sustaining or suffering of another person's actions – the peasants speaking here obviously did not see themselves as empowered and self-reliant.

In the RCMP programme, a similar tendency was obvious in regard to the issue of subsidies for farm implements. Appeals to "have prices reduced" (Wanaomba wapunguziwe bei) (cf previous section) reflect a similar experience of being a passive recipient to powerful organization or governments.

Tendencies among peasant farmers' to re-enact clientilist relationships were particularly salient in contexts where the two programmes reserved their right to preclude peasant farmers from expressing essential concerns in debate.

6.4.3. Inner-organizational processes

Finding themselves between peasant farmers' requests and their organization's policy, development workers were part of a process of negotiating feedback and organizational response. However, in both the SRAP and the RCMP programmes, flexibility was limited, as the following three examples illustrate.

Sticking to principles: In this example, the Advisor of the Women's Group reported in a staff meeting how group members had on various occasions proposed to set up a coffee shop. She made it clear that the women were serious and committed about this. The Agricultural Advisor, however, told her to ignore the requests.

Msemwa: kuna siku moja waliuliza sasa tutajenga lini kibanda cha kuwa na mkahawa hapa? / *(Msemwa na Nyange wanacheka)* / sasa nika — / ni Flora / Flora nikamwambia sawa we Flora / mbona hata tukifanya hata mafunzo ya +++ letu unahitaji? / sasa mbona unapendekeza kuwa na kibanda / kwa kweli kila mtu ana— / walivyosema **wana mawazo kwamba wao wanaan-**

6.4. Participation as entitlement to material benefits 233

> **zisha mkahawa kabisa** xxx / sasa nilivyowauliza wanipe mapendekezo yao juu ya mambo wanayotaka kujifunza / naona kuna moja lilijitokeza / **wanataka kuelewa mahesabu**
>
> *(the following turn is supported by Msemwa using utterances as: mhm, aha)*
>
> Fischer: don't try — / **be careful** not to get blackmailed / **kick back** very hard / you have enough space / they know they benefit a lot if they undergo training / kick back hard / **don't be afraid** if anybody leaves / **we have to stick to our principles** / be careful not to get lost yourself / otherwise you are — you will be in a difficult position later (M02 SRAP:10-11)
>
> Msemwa, aware of the programme's stance on income-generating projects, shyly narrates her experiences of discussions with the women's group in B: "walivyosema wana mawazo kwamba wao wanaanzisha mkahawa kabisa" (as they say, they have this idea that to just set up a coffeeshop). She then relates her discussion with the group, concluding with the women's emerging interest in numeracy: "/ wanataka kuelewa mahesabu" (they want to understand calculations). But Fischer ignores the account of her negotiation with the group. Instead, he takes the role of telling her what to do in a sequence of imperatives: "don't try", "be careful", "kick back", "don't be afraid", as well as expressions of necessity ("we have to stick to our principles"). Msemwa is left with little leeway in this example, and her competence to handle the situation is not recognized.

The Agricultural Advisor cautioned his 'junior' colleague not to raise the expectations of beneficiaries, as the programme would not be able to satisfy them. However, conjuring up a scenario of peasant farmers 'blackmailing' a young and inexperienced colleague served to both assert and cover up power relations that largely worked the other way around: Despite the invitation for peasant farmers to participate in planning processes, most of the agenda was still determined by the SRAP team.

<u>Limited flexibility:</u> The following example from the RCMP network is taken from a staff debate on the draft of the yearly programme report. It relates to an earlier request made by rice farmers: as they found it difficult to afford whole bags of fertilizer, they had asked for a reduction in prices. Management had concluded that it was impossible to reduce the price of the fertilizer, but that smaller amounts could be made available for sale. In the ensuing debate a staff member questioned this step, which in his view amounted to a policy change.

> **Musa** (senior accountant): Mimi nikiendelea kutoa comment yangu [...] tunaingizia **sera mpya** katika mradi / tunasema pengine hatuwezi kupunguza bei ya mbolea lakini tunaweza kurekebisha usambazaji na kuiuza kidogo kidogo kulingana na mahitaji ya wakulima. (M20 RCMP:9)
>
> (if I continue to make my comments [..] we are introducing a new policy into the project / we say that we can not reduce the price of fertilizer but we can improve distribution and sell it in small amounts, according to the farmer's needs.)

The accountant continued to argue that the peasant's association rather than the programme's extension agents should organize small-scale distribution. He also cautioned that providing retail sale would increase the work load of the extension agents and that the programme would incur losses. In his response, the manager pointed out that making sure that beneficiaries could participate – in this case in the adequate use of farm implements – could justify the review and change of policy and practice. He considered the peasants' associations to be too weak financially to organize the distribution of fertilizer, as the farmers' ability to spare cash for this purpose greatly varied between individuals and from day to day. He also pointed out that shrinkage was likely to occur anyway, as the fertilizer would rot away in the store if a large percentage of the rice cultivators could not afford it.

Tensions in this debate related not only to the factual issue at stake. The exchange itself resonated with frustrations about hierachy, policy and experiences of failure: Not everyone in an organizational network had the same opportunity to transform policy and practice as a result of his or her experience. In addition, it is likely that the background of the XYs remark was a more general concern about the financial sustainablity of the programme itself. The RRDP had run for nine years and would stop receiving external finance in the following year. It was highly doubtful whether the peasants would be able to pay the market costs of seed, fertilizers and tractor services in the long run.

Dealing with internal problems: In both the SRAP and the RCMP network, transport facilities such as cars and motorbikes constituted highly contested resources. Both programmes were better endowed with transport facilities than the larger organizational units of which they were part. This resulted in pressure to share these facilities, especially from higher levels of the hierarchy. In the SRAP network, the bishop occasionally ordered the project car to be used for other purposes of the Diocese, especially during the absence of the Austrian Agricultural Advisor. The ensuing conflict was still an issue in informal debate, but did not feature in work meetings at the time of research.

In the RCMP network, a similar issue featured in a management meeting. Issa, one of the senior engineers, complained that the Assistant Minister for Agriculture occasionally requested one of the cars, interfering with some of the programme staff's work schedules. He asked the manager to address the issue, polemically suggesting that the car should be handed over to the Assistant Minister for good.

> **Issa** (senior engeneer) halafu nilitaka tulizungumze hili suala la trooper xxx **hatuifahamu hasa** / kama tunampa Naibu waziri basi tumpe Naibu Waziri / kwa sababu wakati mwingine **tunapata lawama**. Wakati mwengine **tunakwama**, hatuna gari ya kutumia / **tunaambiwa** saa nne anaitaka Naibu Waziri / kwa hivyo kwa kweli ni matatizo / kwa hivyo kama **management** imeamua tumpe Naibu Waziri / **bora tumpe** iwe kama tulivyompa Bwana Ibrahim / **tujue hatuna gari** trooper /

The engineer was obviously fed up with having no transport while the Assistant Minister used the project car. Using the pronoun "we", he constructed himself and his co-workers as an entity distinct from the manager, the minister and the beneficiaries they are supposed to serve. Additionally, he used a rhetorical question "hatuifahamu hasa" (we do not quite understand it) in his account of how the Assistant Minister's interference brought his team into difficulties. Generally, he avoided naming actors for the actions he described. He used the passive voice "tunaambiwa" (we are told) or verbs that described processes that his team underwent as a result of other people's activities "tunapata lawama" (lit. we are receiving complaints) or "tunakwama" (we get stuck). When he finally alleged that the manager had already decided to leave this car to the [Assistant] Minister, he talked of the "management" instead of the manager and his assistant, and susequently assumed another more broad "we" that included the whole of RCMP management and staff: "bora tumpe" (it's better for us to hand it over to him) or "tujue hatuna gari" (so that we know that we don't have the car). At the level of linguistic realizations, there were various elements that mitigated the assertion through indirectness and depersonalisation. Yet the proposal which was made was of course unfeasable and with its exaggeration openly expressed Issa's dissatisfaction.

The manager refused to be drawn into the emotional argument, declined the proposal and cut the debate short. The initial concern "halafu nilitaka tulizungumze hili suala la trooper" (I wanted us to talk about the issue of the trooper) was nipped in the bud at that very point.

There was a very clear proposition here that the manager should stop making concessions to the Assistant Minister and ensure that the programme's assets be used according to purpose. This and other examples illustrated that staff members did not hesitate to voice their grievances and criticism. Staff members aware of problematic developments could verbalize their experiences in an open atmosphere – however, this did not necessarily mean that the respective issues were actually resolved.

Last but not least, the example also points to the limits encountered by research through formal meetings. Complaints about misuse are likely to be discussed informally rather than in formal meetings. It should be emphasized here, however, that both networks were selected for analysis on the basis that they were obviously functioning well, and that there were no suspicions of misuse on a larger scale. The objective of the analysis was to get a better understanding of everyday practices within asymmetric relations of development co-operation that are often taken for granted. The analysis had no ambitions to uncover irregularities, and had there been any it would probably have been inappropriate to do so.

6.5. Discussion and results

6.5.1. Participation as dialogic communication

The analysis of interviews and recorded meetings of both programmes confirmed that participation was to a large extent conceptualized in terms of establishing open and democratic forms of communication. Both staff and beneficiaries highly valued the opportunities created by an open exchange of ideas, as well as the dynamics emanating from mutual learning. Peasant farmers valued both the practical advantages of being informed and the spaces opened to reflect on their situation. Staff emphasized the importance of respecting farmers' opinions as well as being informed about their concerns in creating sustainable working partnerships.

Supporting peasant farmers in establishing their own organizational structures and managing meetings and other communicative encounters was therefore a relevant part of programme activities. However, this was also a domain strongly affected by the organizational constraints of the implementing organizations. Through the focus on communication, beneficiaries were under pressure to 'perform' accordingly, for example by conducting their meetings in accordance with the relevant participatory planning modes. Neither of the two programmes explicitly or regularly addressed social inequalities within their target groups – with the exception of the issue of gender relations, as the de-facto absence of women from most activities in the SRAP had led to various efforts. Prevailing organizational hierarchies had a considerable influence on the way encounters were planned and attended, and on the way relationships between development workers and benficiaries were constructed. Peasant farmers occasionally expressed a feeling of dependancy on the development organizations that included patterns of communication between development workers and themselves.

Egalitarian methods of interaction effectively helped peasant farmers engage in democratic decision-making processes. However, the beneficiaries' initiative was invariably channelled into a narrow range of choices within the respective organization's larger policy framework. The occasional moderated brainstorming or voting by hand was rare and served either to focus on activities that had largely been decided on elsewhere, or to legitimize extra efforts. Neither in the SRAP nor the RCMP did staff solicit the beneficiaries' opinion on fundamental questions of policy. Instead, these matters of principle were presented in a persuasive mode as something that prospective beneficiaries necessarily had to accept.

In the realm of communication, images of the other were to a large extent shaped by the normative ideal of egalitarian relations. Intertextual references to democratization, equality and partnership were obviously important points of orientation. As the example of gender illustrates, paternalistic, neoliberal and gender equity arguments blended with male farmers' avowals of progressive attitude. At the same time, they remained caught up with views of women as primarily belonging to the domestic sphere. In a similar vein, development workers expressed commitment to participatory approaches, including egalitarian and democratic relationships within the network, while at the same time blaming farmers as negligent or even lazy if they failed to implement respective planning tools, which were, after all, selected and prescribed by their own organizations.

6.5.2. Participation as obligation

For development organizations and their staff, the peasant farmers' contributions in terms of time, labour and user fees constituted the second major aspect of participation. Both the SRAP's and RCMP's frameworks were not negotiable in everyday implementation, although details could certainly be adapted to ensure more effective work. In semi-official contexts, the peasant farmers' commitment was evaluated in terms of a highly judgmental and stereotyped working morale, as the example from the SRAP illustrates.

An analysis of the planning process revealed why some of the outcomes of participatory planning processes carry little weight for those concerned: The planning routine may have been applied as an end in itself, or may have implied conditions that had to be accepted without any alternatives. Development workers were preoccupied with monitoring the beneficiaries' performance, which often enough lagged behind the organization's expectations. The development workers' coping strategies ulimately included generalizations and stereotyped views of peasant farmers as irrational. The beneficiaries for their part responded with silence and passivity, or constructive criticism.

6.5.3. Participation as entitlement to material benefits

The peasant farmers' primary interest in participating in the programmes was the prospect of obtaining devlopment goods offered by the programme. These centred on meeting basic needs such as food, housing, clothing and education for the children. The development organization's stance in this regard was determined by the wider policy framework of the mid-1990s, particularly by the notion that beneficiaries had to confirm their commitment by contributing user fees or attending common activities.

In their quest to negotiate goods beyond the regular programme offers, peasant farmers used various strategies. They invoked past practices of governmental agricultural subsidies, argued for one-time exceptions, or reworked their proposals to suit the current policy. Participatory planning events were used to develop ideas differently from the respective programme framework. But the beneficiaries also pointed to their dependency and displayed indifference and passivity when their demands were turned down – in stark contrast to notions of participation that emphasized initiative and self-reliance. Overall, neediness and urgency were part of all requests for material support.

The two programmes' ability to deal with the challenge of material redistribution were limited. The organizations stuck to their principles and left it up to the staff to occasionally show flexibility. With respect to the material demands made by less endowed superior organizational units, both organizations made limited concessions.

6.5.4. Conclusion

The analysis confirmed that participation was a discursive node in the implementation of both programmes. Both programmes featured levels of participation that emphasized the sharing of information and consultation in everyday implementation. Significantly, similar 'low key' notions of participation continue to dominate in social development programmes to date.

The linguistic analysis yielded insights into the way asymmetries of power are negotiated in practice. In particular, modal forms, nominalisations, choice of pronouns and transitivity were found to be relevant for an analysis of the individual speakers' linguistic actions on a micro level. Pursuing topics through meetings at several organizational levels revealed how the peasant farmers' voices were edited and reproduced at different levels of the network. It also gave an idea of how dominant development discourses, for example on gender equality, were selectively taken up to legitimize particular steps in programme implementation. There was evidence that participative approaches, as practiced by the RCMP and SRAP, enhanced the quality of communicative encounters, created space for democratic interaction and led to the occasional surfacing of subversive potential. However, the examples analyzed also documented numerous instances in which the development workers and peasant farmers' representatives successfully instrumentalized participatory rhetoric in order to advance their own interests. Therefore, participatory approaches per se did not lead to more equitable relations among actors. Nor did they result in stereotypes being discarded. Rather, familiar notions of industriousness or rationality were found to reconfigure with notions of participation-as-commitment. Finally, the participatory practices proved largely compatible with surrounding neo-liberal discourses on social development, gender and economic progress.

7. Participation, language and discourse: ways forward

Participation is a concept that has, in one way or another, been essential to the idea of development for the past fifty years. In the process, it has endured changing political contexts and acquired a host of different meanings. For the purpose of this study, a broad 'working definition' of participation was adopted at the outset: Participation was defined as a common effort that entailed democratic decision-making processes, equitable access to knowledge, and a fair distribution of the fruits of development. The different theoretical and analytical perspectives adopted in this study confirmed social justice and equity as decisive criteria for the assessment of participatory development work.

Language use is central to all aspects of development co-operation. The choice of languages used in aid delivery in present day Tanzania reflects both the colonial past and the achievements of the postcolonial promotion of Swahili. Today, Swahili constitutes the primary medium of people-oriented development in Tanzania. However, the overall impact of the 'development industry' on language development in Tanzania is at best ambivalent. Anticipation of donors' linguistic preferences means that much of the higher level reporting and planning of programmes is carried out in English, and that the burden of mediating and translating remains largely with Tanzanian development workers. At the same time, higher education and expertise continue to be delivered in English, thereby remaining largely inaccessible to the majority of the population. Although development organizations make some effort to promote Swahili, such measures are often confined to informal domains and not systematically enforced.

Participatory development discourse reflects a multitude of voices that have shaped ideas on participation throughout the last fifty years. While policy documents by leading development agencies are widely available, statements made by peasant farmers are much less accessible. The data corpus collected and analysed in the course of this research provides insight into issues that were of relevance to people at the grass-roots level in a particular situation. It also documents how implementing organizations elicited or silenced peasant farmers' voices, and how they took up the farmers' concerns and represented them in reports and other policy documents.

In the following, the issue of programme implementation as exemplified by the RCMP and the SRAP will be discussed in greater detail. The focus of the analysis is the impact of participatory approaches on social inequality.

7.1. The examples of the SRAP and the RCMP: How do participatory processes interact with social inequality?

Measured against the six-stage model of participation proposed by Pretty et al. (1995:61) the programmes ranked at the upper middle level: They clearly met the criteria of (1) information giving, (2) consultation, (3) participation for material incentives and (4) functional involvement through the formation of groups. At the same time, they fell 'below' the stage of (5) interactive participation, as the beneficiaries were not significantly involved in decision making; they were also not engaged in (6) self-mobilization. However, while this exercise of benchmarking the programmes according to the 'participation ladder' gives us useful information, it only tells part of the story. Significantly, it is silent about achievements that go beyond the framework of the linear model, and it also conceals problems attendant in the stages reached.

Striving towards a more differentiated analysis, the recent critical debate on participation with its focus on social justice and oppression indeed offers a more differentiated framework. For the purpose of this study, an approach was sought that would address major issues emanating from the recent 'tyranny or transformation' debate. Given the principal role of interpersonal communication in participatory development, the perspective of language and discourse was identified as promising. In the following, the outcomes of the research will be presented in the form of five propositions that focus on the interaction of participatory approaches with social inequality from the following perspectives: at the community level, in regard to gender relations, in the interaction of development workers and beneficiaries, within the global context and in the historical dimension.

7.1.1. Peasant farmers encountering development intervention: exclusion of the needy

Both programmes can be characterized by a selective perception of social inequality. While the targeted rural communities were regarded as poor and in need of support, there was little consideration of socio-economic stratification within the groups.

An analysis of planning documents pertaining to the two programmes shows that the interventions had primarily been designed outside the communities that implemented them; and that, while the potential beneficiaries were consulted, they did not actively take part in the planning process. This also meant that outside planners largely determined who would participate in the programmes. At the planning stage, the SRAP was designed to address younger farmers (between twenty and forty years of age); and the RCMP was designed to address rice farmers in the areas where the programme operated. There was no consideration of poverty or gender constituting a possible obstacle to participation: Potential beneficiaries were treated as socio-economically homogeneous.

Data from implementation, however, indicate that there was a tangible bias towards more affluent community members. In the RCMP, rice farmers were to gain access to modern technology which they could not otherwise afford. However, user fees hindered poorer households from benefiting from the (heavily subsidised) mechanized services like ploughing and weeding. The exclusion of poorer farmers and related measures of implementation was a constant source of controversy in staff meetings, and several complaints by peasant farmers about the prohibitive nature of user fees were recorded.

In the SRAP, the declared aim was to develop village communities in order to prevent rural-urban migration. The program offered young farmers training in agriculture and rural crafts. Working with enterprising and dynamic persons was in this case justified by making reference to the assumed common interests of the village community at large. Once they joined the programme, peasant farmers had to commit time and resources. This was considered a considerable burden by the active participants, and something the poorer and/or female farmers could less easily afford.

Once they joined the programme, peasant farmers had the opportunity to access goods, services and training in return for modest contributions. While fees, for example, covered only a fracture of the actual cost involved, they tended to exclude poorer individuals and exacerbate social differences in the village communities. In addition, some of the peasant farmers also explicitly complained that some persons within the groups were better positioned and served in regard to the 'development goods' available.

The collected data do not suggest that specific efforts were made to include the marginalized. Planning tools that address differences in social status such as wealth rankings were not part of the methodology used. Unfortunately, it was also beyond the scope of this study to undertake a systematic comparative enquiry into the socio-economic background of participants and non-participants of the respective communities; the study had to rely on information provided by participants to establish poverty and the gendered division of labour as reasons for the non-participation of other community members.

Within the programmes, the discourse on inequality and social justice was relegated to staff meetings concerned with minor policy adaptations. Many development workers were deeply concerned about the exclusion of poorer community members and questioned the "myth" (Guijt and Shah 1998) that understood the community as a socio-economically homogenous entity. However, the management of neither of the two implementing organizations had the political will to question matters of principal policy orientation, and the prevailing neo-liberal agenda was not primarily concerned with social inequality in program implementation.

Our data does not suggest that the language used in programme implementation was part of the exclusionary mechanism within the rural communities. Swahili was the language used in programme implementation in both the SRAP and RCMP. In the SRAP program, Jita or Haya was occasionally used in informal interaction. None of the interviewees mentioned limitations in regard to language. However, as already stated, no interviews were conducted with villagers outside the programme.

7.1.2. Gendered power differences: superficial progress, underlying gaps

Among the beneficiaries of both the SRAP and the RCMP programmes, male farmers by far outnumbered female ones. In both programmes, there was a tendency to explain this away as an inevitable consequence of 'given' socio-cultural settings. The inadequate involvement of women was in any case not taken as an opportunity to fundamentally question the inherent gender bias of the programmes.

Officially, both programmes were targeted at female and male farmers alike. Not far under the surface, however, the idea of the 'mainly male' household head continued to shape policy and practice. Prevailing discriminatory patterns in the gendered division of labour, ownership of land and control over profits were not addressed.

In the SRAP, concern about the marginal involvement of women eventually led to the formation of separate women's groups. This, however, did not per se lead to more equitable gender relations. The groups de facto consisted of female household dependents of the previously established core group of 'household heads'. Their activities cautiously explored new spaces for the women involved. The measures taken in support of women's participation, however, were also found to reproduce gendered social norms. For example, in mixed-sex planning meetings, female farmers were (still) represented more by others than they represented themselves; male farmers and (both female and male) development workers spent more time commenting on the women's activities, experience and aspirations than the women themselves.

One fundamental problem lay in the tendency to treat gender in isolation from other social categories. For example, issues like the poverty of female-headed households, or the possibly precarious situation of female household 'dependents' remained unaddressed.

7.1.3. Development workers: creating subaltern voices?

The constructive potential of both programs became most evident in communicative events that brought development workers and peasant farmers together. The fostering of communicative spaces where mutual understanding could be deepened and democratic negotiation cultivated was in itself a major achievement within both programs. In the SRAP, peasant farmers organized and chaired all meetings at the village level. In the RCMP, farmers' organizations elected representatives that attended area meetings. Apart from the efforts made by all participants involved, other factors specific to Tanzanian rural communities played a role. These included language policy that had established Swahili as a national means of communication, an education policy that had led to wide-spread literacy, and a political culture that approved of popular involvement in community

affairs – even if the latter was still biased in regard to gender and socio-economic status.
Yet the grass-roots community institutions were severely restricted by their limited power to influence larger decision-making processes in the programme. Instead of directly fostering grass-roots processes, the development workers primarily functioned as mediators. Their organizations had pre-defined their tasks as communicating outside information and plans to the farmers, negotiating details of implementation, and eliciting progress reports.
Given their orientation towards participatory development, neither of the two organizations could afford to ignore the peasant farmers' opinions. At the same time, they did not intend to entrust the beneficiaries entirely with programme planning and implementation. Instead, development workers were assigned the task of interpreting and mediating the peasant farmers' opinions. Staff members then decided which of the farmers' observations and demands would be accepted as worthwhile and important, while others were dismissed as illogical and contradictory. It is at this level that the views and needs of the beneficiaries were (re)constructed and represented to an outside world of implementing organizations, donors and Northern taxpayers (cf Maral-Hanak 2006a). In many cases, filtering and editing through the staff also coincided with a change in languages, as reporting to donors required the use of English. Thus, even if organizational provisions had been made for peasant farmers in order for them to track and follow the information produced about them, these would have failed in face of the linguistic barrier. The peasant farmers also depended on the development workers when seeking information on their partners in the North – once again, language and institutional filters within the aid industry restricted the flow of information conducive to partnership and mutual understanding.

7.1.4. The changing role of the state as an actor in participatory development

In Tanzania's early postcolonial history, participatory initiatives took on a remarkable model role that influenced policy development at the national level. From the early 1960s onwards, the villages of the Ruvuma Development Association established communities that were in many ways reminiscent of a radical Freirean pedagogy of the oppressed. Among them, the community of Litowa is said to have inspired Nyerere's vision of the Ujamaa village. As Jennings (2003) argues, the communities' model character was so powerful that they were eventually considered a threat to established party and government hierarchies. By the end of the decade, Litowa was dismantled by jealous TANU officials, and self-help initiatives were largely replaced by coercion from above. Thus, by the late 1960s, as the country was only beginning to embark on a broad-based policy of participation passed down 'from above', some of its truly autonomous initiatives had already been nipped in the bud.

There is no doubt that the Tanzanian government made remarkable progress in the realm of health and education throughout the following years. It is worth noting that Paulo Freire, who visited the country in 1971, was impressed by the government's achievements in emancipatory pedagogy. The support given to Swahili in the domain of primary education and politics was important in enhancing the language as a national medium of communication; however, persistent reservations about its introduction to secondary and higher education continue to constitute a significant problem today.

The 1970s also mark the beginning of economic deterioration, coercion and corruption in the country. Throughout the following decades, however, the ideal of the enlightened and democratic Ujamaa community continued to dominated political discourse, even long after the government had turned to economic and political liberalisation.

Tanzania welcomed foreign development aid, including new technical approaches to participation such as the 'Participatory Rural Appraisal' and other concepts commonly applied in the 1990s. Governmental departments involved in participatory programmes, such as the RCMP in this research, adopted much of the related participatory discourse promoted by donors. Yet, once again, models and ideals were possibly more important than the concrete outcomes of the interventions in question. Case studies of participatory projects and programs of this period point to the following problems: Planning in participatory initiatives was dominated by outsiders (Pottier 1997:217); local elites benefited more than poorer sections of the community, and participation was confounded with mobilisation of support (Kelsall and Mercer 2003:298); people did not identify with participatory approaches, but regarded them as one of the many inevitable impositions by donors and implementers (Green 2000:84). Many of the problematic features of the SRAP and RCMP do not seem to have been particular to these specific programmes. To date, participatory approaches in programme implementation have lost little of their challenge and relevance. Donor and recipient countries continue to emphasize participation as a principle in co-operation. The underlying idea that people should have a say in the design and planning of programmes that concern them is therefore as valid as ever.

In recent years, participation has increasingly been put forth in processes and relations at the national and global levels. Here, PRSP processes constitute a case in point: The Tanzanian government, has invited selected NGOs to represent national civil society in consultatory processes on poverty reduction strategies. Efforts to translate key PRSP documents into Swahili as well as provide colloquial language versions of sophisticated policy documents are worth mentioning here. However, the government has not allowed allowed civil society organizations to take an active role in preparing the agenda, let alone influence related decision-making (Evans and Ngalwea 2003:277).

7.1.5. Asymmetries in global aid relations and tangible local repercussions

The research focussed on communicative events in rural communities and organizations' offices in related urban centres, and only a few written documents emanating from donors and implementing agencies were included in the analysis. Yet global asymmetries were present in rural communicative events, and eurocentric language policies emerged as a tangible obstacle to development efforts in rural Tanzanian communities.

The fact that development workers tend to scan communication with farmers for elements compatible with donor policy has already been mentioned. Also, development workers cannot escape being part of the aid industry and related labour market. Their linguistic qualifications and development-related expertise (for example, knowledge of accounting schemes such as the LFA and PCM) are biased towards eurocentric standards.

Finally, global trends in development discourse on gender and participation do influence practice. If the World Bank or DAC promote concepts of gender and participation that veil rather than address inequalities, it is not surprising that similar trends surface at recipient points of the aid industry.

7.2. Language use in development organizations: Can recommendations be made for practice?

Although this research confirms some of the systemic shortcomings of participatory approaches, it is also underscores the usefulness of theoretical insights for practice and implementation. The tentative proposals made in the following focus on fostering awareness and certain elementary measures at the level of organizational policy. Those who shape policy in development co-operation – donors as well as implementing organizations in the North and South – have a particular responsibility in regard to language use in co-operation. Strategies should be developed to ensure that development interventions strengthen languages of popular participation rather than those of elite control.

7.2.1. Organizations and language use

Southern development organizations should reflect on their language policy in various respects. In order to be truly accountable to beneficiaries, important communication and documents should ideally be made accessible in languages of wider communication. In some cases, this may entail the use of two or more languages simultaneously, to make important information accessible to the beneficiary group. At the same time, the linguistic skills of development workers should be systematically analyzed and developed. In regard to the findings of this study in Tanzania, for example, this would mean that resources going into the improvement of language and communication skills should not be limited to

English, but also be made available to foster the use of Swahili and other Tanzanian languages, for example, by enhancing knowledge of technical terminology. In employment policy, the value attached to language proficiency in English should be reconsidered and extended to the knowledge of Swahili and other Tanzanian languages. Exploring the possible use of Swahili and other Tanzanian languages in development co-operation is part of the task at hand, just as well as creating awareness for the fact that prevailing language patterns may exacerbate existing inequalities. Knowledge of the background of colonial and postcolonial language policy could help to attain a critical awareness about the position of former colonial languages. Their dominant position in development co-operation could then be understood as part of the problems developing societies face.

Northern development organizations, too, have the option of actively supporting the use of languages facilitating popular participation, and pushing the boundaries of existing language domains. Accepting prevailing patterns of Western language domination is a way of reinforcing them. Of course, respective changes in policy and practice should be negotiated and not imposed. Additionally, such measures should not be naïvely overestimated. However, organizations working in social development have good reasons "to create communicative contexts that would enhance people's abilities to carry out their activities to improve their social welfare" (Makoni and Mashiri 2006:62).

7.2.2. Mainstream discourse and the power to define

Development organizations should support critical reflection on the challenges posed by participatory development. North-South co-operation is presently characterised by asymmetric relations. An awareness of inequality and donor dominance could correct inflated and idealised ideals that often burden participatory development. A critical approach towards participation and other key concepts of mainstream development discourse, such as gender, empowerment or sustainability, should help to establish realities behind the often rhetorical claims.

Interpersonal interaction in development co-operation is to a large extent shaped by uniform planning tools such as the Logframe and Project Cycle Management. These instruments play an important role in communicating donors' demands towards recipients. Despite their claim to participatory qualities, they often bias communicative practices in favour of donors or intermediate organizations.

Stereotypes often constitute perpetuations of colonial misconceptions, for instance in regard to working morale or hierarchical value attached to languages. The debate on racism and discrimination in development co-operation has only recently begun. Development organizations should encourage a critical attitude towards stereotypes and related forms of discrimination.

Proposing reflexivity as a strategy for practice does not provide simple solutions, but long-term processes of mutual learning. As Christine Sylvester (1999:717) has pointed out, bringing together insights of postcolonial and poststructural thought and development practice constitutes a challenge. However, as she has also emphasized, the potential gains from a critical dialogue between the two approaches are too promising to be ignored.

8. Bibliography

AAWORD Association of African Women for Research and Development.1982. The Experience of the Association of African Women for Research and Development. AAWORD. In: Development Dialogue 1-2, 101-113.

Abdulaziz, Mohammed H. 1971. Tanzania's National Language Policy and the Rise of Swahili Political Culture. In W. H. Whiteley (ed.) Language Use and Social Change. London: Oxford University Press, 160-178.

Abdulaziz, Mohammed H. 1980. The Ecology of Tanzanian National Language Policy. In C. P. Hill and Edgar C. Polomé (eds.) Language in Tanzania. London: Oxford University Press, 139- 175.

ANC (African National Congress). 1955. The Freedom Charter. Adopted at the Congress of the People, Kliptown, on 26 June 1955. http://www.anc.org.za/ancdocs/history/charter.html, 1/2/2007

Ashley, Caroline and Simon Maxwell. 2001. Rethinking rural development. Development Policy Review 19/4, 395-425.

Aune, Jens. 2000. Logical Framework Approach and PRA – mutually exclusive or complementary tools for project planning? Development in Practise 10/5, 687–690.

Baaz, Maria Eriksson. 2005. Paternalism of partnership. A postcolonial reading of identity in development aid. London: Zed Books

Bagachwa, M.S.D. 1997. The rural informal sector in Tanzania. in: Bryceson, Deborah and V. Jamal (eds) Farewell to farms: de-agrarisation and employment in Africa. Aldershot, UK: Ashgate.

Bahiigwa, Godfrey, Ntengua Mdoe and Frank Ellis. 2005. Livelyhoods research findings and agriculture-led growth. IDS Bulletin 36/2, 115-120.

Bakewell, Oliver and Anne Garbutt. 2005. The use and abuse of the logical framework approach. Stockholm: SIDA.

Banda, Felix. 2004. Multilingualism and its implications for transformation in the South African workplace: promoting positive difference and closing the gap between theory and practise. In: Pfaffe, Joachim Friedrich (ed). 2004. Making multilingual education a reality for all – operationalizing good intentions. Proceedings of the Third International Conference of the Association for the Development of African Languages in Education, Science and Technology (ADALEST) held at Mangochi, Malawi, 2004, 268-280.

Barrientos, Stephanie, Andrienetta Kritzinger, Maggie Opondo and Sally Smith. 2005. Gender, Work and Vulnerability in African Horticulture. IDS Bulletin 36/2, 74-79.

Barrow, Ondine and Michael Jennings. 2001. The Charitable Impulse: NGOs and Development in East and North-East Africa. James Currey.

Batibo, Herman. 1992. The fate of ethnic languages in Tanzania. In: Brenzinger, Matthias (ed.). 1992. Language death – factual and theoretical explorations with special reference to East Africa. Berlin: Mouton de Gruyter, 85-98.

Batibo, Herman. 2006. Marginalisation and empowerment through educational medium. The case of linguistically disadvantaged groups of Botswana and Tanzania. In: Pütz, Martin, Joshua Fishman, JoAnne Neff-van Aertselaer (eds). 2006. Along the Routes to Power: Explorations of the Empowerment through Language. New York, Berlin: Mouton de Gruyter, 261-283.

Bearth, Thomas and Diomandé Fan. 2006. The local language – a neglected resource for sustainable development. In: Ernest W.B. Hess-Lüttich (ed.), Eco-Semiotics. Umwelt- und Entwicklungskommunikation. Tübingen/Basel: Francke, 273-293.

Beck, Rose Marie. 2006. "We speak Otjiherero but we write in English", 'Doing Elite' at the Grassroots (Herero, Namibia). In: Pütz, Martin, Joshua Fishman, JoAnne Neff-van Aertselaer (eds). 2006. Along the Routes to Power: Explorations of the Empowerment through Language. New York, Berlin: Mouton de Gruyter, 305-331.

Bell, Emma. 2003. Gender and PRSPs: with experience from Tanzania, Bolivia, Viet Nam and Mozambique. Prepared for the Ministry of Foreign Affairs, Denmark. Bridge (Development-Gender), Institute of Development Studies, Sussex. http://www.eldis.org/static/DOC12249.htm 11.10.2005.

Benke, Gertraud and Ruth Wodak 2003. The discursive construction of individual memories. How Austrian "Wehrmacht" soldiers remember WWII. In: Wodak, Ruth and James Martin (eds). 2003. Re/reading the past: critical and functional perspectives on time and value. Amsterdam: Benjamins 115-138.

Bergdall, Terry. 1993. Methods for active participation. Nairobi: Oxford University Press.

Beukes, Anne-Marie. 2004. The first ten years of democracy: language policy in South Africa. Paper read at Xth Linguapax Congress on Linguistic Diversity, Sustainability and Peace, 20-23 May, Barcelona.

Bgoya, Walter. 2001. The effect of globalisation in Africa and the choice of language in publishing. International Review of Education No 47/3-4, 282-292.

Bhabha, Homi. 1983. Difference, discrimination, and the discourse of colonialism. In F. Barker (ed.) The politics of theory. Colchester, University of Essex, 194-211.

Bhabha, Homi. 1994. The location of culture. London: Routledge.

Biggs, Stephen and Sally Smith. 2003. A paradox of learning in project cycle management and the role of organisational culture. World Development 31/10: 1743-1757.

Bigsten, Arne and Anders Danielson. 2001. Tanzania: Is the Ugly Duckling Finally Growing Up? Uppsala: Nordiska Afrikainstitutet.

Blackburn, Jeremy and James Holland (eds) 1998. Who changes? Institutionalizing participation in development. London: Intermediate Technology Publications.

Blackden, Mark and Chita Bhanu. 1999. Gender, growth and poverty reduction. Special programme for assistance for Africa, 1998 Status report on poverty in Sub-Sahara Africa. Washington DC, World Bank.

Blommaert, Jan. 1992. Codeswitching and the exclusivity of social identities: Some data from Campus Kiswahili. In: Eastman, Carol (ed.), Codeswitching. Clevedon: Multilingual Matters, 57-70.

Blommaert, Jan. 2005a. Discourse. A critical introduction. Cambridge University Press.

Blommaert, Jan. 2005b. Situating language rights: English and Swahili in Tanzania revisited. Journal of Sociolinguistics 9/3, 390-417.

Blommaert, Jan. 2006. Language policy and national identity. In: Ricento, Thomas (ed.). 2006. An introduction to language policy: theory and method. Malden, Massachusetts: Blackwell, 238-254.

Bluhm, Claudia, Dirk Deissler, Joachim Scharloth, Anja Stukenbrock. 2000. Linguistische Diskursanalyse: Überblick, Probleme, Perspektiven. Sprache und Literatur in Wissenschaft und Unterricht 88, 2000, 3-19.

BMaA (Bundesministerium für auswärtige Angelegenheiten). 1999. Gender und Entwicklung – Grundlagen für die Gleichstellung von Frauen und Männern in der Entwicklungszusammenarbeit. Wien: Bundesministerium für auswärtige Angelegenheiten.

BMaA. (Bundesministerium für auswärtige Angelegenheiten) 2005. EZA-Statistik der Homepage des Bundesministeriums für auswärtige Angelegenheiten. www.bmaa.gv.at/up-media/1149_pph_2004.pdf, 1/6/2005.

Boesen, Jannik. 1979. From Ujamaa to villagization. In: Mwansasu, Bismarck und Cranford Pratt (eds.) Toward socialism in Tanzania. Toronto: University of Toronto Press, 125-144.

Booth, D., F. Lugangira, P. Masanja, A. Mvungi, R. Mwaipopo, J. Mwami and A. Redmayne. 1993. Social, Economic and Cultural Change in Contemporary Tanzania - a people oriented focus. Stockholm: SIDA.

Booth, David. 2004. Bridging the 'macro-micro' divide in policy oriented research: two African experiences. In: Eade, Deborah 2004. Development methods and approaches: critical reflections. Oxfam: A development in Practise Reader.

Boserup, Esther. 1970. Women's role in economic development. New York: St. Martin's Press.

Boussofara-Omar, Naima. 1999. Arabic Diglossic Switching in Tunisia: An Application of Myers-Scotton's Matrix Language Frame Model. Unpublished PhD. Dissertation, The University of Texas at Austin.

Brock-Utne, Birgit and Rodney Kofi Hopson (ed.). 2005. Languages of instruction for African emancipation: focus on postcolonial contexts and considerations. Tanzania: Mkuki na Nyota Publishers.

Brock-Utne, Birgit, Zubeida Desai and Martha Qorro (eds) 2003. Language of Instruction in Tanzania and South Africa. Dar es Salaam: E & D Publishers.

Brock-Utne, Birgit. 2002. Language, democracy and education in Africa. Discussion paper 15. Uppsala: Nordiska Afrikainstitutet.

Bromber, Katrin. 2003. Disziplinierung - eine europäische Erfindung? Das elementare islamische Bildungswesen an der ostafrikanischen Küste des späten 19. Jahrhunderts. In: Wirz, Albert/Andreas Eckert/Katrin Bromber (Hg.): Alles unter Kontrolle. Disziplinierungsprozesse im kolonialen Tanzania (ca. 1850 - 1960). Köln: Rüdiger Köppe Verlag, 37-53.

Brown, David. 2004. Participation in Poverty Reduction Strategies: Democracy Strengthened - or Democracy Undermined? in Sam Hickey and G. Mohan (eds) Participation: From Tyranny to Transformation? London: Zed Press, 237-251.

Bryceson, Deborah Fahy. 1999. Sub-Sahara Africa betwixt and between: rural livelyhood practices and policies. Leiden: Afrika-Studiecentrum Working Papers 43/1999.

Bryceson, Deborah Fahy. 2002a. Multiplex livelyhoods in rural Africa: recasting the terms and conditions of gainful employment. In: Journal of Modern African Studies, 40/1, 1-28.

Bryceson, Deborah Fahy. 2002b. The scramble in Africa: Reorienting rural livelihoods. In: World Development, 30/5, 725-739.

Bryceson, Deborah Fahy. 2004. Agrarian vista or vortex: African rural livelyhood policies. Review of African Political Economy 102, 617-629.

Bublitz, Hannelore u.a. 1999. Das Wuchern der Diskurse. Perspektiven der Diskursanalyse Foucaults. Frankfurt: Campus Verlag.

Burbridge, John (ed.). 1988. Approaches that work in rural development: emerging trends, participatory methods and local initiatives. München: Saur.

Burkey, Stan. 1993. People first – a guide to self-reliant participatory development. London: Zed Books.

Butler, Judith. 1990. Gender trouble – feminism and the subversion of identity. London: Routledge. Frey, Regina 2003 : Gender im Mainstreaming – Geschlechtertheorie und -praxis im internationalen Diskurs. Königstein/Taunus: Ulrike Helmer Verlag.

Butler, Judith. 1990. Gender Trouble: Feminism and the Subversion of Identity, London, Routledge.

Calvet, Louis-Jean. 1978. Die Sprachenfresser: ein Versuch über Linguistik und Kolonialismus. Berlin: Arsenal.

Calvet, Louis-Jean. 1987. La guerre des langues et les politiques linguistiques. Paris: Payot.

Cameron, Greg. 2004. Political Violence, ethnicity and the agrarian question in Zanzibar. In: Caplan, Pat and Farouk Topan (eds). 2004. Swahili Modernities: Identity, Power and Development on the East African Coast) Trenton, NJ: Africa World Press.

Canagarajah, Suresh. 1999. Resisting linguistic imperialism in English teaching. Oxford: Oxford University Press.

Canagarajah, Suresh. 2000. Negotiating ideologies through English: strategies from the periphery. In: Thomas Ricento (ed). 2000. Ideology, Politics, and Language Policies: Focus on English. Amsterdam: John Benjamins, 121-132.

Caplan, Pat and Farouk Topan (eds) Swahili Modernities: Identity, Power and Development on the East African Coast) Trenton, NJ: Africa World Press 2004.

Chambers, Robert and Jethro Pettit. 2004. Shifting Power to Make a Difference. In: Groves, Leslie and Rachel Hinton (eds). Inclusive aid. Changing power and relationships in international development. London: Earthscan, 137-162.

Chambers, Robert. 1983/1995. Rural Development – Putting the last first. London: Longman.

Chambers, Robert. 1994a. The origins and practise of Participatory Rural Appraisal. In: World Development. 22/7, 953-969.

Chambers, Robert. 1994b. Participatory Rural Appraisal (PRA) : Analysis of experience. In: World Development. – 22/9, 1253-1268.

Chambers, Robert. 1994c. Participatory Rural Appraisal (PRA): Challenges, potentials and paradigm. In: World Development. – 22/10, 1437-1454.*

Chambers, Robert. 1995. NGOs and development: the primacy of the personal. IDS Working Paper 14. Brighton: Institute of Development Studies.

Chambers, Robert. 1997a. Whose reality counts? Putting the first last. London: Intermediate Technology Publications.

Chambers, Robert. 1997b. Responsible well-being: A personal agenda for development. In: World Development. 25/11, 1743-1754.

Chambers, Robert. 2004. Ideas for development: reflecting forwards. IDS working paper 238. Sussex: Institute for Development Studies.

Chambers, Robert. 2007. From PRA to PLA and Pluralism: Practise and Theory. IDS Working Paper 286. http://www.ids.ac.uk/ids/bookshop/wp/wp286.pdf 1/10/2007

Chilton, Paul and Ruth Wodak. 2007. Preface. In: Ruth Wodak & Paul Chilton (Eds.) A new Agenda in (Critical) Discourse Analysis. Amsterdam: Benjamins (DAPSAC series), i-ix.

Cleaver, Frances. 2001. Institutions, agency and the limitations of participatory approaches to development. In: Cooke, Bill and Uma Kothari (eds). 2001. Participation – the new tyranny. London: Zed Books, 36-55.

Cooke, Bill and Uma Kothari (eds). 2001. Participation – the new tyranny. London: Zed Books.

Cooke, Bill and Uma Kothari. 2001. The case for participation as tyranny. In: Cooke, Bill and Uma Kothari (eds). 2001. Participation – the new tyranny. London: Zed Books, 1-15.

Cooke, Bill. 2001. The social psychological limits to participation. In: Cooke, Bill and Uma Kothari (eds). 2001. Participation – the new tyranny. London: Zed Books, 102-121.

Cooke, Bill. 2003. A new continuity with colonial administration: Participation in development management In: Third World Quarterly, 24/1, 47-61.

Cooksey, Brian. 2004. Can PRS succeed where SAP failed? Dar es Salaam: HakiElimu Working Paper No. 3/04. http://www.hakielimu.org/WP/WPSeries3_2004.pdf 4/4/2008

Cornwall, Andrea, Samuel Musyoki and Garett Pratt. 2001. In search of a new impetus: practicioners' reflections on PRA and participation in Kenya. Brighton: IDS Working Paper 131.

Coulson, Andrew. 1979. African Socialism in Practice - the Tanzanian Experience. Spokesman Books, Nottingham, England.

Coulson, Andrew. 1985. Tanzania: a political economy. Oxford: Clarendon Press.

Crehan, Kate A.F. 1997. The fractured community: landscapes of gender and power in rural Zambia. Berkeley: University of California Press.

Crewe, Emma; Harrison, Elisabeth. 1998. Whose Development? An Ethnography of Aid. London: Zed Books.

Dale, Reidar. 2003. The logical framework: an easy escape, a straitjacket, or a useful planning tool? In: Development in Practice. 13/1, 57-70.

Degnbol-Martinussen John and Poul Engberg-Pedersen. 2003. Aid – understanding international development co-operation. London: Zed Books.

Desai, Zubeida. 2001. Multilingualism in South Africa with particular reference to the role of African languages in education. International Review of Education No 47/3-4, 323-339.

Dichter, Thomas. 2003. Despite good intentions: Why development assistance to the third world has failed. Amherst: University of Massachusetts Press.

Dick, Gundi. 1998. Mainstreaming – aktuelle Genderpolitik in der Entwicklungszusammenarbeit. In: Frauensolidarität 64/2, 15-16.

Eastman, Carol (ed.). 1992. Codeswitching. Clevedon: Multilingual Matters Ltd.

Eastman, Carol M. 1991. The Political and Sociolinguistics of Status Planning in Africa. In: Marshall, David F. (ed.) 1991. Focus on Language Planning, Essays in Honour of Joshua Fishman, John Benjamins, 135-152.

Eastman, Carol. 1992. Introduction. In: Eastman, Carol (ed.). 1992. Codeswitching. Clevedon: Multilingual Matters Ltd, 1-18.

Escobar, Arturo. 1994. Encountering development. The making and unmaking of the Third World. Princetown: Princetown University Press.

Esteva, Gustavo and Madhu Prakash, 1998. Grassroots post-modernism: Remaking the soil of culture. London: Zed Books.

EuropeAid Co-operation Office. 2006. Homepage of the EuropeAid Co-operation Office, European Comission, Brussels, Aid Delivery Methods, Logframe, http://europa.eu.int/comm/europeaid/qsm/project_en.htm#2.%20Logical%20 Framework%20Approach 5/1/2006.

European Commission. 2004. Project Cycle Management Guidelines – Aid Delivery Methods Volume 1. Brussels: Europe Aid Co-operation Office. http://europa.eu.int/comm/europeaid/qsm/documents/pcm_manual_2004_en.pdf 20/1/2006

Evans, Alison and Erasto Ngalwea. 2003. Tanzania. In: Development Policy Review. 21/2, 271-287.

Eyben, Rosalind. 2004. Battles over booklets. Gender myths in the British aid programme. In: Cornwall, Andrea, Harrison, Elizabeth, Whitehead, Ann (eds) Repositioning Feminisms in Gender and Development. IDS Bulletin 35/4, 73-81.

Eyben, Rosalind. 2005. Donors' learning difficulties: results, relationships and responsibilities, IDS Bulletin, 36/3, 98-107.

Fairclough, Norman and Ruth Wodak. 1997. Critical discourse analysis. In: T. A. van Dijk (ed.), Discourse Studies. A multidisciplinary introduction. Vol. 2: Discourse as social interaction. London: Sage, 258-284.

Fairclough, Norman. 1995. Critical Discourse Analysis. The Critical Study of Language. London: Longman.

Fairclough, Norman. 2001. Critical discourse analysis as a method in social scientific research. In: Meyer, Michael and Ruth Wodak (eds). 2001. Methods of critical discourse analysis. London: Sage, 121-138.

Fairclough, Norman. 2003. Analysing discourse. Textual analysis for social research. London: Routledge.

Fairclough, Norman. 2006. Language and globalization. London: Routledge.

Fals-Borda, Orlando. 2000. People's SpaceTimes in global processes: the response of the local. Journal of World-Systems Research, Vol. 3, Fall/Winter 2000, 624-634. http://jwsr.ucr.edu 1/12/2005

Farrington, John, Christine Okali and James Sumberg. 1993. Farmer participatory research. London: Intermediate Technology Publications.

Ferguson, Charles. 1959. Diglossia. In: Word 15, 325-337.

Fishman, Joshua. 1967. Bilingualism with and without diglossia; diglossia with and without bilingualism. Journal of Social Issues 23, 29-38.

Forster, Peter G.and Sam Maghimbi (ed). 1999. Agrarian economy, state and society in contemporary Tanzania. Aldershot: Ashgate.

Foucault, Michel. 1980. Power / Knowledge – Selected interviews and other writings, 1972-1977. Brighton: Harvester Wheatsheaf.

Foucault, Michel. 1976. Mikrophysik der Macht. Über Strafjustiz, Psychiatrie und Medizin. Berlin: Merve.

Fowler, Roger and Gunther Kress. 1979. Critical Linguistics. In: Fowler, Robert., Hodge, Robert, Kress, Gunther. und Tony Trew (eds). 1979. Language and Control. London: Routledge and Kegan, 185-213.

Fowler, Roger. 1985. Power. in: Handbook of Discourse Analysis, ed. by Teun van Dijk, 1985., Vol. 4, Discourse Analysis in Society, London: Academic Press, 61-82.

Francis, Paul. 2001. Participatory development at the World Bank: the primacy of process. In: Cooke, Bill and Uma Kothari (eds). 2001. Participation – the new tyranny. London: Zed Books, 72-87.

Freire, Paulo. 1970. Pedagogy of the oppressed. New York: Continuum.

Freire, Paulo. 1971. "A talk by Paulo Freire" in Studies in Adult Education No 2, Dar es Salaam, Institute for Adult Education.

Freire, Paulo. 1985. The Politics of Education - culture, power, and liberation. New York: Bergin and Garvey.

Frey, Regina. 2003. Gender im Mainstreaming – Geschlechtertheorie und -praxis im internationalen Diskurs. Königstein/Taunus: Ulrike Helmer Verlag.

Gasper, Des. 2000. Evaluating the 'logical framework approach' – towards learning-oriented development evaluation. In: Public Administration and Development 20/1, 17-28.

Gibbon, Peter. 1995. Mechanization of production and privatization of development of Post-Ujamaa Tanzania – an introduction. In: Gibbon, Peter (ed). 1995. Liberalised Development in Tanzania: studies on accumulation processes and local institutions. Uppsala: Nordiska Afrikainstitutet, 9-36. 109-176.

Gomes, Bea. 2006. Geber-Empfänger Beziehungen: Partnerschaften und Hierarchien. In: Bea de Abreu Fialho Gomes, Irmi Maral-Hanak, Walter Schicho (eds.). 2006. Entwicklungszusammenarbeit - Akteure, Interessen, Handlungsmuster. Wien: Mandelbaum - Edition Südwind, 11-24.

Gramsci, Antonio. 1971. Selection from the prison notebooks. London: Lawrence and Wishart.

Grau, Ingeborg. 1993. Die Igbo-sprechenden Völker Südostnigerias: Fragmentation und fundamentale Einheit in ihrer Geschichte. Zentrale Themen der Igbo-Forschung: Igbo-Ukwu Nri, Aro und der Krieg der Frauen. Wien: VWGÖ.

Grau, Ingeborg. 2006. Scramble for Africa, koloniale Machtergreifung und Wandel gesellschaftlicher Rollen im Kolonialismus. In: Englert, Birgit, Ingeborg Grau und Andrea Komlosy. Nord-Süd Beziehungen. Kolonialismen und Ansätze zu ihrer Überwindung. Wien, Mandelbaum, 75-97.

Green, Maia. 2000. Participatory development and the appropriation of agency in Southern Tanzania. Critique of Antropology, 20/1, 67-89.

Grewal, Inderpal. 1998. On the new global feminism and the family of nations: dilemmas of transnational feminist practice. In: Shohat, Ella ed. : Talking visions – multicultural feminism in a transnational age. Massachusetts: Massachusetts Institute of Technology Press, 501-530.

Grillo, R.D. und R. Stirrat (eds) 1997. Discourses of Development. Oxford: Berg.

Groves, Leslie. 2004. Questioning, learning and 'cutting edge' agendas: some thoughts from Tanzania. In: Groves, Leslie and Rachel Hinton (eds.) 2004. Inclusive aid: changing power and relationships in international development. London: Earthscan, 76-86.

GTZ. 1997. Zielorientierte Projektplanung. Eine Orientierung für die Planung bei neuen und laufenden Projekten und Programmen. Eschborn: GTZ http://www.zit.tu-darmstadt.de/cipp/tudzit/lib/all/lob/return_download,ticket,guest/bid,312/check_table,it_chap_downl_embed/~/zopp.pdf#search='ZOPP%20GTZ'.

Guijt, Irene and Meera Kaul Shah. 1998. The Myth of Community: Gender Issues in Participatory Development. London: IT Publishing.

Gumperz, John. 1982. Discourse Strategies. Cambridge: Cambridge University Press.

Habermas, Jürgen. 1970. Zur Logik der Sozialwissenschaften. Frankfurt: Suhrkamp.

Habermas, Jürgen. 1971. Erkenntnis und Interesse. Frankfurt: Suhrkamp.

Habermas, Jürgen. 1986. Erläuterungen zur Diskursethik. Frankfurt: Suhrkamp.

Hailey, John. 2001. Beyond the Formulaic: Process and Practice in South Asian NGOs. In: Cooke, Bill and Uma Kothari (eds.) Participation. The New Tyranny? London: Zed Books, 88-101.

Hall, Budd. 1997. Looking back, looking forward - reflections on the origins of the International Participatory Research Network and the Participatory Research Group in Toronto, Canada. Prepared for the Midwest Research to practise conference in adult, continuing and community education, Michigan State University, East Lansing, Michigan.

Hall, Stuart. 1996. Introduction: who needs identity? In: Stuart Hall and P. du Gay (eds). 1996. Questions of cultural identity. London: Sage.

Halliday, Michael. 1970. The lingustic sciences and language teaching. London: Longman.

Halliday, Michael. 1994. An introduction to functional grammar. London: Edward Arnold.

Hanak, Irmi, Barbara Nöst und Walter Schicho. 1995. Kommunikation und Entwicklung. Forschungsbericht. (Communication and Development. Unpublished Research Report). Wien.

Hanak, Irmi. 1997. Speech strategies and gender exclusion in a rural development project. In: JEP - Austrian Journal for Development Studies, Vienna, No 3/1997, 257-281

Hanak, Irmi. 1998. Chairing meetings: turn and topic control in development communication in rural Zanzibar. In: Discourse and Society, Amsterdam, No 1/1998, 33-56.

Hanak, Irmi. 2000. "Working her way out of poverty." Micro-credit programs' undelivered promises in poverty alleviation. In: JEP - Austrian Journal for Development Studies, 16/3, 303-328.

Havnevik, Kjell J. 1993. Tanzania: the limits to development from above. Uppsala: Nordiska Afrikainstitutet. Dar-es-Salaam: Mkuki na Nyota.

Heine, Bernd. 1979. Sprache, Gesellschaft und Kommunikation in Afrika. Weltforum Verlag: München.

Hersoug, Bjørn. 1996. 'Logical Framework Analysis' in an illogical world. Forum for Development Studies No 2/1996, 377-404.

Hess-Lüttich, Ernest W.B. (ed.), 2006. Eco-Semiotics. Umwelt- und Entwicklungskommunikation. Tübingen/Basel: Francke.

Heugh, Kathleen, 2003. Can authoritarian seperatism give way to linguistic rights? A South African case study. Current issues in language planning, Vol 3/2, 126-145.

Hickey, Samuel and Giles Mohan (eds). 2004. Participation - From Tyranny to Transformation? Exploring New Approaches to Participation in Development. London: Zed Books.

Hickey, Samuel and Giles Mohan. 2004a. Towards participation as transformation: critical themes and challenges. In: Hickey, Samuel and Giles Mohan (eds). 2004. Participation - From Tyranny to Transformation? Exploring New Approaches to Participation in Development. London: Zed Books, 3-24.

Hickey, Samuel and Giles Mohan. 2004b. Relocating participation within a radical politics o development: critical modernism and citizenship. In: Hickey, Samuel and Giles Mohan (eds). 2004. Participation - From Tyranny to Transformation? Exploring New Approaches to Participation in Development. London: Zed Books, 59-74.

Hickey, Samuel and Giles Mohan. 2004c. Relocating participation within a radical politics o development: insights form political action and practice. In: Hickey, Samuel and Giles Mohan (eds). 2004. Participation - From Tyranny to

Transformation? Exploring New Approaches to Participation in Development. London: Zed Books, 159-174.

Hickey, Sam and Giles Mohan. 2005. Relocating participation within a radical politics of development. In: Development and Change 36/2, 237-262.

Hickey, Sam and Sarah Bracking. 2005. Exploring the Politics of Chronic Poverty: From Representation to a Politics of Justice? World Development, 33/6, 851-865.

Hödl, Gerald. 2006. Die Anfänge - vom Empfänger zum Geberland. In: Bea de Abreu Fialho Gomes, Irmi Maral-Hanak, Walter Schicho (Hg.). 2006. Die Praxis der Entwicklungszusammenarbeit - Akteure, Interessen, Handlungsmuster. Wien: Mandelbaum - Edition Südwind, 25-42.

Hooks, Bell. 1981. Ain't I a woman. Boston, MA: South End.

Hughes, Alexandra, Joanna Wheeler and Rosalind Eyben. 2005. Rights and Power: The Challenge for International Development Agencies IDS Bulletin 36/1, 63-72.

Hyden, Goran. 1980. Beyond Ujamaa in Tanzania: underdevelopment and an uncaptured peasantry in Tanzania. London: Heinemann.

Hymes, Dell. 1972. On Communicative Competence. In: Pride, J.B. and J. Holmes (eds) 1972. Sociolinguistics. Harmondsworth: Penguin, 269-93.

Iedema Rick. 1999. Formalizing organizational meaning. Discourse and Society 10/1, 49-66.

IIZ. 1994. Informationsmappe: Das IIZ als Kooperationspartner. Wien IIZ.

Illiffe, John. 1979. A history of modern Tanganyika. African Studies Series 25. Cambridge: Cambridge University Press.

IMG (Independent Monitoring Group). 2005. Enhancing Aid Relationships in Tanzania: IMG Report 2005. Dar es Salaam: Economic and Social Research Foundation.

Irish, Leon and Karla Simon. 2003. Comments on the Non-Governmental Organizations Act, 2002, for the United Republic of Tanzania, Gazetted in the Official Gazette 4 October 2002. In: International Journal of Civil Society Law, Vol 1/1, 71-75. http://www.nesst.org/documents/IJCSLVolume1-1. pdf#search='Karla%20Simon%20NGO%20Tanzania' 4/4/2008.

Jäger, Siegfried. 2001a. Kritische Diskursanalyse - eine Einführung. Münster: Unrast-Verlag.

Jäger, Siegfried. 2001b. Discourse and knowledge: theoretical and methodological aspects of a critical discourse and dispositive analyis. In: Meyer, Michael and Ruth Wodak. 2001. Methods of critical discourse analysis. London: Sage, 32-62.

Jennings, Michael. 2001. Development is very political in Tanzania. In: Barrow, Ondine and Michael Jennings. 2001. The Charitable Impulse: NGOs and Development in East and North-East Africa. James Currey., 109-132.

Jennings, Michael. 2003. 'We must run while others walk': popular participation and development crisis in Tanzania, 1961-9, Journal of Modern African Studies 41/2, 163-187.

Jones, J. 1925. Education in East Africa: A study of East, Central and South Africa by the Second African Education Commission. New York: Phelps Stokes Fund.

Jones, Monty. 2005. Key Challenges for Technology - development and agricultural research in Africa, In: IDS Bulletin 36/2, 46-51.

Kabeer, Naila. 1994. Reversed realities. Gender hierarchies in development cooperation. London: Verso.

Kabeer, Naila. 1999. Resources, agency, achievements. Reflections on the measurement of women's empowerment. In: Development and Change 30 , 435-464.

Kabeer, Naila and Ann Whitehead. 2001. From uncertainty to risk: poverty, growth and gender in the rural African context. IDS Working Paper 134.

Kanogo, Tabitha. 1992. Women and environment in history. In: Khasiani, Shanyisa (ed.) Groundwork – African Women as Environment Managers. Nairobi: African Center for Technology Studies, 7-18.

Kelsall, Tim. 2001. NGOs, donors and the state. In: Barrow, Ondine and Michael Jennings. 2001. The Charitable Impulse: NGOs and Development in East and North-East Africa. Oxford: James Currey.

Kelsall, Tim. 2002. Shop windows and smoke-filled rooms: governance and the re-politicization of Tanzania. Journal of Modern African Studies, 40, 4: 597-619 2002.

Kelsall, Tim and Claire Mercer. 2003. Empowering People? World Vision and transformatory development in Northern Tanzania. Review of African Political Economy 96, 293-304.

Kesby, Mike. 2003. Tyrannies of transformation: a post-structural and spatialised understanding of empowerment through participation. Paper presented at the conference 'Participation - from tyranny to transformation', held a the Institute for development Management and Research, Manchester, Februar 2003.

Khamisi, Abdu Mtajuka. 1991. Current trends in language standardization in Tanzania. In: Cyffer, Norbert, Klaus Schubert, Hans-Ingolf Weier, Ekkehard Wolff. Language standardization in Africa. Hamburg: Helmut Buske Verlag, 207-214.

Kiango, John.G. 2004. Uundaji wa msamiati mpya katika Kiswahili: zoezi lenye njia mbalimbali. Mradi wa kuswahilisha programu huria – warsha Arusha 1-5 Novemba 2004.

Kiondo, Andrew. 1995. When the state withdraws – local development, politics and liberalisation in Tanzania. In: Gibbon, Peter. 1995. Liberalised development in Tanzania. Uppsala: Nordiska Afrikainstitutet,109-176.

Kiondo, Andrew. 2000. Policy advocacy: the case of Tanzania Media Women's Association (TAMWA). Campaigning for women's rights in Tanzania. Civil Society and Governance Programme, IDS, 2000. http://www.ids.ac.uk/ids/civsoc/ 9/11/2005

Kothari, Uma. 2001. Power, knowledge and social control in participatory development. In: Cooke, Bill and Uma Kothari (eds). 2001. Participation – the new tyranny. London: Zed Books, 139-152.

Krings, Sabine, Neuhold, Brita, Perlaki, Gerti. 1994. Gender-Training Seminar: Seminarbericht. Wien: VIDC.

Labov, William, 1970. The Logic of Nonstandard English. in: Alatis (ed.), Report of the Twenty-First Annual Round-Table Meeting on Liguistic and Language in Contact, Washington D.C.

Laitin, David. 1992. Language Repertoires and State Construction in Africa. Cambridge: Cambridge University Press.

Lange, Siri, Hege Wallevik und Andrew Kiondo. 2000. Civil society in Tanzania. Bergen: Christian Michelsen Institute. www.cmi.no 4/4/2008

Lawson, Andrew, David Booth, Meleki Msuya, Samuel Wangwe and Tim Williamson. 2005. Does general budget support work? Evidence from Tanzania. London: Overseas Development Institute (ODI). www.mof.go.tz or www.tzdac. or.tz/budget support (full report and summary available).

Legère, Karsten. 1992. Language Shift in Tanzania. In: Brenzinger, Matthias (ed.). 1992. Language death – factual and theoretical explorations with special reference to East Africa. Berlin: Mouton de Gruyter, 99-116.

Legère, Karsten. 2002. The "Languages of Tanzania" project: background, resources and perspectives. In: Africa & Asia No 2, 163-186, Dept of Oriental and African Languages, Göteborg University.

Legère, Karsten. 2004. "Simu ya mkononi" and "ifungandedzi". Against the myth of African languages lacking terminologies. In: Pfaffe, Joachim Friedrich (ed). 2004. Making multilingual education a reality for all – operationalizing good intentions. Proceedings of the Third International Conference of the Association for the Development of African Languages in Education, Science and Technology (ADALEST) held at Mangochi, Malawi, 2004, 37-58.

Legère, Karsten. 2006a. JK Nyerere of Tanzania and the empowerment of Swahili. In: Pütz, Martin, Joshua Fishman, JoAnne Neff-van Aertselaer (eds). 2006. Along the Routes to Power: Explorations of the Empowerment through Language. New York, Berlin: Mouton de Gruyter, 373-403.

Legère, Karsten. 2006b. Formal and informal development of the Swahili language: focus on Tanzania. In: Selected proceedings of the 36th Annual Conference of African Linguistics ed. Olaoba Arasanyin and Michael Pemberton, 174-184. Somerville, MA: Cascadilla Proceedings Project.

Lewis, Arthur. 1954. Economic Development with Unlimited Supplies of Labour. In: The Manchester School, Vol. 22, 139-191.

Li, Tania Murray. 1996. Images of community. Discourse and strategy in property relations. Development and Change 27/3, 501-527.

Lyimo, Francis. 1999. Peasant Agriculture in Tanzania: access to and use of ressources to improve agricultural production. In: Forster, Peter and Sam Maghimbi. 1999. Agrarian economy, state and society in contemporary Tanzania. Aldershot: Ashgate Publishing Ltd., 160-183.

Maghimbi, Sam. 1999. Revolution and Stagnation in the Peasant Economy of Zanzibar. In: Forster, Peter and Sam Maghimbi. 1999. Agrarian economy, state and society in contemporary Tanzania. Aldershot: Ashgate Publishing Ltd., 89-104.

Makoni, Sinfree and Pedzisai Mashiri. 2006. Critical historiography: does language planning in Africa need a construct of language as part of its theoretical apparatus? Makoni, Sinfree and Alastair Pennycook (eds). 2006. Disinventing and reconstituting languages. Clevedon: Multilingual Matters, 62-89.

Malekela, George. 2003. English as a medium of instruction in post-primary education in Tanzania: is it a fair policy on the learner? In: Brock Utne, Birgit, Zubeida Desai and Martha Qorro (eds.). 2003. Language of instruction in Tanzania and South Africa. Dar es Salaam: E & D Publishers, 102-112.

Mama, Amina. 2002. Gains and Challenges. Linking Theory and Practice. Keynote Address presented at opening ceremony, Women's World's Congress, Makerere University, 21 July 2002. http://www.uct.ac.za/org/agi/new/mama.htm, 3/10/2003.

Mamozai, Martha. 1989. Schwarze Frau, weiße Herrin. Reinbek: Rowohlt Verlag.

Mapolu, Henry. 1973. The social and economic organisation of Ujamaa Villages, M.A. Thesis. University of Dar es Salaam.

Maral-Hanak Irmi. 2006a. Entwicklung kommunizieren: Öffentlichkeits- und Bildungsarbeit. (Communicating development: public relations and educational approaches) In: Bea de Abreu Fialho Gomes, Irmi Maral-Hanak, Walter Schicho (eds.). 2006. Entwicklungszusammenarbeit - Akteure, Interessen, Handlungsmuster. Wien: Mandelbaum - Edition Südwind, 103-122.

Maral-Hanak Irmi. 2006b. Gender-Mainstreaming in der österreichischen Entwicklungszusammenarbeit – zur Etablierung frauenpolitischer Planungsinstrumente in Geberorganisationen. (Gender-Mainstreaming in the Austrian development cooperation – establishing gender planning tools in donor organisations) In: Bea de Abreu Fialho Gomes, Irmi Maral-Hanak, Walter Schicho (eds.). 2006. Entwicklungszusammenarbeit - Akteure, Interessen, Handlungsmuster. Wien: Mandelbaum - Edition Südwind, 65-88.

Maral-Hanak, Irmi. 2004. Feministische Entwicklungstheorien. (Feminist development theories) In: Fischer, Karin, Irmi Maral-Hanak, Gerald Hödl und Christof Parnreiter (Hg.) 2004. Entwicklung und Unterentwicklung. Eine Einführung in Probleme, Theorien und Strategien. Wien: Mandelbaum Verlag, 179-198.

Marsden, Ruth. 2004. Exploring power and relationships: a perspective from Nepal. In: Groves, Leslie and Rachel Hinton (eds.) 2004. Inclusive aid: changing power and relationships in international development. London: Earthscan, 97-107.

Masaiganah, Mwajuma. 2000. A story to tell: 'hili li mama' meaning 'this mama…'. PLA Notes 39, 38-41.

Mazrui, Ali and Alamin Mazrui. 1998. The power of Babel – language and governance in the African experience. Oxford: James Currey.

Mbilinyi, Marjorie. 1974. The Transition to Capitalism in Tanzania. Dar es Salaam. Department of Education, University of Dar es Salaam.

Mbilinyi, Marjorie. 2000. The new face of IMF structural adjustment (Tanzania). Excerpt from a paper prepared for the U.N.'s recent review of its 1995 Beijing Women's Summit. https://www.nadir.org/nadir/initiativ/agp/free/imf/africa/tanzan.htm 3/4/2008

McClintock, Anne. 1997. "No longer in a future heaven" – gender, race and nationalism. In: McClintock, Anne/Mufti, Aamir/Shohat Ella (eds.): Dangerous liaisons: gender, nation and postcolonial perspectives. Minneapolis: University of Minnesota Press, 89-112.

McFadden, Patricia. 2000. Radically Speaking: The Significance of the Women's Movement for Southern Africa. Paper presented in Vienna, Austria,

October 2000. http://www.wworld.org/ programs/regions/africa/patricia_mcfadden3.htm, 20/1/2004.

MEC (Ministry of Education and Culture Tanzania). 1997. Sera ya Utamaduni. Dar-es-Salaam. Ministry of Education and Culture. http://www.tanzania.go.tz/policiesf.html 4/4/2008

Meena, Ruth. 2003.The politics of quotas in Tanzania. A paper presented at the International Institute for Democracy and Electoral Assistance (IDEA) Parlamentary Forum Conference, Pretoria 2003. www.quoataproject.org/CS/CS_Tanzania_Meena_27_7_2004.pdf 19/1/2006

Meier, Christoph. 1997. Arbeitsbesprechungen. Interaktionsstruktur, Interaktionsdynamik und Konsequenzen einer sozialen Form. Opladen: Westdeutscher Verlag.

Melkote, Srinivas and Leslie Steeves. 2001. Communication for development in the Third World: theory and practice for empowerment. London: SAGE.

Mendoza, Breny. 2002. Transnational feminisms in question. In: Feminist Theory 3 /3, 295-314.

Menz, Florian. 1991. Der geheime Dialog. Medizinische Ausbildung und institutionalisierte Verschleierung in der Arzt-Patienten-Kommunikation – eine diskursanalytische Studie. Frankfurt: Lang.

Menz, Florian. 2000. Selbst- und Fremdorganisation im Diskurs. Interne Kommunikation in Wirtschaftsunternehmen. Wiesbaden: Deutscher Universitäts-Verlag.

Menz, Florian. 2003. The languages of the past. On the reconstruction of a collective history through individual stories. In: Wodak, Ruth and James Martin (eds). 2003. Re/reading the past: critical and functional perspectives on time and value. Amsterdam: Benjamins 139-176

Mercer, Claire. 1999. Reconceptualizing state-society relations: Are NGOs 'making a difference'? Area,31/3, 247-258.

Mercer, Claire. 2002a. 'Deconstructing development: the discourse of maendeleo and the politics of women's participation on Mount Kilimanjaro', Development and Change 33/1,101-127

Mercer, Claire. 2002b. 'NGOs, civil society and democratisation: a critical review of the literature', Progress in Development Studies, 2/1, 5-22 *

Meyer, Michael. 2001. Between theory, method and politics: positioning of the approaches to CDA. In: Meyer, Michael and Ruth Wodak. 2001. Methods of critical discourse analysis. London: Sage, 14-31.

Michael, Sarah. 2004. Undermining development. The absence of power among local NGOs in Africa. Oxford: James Currey.

Mies, Maria. 1982. The lace-makers of Narsapur: Indian house- wives produce for the world market. Westport, CT: Lawrence Hill.

Miller, Valerie, VeneKlasen Lisa and Cindy Clark. 2005a. Rights-based development. Linking rights and participation challenges in theory and action. IDS Bulletin 36/1, 31-40.

Miller, Valerie, VeneKlasen Lisa and Cindy Clark. 2005b. Rights-based Approaches: Recovering Past Innovations. IDS Bulletin 36/1, 52-62.

Mills, Sara. 1997. Discourse. London: Routledge.

Mogella, Cosmas. 2000. The State and Civil Society Relations Civil Society and Governance Programme, IDS , 2000. http://www.ids.ac.uk/ids/civsoc/ 9/11/2005

Mohan, Giles and Kristian Stokke. 2000. Participatory Development and Empowerment - the dangers of localism. Third World Quarterly 21/2, 266-80.

Mohan, Giles. 2001. Beyond participation - strategies for deeper empowerment. In: Cooke, Bill and Uma Kothari (eds). 2001. Participation – the new tyranny. London: Zed Books, 153-167.

Mohanty, Chandra Talpade. 1988/1997. Under western eyes: feminist scholarship and colonial discourses. In: Visvanathan (ed) 1997, 79-86.

Mohanty, Chandra Talpade.1997. "Feminist Encounters: Locating the Politics of Experience". In: McDowell, Linda. & J. P. Sharp (eds). 1997. Space, Gender, Knowledge. Feminist Readings. Arnold.

Moser, Caroline. 1989. Gender Planning in the Third World: Meeting Practical and Strategic Gender Needs. In: World Development 17/2, 1799-1825.

Moser, Caroline. 1993. Gender Planning and Development. Theory, Practice and Training. New York: Routledge.

Mosse, David. 1995. Social analysis in participatory rural development. In: PLA Notes No 24, IIED, London.

Mosse, David. 2005. Cultivating Development - an ethnography of aid policy and practice. London: Pluto Press.

Msanjila, Yohana. 2005. Hali ya Kiswahili katika shule za sekondari Tanzania: udhalilishaji wa lugha ya taifa? Swahili Forum 12, 205-218.

Mtesigwa, Peter C.K. 2004. Uundaji wa istilahi: uzoefu wa Baraza la Kiswahili la Taifa (BAKITA) Mradi wa kuswahilisha programu huria – warsha Arusha 1-5 Novemba 2004.

Mulokozi, Mugyabuso M. 2002. Kiswahili as a national and international language. Dar-es-Salaam: Institute of Kiswahili Research. accessible at www.helsinki.fi/hum/aakkl/documents/Kiswahili.pdf 6/7/2008

Muna, Rebecca. 2001. Civil Society participation in the PRSP: A case study of Tanzania. Paper presented at the Gender Festival, Dar-es-Salaam 2001. http://www.tgnp.co.tz/index.html 20/7/2003

Mutasa, Vidah. 2003. The issue of language of instruction in Tanzania. Brock-Utne, Birgit, Zubeida Desai and Martha Qorro (eds.). 2003. Language of instruction in Tanzania and South Africa. Dar es Salaam: E & D Publishers, 197-202.

Mutter, Theo. 1995. Kritische Rückfragen an den Methodenboom in der Entwicklungspolitik. Peripherie 57/58, 165-175.

Muysken, Pieter. 2000. Bilingual Speech. A Typology of Code-Mixing. Cambridge: CUP.

Mwinsheikhe, Halima Mohammed. 2003. Using Kiswahili as a medium of instruction in science teaching in Tanzanian secondary schools. In: Brock-Utne, Birgit, Zubeida Desai and Martha Qorro (eds.). 2003. Language of instruction in Tanzania and South Africa. Dar es Salaam: E & D Publishers, 129-148.

Myers-Scotton, Carol. 1992. Comparing codeswitching and borrowing. In: Eastman, Carol (ed.). 1992. Codeswitching. Clevedon: Multilingual Matters Ltd, 19-40.

Myers-Scotton, Carol. 1993a. Social motivations for code-switching – evidence from Africa. Oxford: Clarendon Press.

Myers-Scotton, Carol. 1993b. Duelling Languages. Grammatical structures in codeswitching. Oxford: Clarendon Press.

Myers-Scotton, Carol. 2000. Comparing verbs in Swahili-English codeswitching with other data sets. Kahigi, Kulikoyela, Yared Kihore and Maarten Mouse. 2000. Lugha za Tanzania – Languages of Tanzania. Leiden: CNWS.

Myers-Scotton, Carol. 2002. Contact linguistics: Bilingual encounters and grammatical outcomes. Oxford: Oxford University Press.

Nandi, Snehanshu Sekhar and Wouter Schaap. 2005. Beyond PRA: experiments in facilitation local action in water management. Development in Practice, 15/5.

Narayan, Deepa and Jennifer Rietbergen-McCracken. 1998. Participation and social assessment: tools and techniques. Washington: World Bank.

Narayan, Deepa and Patti Petesch. 2002. Voices of the Poor: From Many Lands. New York, N.Y: Published for the World Bank, Oxford University Press.

Narayan, Deepa with Raj Patel, Kai Schafft, Anne Rademacher and Sarah Koch-Schulte. 2000. Voices of the Poor: Can Anyone Hear Us? New York, N.Y.: Published for the World Bank, Oxford University Press.

Narayan, Deepa, Robert Chambers, Meera Kaul Shah, and Patti Petesch. 2000. Voices of the Poor: Crying Out for Change. New York, N.Y: Published for the World Bank, Oxford University Press.

Nauheimer, Holger. 1997. Project Cycle Management (PCM) - New Project Management Tools or recycled tools from yesterday? AT-Forum No 9; http://www.change-management-toolbook.com/tools/pcm.html 19/1/2006.

Neke, Stephen Mugeta. 2003. English in Tanzania - an anatomy of hegemony. Unpublished PhD thesis, University of Gent. http://cas1.elis.rug.ac.be/avrug/pdf03/neke.pdf 4/4/2008

Nelson, Nici and Susan Wright (eds). 1995. Power and Participatory Development. Theory and Practice. London: Intermediate Technology Publication.

Nelson, Nici and Susan Wright. 1995. Introduction: participation and power. In: Nelson, Nici and Susan Wright (eds). 1995. Power and Participatory Development. Theory and Practice. London: Intermediate Technology Publication, 1-18.

Netherlands, Ministry of Foreign Affairs, Policy and Operations Evaluation Department Poverty, policies and perceptions in Tanzania : An evaluation of Dutch aid to two district rural development programmes . The Hague: Ministry of Foreign Affairs (Netherlands), 2004.

Ngugi wa Thiong'o. 1993. Moving the Center – the struggle for cultural freedoms. London: James Currey.

Nöst, Barbara. 1997. Partizipation oder Instrumentalisierung. Das Agricultural Extension Service in Zanzibar. Journal für Entwicklungspolitik 3/97, 237-256.

Novellino, Dario. 2003. From seduction to miscommunication: the confession and presentation of local knowledge in 'participatory development'. In: Pottier, Johan, Alan Bicker and Paul Sillitoe (eds). Negotiating local knowledge - power and identity in development. London: Pluto Press.

Nyamu-Musembi, C. and Andrea Cornwall. 2004. What is the "rights-based approach" all about? Perspectives from international development agencies. IDS Working Paper 234. Brighton, England, Institute of Development Studies.

Nyamu-Musembi, Celestine and Andrea Cornwall. 2005. Why rights? Why now? Reflections on the rise of rights in the international development discourse. IDS Bulletin 36/1, 9-18.

Nyerere, Julius Kambarage. 1962. Ujamaa -the basis of African socialism, TANU Pamphlet.

Nyerere, Julius Kambarage. 1966. President's Inaugural Address. In: Nyerere, Julius Kambarage.1966. Freedom and Unity. A selection from writings and speeches 1952-65, Oxford University Press, 176-187.

Nyerere, Julius Kambarage. 1968. Socialism and Rural Development. In: Freedom and Socialism 1968, 337-366.

Oakley, Ann. 1972. Sex, Gender and Society. London: Temple and Smith.

O'Barr, William. 1976. Language Use abd Language Policy in Tanzania: An Overview. In: William O'Barr and Jean F. O'Barr (eds) Language and Politics, Paris: Mouton, 35-48.

ODA (Overseas Development Administration). 1995. Guidance note on how to do stakeholder analysis of aid projects and programmes. Social Development Department, London. http://www.euforic.org/gb/stake1.htm

ODA. 1986. Women in development and the British aid programme. London: Overseas Development Administration.

OECD-DAC. 1995. Participatory Development and Good Governance. DAC Development Cooperation Guideline Series. Paris: OECD.

OECD-DAC. 1999. DAC Guidelines for Gender Equality and Women's Empowerment in Development Co-operation. Development Co-operation Guideline Series. Paris: OECD Publishing.

OECD-DAC. 2005. Aid activities in support of gender equality 1999-2003. Creditor reporting system on aid activities, Volume 2005, Issue 6, OECD Publishing.

OEZA (Austrian Development Co-operation). 2006a. Leitlinien der Evaluierung in der österreichschen Entwicklungszusammenarbeit (Guidelines for Evaluation in the Austrian Development Co-operation. Vienna: Federal Ministry of Foreign Affairs. www.bmaa.gv.at/up-media/1_leitlinien_dt_.pdf

OEZA. (Austrian Development Co-operation). 2006b. Good Governance – policy document. Vienna: Federal Ministry of Foreign Affairs. www.ada.at

Ohly, Rajmund. 1987. Primary Technical Dictionary English - Swahili. Dar es Salaam: Institute of Production Innovation.

Okali, Christine, Sumberg, James and Farrington, John. 1994. Farmer Participatory Research: Rhetoric and Reality. Intermediate Technology Publications, London.

Parfitt, Trevor. 2004. The ambiguity of participation: a qualified defence of participatory development. Third World Quarterly, 25/3, 537-556.

Pennycook, Alastair. 1994. The cultural politics of English as an international language. London: Longman.

Pennycook, Alastair. 1998. English and the Discourses of Colonialism. London: Routledge.

Pennycook, Alastair. 2000. Language, ideology and hindsight: Lessons from colonial language policies. In: Thomas Ricento (ed). 2000. Ideology, Politics, and Language Policies: Focus on English. Amsterdam: John Benjamins, 49-66.

Pennycook, Alastair. 2001. Critical applied linguistics: a critical introduction. Mahwah, New Jersey: Erlbaum.

Petzell, Malin. 2005. Expanding the Swahili Vocabulary. Africa & Asia – Dept. of Oriental and African Languages, Göteborg University.

Philippson, Robert and Tove Skutnabb-Kangas. 1995. Language rights in postcolonial Africa. In: Phillipson, Robert and Tove Skutnabb-Kangas. Linguistic human rights – overcoming linguistic discrimination. Berlin: Mouton de Gruyter, 335-346.

Philippson, Robert. 2001. English for globalisation or for the world's people? International Review of Education, 47/3-4, 185-200.

Pieterse, Jan Nederveen. 1998. 'My paradigm or yours? Alternative development, post-development, reflexive development. Development and Change, 29:343-73.*

Pieterse, Nederveen Jan. 2000. After Post-Development. Third World Quarterly 21/2, 175-91.

Polomé, Edgar C. and C. P. Hill (eds). 1980. Language in Tanzania. Oxford University Press.

Polomé, Edgar C. 1980. Tanzania: A Socio-Linguistic Perspective. In C. P. Hill and Edgar C. Polomé (eds.) Language in Tanzania. London: Oxford University Press, 103-138.

Ponte, Stefano. 2002. Reply to van Donge. In: Journal of Modern African Studies 40/2, 313-320.

Pottier, Johan. 1997. Towards an ethnography of participatory appraisal and research. In: Grillo, R.D. und R. Stirrat (eds) 1997. Discourses of Development. Oxford: Berg, 203-228.

Potts, David. 2002. Project planning and analysis for development. Boulder: L. Rienner

Pretty, Jules, Irene Guijt, John Thompson, Ian Scoones.1995. The Trainers Guide for Participatory Learning and Action. London: IEED.

Puja, Grace Khwaya. 2003. Kiswahili and Higher Education in Tanzania: Reflections based on a sociological study from three Tanzanian university campuses. In: Brock-Utne, Birgit, Zubeida Desai and Martha Qorro (eds.).

2003. Language of instruction in Tanzania and South Africa. Dar es Salaam: E & D Publishers, 113-128.

Pütz, Martin, Joshua Fishman, JoAnne Neff-van Aertselaer (eds). 2006. Along the Routes to Power: Explorations of the Empowerment through Language. New York, Berlin: Mouton de Gruyter.

Qorro, Martha and Roy Campbell, Zaline. 1997. Language crisis in Tanzania: the myth of English versus education, Mkuki Na Nyota Publishers. Dar es Salaam.

Qorro, Martha. 2003. Unlocking Language Forts: The Language of Instruction in Post Primary Education in Africa with Special Reference to Tanzania. In Birgit Brock-Utne, Zubeida Desai, and Martha Qorro (eds.) Language of Instruction in Tanzania and South Africa. Dar-es-Salaam E&D Limited, 187-196.

Ricento, Thomas (ed.). 2006. An introduction to language policy: theory and method. Malden, Mass.: Blackwell.

Robb, Caroline. 2004 . Changing power relations in the history of aid. In: Groves, Leslie and Rachel Hinton (eds.) 2004. Inclusive aid: changing power and relationships in international development. London: Earthscan, 21-41.

Robinson, Clinton. 1996 .Language use in rural development: an African perspective. Berlin – New York: Mouton de Gruyter.

Roy-Campbell, Zaline. 2001a. Empowerment through language. The Tanzanian experience and beyond. Trenton NJ: Africa World Press.

Roy-Campbell, Zaline. 2001b. Globalisation, language and education: a comparative study of the United States and Tanzania. International Review of Education, 47/3-4, 267-282.

Rubagumya, Casmir M. (ed.) 1990. Language in education in Africa – a Tanzanian perspective. Clevedon: Multilingual matters.

Rubagumya, Casmir. 2003. English medium primariy schools in Tanzania: a new 'linguistic market' in education? Brock-Utne, Birgit, Zubeida Desai and Martha Qorro (eds.). 2003. Language of instruction in Tanzania and South Africa. Dar es Salaam: E & D Publishers, 149-169.

Rugemalira, Josephat, Casmir Rubagumya, M.K. Kapinga, Azaveli Lwaitama and J.G.Tetlow. 1990. Reflections on recent developments in language policy in Tanzania In: Rubagumya, Casmir M. (ed.) 1990. Language in education in Africa – a Tanzanian perspective. Clevedon: Multilingual matters, 25-35.

Rugemalira, Josephat. 2005. Theoretical and practical challenges in a Tanzanian English medium primary school. In: Africa & Asia, Department of Oriental and African Languages at Göteborg University, No 5/2005, 66-84.

Rugumamu, Severine M. 1997. Lethal Aid: The Illusion of Socialism and Self-Reliance in Tanzania. Africa World Press.

Said, Edward. 1978. Orientalism. New York: Vintage Books.

Salamon L.M. und H.K. Anheier. 1992. In Search of the non-profit sector I: the question of definition. Voluntas 3/2, 125-153.

Samsom, Ridder. 1988. Ufundi (Wa) Magari. Leiden: M. A. thesis, Leiden University.

Schegloff, E.A. 1997. Whose Text? Whose Context? Discourse and Society 8/2, 165-187.

Schicho. Walter und Barbara Nöst. 2006 Entwicklungsdiskurs und Praxis der EZA. Konzepte, Akteure und Widersprüche. In: Bea de Abreu Fialho Gomes, Irmi Maral-Hanak, Walter Schicho (eds.). 2006. Entwicklungszusammenarbeit - Akteure, Interessen, Handlungsmuster. Wien: Mandelbaum - Edition Südwind, 43-64.

Scoones, Ian and Thompson, John. 1994a. Introduction. In: Scoones, Ian and Thompson, John. (eds). 1994. Beyond farmer first: rural people's knowledge, agricultural research and extension practice. London: Intermediate Technology Publications, 1-12.

Scoones, Ian and Thompson, John. 1994b. Knowledge, power and agriculture – towards a theoretical understanding. In: Scoones, Ian and Thompson, John. (eds). 1994. Beyond farmer first: rural people's knowledge, agricultural research and extension practice. London: Intermediate Technology Publications, 16-32.

Scoones, Ian and Wolmer, William. 2003. The politics of livelihood opportunity. IDS Bulletin 34/3, 112-115.

Sen, Gita/Grown, Caren. 1987. Development, crises and alternative visions for DAWN. London: Earthscan Publications.

Senkoro, F.E.M.K. 2004. Language of instruction: the forgotten factor in education quality and standards in Africa. Paper presented at the CODESRIA general assembly, Maputo, December 2004.

Shanin, T. 1976. Introduction. In T. Shanin (ed.) 1976. Peasants and Peasant Societies. Middlesex, Penguin Books (first edition 1971).

Sheriff, Abdul. 1987. Slaves, spices & ivory in Zanzibar - integration of an East African commercial empire into the world economy, 1770 – 1873. London: Currey.

Shivji, Issa. 2002. From liberation to liberalization - intellectual discourses at the University of Dar es Salaam, Tanzania. Austrian Journal for Development (JEP) 20/3, 281-294.

Shivji, Issa. 2004. Reflections on NGOs in Tanzania: what are we, what we are not, and what we ought to be? Dar es Salaam: HakiElimu Working Paper No. 9/04 http://www.hakielimu.org/WP/WPSeries9_2004.pdf 1/10/2007

Slater, David and Morag Bell. 2002. Aid and the geopolitics of the post-colonial: Critical reflections on New Labour's overseas development strategy. In: Development and Change 33/2, 335-360.

Spivak, Gayatri. 1988. Can the subaltern speak? In C. Nelson and L Grossberg. (eds) Marxism and the interpretation of culture, University of Illinois Press, Urbana, 271-313.

Stroud, Christopher. 2001. African mother tongues and the politics of language: linguistic citizenship versus linguistic human rights. Journal of Multilingual and Multicultural Development, 22/4, 339-355.

Stubbs, Michael. 1997. Whorf's children: critical comments on critical discourse analysis. In: Ryan, Ann and Alison Wray (eds.) 1997. Evolving models of language. Clevedon: Multilingual Matters, 100-116. http://www.uni-trier.de/uni/fb2/anglistik/Projekte/stubbs/whorf.htm 3/8/2006

Swigart, Leigh. 1992. Two codes or one? The insider view and the description of code-switching in Dakar. In: Eastman, Carol (ed.), Codeswitching. Clevedon: Multilingual Matters, 83-102.

Sylvester, Christine. 1999. Development Studies and Postcolonial Studies: Disparate Tales of the Third World. Third World Quarterly 20/4, 703-21.

Threadgold, Terry. 2003. Critical Studies, Critical Theory and Critical Discourse Analysis: Histories, Remembering and Futures. Linguistik online, 14, 2/03.

Thürmer-Rohr, Christina. 1987. Vagabundinnen. Berlin: Orlanda Frauenverlag.

Titscher, Stefan, Ruth Wodak, Michael Meyer, Eva Vetter. 1998. Methoden der Textanalyse. Opladen: Westdeutscher Verlag.

Titscher, Stefan, Ruth Wodak, Michael Meyer, Eva Vetter. 2000. Methods of text and discourse analysis. Sage Publications.

Tollefson, James. 2006. Critical theory in language policy. In: Ricento, Thomas (ed.). 2006. An introduction to language policy: theory and method. Malden, Massachusetts: Blackwell, 42-59.

Torres, Carlos Alberto.1993. From the 'Pedagogy of the oppressed' to 'A luta continua': the political pedagogy of Paulo Freire. In: McLaren, Peter and Peter Leonhard. 1993. Paulo Freire – a critical encounter. London: Routledge.

Tripp, Aili Mari. 2000. Political Reform in Tanzania: The Struggle for Associational Autonomy. Comparative Politics. 32/2, 191-214.

Tripp, Aili Mari. 2001. Women's movements and challenges to neopatrimonial rule: preliminary observations from Africa. In: Development and Change 32, 33-54.

Tripp, Aili Mari. 2005. Regional Networking as Transnational Feminism: African Experiences. In: Feminist Africa, Vol. 4. http://www.feministafrica.org/index.php/regional-networking 4/4/2008

Tripp, Robert. 2001. Agricultural technology policies for rural development. Development Policy Review 19/4, 479-489.

TUKI (Taasisi wa Uchunguzi wa Kiswahili). 2001. Kamusi ya Kiswahili-Kiingereza. Dar es Salaam: TUKI.

Tvedt, Terje. 1998. Angels of Mercy or Development Diplomats? NGOs and Foreign Aid. Trenton: James Currey LTD. Oxford: African World Press.

UNESCO 2003. Education for a multilingual world. Paris: UNESCO. http://unesdoc.unesco.org/images/0012/001297/129728e.pdf 4/4/2008

Uvin, Peter. 2002. On high moral ground. The incorporation of human rights by the development enterprise. In: Praxis – The Fletcher Journal of Development Studies 17, 1-11.

Van Dijk, Teun A. (ed.). 1993. Principles of critical discourse analysis. Discourse and Society 4/2, 249-283.

Van Dijk, Teun A. 2001. Multidisciplinary CDA. A plea for diversity. In: Meyer, Michael and Ruth Wodak. 2001. Methods of critical discourse analysis. London: Sage, 95-120.

Van Dijk, Teun A. 2007. Discourse studies. London: Sage Publications.

Van Donge, Jankees. 2002. Trading images? A comment on Ponte's reassessment of agrarian change in the Uluguru Mountains. Journal of Modern African Studies, 40/2, 303-311.

Wardhaugh, Ronald. 1992. An introduction to sociolinguistics. Second Edition. Oxford: Blackwell.

Webb, Vic. 2004. The non-promotion of the indigenous languages of Africa: Why? In: Pfaffe, Joachim Friedrich (ed). 2004. Making multilingual education a reality for all – operationalizing good intentions. Proceedings of the Third International Conference of the Association for the Development of African Languages in Education, Science and Technology (ADALEST) held at Mangochi, Malawi, 2004, 105-116.

Wedgwood, Ruth. 2005. Education and Poverty Reduction in Tanzania. Paper presented at the UKFIET Oxford Conference on Education and Development,

September 2005. http://www.cas.ed.ac.uk/research/OXCON_Wedgwood_final. pdf 20/11/2005

Weick, Karl. 1979. The social psychology of organizations. Reading, Mass: Addison-Wesley.

Whitehead, Ann. 2000. "Continuities and Discontinuities in Political Constructions of the Working Man in Rural Sub-Saharan Africa: The 'Lazy Man' in African Agriculture" in the European Journal of Development Research.

Whiteley, Wilfred. 1969. Swahili – the rise of a national language. London: Methuen.

Widdowson, H.G. 1995. Discourse analysis: a critical review. Language and Literature 4/3, 157-172.

Wiggins, Steve. 2005. Success stories from African agriculture. What are the key elements of success? In: IDS Bulletin 36/2, 17-22.

Win, Everjoice (2004), "If it doesn't fit on the blue square it's out! An open letter to my donor friend", in Leslie Groves and Rachel Hinton (editors) (2004), Inclusive Aid: Changing Power and Relationships in International Development, Earthscan, London 123-127.

Winford, Donald. 2003. An introduction to contact linguistics. Malden, Mass. Blackwell.

Wodak, Ruth. 1997. Some important issues in the research of gender and discourse. In: Wodak, Ruth (ed.) Gender and Discourse, London, Sage Publications.

Wodak, Ruth. 2001a. What CDA is about - a summary of its history, important concepts and its developments. In: Wodak, Ruth and Michael Meyer (eds.) 2001. Methods of Critical Discourse Analysis. Sage Publications, 1-13.

Wodak, Ruth. 2001b. The discourse-historical approach. In: Wodak, Ruth and Michael Meyer (eds.) 2001. Methods of Critical Discourse Analysis. Sage Publications, 63-94.

Wodak, Ruth, Rudolf de Cillia, Martin Reisigl, Karin Liebhart, Klaus Hofstätter, Maria Kargl. 1998. Zur diskursiven Konstruktion nationaler Identitäten. Frankfurt: Suhrkamp.

Wodak Ruth and James Martin. 2003. Introduction. In: Wodak, Ruth and James Martin (eds). 2003. Re/reading the past: critical and functional perspectives on time and value. Amsterdam: Benjamins, 1-18.

Wodak, Ruth and James Martin (eds). 2003. Re/reading the past: critical and functional perspectives on time and value. Amsterdam: Benjamins.

Wodak, Ruth and Bernd Matouschek. 1993. We are dealing here with people whose origins one can clearly tell by looking": critical discourse analysis and the study of neoracism in contemporary Austria. In: Discourse and Society 2/4, 225-248.

Wodak, Ruth and Michael Meyer (eds.) 2001. Methods of Critical Discourse Analysis. Sage Publications.

Wodak, Ruth, Peter Novak, Johanna Pelikan, Helmut Gruber, Rudolf de Cillia, Richard Mitten. 1990. Wir alle sind unschuldige Täter. Diskurshistorische Studien zum Nachkriegsantisemitismus. Frankfurt: Suhrkamp.

Wodak, Ruth and Gilbert Weiss. 2003. Critical Discourse Analysis: Theory and Disciplinarity. Palgrave Macmillan.

Wood, Linda A. and Rolf O. Kroger. 2000. Doing Discourse Analysis: Methods for Studying Action in Talk and Text. Corwin Press.

Woodford-Berger, Prudence. 2004. Gender mainstreaming: what is it and should we continue doing it? In: Cornwall, Andrea/ Harrison, Elizabeth/Whitehead, Ann (eds) Repositioning Feminisms in Gender and Development. IDS Bulletin 35/4, 65-72.

World Bank. 1996. The World Bank Participation Sourcebook. Environmentally Sustainable Development. Washington DC: World Bank. http://www.worldbank.org/wbi/sourcebook/sbintro.pdf 17/4/2008

World Bank. 2000. The PRSP Sourcebook. Washington DC: World Bank.

World Bank. 2001. 'Gender in the PRSP: a stocktaking', World Bank Poverty Reduction and Economic Management Network, Gender and Development Group, Washington DC: World Bank.

Yahya-Othman, Saida. 1990. When International Languages Clash: The Possible Detrimentral Effects on Development of the Conflict between English and Kiswahili in Tanzania, in: Rubagumya, Casimir M. (ed) 1990. Language in education in Africa: a Tanzanian perspective. Philadelphia: Multilingual matters, 42-53.

Ziai, Aram, 2006. Zwischen Global Governance und Post – Development. Entwicklungspolitik aus diskursanalytischer Perspektive. Münster: Westfälisches Dampfboot.

Notes on Transliteration

xx	Interval of 2 seconds.
xxx	Interval of 3 or more seconds.
-	Interruption of word or sentence.
++	Inaudible or incomprehensible utterance.
(...)	Situational comments, e.g. on non-verbal interaction.
/	separation of two utterances
:,::,:::,	lengthening of vowels
<..>	Speech overlap by following speaker(s).
<<..>>	From << to >> Speech overlap with previous speaker.
<<<..>>>	From <<< to >>> Overlap with both previous speakers.

Example:
A: Will you come to the park <tomorrow?>
B: <<At what>> time? I am quite busy.
In this example, the last part of A's question (tomorrow) overlaps with the first part of B's answer (At what). This way of transliteration does not provide an exact indication of which sounds are uttered simultaneously, but it is sufficient for our purpose here.

(Footnotes)
1 In the left column, the transliteration of the original taped material is given; the right column contains an English translation.
2 Passages codeswitched to English are printed **bold**
3 Passages that are in English in the original are printed in *italics*

List of Abbreviations

AAWORD	Association of African Women for Research and Development
ADB	African Development Bank
ANC	African National Congress
BAKITA	Baraza la Kiswahili la Taifa (National Swahili Council)
BAWATA	Baraza la Wanawake Tanzania
CAES	Comprehensive Agricultural Extension Service
CBO	Community Based Organisations
CDF	Comprehensive Development Framework
CEDAW	Convention for the Elimination of all Forms of Discrimination Against Women
CIDA	Canada International Development Organisation
DAC	Development Assistance Committee
DARE	De-Agrarization and Rural Employment
DAWN	Development Alternatives with Women for a New Era
DfID -	Department for International Development
ERP	Economic Recovery Program
ESAP	Economic and Social Action Program
EU	European Union
FAO	Food and Agricultural Organization
GTZ	Deutsche Gesellschaft für Technische Zusammenarbeit
HAKIARDHI	Land Rights Research and Resources
HIPC	Highly Indebted Poor Countries
IDA	International Development Association
ILO	International Labour Organisation
IMF	International Monetary Fund
INSTRAW	International Research and Training Institute for the Advancement of Women
LEAT	Lawyers' Environmental Action Team
LFA	Logical Framework Approach
MDG	Millennium Development Goals
NESP	National Economic Survival Programme
NGO	Non-governmental Organisation
ODA	Overseas Development Administration
OECD	Organization of Economic Co-operation and Development
OEZA	Österreichische Entwicklung- und Ostzusammenarbeit
OOPP	Objective-Oriented Project Planning
PCM	Project Cycle Management
PRA	Participatory Rural Appraisal
PRGF	Poverty Reduction and Growth Facility

PRSP	Poverty Reduction Strategy Papers
RCMP	Rice Cultivation Mechanization Program
RDA	Ruvuma Development Association
RRA	Rapid Rural Appraisal
SRAP	Sustainable Rural Agriculture Program
SWOT	Strength-Weakness Opportunities-Threats Analysis
TAMWA	Tanzania Media Women's Association
TANGO	Tanzania Association of Non-Governmental Organisations
TANU	Tanzania African National Union
TAZARA	Tanzania-Zambian Railway
TCDD	Tanzania Coalition on Debt and Development
TGNP	Tanzania Gender Networking Programme
TUKI	Taasisi ya Uchunguzi wa Kiswahili (Institute of Swahili Research)
UN	United Nations
UNIFEM	United Nations Development Fund for Women
USAID	United States Agency for International Development
UWT	Umoja wa Wanawake Tanzania (Tanzania Women's Union)
WID	Women in Development
IBRD	International Bank for Reconstruction and Development
ZOPP	Zielorientierte Projektplanung

List of Illustrations

Figure 1: The Project Cycle	81
Figure 2: The Logical Framework Approach	83
Figure 3: The Logical Framework Matrix	84
Figure 4: Importance/influence analysis grid for Stakeholder Analysis	89
Figure 5: Example of SWOT-Analysis	90
Figure 6: SRAP: Organizational Network	144
Figure 7: RCMP - Organizational Network	152
Figure 8: Fairclough's model of discourse	198

Beiträge zur Afrikaforschung

hrsg. vom Institut für Afrika-Studien der Universität Bayreuth

Markus Verne
Der Mangel an Mitteln
Konsum, Kultur und Knappheit in einem Hausadorf in Niger
Die Allgegenwart von Knappheit und Mangel prägt die Lebensumstände in Berberkia, einem Dorf im westafrikanischen Sahel: Permanent fehlt es an Geld, und deshalb immer auch am Grundsätzlichen, an Kleidung, an Hausrat, und nur zu oft auch an Nahrung. Ethnographisch dicht zu beschreiben, was dieser umfassende Mangel nicht nur für die alltägliche Konsumpraxis, sondern auch in Hinblick auf das gesellschaftliche Zusammenleben bedeutet, ist eines der Anliegen des vorliegenden Buches; ein anderes ist es, den Ursachen und Bedingungen dieser allgegenwärtigen Knappheit nachzuspüren. Nicht nur, so lautet dabei die zentrale These, wird in Berberkia jeglicher Konsum durch den Mangel an Mitteln deutlich begrenzt. Weil „Konsum" in Berberkia eine Art sozialen Handelns darstellt, die sich zwar um den einzelnen Haushalt zentriert, dessen Grenzen jedoch permanent transzendiert, trägt auch die lokale Konsumpraxis ihrerseits zur Omnipräsenz des Mangels bei. Vermittelt über kulturelle Vorstellungen des Gebens und des Nehmens bestimmen sich Konsum und Knappheit in Berberkia wechselseitig, was Knappheit zu einer notwendigen Bedingung für das gemeinschaftliche Zusammenleben im Dorf werden lässt. *„Plausibel zu machen, dass und wie das in sich träge Kulturelle in seiner spezifischen, Berberkia betreffenden Gestalt die wechselseitige Beziehung von Konsum und Knappheit bestimmt, ohne dabei selbst unabhängig zu sein, ist Ziel dieser Arbeit."*
vol. 29, 2007, 584 pp., 39,90 €, pb.,
ISBN 978-3-8258-9787-1

Kerstin Bauer
Kleidung und Kleidungspraktiken im Norden der Côte d'Ivoire
Geschichte und Dynamiken des Wandels, Ende 19. Jahrhundert bis Anfang 21. Jahrhundert
Warum verschwinden handgewebte Textilien in Westafrika mehr und mehr aus dem Alltagsgebrauch? Wieso werden sie in rituell-zeremoniellen Kontexten hingegen bewahrt? Diese Fragen bilden den Ausgangspunkt für die vorliegende Arbeit über Geschichte und Wandel von Kleidung im Norden der Côte d'Ivoire. Im Mittelpunkt stehen die renommierten Textilhandwerker und Händler der muslimischen Dyula und ihre Bezüge zu anderen Gesellschaftsgruppen. Der Fokus der Untersuchung liegt auf den Akteuren und ihren Kleidungspraktiken in unterschiedlichen Handlungskontexten. Kerstin Bauer identifiziert verschiedene vestimentäre Sphären, die jeweils eigenen Dynamiken des Wandels unterliegen, und zeigt auf, wie diese ineinander greifen. Ihre Studie stützt sich auf historische Quellen und eigenen Feldforschungen in der Côte d'Ivoire und im Süden Burkina Fasos.
vol. 30, 2007, 592 pp., 49,90 €, pb.,
ISBN 978-3-8258-0301-8

LIT Verlag Berlin – Münster – Wien – Zürich – London
Auslieferung Deutschland / Österreich / Schweiz: siehe Impressumsseite

Gudrun Miehe; Jonathan Owens; Manfred von Roncador (eds.)
Language in African Urban Contexts
A Contribution to the Study of Indirect Globalisation
This volume contains the results of the Bayreuth SFB research program "Effects of globalisation processes on the vitality of languages in West African cities". Two towns with different historical and colonial background, Maiduguri in Nigeria and Banfora in Burkina Faso, were selected as research areas. The contrast between language and social institutions is most obvious in the colonial and post-colonial world in Africa. Colonization was characterized by the importation of European institutions which were of a qualitatively new nature linked to the globalising forces. This qualitative newness is captured in our term "direct globalisation". A basic observation is that the globalising forces led to a hierarchicalisation of languages in Africa which is not obviously attested in the institutions of direct globalisation. Our term "indirect globalisation" describes the alignment of local practices to the external forces and institutions introduced during a globalising colonial and post-colonial experience.
vol. 31, 2007, 392 pp., 39,90 €, pb.,
ISBN 978-3-8258-0388-9

Hans Peter Hahn; Georg Klute (eds.)
Cultures of Migration
African Perspectives
International Migrations have become a central topic in the Humanities in the last years. Understanding migration requires a closer look at the migratory phenomena and the continuities within the societies involved in the migration process. This volume intends to overcome simplistic views on migration and the shortcomings of a push and pull-factor analysis. Instead, the perspective of the migrants themselves orients the approach of "cultures of migration". In this view, migration becomes a complex issue, and motives and acceptance of migration appear to be a matter of negotiations, in the migrants' societies of origin and in the host societies as well. The present volume brings together a number of essays exploring the cultures of migration in various contexts. It is organised in three sections, dealing with "Migrations as Encounters", "Migration as Challenge", and "Transcontinental Migrants". Ten contributions, each based on original fieldwork in various parts of Africa, examine the validity of the concept of "cultures of migration", as explained in the introduction.
vol. 32, 2007, 296 pp., 29,90 €, pb.,
ISBN 978-3-8258-0668-2

LIT Verlag Berlin – Münster – Wien – Zürich – London
Auslieferung Deutschland / Österreich / Schweiz: siehe Impressumsseite

Erdmute Alber; Sjaak van der Geest; Susan R. Whyte (Eds.)
Generations in Africa
Connections and Conflicts
Though long neglected in anthropological research, the connections and conflicts between generations are at the heart of social processes. In this book, sixteen studies examine relations between generations of kin and between historical and political generations. The topics range from grandmother's cooking, migrant remittances, youth unemployment, teenage pregnancy, Valentine's Day, and hip hop music, to respect, religious virtue, gerontocracy, memory, wisdom, complaint, and the meaning of tradition. Together they reinvigorate and expand the old anthropological interest in generation, showing how necessary it is to understanding contemporary African societies.
vol. 33, 2008, 432 pp., 39,90 €, pb., ISBN 978-3-8258-0715-3

LIT Verlag Berlin – Münster – Wien – Zürich – London
Auslieferung Deutschland / Österreich / Schweiz: siehe Impressumsseite

Afe Adogame; Magnus Echtler; Ulf Vierke (Eds.)
Unpacking the New
Critical Perspectives on Cultural Syncretization in Africa and Beyond
In a world supposedly characterized by the production of new differences and cultural permutations resulting from the twin processes of globalization and cultural syncretisation, hardly anything has remained as obscure and theoretically under-theorized as the very notion of the "new" itself. An inherent relativity often accompanies any contemplation of what is new or old, as well as the question at which point the old turns into the new. Syncretism as both process and description hinges largely on the assumption and premise that what is observed has appropriately or inappropriately mixed categories – culture, religion, language – that are intrinsically alien to each other. Such a syncretic constellation is bound to result in something that may be considered new. Any definition of "syncretism", the syncretisation process and the appropriation of the notion "new" as useful heuristic tools must indeed be located within specific local contexts, as such terms are unlikely to serve as adequate descriptions of homogenous sets of phenomena. Syncretism as a process is intertwined with processes of contextualization. Against this backdrop, this book seeks to unravel and demystify the ideology of the new on the basis of concrete case studies from various regions across Africa and beyond. Contributors: Afe Adogame, Peter Beyer, Astrid Bochow, Simon Coleman, André Droogers, Magnus Echtler, Hans Peter Hahn, Peter Gottschligg, Dymitr Ibriszimow, Said A.M. Khamis, Karina Kopatsch, Selome Kuponu, Roman Loimeier, Elísio Macamo, Dieter Neubert, Jonathan Owens, Farouk Topan, Ulrich Rinn, Dana Rush, Hans-Jörg Schmid, Ulf Vierke.
vol. 36, 2008, 384 pp., 29,90 €, pb., ISBN 978-3-8258-0719-1

LIT Verlag Berlin – Münster – Wien – Zürich – London
Auslieferung Deutschland / Österreich / Schweiz: siehe Impressumsseite

Hans Peter Hahn (Ed.)
Consumption in Africa – Anthropological Approaches
The study of consumption, including such aspects as social differentiation, communication and the change of needs, has become a major field of study within material culture research. This volume unites a number of ethnographic case studies documenting a wide range of local practices with regard to consumer goods. Although based on the acquisition of globally circulating goods, consumption in Africa is appropriated and, thus, becomes part of the local material culture. The contributions of this volume are the outcome of a workshop held at the African Studies Centre at Bayreuth University. Each chapter deals with the social dynamics engendered by new modes of consumption in specific areas (Côte d'Ivoire, Zambia, Tanzania, Nigeria, Burkina Faso and Niger). Cover Photos: Bicycle owner and vendor of locally brewed beer in Kollo (Dép. de Tiébélé) on the way to the market, woman selling millet on the market of Zabré (both Burkina Faso)
vol. 37, 2008, 208 pp., 29,90 €, pb., ISBN 978-3-8258-0725-2

LIT Verlag Berlin – Münster – Wien – Zürich – London
Auslieferung Deutschland / Österreich / Schweiz: siehe Impressumsseite

Ethnologie: Forschung und Wissenschaft

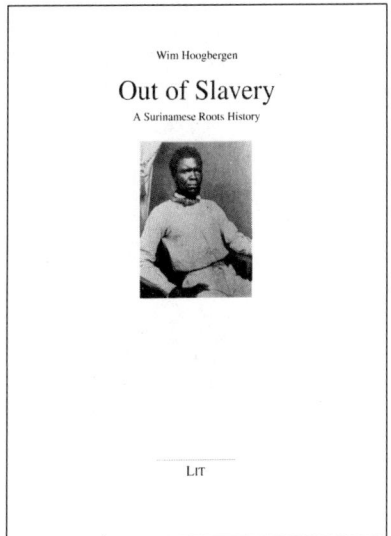

Wim Hoogbergen
Out of Slavery
A Surinamese Roots History
vol. 6, 2008, 256 pp., 19,90 €, pb.,
ISBN 978-3-8258-8112-2

Franz von Benda-Beckmann;
Keebet von Benda-Beckmann
Social Security Between Past and Future
Ambonese Networks of Care and Support
Social security is a particularly precarious issue where states hardly provide any services in periods of need and distress. The book analyses the arrangements relationships through which food, shelter and care are provided on the island of Ambon, famous spice island in Eastern Indonesia. It also shows how relations of support tie Ambonese migrants in the Netherlands to their home villages, and how normative conceptions of need and care among kinsmen and villagers change over time. Though special in their own historical setting, Ambonese networks of care and support are illustrative of poor rural populations in the Third World. Focusing on the precursors of the violent conflict that erupted in 1998, the book shows that social security is like a magnifying glass linking past, present and future.
vol. 13, 2007, 344 pp., 29,90 €, pb.,
ISBN 978-3-8258-0718-4

LIT Verlag Berlin – Münster – Wien – Zürich – London
Auslieferung Deutschland / Österreich / Schweiz: siehe Impressumsseite

Gerd Spittler
Founders of the Anthropology of Work
German Social Scientists of the 19th and Early 20th Centuries and the First Ethnographers
Work is vital for most individuals and for every society. Yet it leads a Cinderella-like existence within social anthropology. Even today we can learn from older social scientists like Karl Marx, Wilhelm Heinrich Riehl, Karl Bücher, Eduard Hahn, Wilhelm Ostwald, and Max Weber. Comparing industrial and non-industrial work, they were interested in the character of work as performance, play or ethical deed, and as rational action. Due to a lack of ethnographic studies, the empirical basis of their analysis remained weak. A serious ethnography of work was started by Karl Weule, Richard Thurnwald, and Bronislaw Malinowski. Having close links to the older social scientists they introduced new perspectives based on fieldwork in Africa and Melanesia.
vol. 14, 2008, 320 pp., 29,90 €, pb.,
ISBN 978-3-8258-0780-1

Elizabeth Challinor
Bargaining in the Development Market-Place
Insights from Cape Verde
The process of ethnographically detailing how individuals encounter institutions is a complicated task. Few are those accounts that manage to clearly elucidate how new institutional knowledge passes through individuals within the course of normative, everyday living. Elizabeth Challinor's ethnography of rural Santiago, Cape Verde does an outstanding job of revealing how the introduction of new institutional procedures are felt and experienced in non-suspecting places, in non-suspecting ways and with non- suspecting outcomes. Challinor's descriptions of the encounter between new policies and daily practice provide an important lesson on the power in ethnographically informed theorization.
Kesha Fikes, University of Chicago
vol. 15, 2008, 216 pp., 24,90 €, pb.,
ISBN 978-3-8258-1410-6

LIT Verlag Berlin – Münster – Wien – Zürich – London
Auslieferung Deutschland / Österreich / Schweiz: siehe Impressumsseite